REMARKABLE HIGH TORIES

Supporters of King and Parliament
in Revolutionary Massachusetts

William H. B. Thomas

HERITAGE BOOKS
2008

HERITAGE BOOKS
AN IMPRINT OF HERITAGE BOOKS, INC.

Books, CDs, and more—Worldwide

For our listing of thousands of titles see our website
at
www.HeritageBooks.com

Published 2008 by
HERITAGE BOOKS, INC.
Publishing Division
100 Railroad Ave. #104
Westminster, Maryland 21157

Copyright © 2001 The Estate of Beverley T. Thomas

Please Note - Disregard the reference to a genealogical chart in the acknowledgements of this book. No such chart exists as part of this publication.

All rights reserved. No part of this book may be reproduced or transmitted in any form or by any means, electronic or mechanical, including photocopying, recording or by any information storage and retrieval system without written permission from the author, except for the inclusion of brief quotations in a review.

International Standard Book Numbers
Paperbound: 978-0-7884-1705-4
Clothbound: 978-0-7884-7206-0

To
the memory of my father
John Dana Thomas
and to my wife
Beverley
and to my children
Anthony Thomas and Constance Thomas Terriberry
and my grandson
Nathaniel Ray Thomas
the fourth of this name
since 1731

"REMARKABLE HIGH TORIES"

It seems impossible, in all common sense, to get rid of the old terms 'Whig' and 'Tory,' familiar as they are, even nowadays, to all readers of American history. The names, of course, are echoes of those of the two English parties; but so opprobrious has the word 'Tory' been in our history that some writers have tried to substitute the term 'Loyalist,' with 'Whig' changed to 'Patriot.' ...That Whigs were always patriots, particularly when they took to mobbing and violence, the present writer questions. It seems to him unnecessary squeamishness never to use the word Tory, consequently he uses it, particularly in the sense of an aggressive loyalist.
- Allen French, The First Year of the American Revolution (1934)

A second circumstance which smoothed the way for the progress of the revolutionary movement in rural New England was the ineffectiveness of the Tory opposition. Whereas Boston patriots could be called together at a few moments' notice, the ablest Tory leaders such as Timothy Ruggles of Hardwick, James Putnam and the Chandlers of Worcester, the Winslows and Thomases of Plymouth County, and John Worthington of Springfield were too remote from each other to take concerted action.
- John C. Miller, Sam Adams: Pioneer in Propaganda (1936)

Contents

Preface xiii

I   "That Most Loyal Town" 1

II   Tension Mounts 11

III   Of Generations Past 45

IV   Young Ray 64

V   Marriage and Country Life 79

VI   The Provincial Gentry 102

VII   "Continual Uneasiness of Mind" 136

VIII   The Storm Breaks 151

IX   War 166

X   Years of Separation 192

XI   Reunion 217

XII   Refuge 230

XIII   A New Century 254

XIV   Aftermath 279

A Note on Sources and Methods 280

Index 276

List of Illustrations

facing page

Deacon Nehemiah Thomas's house	2
Careswell	12
Winslow House in Plymouth	13
Secret Passage	22
Eagles Nest	39
Dr. Isaac Winslow	23
Discharge by Nathaniel Ray Thomas of his guardian	68
Nathaniel Ray Thomas	72
Sarah *Dering* Thomas	73
General John Winslow	96
Judge Martin Howard	97
Mary *Sylvester* Dering	122
Thomas Dering	123
Nathaniel Ray Thomas's house	128
Nathaniel Ray Thomas's house with additions	129
Sarah *Dering* Thomas's letter	124
General John Thomas	138
Colonel Anthony Thomas's house	139
Lieutenant Joshua Winslow	144
Ebenezer Storer	145
Hammersmith House	186
Prospect Place	200
Gravestone of Nathaniel Ray Thomas	208
Lieutenant Charles Thomas	218
Lady Frances Wentworth	220
John Briggs Thomas	221
Major Briggs Thomas's house	226
Nathaniel "Nat" Thomas	after p.254
Elizabeth *Packer* Thomas	after p.254
Mt. Uniacke	after p.254
Sarah *Thomas* Francklin	after p.254
Elizabeth Gould Francklin	after p.254
Ann *Thomas* Porter	after p.254

PREFACE

First and foremost, I want to acknowledge the very special debt of gratitude I owe my father, John Dana Thomas. Not only did he very early in my life acquaint me with the story of the Thomas family - and he was a good storyteller - but also he urged me to tell that story. It was his inspiration that finally encouraged me to start. Likewise, throughout my childhood and adolescence, I was excited by the fragments of a family letter or deed dating from the 18th century which my cousin, Louise Ames Norman, bestowed upon me each Christmas.

In 1947, back from World War II, I was anxious to see for myself the extensive collection of Thomas family papers with which Mrs. Norman had enticed me as a child. I called upon her. She was eager to show me the papers. After sharing a pleasant tea, she brought out a sea chest filled with letters, receipts, deeds, manuscripts and legal documents of five generations of the Thomas family in Marshfield. She said she had no one interested in retaining them and offered to let me have them as long as she could keep the chest they were stored in. I could hardly believe my good fortune!

This gift gave evidence to the intriguing stories my father had told me through the years, particularly when we were at the Rexhame farmhouse in Marshfield during the summers. Colonel Anthony Thomas (my Patriot fourth great-grandfather) had bought the 200-acre farm at Rexhame in the 1750's and by 1915 my father owned it. Colonel Anthony and Nathaniel Ray Thomas (my Loyalist or Tory fourth great-grandfather) were so real to me that as a small child I thought they lived nearby and would come through the door at any minute.

After the War, I located in Virginia and throughout the years that I farmed and worked there on various history projects, the Thomas papers were in my thoughts. My children urged me to write the story of the two Thomas families in Marshfield - one Loyalist and one Patriot - who were eventually joined in marriage. The granddaughter of the Loyalist married the grandson of the Patriot and started their married life at the farm at Rexhame, and I had papers and documents which could give substance to the stories of my childhood.

Although I have over 1,000 documents, I have never found any existing letters from Nathaniel Ray Thomas and his wife Sarah to each other. However, the letters which they wrote to their relatives and friends reveal their feelings for each other clearly. The letters also reveal the details of the life of the provincial gentry in Marshfield and the mounting tension of the years immediately preceding the American Revolution. They add to our knowledge of Nathaniel Ray's position as a Councilor of the Province, his departure from Boston with the withdrawing British Army, his subsequent efforts in Halifax, Nova Scotia, and in New York, and his ultimate refuge in England. The years of separation from his wife and children and the reunion of them all in Nova Scotia prior to his death are vividly depicted in the correspondence that we have, much of it the frequent letters of Sarah, his wife, to her many relatives and friends. Their children, too, corresponded from Nova Scotia with their relatives in America and those letters show the closeness which they maintained over the years.

Nathaniel Ray Thomas was a member of His Majesty's Council of Massachusetts and an ardent supporter of the Royal cause. He was one of the eleven hundred Tories or Loyalists - those who professed loyalty to England, to King and to Parliament - who left Boston, Province of Massachusetts Bay, upon the evacuation of that city by British forces in March, 1776. In Marshfield he had neighbors and friends who thought as he did - particularly Major General John Winslow and his son Dr. Isaac Winslow of Careswell who were "likewise remarkable high Tories" but whose lives took a different direction.

I recall a passage from Lysander Richard's History of Marshfield, bearing on the Tories, which made me as a boy all the more anxious to tell the story of Nathaniel Ray Thomas and the Tories. The passage went as follows: "What more stirring and patriotic utterance was given to the people than this, [a protest against Tory resolutions] proclaimed a year and a quarter before the signing and issuing of the Declaration of Independence and promulgated in a town (our town, it must be said, with a pang of sorrow) yes, a town which was the hotbed of toryism."

I am glad to finally have my Thomas ancestors walk through the door. It has been a long wait.

Acknowledgements

I want to express my appreciation to William H. Runge, former Curator of Rare Books at Alderman Library, the University of Virginia in Charlottesville, Virginia for much assistance; and also Conley Edwards of the Virginia State Library for his help in many ways. I also benefited greatly from the mature advice of Elizabeth Schneider, Bloomingdale Farm, Somerset, Virginia.

Upon returning to live in Marshfield, Massachusetts after an absence of more than forty years I made the acquaintance of many friends, new and old. I want to acknowledge the professional assistance of Ernest Buchner, former Director of the Pilgrim Society, Pilgrim Hall, Plymouth. His critical reading of the book in manuscript was very helpful and his apt suggestions very pertinent and welcome. Likewise I thank Peggy Timlin Baker, Curator of Books and Manuscripts for the Pilgrim Society, for reading the manuscript and furnishing me with appropriate insight in regard to many matters. I do appreciate the assistance of Cynthia Krusel and Joan Scolponeti, both of the Historical Commission of Marshfield, for reading the book and commenting critically on various aspects of it.

I am indebted to many people. I must acknowledge the aid and particularly the constant encouragement and support given me by my wife, Beverley and my children, Anthony and Constance. She and they have been very understanding particularly when I was vexed at critical points. Furthermore my wife assisted very materially with typing and editing the manuscript. I want also to acknowledge the very important contribution of Jean Bouton, Quincy, Massachusetts, my research assistant for providing important information from various institutions. Particularly useful was her assistance in preparing the Index. Her unfailing good cheer and her willingness to do all asked of her was noteworthy; much of the book is the result of her good and faithful efforts. I appreciate the efforts of Ann Lariviere for helping me with the Marshfield town records, obviously a vital matter in a history such as this, and I am particularly grateful to the immediate past Town Clerk of Marshfield, Mrs. Constance C. Donohue, for an important analysis of the records in her charge.

I must acknowledge also for his encouragement and support and for making available his much-to-be-admired library's resources, Dennis Corcoran, the former Director of the Ventress Memorial Library in Marshfield.

For putting the book in final form I had the good assistance of Mary Doyle and Grace Buscher, the former in actually providing a computer on which to type originally the draft of the book and in clearing the way when technical problems confronted me; and the latter for preparing the all important final version of the manuscript and for her ready availability in solving highly technical problems. I must also thank Harrison Longhi for his fine work in preparing photographs to be used as illustrations, Claire Bouton for researching possible illustrations, and

Ralph Poland and Kathy Sylvester of Coastal Copy in Marshfield for their cheerful and interested help in getting the illustrations ready for publication.

Linda Ashley and her family are to be commended for their expertise in managing to condense and print out the genealogical chart which makes clear the interconnections of all the families and friends.

Further, I thank Gerald McCluskey for his hospitality in letting Beverley and me stay in his house, which happens to be my fourth great-grandfather, Colonel Anthony Thomas's house, while I was working on the book. Likewise I do want to express my appreciation to John and Barrie Gleason, owners of the farm at Rexhame, Marshfield where I spent so many summers as a boy, for their kindness in giving me the run of the place, so to speak.

In Halifax, Nova Scotia, I was assisted very materially by Barry Cahill, Manuscripts Archivist, at the Public Archives of Nova Scotia which I do acknowledge with thanks. In Windsor, Nova Scotia, I had many hours of delightful and constructive conversation with L. S. Loomer, proprietor of a book store. In Windsor also I acknowledge the pleasant visit with, and warm hospitality of, a relation, my sixth cousin, A. G. Macdonald, who likewise descended from Nathaniel Ray Thomas.

Lastly, I want to acknowledge the very useful role of Tammy and Stuart Nixon of Hearthstone Bookshop in Alexandria, Virginia for their very kind introduction and recommendation of myself to Laird Towle of Heritage Books, Inc. and to thank Karen Ackermann, President of Heritage Books, for her thoughtful and careful assistance in guiding the book through the press and for her many practical and pertinent suggestions.

I would be remiss if I did not acknowledge the understanding and courteous assistance of the Board of Governors of the Historic Winslow House Association, Marshfield, Massachusetts. They have been very supportive and generous in their relations with me. I appreciate this.

"That Most Loyal Town"

Word of the Boston Tea Party - an event "so bold, so daring" John Adams declared - spread rapidly and with electrifying effect. Even outlying towns learned within a day or so of the dumping of the tea from the tea ships in Boston Harbor that Thursday night, December 16, 1773. By Sunday night the 19th, a town such as Marshfield, some thirty-five miles south of Boston on the Province of Massachusetts coast, not only had the news but there had been time for some townspeople, patriots to be sure, to gather and plan sympathetic action.

Such patriotic enthusiasm was quick to surface. Destruction of the tea was in open defiance of England and her colonial policy. By destroying the tea and hence not paying the duty imposed on that commodity when imported into America, the Patriots effectively squashed any notion that, if they had accepted the tea and paid the duty, they would have impliedly acknowledged the right of Parliament to tax them.

Even before the Boston Tea Party, towns in New England had taken steps to ferret out and destroy dutied tea. Patriot leaders at Marshfield knew that quantities of that commodity had been stored at certain locations in the town, presumably to forestall any effort to destroy the tea which enjoyed vast popularity among the people. Chests of the tea were secured in the building used as a store by John Bourne near the First Church and militia training field - the center of town activities - and in the cellar of Deacon Nehemiah Thomas's house a short distance to the southeast. Nehemiah Thomas, a prudent, industrious man of sixty-one years, a deacon of the First Church for some twenty-one years, and active in town affairs, was both Town Clerk and Town Treasurer. Contemporaries would later recall the Deacon as one "in whom each grace, each lovely virtue shone." One might have supposed the cellar of his house would be a secure place for the dutied tea to be stored, safe from any who might be tempted to destroy it.

That evening, the 19th of December, the Patriots formed a small group on the road that led by the First Church. They brought ox carts. The procession turned into the lane that led to Deacon Thomas's. In the chill winter air that Sunday evening, the men quickly and silently removed chests of the tea from the cellar and loaded them onto the carts. The

"That Most Loyal Town"

Deacon himself was not at home nor, for that matter, had he thought that the tea would be seized and destroyed. By nature a cautious man, he feared the consequences. But the Patriots, undaunted, went on anyway.

They moved on to John Bourne's store near the First Church. They repeated the rifling begun at the Deacon's. Expeditiously the tea chests were taken out of the store and loaded on the carts. By now word of the undertaking had been noised about town. Women, even children, hurried to join the men. Possibly by pre-arranged plan, the carts were headed toward a small hill immediately opposite the training field. The drovers urged on the oxen up the hill. Near the summit they paused. The men unloaded the chests of tea, broke them open and scattered the tea on top of a rock "quite flat on top." In the dim flickering light of lanterns, those present knelt in prayer. Benjamin White and Jeremiah Low, leaders of the Patriots, applied torches to the heaped-up tea. It burned quickly. Both participants and on-lookers were well satisfied with the night's work.

News of the burning of the tea circulated fast. Many were excited and joyous over this overt defiance of the customs laws, this thwarting of the duty collectible on tea. Not all, however, were pleased by such precipitous action. Marshfield, a town of a thousand or so souls, was by 1773 sharply divided in its sentiments. Certainly one group who welcomed news of the Boston Tea Party, and the action that Sunday night in Marshfield were the Patriots, or Whigs as they were called to distinguish them unmistakably from Tories who supported King and Parliament. And yet there was a sizable number of Tories in Marshfield, those known or at least suspected, of loyalty to the King. The more aggressive of the Patriots were clearly eager for independence from the Crown. In between were those who had inclinations toward one side or the other, but in those early days of tension either kept their feelings to themselves or felt it the better part of wisdom to wait and see which party, the Patriots' or the Kings', would prevail.

Of the group loyal to the King were those of varied occupation and circumstance. Some were small farmers, owning and working a few acres; some were artisans; some tradesmen; a few more were farmers with farms of several hundred acres or merchants doing a substantial business. Some were professional men, others minor officials in town or Provincial government. Nor was it surprising that many were loyal simply because loyalty to the Crown was inbred, natural for them.

Deacon Nehemiah Thomas's house, Marshfield, where the tea was stored. No longer standing. Photograph by William H.B. Thomas, 1938.

"That Most Loyal Town"

Likewise, throughout the Province of Massachusetts Bay, the wealthy, large landowners with a tradition of holding office under the Crown tended to be loyal. Two such men in Marshfield were Nathaniel Ray Thomas and Dr. Isaac Winslow, "remarkable high Tories" a contemporary called them. Both were of families of long standing in the town. Both descended from families which had provided men prominent in the civil and military life of town and Plymouth Colony and later the Province of Massachusetts Bay. Both possessed extensive property, larger by far than that owned by most. This latter situation - carried over from the old country, England, where possession of land was the mark of gentility and station, one to which many aspired and one which most never achieved - was even then still pervasive among the early settlers of the New World. Ray Thomas and Dr. Winslow were clearly of the gentry, as that word was understood.

Tory reaction to the burning of the tea on what was ever after known as Tea Rock Hill was swift and forthright. They initiated a move for an immediate town meeting. Notice was posted. The date set was January 31, 1774. The place of the meeting was chosen as the First Church facing on the town common and militia training ground. The ferment by now stirred up in Marshfield erupted. Numerous partisans of both Loyalist and Patriot persuasion appeared at the meeting. It soon became apparent that the Tories outnumbered their opponents. Both Ray Thomas and Dr. Isaac Winslow, cousins and neighbors, were present. Others known to share their views mingled in the crowd. The meeting was called to order. First on the agenda was the selection of a Moderator to chair the meeting. "Nathl Ray Thomas Esq., was chosen Moderator."

Upon taking the chair, Ray Thomas immediately put to the townspeople this question: "to know the town's mind whether he should have leave to speak his mind and declare his sentiments relating to the things mentioned in the warrant." [The wording of the warrant is not known.] That passed in the affirmative.

What "the things mentioned in the warrant" were - the reasons stated for calling the meeting - soon became obvious to those in attendance. As Moderator, Ray Thomas spoke warmly and with conviction. Then there was put to a vote the town's mind whether it would act upon the warrant. That also passed in the affirmative. Accordingly, the town chose a committee "to take into consideration and draw up what they think

"That Most Loyal Town"

proper for the town to vote, and to make their report..." This related to "the things mentioned in the warrant," the subject to which Ray Thomas had addressed his "insinuations," as a contemporary newspaper account put it. The committee chosen consisted of Dr. Isaac Winslow, Nathaniel Ray Thomas, Esq., and Messrs. Elisha Ford, Seth Bryant, William Stevens, John Baker, and Ephraim Little. These men were of known, or strongly suspected, Loyalist sympathy. The meeting was then adjourned for an hour to enable the committee "to consider the things mentioned in the warrant" and draft its report.

When the town meeting reconvened an hour later, amid murmuring and restless shufflings of anticipation, one of the committee read the report. There was a preamble, from which people quickly sensed what was to come:
> This town taking into consideration the late tumultuous, and as we think illegal proceedings in the town of Boston in the detention and destruction of the teas belonging to the East India Co., which we apprehend will effect our property, if not our liberties, think it our indispensable duty to show our disapprobation of such measures and proceedings, therefore voted and resolved as the opinion of this town;

There was quiet in the church, the townspeople instinctively aware that something of moment was about to be uttered. The reader went on:
> That this town ever have and always will be good and loyal subjects to our Sovereign Lord, King George the 3rd, and will observe, obey and enforce all such good and wholesome laws as are or shall be constitutionally made by the Legislature or the Community of which we are members; and by all legal ways and means, to the utmost of our powers and abilities will protect, defend and preserve our liberties and privileges against the machinations of foreign or domestic enemies.

Thus far what had been said was familiar and expressive of what they believed. For after all, most colonists still professed loyalty to the Crown and obedience to the laws by which they were governed. They had a willingness, more likely a strong determination, to protect, defend, and preserve their liberties and privileges as British subjects. But to those same colonists so determined to keep their liberties and privileges

"That Most Loyal Town"

inviolate, the resolutions which followed only aroused anger and bitter resentment. The first of those resolutions was straightforward:

> Resolved, that the late measures and proceedings in the town of Boston in the detention and destruction of the teas belonging to the East India Co. were illegal and unjust, and of a dangerous tendency.

Not only had most Massachusetts towns applauded the Boston Tea Party but Marshfield Patriots who had taken the initiative in the town to seize and burn the tea were among those at the town meeting. They seethed with realization of what the Tory leaders, obviously in control of the meeting, were putting before it. The next resolution was even more pointed:

> Resolved, that Abijah White, Esq., the present Representative of this town, be and hereby is instructed and directed to use his utmost endeavors that the perpetrators of those mischiefs may be detected and brought to justice, and as the country has been heretofore drawn in to pay their proportionable part of the expense which accrued from the riotous and unruly proceedings and conduct of certain individuals in the town of Boston, if application should be made to the General Court by the East India Co., or any other persons for a consideration for the loss of said teas, you are by no means to acquiesce, but bear you testimony against any measures by which expense may accrue to the province in general, or the town of Marshfield in particular; and those people, only, who were active, aiding and assisting or conniving at the destruction of said teas, pay for the same.

This was particularly galling to Marshfield Patriots because a town's instructions to its representative at the General Court, the Province legislature, were binding. The instructions to Abijah White, himself a strong Tory, were hardly expressive of Patriot sentiment in the town.

The final resolution stated that White be directed to see that Provincial laws be carried out and that all offenders against those laws be properly punished. But it continued:

> And we further declare it as our opinion that the grand basis of Magna Charta and reformation of Liberty of Conscience, and rights of Private Judgment is just,

"That Most Loyal Town"

> wherefore, we do renounce all method of imposition, violence and persecution, such as has been most shamefully exercised upon a number of inhabitants of the town of Plymouth by obliging them to sign a recantation, as called, and in case of refusal to have their houses pulled down, or they tarred and feathered, and all this under the specious Mask of Liberty.

The report, having been read, was accepted. It was voted that the Town Clerk record it and send a copy to Abijah White and that he put it in the Boston newspapers.

With their publication in the Boston press, the resolves quickly achieved notoriety and sharp rebuttal. Neighboring Duxbury was a town of as strong Whig sentiment as Marshfield was of Tory sympathy. A Duxbury correspondent wrote a letter for publication in the <u>Boston Gazette and Country Journal.</u> It appeared February 5, 1774:

> I imagine you have by this time heard of the very remarkable Resolves of the town of Marshfield respecting the destruction of the teas, &c. which was effected principally by the insinuating act of a certain man, who having lately rendered himself odious to the Province by his conduct in a public station, is endeavoring to wipe off the infamy on the people of that town. His insinuations are (as I am informed by people of veracity) that the tea must be paid for; that any town remonstrating against the destruction of it, will effectually secure them against paying any part of the expenses and if it is paid for that his particular share will be £40 who commonly pays scarce £3 annum of the Province tax. However the sentiments of the Old Colony are not to be collected from those of Marshfield.

Following this communication, the same paper published an item two days later with further news:

> We are informed that the Resolves of the town of Marshfield were carried by a majority of only one vote, and we soon expect a more intelligible account of the meeting than has yet been given in a public paper.

Ray Thomas's part in persuading the Marshfield town meeting to adopt the Resolves was quite obviously well understood. He was singled out

"That Most Loyal Town"

by Whig scribes for derisive and, even more telling, malicious comment. But he was not alone. Abijah White, the Tory leader and Marshfield representative to the General Court who was instructed by the town to give the Resolves to the press, likewise became the butt of Whig denunciation. Also in the February 5th issue of <u>The Boston Gazette and Country Journal</u> appeared a satirical story about that gentleman:

> We hear from Marshfield that the puissant A - -W - -Esq. lately went into a neighbor's house and being seated, though very uneasy, he was inquired of what made him so, when he instantly arose and drew forth a sword (being formerly a valiant soldier) declaring he would make daylight shine through 'em but what he would carry his point, giving as a reason that he was afraid of his life without being arm'd, tho' never assaulted. Being thus accout'red one day on going to his barn, his cattle being affrighted and taking him to be a stranger, surrounded him and we hear 'twas with difficulty that he escaped with his life and the loss of his sword.

In another newspaper item stemming from White's presenting for publication the Marshfield Resolves, a Whig with poetic fancies contributed this bit of verse:

> *Abijah White, when sent*
> *Our Marshfield friends to represent*
> *Himself while dread array involves,*
> *In awful pomp descending down*
> *Bore terror on the factious town.*

With feeling in the town so sharply divided and both Whig and Tory adherents so quick to express their views, the rapidity with which the Patriots responded to the Resolves adopted on January 31st was not surprising. The <u>Massachusetts Spy</u> of February 23rd reported a protest signed by "a large number of the prominent inhabitants of the town of Marshfield":

> We the subscribers think ourselves obliged in faithfulness to the community, ourselves and posterity, on every proper occasion to bear our public testimony against every measure calculated to destroy that harmony and unanimity which subsists through the colonies and so eventually to the destruction of those liberties wherewith the Author of Nature and our happy constitution has made us free. Were they not already

> notorious, it would give us uneasiness to mention the Resolves which were voted in this town the 31st of January last.

With this preamble, the Whigs then set forth their reactions to and objections to the separate resolutions as passed:

> To the first of these Resolves we do not object; but do heartily join in recognizing our loyalty and subjection to the King of Great Britain and our readiness to be ever subject to the laws of our legislature. In their second Resolve, they say that the measures and proceedings in the town of Boston in the detention and destruction of the teas, belonging to the East India Company, are illegal, unjust and of a dangerous tendency, against which we take the liberty to protest. We have long groaned under the weight of an American Revenue Act and when by the virtue of the people in not purchasing any goods loaded with a duty, the malignity of the act was in some measure evaded, a scheme was devised and prosecuted by the ministry, to enforce said act by permitting the East India Company to force their infectious teas upon us, whether we would or not. At this, not only the inhabitants of Boston, but of the whole province were very much and very justly alarmed and while they were prosecuting every method that the human wisdom would devise that the tea should be sent back undamaged, it was destroyed, but whether by the people of that town, or any other town of this province do not appear.

By the next resolution, the third, the town had resolved to instruct their representative to the General Court, the Tory Abijah White,

> lst, to endeavor that the perpetrators of these mischiefs be brought to justice. This appears to us to be the business of another department. We have executive courts and officers, whose duty it is to punish offenders and we trust they are faithful.
>
> 2dly, They instruct him to endeavour that this town be excused from paying for said teas, which we think might have been omitted, at least, till there was a probability of a requisition from proper authority for payment. They conclude with a denunciation "of all methods of imposition, violence and persecution, such as has been

"That Most Loyal Town"

most shamefully exercised upon a number of inhabitants of Plymouth by obliging them to sign a recantation" &c. Such bitter, virulent and injurious reflections on our brethren at Plymouth, ought not to have taken place until some shadow of proof had been adduced to the town, that any such violence &c. was ever practiced by them on a single person. The occasion of this our protest has given us great uneasiness and we were confident those extraordinary resolves would not have taken place but by the insinuations of a certain gentleman who seems willing his constituents should share in the resentment of the whole country, which he had incurred by his conduct in a public character. We mean not to countenance riotous and disorderly conduct, but, being convinced that liberty is the life and happiness of a community, are determined to contribute our last mite in its defence, against the machinations of assuming, arbitrary men, who stimulated with a lust of dominion and unrighteous gain are ever studying to subjugate this free people.

The protest was dated at Marshfield, February 14, 1774. Fifty-one Whig householders signed. Colonel Anthony Thomas, head of the town's militia and colonel of the Second Plymouth County Regiment of militia, was among the first. Nehemiah Thomas, his cousin and a man likewise prominent in town affairs at the time, and Briggs Thomas, the Colonel's son and the Deacon's son-in-law, signed. Both Benjamin White and Jeremiah Low, leaders of the group who had seized and burned the tea, joined in the protest. But others of the White family and members of the Little family, both predominately Tory in sympathy, refused to add their names.

For his participation in the town meeting of January 31st and for his "insinuations" that prompted adoption of the "very remarkable Resolves" of Marshfield, Ray Thomas gained widespread notoriety among Massachusetts Patriots. But his loyalty to the Crown was also noted and remembered by those in authority in Government circles. Whether one's feelings were Tory or Whig, Ray Thomas was a marked man.

It was neither popular, certainly, nor altogether safe to be loyal to King and Parliament on the eve of the American Revolution. But for some who were loyal, it was destiny.

II

Tension Mounts

Marshfield, "that most loyal town," was a small country town some thirty-five miles south of Boston in the Province of Massachusetts Bay and roughly fifteen miles north of Plymouth in Plymouth County. Plymouth had been the chief town of Plymouth Colony, the Old Colony, since the landing there in 1620 of those who would become known as the "Old Comers." It was, indeed, the capital of the Old Colony until that Colony was absorbed into the larger, more important Province of Massachusetts Bay in 1691 after nearly seventy-five years of independent existence.

Plymouth was now, in the first quarter of the eighteenth century, a shire town, the county seat of the county of that name. Marshfield, incorporated in 1640 in Plymouth while the Colony still persisted, was by the 1770's a town of some 1,000 inhabitants. It was a farming community, with shipbuilding an important and flourishing business on the North River, the boundary with the town of Scituate. The terrain was rolling, rising from low land along the coast to a hilly section to the north. The southern part of town had been the earliest settled and was still the center of town activities. Here the First Church stood by the training field where the militia went through the manual of arms and pirouetted in the mysteries of the drill. Here too stood Bourne's Ordinary, where man and beast could find refreshment and Mr. Bourne dispensed staples hard to locate in the surrounding countryside.

One of the narrow dirt roads that radiated out from First Church and training field led easterly to the Duxbury marshes. It crossed Green Harbor River (formerly Greene's Harbor River) where that river was hardly larger than a stream, some two miles from the center of town. Green Harbor River, winding and meandering, broadened out through salt marshes till it reached the sea. The road, although south of and some distance from the river, generally followed the river's course. Skirting the marshes, it traversed higher ground suitable for tillage and pasturage and even higher ground covered in woods. This area of the town was known to William Bradford, governor of the Plymouth Colony and chronicler of its early history, as early as 1632 as "a place very well

Tension Mounts

meadowed and fit to keep and rear cattle good store [in abundance]." Appropriately enough, this area of Marshfield was known as Green's Harbor. It was in 1640, that Green's Harbor was denominated a "town with the name Rexham, now Marshfield..."

That road which led out from the center of town toward the Duxbury marshes was the site of the farms and homes of some of the earliest settlers. Edward Winslow, one of the Mayflower company in 1620 and thereafter important in the affairs of the Colony, acquired a large grant from the Colony at the end of that road abutting on the Duxbury marshes. The total of his holdings was about one thousand acres. By 1774 this land had descended to General John Winslow, his great-grandson and a staunch upholder of the Crown. That was the year of the General's death and his property became vested in his sons, Pelham and Dr. Isaac Winslow. Edward Winslow's house by then was no longer in existence. It had stood nearer the marsh than the existing house which was built in 1699 by Edward's grandson, Judge Isaac Winslow.

About a mile nearer town, situated on the edge of Greens' Harbor marsh and extending over adjoining higher ground suitable for tillage and pasturage and even more distantly to a low ridge of hills paralleling the river, was the land granted by the Colony to William Thomas in 1641. This was a large grant for the time and place, some twelve hundred acres in extent, when most allocations of land were for less than one hundred acres or at the most one or two hundred. The Winslows and Thomases received sizable grants because of their prominence in the Colony - Winslow as a Governor and outstanding political and diplomatic leader and William Thomas as one of the "Merchant Adventurers" who underwrote financially the voyage of the Mayflower and the additional costs of settlement. William Thomas also was one of the Assistants for a number of years, which in effect made up the Governor's Council of the Colony. He also held several other important posts in the government.

In the general vicinity of the lands of Edward Winslow and William Thomas were those of other early settlers. Among these was the farm of John Thomas, who although bearing the same name, was not related to William Thomas as far as is known. He was a trusted servant of Edward Winslow. His was a small farm of under a hundred acres and in the early 1770's was divided among the four grandchildren of the first John. One of these was Colonel Anthony Thomas, head of the military establishment in Marshfield and another was John Thomas, a doctor and long

Tension Mounts

a town leader, and soon to be named a general officer of Massachusetts Provincial forces by the Provincial legislature.

Still further to the eastward along that road leading out from the First Church and the training field was the mansion then in possession of Dr. Isaac Winslow. Built on land which descended to him from his great-great-grandfather Edward Winslow, the <u>Mayflower</u> passenger and three times governor of Plymouth Colony. The house had been built by the governor's grandson, Judge Isaac Winslow, who had held the post of Chief Justice of the Plymouth County Inferior Court of Common Pleas and Quarter Sessions of the Peace and also the presidency of the Provincial Council. It stood at the end of a narrow dirt road.

In the mid-1750's or early 1760's Dr. Winslow's father, General John Winslow, added architectural features then popular and based upon English prototypes. On the exterior of the house he introduced quoins or wooden squares simulating stone at the corners of the main building and the enclosed portico. In the interior he added wallpaper, fireplace tiles, plaster, wainscoting and paneling.

Altogether, Careswell, the "Winslow Mansion," as it would be called, gave the appearance of having been the commodious establishment of an early worthy, a gentleman of means, with refinements added in the eighteenth century to conform to then-fashionable notions.

Going back on that road from town about a mile, one would have come to a dirt lane that led through a rolling meadow to Ray Thomas's house. Surrounding this were the extensive acres of property, some twelve hundred that had been his family's since 1641. His house, his "new Mansion House" he would call it, had been completed in 1772. He was very likely influenced in the design of the house by that of the house of his long-time friend and boyhood neighbor Edward Winslow, brother of General John Winslow of Careswell. Edward Winslow's house was in Plymouth, erected on a commanding position overlooking the harbor. Ray Thomas's "New Mansion House" was commodious and architecturally a modestly distinguished Georgian country house.

Ray Thomas and Isaac Winslow were not far apart in age. Ray, at 42, had been born in 1731; Winslow, at 34, was born in 1739. A miniature of Thomas, done probably about this time, shows a gentleman of regular rather than decidedly handsome features, with a plain wig and wearing a plum-colored waistcoat. A contemporary portrait of Winslow is of an

Careswell, the residence of the Winslow family. Still standing at the intersection of Careswell and Webster Streets. Courtesy of the Historic Winslow House Association.

House of Edward Winslow in Plymouth before alterations. Now the headquarters of the General Society of Mayflower Descendants. Courtesy of the General Society of Mayflower Descendants.

Tension Mounts

older man whose eyes, saddened, have seen much of life's suffering. He, too, wears a wig and a white stock at the neck.

Both men had been friends since childhood. Not only had their families been friends and neighbors since the earliest days, even before the town was founded, but Ray and Isaac had been thrown together as boys, living as they did on adjoining estates. Since Ray was left an orphan at an early age, both his parents having died when he was six, Isaac's father, General John Winslow occupied a position of father to the young man, in loco parentis the lawyers called it. Indeed, the families were very close, all the more so because General Winslow had married a cousin of Ray's, making the boy a third cousin to Isaac.

At the Winslow's, where Ray was a frequent guest, there must have been talk of England and relations between the colonies and the Mother Country. General Winslow had been in the service of the Crown for much of his adult life and he spoke of soldiering and wars fought for the King, talk which made a vivid impression on young Ray. This was another bond between young Ray and Isaac and Isaac's brother, Pelham. The influence of General Winslow was very great on the boys. There was instilled in them a deep regard for England and all things English. In that period of friction between England and her American colonies, particularly the Province of Massachusetts Bay, the influence of General John Winslow was very strong and instrumental in shaping the minds not only of his sons Pelham and Isaac, but also of their boyhood friend Nathaniel Ray Thomas.

Marshfield, with its strong Tory faction led by Ray Thomas and Dr. Isaac Winslow, was one of few - and certainly the most notorious - of the Massachusetts towns openly expressing disapproval of the Boston Tea Party. But the Patriots saw in the East India Company's tea plan a conspiracy with the British ministry to force Americans to accept Parliament's right and power of taxation. When full details of the Tea Party reached England, the government was not long in adopting a hard stance toward the Bostonians. Initially it had broad support among the British people who felt strong measures should be taken against the Americans.

The government of the Prime Minister, Lord North, brought into Parliament a bill designed to close the port of Boston. It was punitive in nature, aimed at making the Bostonians scapegoats for what legal authorities in England considered an act of treason. Coercion was the

Tension Mounts

theme of the ministry. Despite modest opposition, the bill passed. The King gave the royal assent on March 31, 1774.

Alteration of the Massachusetts Charter, the Charter of 1692, the so-called Second Charter, had been under consideration by the ministry for some time. One provision of the Charter - election of the Governor's Council by the General Court, the legislature - seemed particularly objectionable. The councils of other provinces were appointed by the Crown and held office at the Sovereign's pleasure. Appointment by the Crown certainly seemed to Lord North's government preferable to what amounted to the peoples' choice. The ministry desired the charter altered to accomplish this. The Royal will would surely be strengthened. Another provision of the Massachusetts Government Bill was aimed at curbing expressions of popular discontent about government policy. This limited towns to one town meeting each year, held solely for the purpose of electing officers and adopting rules and regulations for purely local administration.

Lord North introduced the bill pursuant to a message from the King to both Houses of Parliament. King George III had urged them to "take into their most serious consideration, what further regulations and permanent provisions may be necessary to be established for better securing the execution of the Laws, and the just dependence of the Colonies upon the Crown and Parliament of Great Britain." In introducing the bill on March 28, 1774, Lord North foretold what was to come: "I propose, in this Bill, to take the executive power from the hands of the democratic part of the government." Lord George Germain commented in approval: "There is a degree of absurdity, at present, in the election of the Council." So was the majority feeling in Parliament, which concerned colonists were to learn shortly. But there was immediate and strenuous opposition. It was formidable opposition.

On the first reading of the bill, William Dowdeswell, veteran leader of the Opposition in the House of Commons, rose to object. After noting that the Americans had labored and flourished for fourscore years "under that democratic charter...and we have reaped the benefit of their labour, yet you are now going to destroy that very charter which has subsisted to the mutual benefit of both countries..."

On the second reading of the bill there was continued opposition by members of the Commons. Three of those members - General Henry Conway, Thomas Pownall, former governor of Massachusetts, and

Tension Mounts

Charles James Fox - were known to be friendly to the colonies. Governor Pownall, well versed in colonial affairs, pointed out that "the Committees of Correspondence in the different Provinces, are in constant communication...As soon as intelligense of these affairs reach them, they will judge it necessary to communicate with each other...They will hold a conference - and to what these Committees, thus met in Congress, will grow up, I will not say." Lord North countered these observations with comments of his own. "The Americans have tarred and feathered your subjects, plundered your merchants, burnt your ships, denied all obedience to your laws and authority...The measure now proposed, is nothing more than taking the election of Counsellors out of the hands of those people, who are continually acting in defiance and resistance of your laws."

After the third reading, the bill passed and was sent to the House of Lords for its concurrence. But before that occurred, Edmund Burke protested against the bill because the parties aggrieved were not heard. "Repeal, sir, the Act which gave rise to this disturbance; this will be the remedy to bring peace and quietness, and restore authority; but a great black book, and a great many red coats, will never be able to govern it."

Early in May the House of Lords, after much debate, passed the bill. Among those dissenting, the Bishop of St. Asaph observed, "would to God, my Lords, we had governed ourselves with as much economy, integrity, and prudence, as they have done. Let them continue to enjoy the liberty our fathers gave them. Gave them, did I say? They are the coheirs of liberty with ourselves; and their portion of the inheritance has been much better looked after than ours..."

Then William Pitt, the Great Commoner, now the Earl of Chatham, arose. Long known as a friend to America, he spoke from much experience and with depth of feeling. It was a moving scene:

> My Lords, I am an old man, and would advise the noble Lords in office to adopt a more gentle mode of governing America; for the day is not far distant, when America may vie with these Kingdoms, not only in arms, but in arts also. It is an established fact, that the principal towns in America are learned and polite, and understand the constitution of the empire as well as the noble Lords who are now in office; and consequently, they will have a watchful eye over their liberties, to prevent the least encroachment over their hereditary rights.

Tension Mounts

The gist of the debates in Parliament over the Massachusetts Bay Government Act quickly appeared in the British press. Newspapers together with letters from England to American correspondents began arriving in late May and early June. That act, with its predecessor the Port Act and the two successive acts relating to the administration of justice and the quartering of troops, collectively and quickly became known as the Coercive Acts.

General Thomas Gage, commander in chief of British military forces in the Colonies, was appointed governor of Massachusetts Bay on April 7, 1774, replacing Thomas Hutchinson. He arrived in Boston in mid May. Hutchinson left that town on June 1st, destined never to return to his native land. This was a sad day for the former governor. But he took with him several addresses of support and thanks, and personal letters, from Loyalists and from moderates who generally favored a traditional government. One of those who viewed Hutchinson's departure with regret was Nathaniel Ray Thomas.

Ray's feeling was both political and personal in nature. It was political because Ray was closely allied in Loyalist sentiment with the Hutchinson-Oliver dominated government in Massachusetts. This was the Tory oligarchy, sometimes thought of as the "court" party as distinguished from the "country" party. Allied as he was with the ruling power in the Province, Ray had been earlier commissioned by the then governor, Sir Francis Bernard, on January 28, 1762 as a Justice of the Peace for Plymouth County. Commissioned with him at the same time were his neighbor at Careswell, General John Winslow; his cousin and college classmate, "Will" Watson; and Abijah White of Marshfield. Of the political hierarchy acquainted with Ray Thomas, the most prominent was Peter Oliver of Middleborough in his own county of Plymouth, who was Associate Justice of the Superior Court of Judicature and brother of the lieutenant governor of the Province, Andrew Oliver.

Ray had another tie with Thomas Hutchinson, a personal one, a relationship through Ray's wife, Sarah. Elizabeth, the daughter of Sarah's sister Elizabeth Wentworth, had married Hutchinson's nephew Nathaniel Rogers as her second husband. Left an orphan at an early age, Rogers was brought up by Hutchinson, his legal guardian, in his own family and was regarded by the governor as one of his own sons. Rogers had sought the office of Secretary of the Province after the governor's brother-in-law Andrew Oliver vacated that position to become

Tension Mounts

lieutenant governor. Rogers' commission was seriously under consideration when he suddenly died in 1770. Because of his activities in support of government and his association with the Hutchinson-Oliver family faction, Rogers was denounced and ill treated by the Patriots. His wife, Sarah's niece Elizabeth Rogers, had been so harshly threatened that she had to leave her home.

Ray's action as Moderator of the January 31st Marshfield town meeting in persuading adoption of the resolves critical of the Boston Tea Party had called attention to his determined Loyalist sentiment. He was a firm "Friend to Government." His strong stand brought its reward. In March 1774, Governor Thomas Hutchinson wrote to the Earl of Dartmouth, Secretary of State for the Colonies, advising him about the matter of appointments to the so-called Mandamus Council, now Royal appointments by virtue of the Massachusetts Government Act. It was called the Mandamus Council because the King had issued a writ of mandamus [an authorative order of law] directing members of the council to serve. Discussing the local politicians involved, Hutchinson suggested names of those deserving of that honor. Nathaniel Ray Thomas was one.

On June 3, 1774 Lord Dartmouth wrote to Thomas Gage, Hutchinson's successor. Noting that "Parliament has made a very considerable progress in the American business," Dartmouth told Gage that he had sent on the Massachusetts Bay Government Act and His Majesty's Additional Instruction, which listed the thirty-six persons nominated by the King, with the advice of the Privy Council, to be the Council of Massachusetts Bay, "the best qualified for that Trust." His Lordship observed also that "there is little room to hope that every one of the persons whom His Majesty has appointed to be of his Council, will be induced to accept the honour; for there can be no doubt that every art will be practiced to intimidate and prejudice."

By what the Earl of Dartmouth called "a very unlucky circumstance," his letter of June 3rd, transmitting the Government Act and the instructions regarding the Council, did not reach Governor Gage until August 6th. On June 26th the Governor had informed Dartmouth that "the contrivers of all the mischief in the town of Boston, I am informed, are now spiriting up the people throughout the Province to resistance." Gage felt the reason was that the rough drafts of the acts of Parliament - the Coercive or Intolerable Acts - had already been printed in Massachusetts on June 4th. A month later Gage still had not received "the new Act for the better Government of this Province, tho' it is printed here, and many tell me, I

Tension Mounts

must expect all the Opposition to the Execution of it that can be made." Then he added in his letter to Dartmouth: "I hope the new Councillors and the Magistrates will be firm, but I have experienced much Timidity & Backwardness when People are wanted to stand forth openly."

As soon as Thomas Gage received the Massachusetts Bay Government Act and King's instructions regarding the Council, he lost no time, as he informed Dartmouth, in forming the "New Council." On August 8th, two days after receiving his instructions, he assembled all those members he could and directed that all the Councilors meet on August 16th. The Boston Evening-Post of the 15th, carrying a dispatch dated the 9th, furnished its readers with a "List of the Gentlemen appointed by His Majesty, Councillors of this Province," perhaps the first official notice in the press. Among those named was Nathaniel Ray Thomas. At the Council meeting on the 16th he took the required oaths and was sworn in a member.

Reporting to Dartmouth on August 27th of the progress he had made in forming the "new Council," Gage stated that "the twenty four who have accepted the honor the King has conferred upon them, are as respectable Persons as any in the Province." Recalling the Colonial Secretary's earlier comment, he acknowledged: "Your Lordship judged right that Art would be practised on this occasion to intimidate & prejudice." At the Council meeting, August 16th, several members gave an account of the state of their respective counties, "from whence it appeared that the Phrenzy had spread in a greater or less degree thro' all."

On Wednesday, August 31, 1774 the Council met in the Council Chamber of the Town House in Boston. Present were His Excellency the Governor, Thomas Gage; His Honor the Lieutenant Governor, Thomas Oliver; and fourteen members of the Council. The remaining two Councillors who had accepted seats on the Council and had been sworn in were not in attendance. They were Colonel Abijah Willard and Nathaniel Ray Thomas. As the first order of business, "His Excellency represented to the Board the very great tumults and disorders prevailing in many parts of the Province, tending to the entire subversion of Government, and particularly the attacks made upon diverse Members of the Board (residing in the Country) which had arisen to such a height, as that several of them had thought it necessary for the safety of their persons, to repair to and continue in the town of Boston." The Governor referred the Board to first-hand accounts submitted by harassed Coun-

Tension Mounts

cilors and others and filed with the Secretary. As a result of Patriot threats and intimidation, some of those appointed to the Council by the King refused to accept and others, having accepted, resigned.

A few days earlier, on August 25th, the Governor had written to Dartmouth the news that already several of those appointed had declined to accept. One refused from timidity, Gage said, and three more "plead age and infirmities, but I believe choose to avoid the present disputes." Still another, Gage added, "had connections with all sides, and would keep well with all, and I apprehend wants to see what turn affairs will take before he gives a positive answer." A week later the governor reported to the Colonial Secretary a half dozen resignations of men who had originally accepted and been sworn in.

Nathaniel Ray Thomas was not at the Council meeting though the plight of those Councilors around the Province was undoubtedly known to him. Still he remained steadfast in his determination to obey the King's instructions and to stay with the Council. It is doubtful he would have changed his mind even if he had known the details of the other Councilors' problems.

Among those resigning was Joseph Lee of Cambridge. In his letter of resignation of September lst, he echoed the governor's representations to the Council at its meeting the previous day, particularly as to the state of the Province: "...I find the establishing such a Council has so universally inflamed the minds of the People of the Province, and excited such tumults and disorders in various parts of it, as threatens a catastrophe greatly to be dreaded, and exposes the Members of the Council to such continual injurys and insults as I am unable to sustain. I am therefore obliged to submit to the rage of the time, and must beg Your Excellency to accept a Resignation of my Seat at the Board..."

Also on file in the Secretary's office was the letter of resignation of Timothy Paine of Worcester, written the last week of August and setting forth in considerable detail the circumstances that caused him to withdraw. More than two thousand men, Paine said, assembled on the town common. Nothing would satisfy them except that he resign and, he added in his letter to Gage, he was told they would not answer for the consequences if he did not. Accordingly, he signed a resignation and, at their insistence, was "escorted by the Grand Committee to the main Body, who were drawn up in the form of a hollow square, and there was obliged to read said resignation." Paine informed the governor that when

Tension Mounts

the assemblage broke up, a large detachment went to nearby Rutland to "wait upon" Colonel John Murray, who had accepted a seat on the Council.

When a body of some 1,500, "most of them armed with sticks, in general heavy enough to have levelled a man at a stroke" arrived at Colonel Murray's on Saturday, the 27th, they were told the Colonel was gone. They insisted on searching his house. "Rather than suffer such a rabble to enter the house," the Colonel's son Daniel wrote his father, "I would defend it with the little force I had (which was only our own family, which you are sensible could have made but a poor defence) to the last extremity." But in the face of superior and obviously determined numbers, the younger Murray let some of the leaders enter and search the house. The mob thereupon left. Daniel Murray was on the spot and knew the temper of the people firsthand. He warned his father: "...I have been told, and have not the least doubt but it will be put in execution, that if you do not make a Public Recantation (as they express it) of your Seat at the Council Board by the 10th of September next, they will make you another visit and destroy all your buildings, etc; and should you be at home, the greatest indignities would be offered to you; and I have too much reason to fear you might expect nothing short of death." But Colonel Murray did not resign from the Council.

The remaining qualified Councilors who were not present at the August 31st Council meeting at the Town House in Boston were Colonel Abijah Willard and Nathaniel Ray Thomas. The former had been personally harassed on his return trip from business in Connecticut. "Arms were put to his breast with threats of instant death, unless he signed a paper, the contents of which he did not know, nor regard." He managed to get to his house in Lancaster, however, he reported to Gage; but the news on September 2nd was that a large body of men was said to be marching on his house to force him to make concessions. Nothing further had been heard from the Colonel himself. Later though, having made his way to Boston, he took his seat on the Council.

Nathaniel Ray Thomas had remained at his house in Marshfield, "that most loyal Town," because of the disruption in the countryside outside of Boston. Ray was, however, very much aware of the Patriot threats and intimidating acts. Nearly a week had passed since the Council meeting of Wednesday, August 1st; two weeks since he had accepted his seat on the Council at his swearing in on August 16th.

Tension Mounts

At about this time Ray Thomas's refusal to resign his appointment by the King to the Mandamus Council had enraged the Patriots of Marshfield.

One late summer day soon after the birth of Dr. Isaac Winslow's first child on July 14, 1774, Ray paid one of his customary and frequent calls on the Winslows at Careswell. Dr. Winslow had inherited the Winslow property on the death of his father, the General, and was then ensconced in the old house. At this juncture of affairs the Tories of Marshfield were in the habit of using Dr. Winslow's house as a place for their meetings. Ray Thomas's appointment to and subsequent swearing in to a seat on the Mandamus Council was by now common knowledge. This was true not only in Marshfield but throughout the Province.

Ray had ridden over from his house and was warmly greeted by the Doctor. After an exchange of greetings and some modest conversation, Dr. Isaac Winslow suggested to his friend that he pay a visit to his wife and young son, John, in the main bedroom upstairs. Mrs. Winslow and her son were in what was always known as the "bridal chamber" because the room was first occupied by the builder of the house, Colonel Isaac Winslow, and his bride, Sarah Wensley, shortly after the house was completed.

Ray went upstairs and greeted Elizabeth Winslow and the new baby. Like all masculine visitors viewing a squirming fresh-faced baby, he "oohed" and "aahed" appropriately and was suitably impressed at the new arrival. He was about to return downstairs and congratulate his old friend on his first-born child when a large group of Whigs or Patriots, suddenly appeared outside the front door and demanded entrance. As their ring-leader announced, they wanted to search the house. They had reason to believe that the notorious and misguided member of the "newfangled" Council as it had been called, the Tory Nathaniel Ray Thomas, had taken refuge in Dr. Isaac Winslow's house. Without knowing the circumstances of Ray's visit, the Whigs burst open the front door of the house and proceeded with their search.

Swarming over the first floor, through the parlor and the hall or dining room and the winter kitchen and even the summer kitchen in the ell, the men went. Then they started upstairs. Ray, in the meantime, fully aware of what the raucous crowd was about, had retreated into the "bridal chamber" and, as an anxious and perturbed Elizabeth Winslow looked on, went to the paneled door to the right of the fireplace and opened it.

Tension Mounts

As Ray well knew, the door opened into a closet and onto a series of apparently appropriate shelves. By using the shelves for footholds, as Ray knew from long familiarity with the house, one could climb up and over into a downward passage that led to a secret room behind the parlor fireplace. This he proceeded quickly and as silently as possible to negotiate. The Whigs burst into the "bridal chamber," with much fanfare. They found the door to the closet closed and access to the secret passage hidden from sight.

They found Elizabeth Winslow in bed nursing her son. The sight rattled the Whigs. They hastily began in a bumbling sort of way to back from the room. "Excuse us, ma'am," they apologized shamefacedly. They quickly and quietly backed down the stairs, without searching the "bridal chamber" with more care. Ray was safe in his hiding place. The Whigs hurriedly left. Marshfield's most notorious Tory, most ardent supporter of the King and Parliament, was safe from the mob.

Then, on Tuesday, September 6th, someone brought him warning that a large party from the neighboring towns was preparing to march on his house and confront him the next day.

There was hasty, emotional talk. Ray and Sarah, and probably their eldest son Nat and eldest daughter Sarah, shared the conference. The younger children were kept out of the way by a servant. Ray was grim. He well knew the situation. It had a familiar ring. No longer was it safe to remain even in Marshfield. He feared for his life, he worried over his family's fate. Whatever the risk, however, he had to take the chance of getting through to Boston to join the Government. The Council must not, as Gage feared, be "annihilated." Recently appointed to that body and sworn in, Ray felt even more strongly than before that the Royal authority had to be preserved. This overrode even concern for himself and his family. Ray decided quickly. Farewells were brief and moving.

It was dark that evening. Hardly aware of the late summer night's familiar reassuring sounds, alert only to the prospect of the morrow's grim uneven tramping and angry hostile muttering of a thousand threatening men, Ray had sent orders to a farmhand to saddle his best horse. Mounting he turned momentarily in the saddle. Nat had gone out with him. Sarah, young Sarah, and the other children stood in the rear doorway. Sarah had her arms around Elizabeth and Charles, holding them close. Ray waved, then turned his horse's head toward the east and rode off. He knew very well how risky it would be to travel by road

Entrance to the secret passage in the Bridal Chamber, Careswell. Photograph by Mary E. Doyle.

Dr. Issac Winslow, Courtesy of the Pilgrim Society, Plymouth, Massachusetts.

Tension Mounts

and so decided to ride across his own land, skirting Greens' Harbor River marsh, and then, crossing the river, headed onto the beach. He continued north along the beach toward Boston. He swam his horse across the mouth of the North River and rode on. He heard the waves breaking, he saw the dim outline of sand dunes. Reaching Hingham Harbor by early morning light, he found boatmen milling about their small craft. Finding one of the men willing to carry him to Boston for a fee, Ray chartered the vessel and so completed his escape to the provincial capital.

It was well indeed that Ray Thomas had fled Marshfield, for true to the warning he had received, a mob had formed and marched on his house the next morning. The <u>Massachusetts Spy</u> of September 22nd carried a firsthand account of the events that transpired:

> On the evening of the 6th instant, a large number of people collected at Plimouth, in consequence of the bells ringing, drums beating, &c. when they were informed, that a visit was proposed the succeding day to N. Ray Thomas, of Marshfield, one of Lord North's new-fangled peace-officers. It was thought preposterous by many, to visit Mr. Thomas 'till there was more certain evidence of the resignation of their own councellor; who had verbaly declared his intention of resigning almost a fortnight, and had dispatched a courier to the Governor for that purpose; but no account of it appearing in the public papers, gave grounds for suspicion, that some intervening circumstance had prevented his surrendering...
>
> Wednesday morning the people assembled, and having marched as far as Kingston, formed a procession, and were joined by large parties in their way to Marshfield, where they found a vast concourse of their brethren, from the several towns of Pembroke, Scituate and Hanover, drawn up in regular battalia, [order of battle] and parading before the Rev. Mr. Shaw's. A committee consisting of thirty-five persons was chosen out of the body to confer with Mr. Thomas, and warn him at the peril of their high resentment immediately to desist acting in a capacity for which nature had rendered him unfit, and to which he had no constitutional claim. The whole body in exact order repaired to Mr. Thomas's house, and the committee going in, were told upon enquiry, that he decamped the preceding evening, and had taken sanctuary in Boston, once the scourge of parricides, but now their only assylum. The most solemn protestations of his wife and son, that he was absent from home,

Tension Mounts

would not satisfy the people out of doors. They must attest the same on oath, or the house must be searched. The former was consented to, and an oath was administered to them both, by one of the eldest and worthiest justices in the county. They then confirmed the truth of what they had before said. One of the committee in behalf of the rest wrote the following letter to Mr. Thomas, and obliged his son by oath to deliver it to him the next day, viz:

"Marshfield, 7th September, 1774
"To Nathaniel-Ray Thomas, Esq:
"Sir,
"WHEREAS you have accepted a seat at the council board, under the new unconstitutional establishement, and have sworn to execute the late oppressive acts of parliament, which has occasioned great uneasiness, and the meeting of a large and respectable number of people from every part of the county, for the purpose of demanding your resignation of the aforesaid obnoxious office: These are to inform you, that we expect you to resign the same, within ten days from this time, and publish it in the Boston papers. Otherwise you may compel us to take measures disagreeable to ourselves, as well as to you.
The County of Plimouth."

The business of the committee being finished, they reported their proceedings to the body, which were unanimously voted to be satisfactory, and having given three cheers in approbation of their conduct, dispersed, each to his respective habitation. No injury was offered to the property or person of any individual; the utmost decorum, propriety, and decency, were observed through the whole day.

Several gentlemen attending, thinking the object of pursuit too insignificant to merit the least degree of notice; one that it would rather gratify his vanity by bringing him from the kennel of security into public view; and this is the reason he has been neglected so long; but however inconsiderable he may be in himself, he has derived so much consequence from his late appointment, that unless he complies with the requisition of the county, and reverts to his primitive nothingness, a

Tension Mounts

storm will break over his head, that no tears of contrition will be able to divert.

Thus did the local populace, the neighbors of Nathaniel Ray Thomas, vent their long-suppressed ill feeling against him. What was even more telling, though probably unknown to Ray, was an open coffin which the crowd had brought along with them. It was symbolic of the punishment that awaited the obdurate councillor if he did not back down and sign a recantation, his resignation from the Council. There was little doubt but that the crowd meant business.

General Thomas Gage, Hutchinson's successor as governor of Massachusetts, issued writs for election for representatives to the General Court, the body which was responsible for governing the Province. The assembly was to sit at Salem on October 5th. Then the governor, considering it unwise to convene the legislature because of the recent and ongoing friction between the Tories and Patriots, endeavored to halt the holding of elections. But they were held anyway. The elected representatives met at Salem and when the governor failed to appear, the representatives went into convention and agreed to form a Provincial Congress. In this sequence of events, Marshfield had held a town meeting on September 26th and had chosen Nehemiah Thomas as representative to the General Court planned for Salem on October 5th. On October 8th, however, with the governor failing to appear at Salem and those in attendance going into convention, a meeting of the inhabitants of Marshfield was held by call of the Selectmen. Nehemiah Thomas was unanimously chosen to cooperate with his colleagues "in order to form themselves into a provincial Congress Committee, and to take into their most serious consideration what may be the most wise and prudent measure to be taken at this most alarming crisis of our public affairs, and what may be most likely to produce a radical change of our public grievances." For all practical purposes, the Provincial Congress of Massachusetts had taken over the functions of the Royal government.

Earlier, following the news of the Boston Port Act closing the port of Boston, sentiment in the colonies grew for calling of a general congress to consider British-American relations. By the end of the summer of 1774, twelve of the thirteen colonies had agreed to the idea of a continental congress to be held in Philadelphia in September; and by the first of that month all had delegates to such a session. When the delegates convened in Philadelphia, they set themselves to the task of

Tension Mounts

formulating a statement of the colonies' rights and grievances and of adopting a measure to force Britain's cooperation. While these matters were under consideration, news arrived from Boston that General Gage was about to fortify the narrow neck of land that connected the town with the mainland, thus blocking access to the capital of the Province and possibly holding its citizens hostage. At that stage the Boston town meeting sought the advice of the Continental Congress.

A committee of Congress informed Gage that "the town of Boston, and province of Massachusetts Bay, are considered by all America as suffering in the common cause." It asked the governor to cease the construction of fortifications. The Congress also advised the Bostonians not to submit to the Coercive Acts, resolving specifically that anyone who took a commission under the Government Act would be abhorred as an instrument of the British ministry, the "despotism" that was threatening to crush American liberties. Among those thus branded by the Congress was, of course, Ray Thomas.

Among other items on the delegates' agenda was the matter of ensuring Britain's compliance with the colonists' position. Economic coercion had long been felt to be an effective way to accomplish this. It would take the form of non-importation and non-exportation of goods from and to England, and the non-consumption of British commodities in the colonies. Of particular importance was the provision for committees - committees in county, town, and city - to enforce the commercial boycott. This program shortly became known as the Continental Association. The Association, through its local committees of inspection and enforcement, gradually provided the sinews of a body politic, a form of revolutionary government supplanting that which had existed previously.

Because of the harsh treatment singled out for Massachusetts by the British ministry, that province responded with vigorous approval of the Association. During the fall of 1774 and early spring of 1775, more committees of inspection and enforcement were formed in the Province of Massachusetts Bay than in any other colony. Not only was approval vigorous but very nearly unanimous among counties and towns expressing their sentiments about the Continental Congress and the Association. The town of Marshfield, however, denied the authority of the Congress and rejected the Association.

Tension Mounts

Because of Ray Thomas's Tory activities, Whig leaders had imposed a boycott against anyone doing business with him. One day in that fall of 1774 Seth Sprague of Duxbury, Province of Massachusetts Bay, by his own account "a great boy about fourteen years old," watched in fascination as an odd-looking procession made its way into town along the Kingston road. A crowd of noisy jeering men and boys, milling about an ox-drawn cart, stopped near Seth. In the cart lay the carcass of a slaughtered ox, so slit open that a man was seated in its belly. Even as Seth watched, the crowd surrounding gathered up the tripe of the ox and hurled it into the man's face and tried to smear him completely from head to foot "to the endangering his life."

Seth ran over to one of the men in the crowd around the cart. Hesitantly, he asked what was going on. The man told him, pointing to the cart and explaining that the poor wretch seated in it was one Jesse Dunbar from near Bridgewater. Then the man went on, saying that Dunbar had bought some fat cattle from the farm of Nathaniel Ray Thomas in Marshfield and driven them to Plymouth for sale. Even young Sprague had heard his father talk of Ray Thomas, who, everyone knew, supported King and Parliament against the American colonies. But also, and worse in the eyes of Patriots, he had accepted an official position from the Crown in his own Province of Massachusetts Bay. For the Whigs, in party parlance of the times, he was a "high" Tory.

After Dunbar and his drove of fat cattle had reached Plymouth, Seth was told, Dunbar killed one of the beeves, skinned the carcass, and hung it up. But by then word had spread from whom the cattle had been bought, and local authorities arrived on the scene. The Whig Committee of Correspondence took stern measures. It vented its immediate wrath on Dunbar, who the Committee suspected of being sympathetic to Britain. But the Committee really wanted to show its scorn, to make a conspicuous mockery, of Ray Thomas, and set out to do just that. Taking the carcass of the slaughtered ox and throwing it into a cart, Committee members slit it open and forced Dunbar to seat himself in the belly of the beast.

The Committee was determined to send the hapless Dunbar and the slaughtered animal to Marshfield and Ray Thomas as evidence of its contempt. Willing hands then carted Dunbar four miles, extracted a dollar from him for the ride, and turned over cart and unwilling passenger to a Kingston mob. These eager participants proceeded four miles farther to the Duxbury line, made Dunbar pay another dollar for

Tension Mounts

their stretch of the journey, and deposited cart and the thoroughly shaken Dunbar before Seth Sprague's eyes. For the last few miles to Ray Thomas's house in Marshfield, Seth declared, "I was among a rabble of boys that went hooting and hollowing behind the cart."

The procession moved on through Duxbury village, past Duck Hill. The road wound into Marshfield through meadows and by woods and marshes, and past Dr. Winslow's house. Bearing to the left, the road continued for a half mile or so to the lane leading to Ray Thomas's "new Mansion House," as he was wont to call it. The cavalcade turned into the lane and went purposely up to the house, stopping only a rod or two before the front door. Dunbar's tormentors collected a final tribute from him, a final dollar, and then tipped up the cart and let the carcass of the ox slide out at Ray Thomas's doorstep.

Ray Thomas was not about, he was in Boston. But his wife was home. What happened next young Seth would not forget. Years later, he recalled: "Mrs. Thomas was a well-informed, prudent, discreet woman. She opened her front window and addressed the company in such a manner as I have reason to think made some of them, at least, very much ashamed...Although it was good fun for me to follow Dunbar with tripe on his head, I got somewhat frightened before I got home."

Young Seth Sprague's was a candid reaction. To a fourteen-year-old it seemed like fun, but to a mere lad who hardly understood the nature of partisan harassment, what went on that day had also been frightening.

Events combined to make the situation both in the Province of Massachusetts and the town of Marshfield increasingly tense and explosive. Considering General Gage's recent dispatches, Lord Dartmouth, Secretary of State for the Colonies, acknowledged on October 17th "the affairs of the Province to be indeed in a very dangerous & critical situation..." Two months later Gage advised Dartmouth that "nothing has been left untryed that could tend to hurt and terrify the mandamus Counsellors to resign, who have withstood all threats against their persons and properties, but they are still obliged to take shelter with the Troops..." Referring then to the admission of three more members into the Council, he added "all the former Counsellors stand firm and deserve the greatest encouragement."

Almost immediately following this, the governor sent the Secretary of State "a List of his Majesty's Council in His Province of the

Tension Mounts

Massachusetts Bay." Named were Thomas Oliver, Esq., Lieutenant Governor; Peter Oliver, Chief Justice; Harrison Gray, Treasurer; Thomas Flucker, Secretary; Foster Hutchinson; William Browne; Timothy Ruggles; Josiah Edson; John Murray; Joshua Loring; John Erving, Jr.; Nathaniel Ray Thomas; Sir William Pepperell; Daniel Leonard; Richard Lechmere; James Boutineau; and John Vassall, Nathaniel Hatch, and George Erving, those admitted but not sworn in.

At about the same time one of the Council, General Ruggles, an outspoken supporter of the Crown, endeavored to muster opposition to the Continental Association. Ruggles circulated a petition to the effect that those signing it pledged neither to acknowledge nor submit to the authority of the Continental Congress "at the risk of our lives if need be." They would reject the Association. There was little favorable response to the petition, however, with one notable exception.

In a letter from Boston about the middle of January, 1775, a New York correspondent was told: "one hundred and fifty of the principal inhabitants of the Town of Marshfield entered into General Ruggles's Association against the Liberty Plan." Tory sympathizers thereupon formed the Associated Loyalists of Marshfield; the group's principal meeting place was Dr. Isaac Winslow's, quite understandably, for he was the leading Tory then in Marshfield. When news of this reached Plymouth, Patriots there "threatened to come down in a body and make them recant, or drive them off their farms..."

General Gage was well aware of such an ominous situation. In a letter to Dartmouth on January 27th, he noted "information often from the Country that the Towns in this Province become more divided, notwithstanding the Endeavors used to keep up their Enthousiasm; and the Tyranny and Oppreassive Acts exercised against Persons deemed Friends of Government, has driven them in Several Places to combine together for their Mutual Defence." He went on to stress: "Where the Majority in a Township has been averse to their Measures, the Faction has employed their adherents in Neighbouring Towns to join and form Bodys sufficient to force them by numbers to sign Recantations, which has been attended with Violence and ill Usage."

With this preamble, General Gage came directly to the point of his letter. "The Town of Marshfield with part of that of Scituate having been lately under Terrors of this kind, from the Threats of their Neighbours, for having form[ed] some Association amongst themselves, applyed to me

Tension Mounts

for Protection; and I have sent a Detachment of one hundred Men to their Relief. I inclose Your Lordship a Copy of their Petition to me on this head..." Gage then observed that "it is the first Instance of an Application to Government for assistance, which the Faction has ever tried to perswade the People they would never obtain, but be left to themselves."

Gage's response to the petition of the Marshfield Loyalists, his dispatching troops for their protection, evoked a variety of comment. A letter from Boston to a New York correspondent remarked on Marshfield inhabitants signing General Ruggles' Association and on the hostile threats from Plymouth, then stated that the Associators in Marshfield had begged Gage's support. The detachment of British troops sent by him landed quietly and no appearance of Plymouth Patriots was noted. The Boston letter continued: "The detachment carried with them three hundred stand of Arms for the use of the gentlemen of Marshfield; one hundred and fifty more having joined the first Associators on advice of the Plymouth threatenings; the whole three hundred have solemnly engaged themselves to turn out in case of an attack."

Finally, the writer from Boston commented: "That the Liberty Rebels in this Town might save their own credit, and that they might have something to say for not opposing the detachment, they, on the first hearing where the Soldiers were going, wisely sent off an express to their Plymouth confederates, begging them to desist from doing what they realy had no mind to; and now they are praising themselves for their peaceable disposition, which they always do when their outrages have raised any opposition against them, and are execrating the Government for wanting to massacre them." The New York newspaper, by printing the letter, made clear its Loyalist persuasion.

The people of Marshfield itself were not without a voice, when it came to the printing of letters by the press. A letter from that town, dated January 24, 1775, was made public by a Boston paper also with Tory leanings.

> Two hundred of the principal inhabitants of this loyal town, insulted and intimadated by the licentious spirit that unhappily has been prevalent amongst the lower ranks of people in the Massachusetts Government, having applied to the Governour for a detachment of his Majesty's Troops to assist in preserving the peace, and to check the unsupportable indolence of the disaffected and turbulent, were happily relieved by the appearance of Captain Balfour's party, consisting of one hundred

Tension Mounts

Soldiers, who were joyfully received by the Loyalists. Upon their arrival, the valour of the Minute-Men was called by Adam's crew; they were accordingly mustered, and to the unspeakeble confusion of the enemies of our happy Constitution, no more than twelve persons presented themselves to bear Arms against the Lord's anointed. It was necessary that some apology should be made for the scanty apperance of their volunteers, and they coloured it over with a declaration that "had the party sent to Marshfield" consisted of half a dozen Battalions, it might have been "worth their attention to meet and engage them" but a "day would come when the courage of their Minute host" would be able to clear the country of all their enemies, "howsoever formidable in numbers."

The letter concluded: "The King's Troops are very comfortably accommodated, and preserve the most exact discipline; and now every faithful subject to his King dare freely utter his Thoughts, drink his Tea, and kill his Sheep as profusely as he pleases."

The Patriot faction was constantly presenting its views and sentiments, usually with even more vigor and vengeance than that of the Tories. James Warren, the Plymouth Whig and leader of anti-government forces, wrote to John Adams at the Continental Congress on January 15th before the Marshfield Associators asked Gage for protection. The Tories, Warren informed Adams, were "more assiduous than Satan was with our first Parents, and equal him in deceit and Falsehood and with many find Success. No stone is left unturned to effect their purposes...The Tories it is observed hold up their heads lately whether from Encouragement taken from the late publications, or a Spirit of delusion diffused among them by the infernal Junto at Boston, I know not."

With his letter to Adams, Warren enclosed for "your Amusement two acts of a dramatic performance. Composed at my particular desire they go to you out of the hand of the Copier, without pointing or marking." This was <u>The Group</u>, a play written by Warren's wife, the versatile Mercy Otis Warren whose pen was conspicuously at the service of American Patriots. It was a satirical piece, whose barbs were aimed at Crown officials, specifically members of the Mandamus Council. The first part of the play, extending through the first scene of the second act, was pre-

Tension Mounts

sented to the public in the <u>Boston Gazette</u> of January 23, 1775. Before the end of the month, the real names of those held up to ridicule through fictional characterization in the play were known. Simple Sapling, Esq., contemporaries all agreed, was Nathaniel Ray Thomas.

When the Whig <u>Essex Gazette</u> of January 31st reported activities in Marshfield earlier that month, its news item mentioned "young Simple Sapling," obviously a derisive reference to Ray Thomas's eldest son Nathaniel. The paper reported that "a Set of the worst Tories" of Marshfield, made up of "about 200 Boys, Negroes, &c." equipped themselves with "two Swivel Guns" and sent "young Simple Sapling to the Governor, to whom they wrote all the falsity possible, and would make him believe they were in danger of being visited on account of signing Brigadier Ruggles's Association...Never was there such a Set collected together before, and shall as soon as possible collect their Names and more of their proceedings, so that their Accounts may be contradicted, as their reigning Principle is Lying." Readers of Whig and Tory newspapers could take their pick, it would seem, of whichever account of Marshfield's appeal to General Gage they fancied.

Gage responded swiftly to that appeal, the petition to which he had referred in his dispatch of January 27th to Dartmouth. He ordered a detachment of troops to proceed by water to Marshfield. Two of his officers, stationed with the British garrison in Boston, recorded in their respective diaries the events of January 23rd. Frederick Mackenzie, first lieutenant and adjutant of the 23rd Regiment, the Royal Welch Fusiliers, noted straightforwardly:

> 23rd. A Detachment consisting of 1C, 3S, 4S, 4C, 2D, 100P embarked this aftnoon on board The Armed Schooner Diana, and the Sloop Britannia, with 7 days provisions, their Barrack bedding, a few necessaries, and baggage sufficient for ten or 14 days. This Detachment is under the Command of Captain Balfour of the 4th Regiment [the King's Own], and is going to some town on the Coast not far distant.

John Barker, lieutenant in the 4th Regiment, the King's Own, elaborated on the facts in his diary:

> [Jan.] 23rd. This day at 3 o'clock P.M. a Detachment of 1C, 3S, 4S, 4C, 2D, 100P, embar'd on board two Vessels, to go to a Place called Marshfield about 30 miles from hence; it is in consequence of about 200 People

Tension Mounts

> there having declar'd themselves for Government, for which the People of Plymouth have threat'ned to attack them and force them to their measures, as they sent to the Cmmr. in Chief to request He wou'd send them some Troops for their protection, and Arms and Ammunition for themselves, both which He has don. Capn. Balfour of the 4th has this Command; we shall not perhaps see whether the Scoundrels will dare put their threats in execution, but I dare say not; they will be the same as they have hitherto been.

John Barker was a young officer, quite different in his outlook and comments from Frederick Mackenzie, older, more mature and experienced, a dispassionate recorder of facts. In his diary entry for the 23rd Barker exhibited his habit of frequent, offhand, and often critical observations of people and places; Mackenzie stuck to the essential facts. Barker continued with information of a sort that suggests he may have written the entry after the day itself:

> Mr. Thomas who lives there has order'd his House to be fitted up for Barracks: it will hold them all, I make no doubt, but they will have a very pleasant time of it, as there are two or three Gentlemen who will be as civil to 'em as they can; indeed it will be for their own sakes, a motive that will carry a Man further than anything I know.

On the 23rd also the Boston Committee of Correspondence sent off by express to the Plymouth Committee an urgent appraisal of the British troop movement. After scratching out words intimating that Marshfield people were apprehensive of injury to their persons or property by some in their vicinity, the Boston Committee set forth what they knew and what they advised.

> Having just received assurances that application has been made to General Gage by Messrs. White, Ford, Phillips, 2 Curtisses, etc., requesting a body of troops to be stationed in Marshfield, in consequence of which application we have received information that a detachment of 130 or 140 men, officers included, are already embarked and fallen down the streat destined for Plymouth or Marshfield. Pursuant to our duty, we thought proper by express to give you the earliest intelligence as we cannot but be alarmed at this dangerous maneuver

Tension Mounts

> of our enemies, which we apprehend is intended to precipitate us into a conflict with Great Britain.
>
> Our friends seem solicitous that, agreeable to the advice of the Grand Congress, you should act upon the defensive. We presume not to dictate, being assured that the wisdom and fortitude of our brethren in your county are equal to every occasion.

This advice from Boston was most likely that referred to in the January 26th letter to New York, which noted that "the Liberty Rebels in this town [Boston]...wisely sent an express to their Plymouth confederates, begging them to desist from doing what they really had no mind to do..."

In its express to Plymouth, the Boston Committee provided the additional information that "the dishonourable fugitive from Marshfield [Nathaniel Ray Thomas] has given the officers particular directions where they may seize the town magazine. We need not advise to take proper precautions for the security of these valuable articles and that our friends at Marshfield be immediately advised of this important matter." A postscript concluded: "We should not have urged you to the trouble of writing to our friends at Marshfield, but they, not having a committee of correspondence, and you from your situation being better acquainted with the sentiments of individuals, may address those persons to whom it may be proper to communicate."

News of General Gage's despatch of troops to Marshfield quickly spread. The following day, January 24th, John Andrews, the Boston merchant, wrote in his diary:

> In consequence of an application from a number of the inhabitants of Marshfield (who are under the influence of Ray Thomas, one of the Mandamus Councellors, and the Winslow family, who are likewise remarkable high Tories) a number of men, drafted from several of the Regiments, to the amount of 100, embark'd on board an arm'd schooner last evening to go there for their protection - they pretending that the neighboring towns had threatened to molest 'em - but cant learn that they had any such intentions. Hope the people will be discreet and prudent enough not to meddle with the Soldiers.

A few days later Ezra Stiles, Congregational minister, president of Yale College in New Haven, Connecticut, and inveterate diary writer, noted:

Tension Mounts

> There is a flying Report in Town, that upon the Petition of a Number of men at Marshfield, the Connexion of Mr. Thomas of that place one of the Mandamus Councellors, Gen. Gage has sent thither by Water a Body of Troops. But it is dubious...

Within the week, however, he had received fresh information:

> The Marshfield affair is true - about 120 Troops having been sent thither. But the Committee at Boston have written thither and to all the surrounding Towns beseeching them not to take fire & withold all Violence. It being resolved to keep still & bear all Insults till news from the Parliament.

The various reports and comments about what Stiles called "the Marshfield affair" differed according to their Whig or Tory source. Tory accounts revealed an immediate apprehension of some form of Patriot retaliation or a ridicule of Patriot efforts. Whig recitals, on the other hand, bearing down particularly on their enemies' "deceit and Falsehood," "their reigning Principle..Lying," nevertheless expressed frequent concern about war with Great Britain, and the danger of provoking or antagonizing the soldiers at Marshfield, and the need generally for maintaining calm. Lord Dartmouth had correctly appraised "the affairs of the Province to be indeed in a very dangerous & critical situation."

The movement of troops to Marshfield, attracting attention as "the Marshfield affair," had been effected by the British navy. The contingent under Captain Nesbitt Balfour of the 4th Regiment (the King's Own) consisted of three subalterns, four sergeants, four corporals, two drummers, and one hundred privates. The men boarded the schooner Diana, armed with "Saint Lawrence" guns and reputed "the best vessel of the kind that has been yet in the King's Service," and the sloop Britannia, at 3:00 P.M. on the afternoon of January 23rd. The ships dropped down Boston Harbor and then coasting southward along the shore, headed for the mouth of the North River dividing the towns of Scituate and Marshfield. Easing upstream to White's Ferry, the vessels disembarked the troops.

Captain Balfour's command was destined to take up quarters at Ray Thomas's house. Arrangements had already been made, on Ray's orders, for his house to be fitted up as barracks. Sarah Thomas and the children - six now that Nat and Henry Dering were not at home - and Mary Gooch, Sarah's sister who had been living with them the past few

Tension Mounts

years, quitted the house to make room for the troops. Sarah's cousin Joshua Winslow, writing to Thomas Dering later that summer of 1775, recalled: "You know that I have been a neighbor of Mrs. Thomas at Marshfield about two years...as you may have heard that Mr. Thomas's House was a Barrack last winter at which time the Family were dispersed." As for their situation, he added: "Mrs. Thomas & Mrs. Gooch with 5 more were with us till the Troops removed. Mrs. Gooch, her maid & Polly Thomas are yet with us." Earlier in the summer, Dr. Isaac Winslow had referred to "the ladies of Mrs. Thomas's family (who are now with us)..."

Once ashore and probably on the 24th, the contingent of the King's Own began its march southward to their intended barracks at Ray Thomas's. The troops tramped down the narrow twisting Green Harbor Path, which in the earliest days was a principal route from Plymouth to Marshfield. Their line of march generally paralleled, though to the westward, the course of the South River. After several hours, Balfour's column crossed that stream on an old footbridge some hundred and fifty rods northwest of the Town Common and the First Church. As the regulars neared the Common, children excitedly spilled out of the grammar school close by the First Church. Ten-year-old Isaac Thomas watched the Redcoats with "boyish curiosity" as they marched past and, with others of his schoolmates, trailed along after the soldiers. It was a remarkably warm day for January, one of the mildest any could remember, the noonday sun reflected on a hundred glittering bayonets, as Isaac Thomas often recalled.

Captain Balfour led his men beyond the Training Field on the Neck Road, turning off to the south in the direction of Ray Thomas's. Almost at that point was the house of Captain William Thomas, more familiarly known to townspeople as "Capt. Willie." In a lower bedroom of the Captain's house was stored Marshfield's supply of powder and shot, some of it said to be under a bed. [When the Captain's granddaughter was asked many years later whether she thought anyone slept in the bed, she replied that if it had been necessary, someone would have slept in that bed.] The Boston Committee of Correspondence on the 23rd had advised the Plymouth Committee that "the dishonourable fugitive from Marshfield [Ray Thomas] has given the officers [of Balfour's detachment] particular directions where they may seize the town magazine." But such notice, if sent on the 23rd even by express, could hardly have been relayed by the Plymouth Committee in time to alert

Tension Mounts

Marshfield leaders to take appropriate action before the British appeared in the town.

With the enemy on the scene and any warning at that point needless, Marshfield Whigs nevertheless acted quickly. Benjamin White and Jeremiah Low, the brothers-in-law who had fired the tea the preceding December 19th, again came to the fore. Around midnight of the 24th, with some of the neighborhood, they hitched up ox teams and, driving them to Captain Thomas's, carefully loaded the town's powder and shot onto the wagons. Moving off as quickly and quietly as they could, they headed for places believed safer than "Capt. Willie's." Benjamin White unloaded as much as his barn, on the outskirts of town, would hold. Marshfield's store of ammunition remained untouched.

III

Of Generations Past

Five generations of his family had preceded Nathaniel Ray Thomas on the Marshfield property. His earliest forbear, William Thomas, "that Godly Gentlemen" as a contemporary described him, had been born about 1573, traditionally of Welsh ancestry. He may have been, indeed, one of "Several Welsh Gentlemen of Good Note" who were induced to settle in the Colony of New Plymouth, which from 1620 to 1691 comprised the southeastern portion of the present Commonwealth of Massachusetts. By 1624, in any event, William Thomas was one of the Merchant Adventurers or investors in a company, which earlier, seeking commercially profitable overseas undertakings, had agreed to finance the Separatists or Pilgrims in their proposed colonial venture in the New World. From this arrangement came the voyage of the Mayflower in 1620.

By 1627 the Merchant Adventurers and the Plymouth colonists had agreed to end their business arrangement, although a number of the former continued to back the venture. Of these, several left England themselves to share in that New World undertaking. One was William Thomas, who, with his son Nathaniel (later known as Captain) and the latter's wife Mary, endured the harsh Atlantic crossing to settle in New Plymouth colony about 1636. Fittingly enough, at the time of William Thomas's death fifteen years later, the inscription on his gravestone in the burying ground at Marshfield described him for posterity as "William Thomas esq/One of the founders of New Plymouth Colony."

On January 7, 1641 the Court of Assistants of the Colony granted to William Thomas, gentleman, a tract of some twelve hundred acres of land in the locality already by then known as "Greenes Harbour" about fifteen miles north of the settlement at Plymouth. Imperious legal language, customary in such grants, nevertheless served to remind William Thomas that his lands, though three thousand miles across the sea from the seat of Empire, were part and parcel of the dominions of his Sovereign Lord Charles I, by the grace of God King of England, Scotland, France and Ireland, Defender of the Faith, etc.

Eagles Nest, the residence of the Thomas family. Burned in 1878. From John Warner Barber, <u>Historical Collections...Of Every Town in Massachusetts</u> (1839).

Of Generations Past

Green's Harbor was, Governor William Bradford reported in 1632, "a place very well meadowed and fit to keep and rear cattle good store [in abundance]." It seemed a pleasing and rich countryside to colonists seeking more land for homesteads and pasture than remained in and around the village of Plymouth.

Lying between Green's Harbor River to the north and the Duxbury town line to the south, the Thomas grant embraced upland, including a neck of land called the Eagles Nest, low wooded hills, and portions of the "great fresh marsh," Green's Harbor River marsh. The upland rose westerly to form a wooded ridge, which continued for more than a mile to the point where the river, curving inland, narrowed to a stream. North of the ridge and between it and the river were meadows, some rising ground here and there, and beyond, the marshes and the sea. One could catch glimpses of water from the high ground, hear the sound of waves as the tide came in, smell the salt sea air when the wind was in the east. One could sense an approaching storm when gulls flew in from the sea, with the sky soon dark and lowering and the rain driving hard across meadow and marsh.

It was here that William Thomas lived. Somewhere on the neck of upland known as the Eagles Nest, which pushed out into the marshes, was the "old house," as he called it. To this he first brought his family. But before his death in 1651 he had established as his residence a house to the west of it, built on a rise and facing south across a meadow to the "heighway" from Plymouth "into the Bay [Massachusetts Bay Colony]" and the wooded ridge beyond. Here, Nathaniel Ray Thomas would later affirm was "where his patrimony was the most considerable and his family residence was coeval with that town." That town was Marshfield, established by the General Court of the Colony on March 2, 1640 and first known as Rexhame.

A mile or so east of William Thomas's was the property granted some years earlier to Edward Winslow, Dr. Isaac Winslow's great-grandfather and one of the three or four leading personages of New Plymouth Colony. Born to a family among the lesser gentry in England, he was a leader from the outset of the Separatist or Pilgrim venture and served variously as governor of the Colony or as an Assistant, one of the governor's council. Winslow also acted as agent for the Colony in negotiations with the home government in London. At Green's Harbor he received tracts of land totaling one thousand acres or more and in

Of Generations Past

1636 had established there his residence, Careswell, named for a family property in England.

Green's Harbor, as that section of Marshfield continued to be known, was the center of early settlement and town activities. Beyond the properties of Edward Winslow and William Thomas to the north and to the west, a number of colonists had acquired land, mostly of small acreage. But the land actually settled was not as yet great. From the outset, however, the town was active in its own affairs and men from Marshfield frequently traveled to Plymouth on town or colony business.

By 1640 Edward Winslow had already been twice governor of the Colony. In June 1641 William Thomas began his active public service as one of two deputies or representatives from Marshfield to the General Court. Then, at March Court 1642, he was elected an Assistant, an office he would hold, with the exception of one year, until his death. In New Plymouth the Assistants comprised, in effect, the governor's council. When William Thomas took the oath of his office as Edward Winslow had done earlier, he swore "to be truely Loyall to our Sovereigne Lord King Charles his heires and Successors...."

Together with Colony affairs - he journeyed to Plymouth at least half a dozen times each year for sittings of the General Court and Court of Assistants - William Thomas involved himself in affairs at home. At a town meeting held February 27, 1644, the inhabitants of Marshfield agreed that there should be a Moderator chosen at the beginning of each session to conduct the business of the day; and they hoped to promote attendance by setting a series of fines for those who would disturb the meeting, arrive late, fail to attend, or leave without being properly dismissed. The first Moderator, chosen that day, was William Thomas; and among the first offenders, fined for not appearing at the hour of the meeting, was his son Nathaniel.

On July 9, 1651 William Thomas made his will. "Being weak in body" - that customary recital was doubtless correct - he could only sign with a mark. The end was near. In August, as the cicadas' shrill pulsing endless notes filled the hot still days and prefaced again the approach of harvest, William Thomas died. He was laid to rest in the burying ground by the church, on land given by him to the town for such use, a small parcel of land surrounded by his own extensive acres, a rise on the edge of Green's Harbor River marsh where the salt sea air moaned softly through the branches of ancient gnarled cedars.

Of Generations Past

Something of the character and quality of his situation is revealed by his will and inventory. The total value of his personal property was larger by far than that of most Plymouth colonists. Particular items are representative. There were, for example, a noteworthy amount of silver plate, utensils for table or domestic use, including "a silver beer bowle"; a "Trunke of fine linnen"; a table, chairs and cushions, chests and a looking glass; a feather bed as well as other beds; and a collection of about seventy-five books, a library of respectable size for the time and place. Among the bequests in his will was one of a "Taffety gowne and allsoe a Chamlett gowne and a fayer red petticoat."

It was with the disposition of his land, however, that William Thomas revealed most clearly his concern for property and material well being. At a time and in a world when there was little in the way of money or corporate shares or government securities, wealth, of necessity, took a tangible form. Land, in particular, had been of incomparable importance since feudal hierarchies were first founded upon it. It provided an income for the possessor of a landed estate; it gave him political and social standing. Even more with the discovery of the New World, it fired the imagination of men, giving promise of wealth to empire builders and speculators, and above all, of a new life to countless thousands. For in that vast New World, land was something which a man could hold for himself - a home, security, property from which he could wrest a living and with which he might reap rich rewards as well. For land and all that it represented, which few men had or could aspire ever to have in the Old World, those countless thousands braved the harsh and fearsome Atlantic voyage.

Whether or not William Thomas possessed or had any rights to a landed estate in old England, it was reasonable for him to expect that he would in New England. Just as wealthy merchants and men of business at home were eager to secure a country estate and the status of a country gentleman, so William Thomas would naturally have envisioned that for himself in New Plymouth. Furthermore, as one of the original adventurers backing the Pilgrim enterprise and a continuing supporter in the colony, and with his wealth and acknowledged rank as a gentleman, he could expect the New Plymouth government to respond favorably with a substantial allocation of land. This the Court of Assistants did in 1641, as it had earlier for Edward Winslow. Just what their grants of some one thousand acres each signified is suggested by the fact that the range of average grants was from less than fifty acres to about three hundred acres on the large size.

Because of the significance of land and the extent and value of his own holdings, William Thomas sought to provide for its preservation intact for his family for as long as possible. In his will, therefore, he had resorted to a solution that had been worked out centuries earlier by the English Crown, the landed families and their lawyers to accomplish that result. It was a solution familiar to him and one to which other landowners in New Plymouth Colony would turn as well. He left some 1,000 of his 1,200-acre grant to his only son Nathaniel in such a way that no part of it could be sold or seized by creditors and possession of the land would descend to Nathaniel's eldest son and successively to the eldest son from generation to generation. For example, if an eldest son died without a male heir, then that eldest son's next oldest brother, if he survived, would take the property. Together, this was known as entail and primogeniture.

To his younger grandson Nathaniel, who would not in due course inherit, William Thomas left some 200 acres of the original grant, including the "house commonly called the old house" with orchard adjoining and meadow and upland as well. Doubtless of more immediate significance to the eight-year-old boy at the time, however, had been his grandfather's gift to him of the "horse foal now sucking on the mare."

More than the "heighway into the Bay," then, the road that passed Edward Winslow's Careswell and William Thomas's property, later to be known as the Eagles Nest, connected those places, their owners, and their owners' families. There were broad and similar patterns. Edward Winslow and William Thomas were friends, neighbors and associates. Both had come from backgrounds - the landed gentry and the London merchants - which differed markedly from those of most of the Plymouth colonists. Both had experienced more of the world. Their respective properties, far larger than those customarily granted, lay adjacent to each other. They gave to Green's Harbor in Marshfield an appearance and feel quite different from any other section of the Colony and this would last, unimpaired and unchanged, for a century and a quarter until the American Revolution.

The families themselves, for that century and a quarter, had the flavor and status of "county families," as they might have been called in England, or gentry. They had country estates and, in the case of the

Of Generations Past

family of William Thomas, an entailed estate. As country gentlemen, members of the families occupied - and it seemed to have been naturally expected - positions of importance, honor and trust. They were magistrates in New Plymouth Colony, in later years, councilors of the Province of Massachusetts Bay. They sat on the bench of the Colony; they were justices of the peace, judges of the Inferior Court of Common Pleas and Quarter Sessions of the Peace, and, in some instances, reached the eminence of the Superior Court of Judicature of the Province. They bore military titles, and a Colonel Thomas or a Colonel Winslow could well have earned their rank and known war firsthand. Some members of the families were to have the distinction of being educated at the college in Cambridge, Harvard; most possessed natural ability and intelligence.

William Thomas and Edward Winslow had come from England, and they never thought of themselves, even in a remote colony, as anything but Englishmen. Courts were held in His Majesty's name. Legal process and writs ran in the name of the King. Oaths of office contained an affirmation of allegiance to him. He who broke the peace broke the King's peace. Theirs was loyalty to the Crown, very real and unswerving, and it would last down through 150 years or five generations.

Following the death of William Thomas in 1651, his son Nathaniel, Captain Nathaniel Thomas as he was usually known, acceded to the Green's Harbor property under the entail established by his father. Captain Nathaniel and his wife had two sons, William II and Nathaniel, Jr.; and several daughters - Elizabeth, Bethiah, and Mary. Both sons were involved with their father in an altercation with the Reverend Samuel Arnold, minister of the First Church, and the town of Marshfield, which sputtered on as the Captain's main preoccupation until his death in 1675 - a quarter of a century later. The controversy typified the seventeenth-century colonist's, in this case, the Thomas's, quick sensitivity to real or imagined wrongs and the stubborn persistence with which they sought relief.

The Captain's father had given one hundred acres of land to the town to help to support the ministry, which became known as the "Minister's Land." Ostensibly at issue was access to the "Minister's Land," but the real conflict centered on the minister himself, the Reverend Samuel Arnold, constantly crossing Thomas land to get to his land. The parsonage was on the north side of Green's Harbor River; the "Minister's Land" on the south, adjacent to Thomas property. The Captain questioned the

Of Generations Past

right of the town and, more particularly, the right of Reverend Mr. Arnold to trespass on Thomas land. The minister, evidently, was in the habit of crossing the river on a cart bridge on his way from the parsonage to the "Minister's Land" to take off hay.

Captain Nathaniel brought suit against Mr. Arnold for trespassing on his land, not once, but three times and to little avail. Mr. Arnold countered with a complaint that William II, the Captain's elder son, had accused him of having "delivered and taught horible blasphemy." The Court of Assistants, concerned because the charge had been made by the grandson of a former magistrate, "that Godly Gentleman," William Thomas, nevertheless found the charge "great arrogancy in Mr. Thomas" and advised him "for the future to carry more soberly..."

The town then entered the controversy by appointing persons to throw down any fence set up to obstruct passage over the bridge to the "Minister's Land." Captain Nathaniel forthwith put up a fence. A meeting with the town was arranged. Captain Nathaniel refused to appear. The town ordered the fence to be taken down and not be put back up.

The Court next ordered the constable of Marshfield to take into custody certain goods belonging to Captain Nathaniel and his son William, which had been attached under legal process. They resisted. Father and son were immediately committed to prison during the pleasure of the Court and ordered to pay the constable twenty shillings for reviling and threatening him. The Reverend Mr. Arnold's son entered the altercation. He assaulted young William Thomas. They came to blows. Both were fined for breaking the King's peace.

Captain Nathaniel adopted a new course of action. He refused to pay his share of the rate due the minister, even disposing of four barrels of cider which had been seized for the amount due. It was possibly about this time that his younger son Nathaniel endeavored to assist his father. Then about to enter the law as a profession, Nathaniel advanced some plan toward settlement. A meeting between the Selectmen of Marshfield and Captain Nathaniel and Nathaniel, later Colonel, was scheduled. The Captain did not appear. Nathaniel did, but the record showed that he had no authority to act.

Captain Nathaniel, stubborn and intransigent, filed suit in 1674 against those who were to collect Mr. Arnold's rate, charging that they had come onto his land and "did then and there hurt and harry" his cattle and took

Of Generations Past

away one of his animals. But even the Captain was tiring, for he failed to prosecute his case and it was dismissed. For his part, the Reverend Mr. Arnold at last could cross the cart bridge to the "Minister's Land" as he pleased.

Following the death of Captain Nathaniel early in 1675, his elder son William II entered upon and took possession of the property at Green's Harbor under the entail established by his grandfather. There he lived, unmarried and unnoticed, until his death in 1718. But his younger brother Nathaniel, shortly and hereafter known as Colonel Nathaniel, though mindful that he himself had inherited a farm outright under his grandfather's will, vigorously undertook to achieve goals of his own. Entail and primogeniture in England had long made it customary, indeed necessary, for younger sons who did not inherit extensive family property to take up a career. The army, government service, law, the Church - all offered traditional opportunities.

By 1665 the young Colonel Nathaniel - he was twenty-two years old - received "the black staffe with a brazen head" that symbolized his duty as one of the constables of Marshfield. This was the lad's first position, one that traditionally started a person toward successively important town offices. Perhaps it was this office with its responsibility for upholding the King's peace and the dignity of law that influenced him in his choice of the law as a profession. Or perhaps it was his recollection of his grandfather, the first William Thomas, who had sat on the bench as a member of the General Court and Court of Assistants, that caused him to embark on a legal career. In any case, his father's long-continuing, tumultuous struggle with the Reverend Mr. Arnold had provided an early opportunity for him to try out his hand at the settlement of disputes.

In the years immediately preceding his father's death, Colonel Nathaniel was engaged in the practice of law. But then, early in the summer of 1675, "The Greate Indian Warre," King Philip's War, began with a sneak attack on a small town in Plymouth Colony. At the outbreak of hostilities Colonel Nathaniel Thomas, then a lieutenant, forwarded from the scene of fighting a report that had originated with certain Indian chieftains to his friend, neighbor and then governor of Plymouth Colony, Josiah Winslow. It was to the effect that, if they captured "six English heads, then all the Indians in the country were engaged [to fight] against the English." Mindful of his wife Deborah, he asked Winslow to reassure her. "I pray, sir, remember me to my wife, and bid her be of good cheer."

Of Generations Past

During the war, throughout Marshfield, watch was kept day and night; and the dread meaning of signal fires or musket shot was known to every man, woman, and child. Guns were kept loaded and within reach. Not since the early days of the Colony had men carried their firearms to Sunday meeting. In addition to Winslow's Careswell, the house of William Thomas II, as it had been a generation earlier, was protected by a guard on constant watch and ever ready as a place of refuge for neighboring families in case Philip invaded Marshfield. Towns were few, small in number, and widely separated. Word traveled slowly. Deep woods covered much of the land. Night was dark and still. So it was that the people, fearful for years of Indian attack, now waited with grim apprehension the stealthy savage onslaught. The war came close to Marshfield - the next town to the north, Scituate, was sacked - and there was a chilling immediacy about that constant threat. But time was running in favor of the English with their better-organized and greater resources. By August 1676, with fighting on the wane, Philip was killed. The war was over.

Shortly before this time Nathaniel Thomas, whether Captain Nathaniel or his son Nathaniel is not clear, was on his way home in August 1658 when neighbors accosted him and urged him to go in a nearby house for shelter from a storm that was brewing. The storm looked black and forbidding. Nathaniel Thomas went in with the others to the house. One of the neighbors, John Phillips, sat down on a stool with his face toward the door and his back to the hearth. Thomas sat down with his face about six feet from Phillips. The narrative of Captain Thomas or his son continued: "The Thunder came quickly up over the house. The Clouds flying exseeding Low & thick soe that the heavens were much darkened. Then in a moment came downe (as it were) a great ball of fire with a Terrible crack of Thunder & fell Just before where the sd [said] Phillips sat, my eye then hapening to be on him saw him once start on the stole he sat on & fell from thence dead on the hearth backward without any motion of life, many bricks of the chiney were beaten downe the principle Rafters split the battens & lineing next the chiney in the chamber broken, one of the maine posts of the house into which the sumer was framed torn in to shivers & great part of it caried severall rod from the house, the dore where the ball of fire came downe Just before the sd Phillips was broken downe, out of the gert or sumer aforesd being a dry oake was peices wonderfully taken, I doe not remember there was any outward appearance of hurt upon the body of the sd Phillips, a young child being at that moment about three foot from sd Phillips had noe harm."

Of Generations Past

An inquest convened in Plymouth, August 4, 1658, found that Phillip's death was "by an Imediate hand of god manifested in Thunder and lightening..."

On June 23, 1666, "it pleased God to go on in a manifestation of his displeasure against New-England, in a very remarkable manner, by striking dead in a moment by a blow of Thundar, three persons in the Town of Marshfield in the Jurisdiction of New-Plimoth, in the month of June, viz. one named William Shirtliff, and a Woman and a Youth;..."

They were among fourteen people sitting in the common room of Mr. Phillips' house when a bolt of lightning came down the chimney, rent it to pieces, and struck all the people. The woman killed was Mr. Phillips' second wife, Grace, and the youth killed was Mr. Phillips' son Jeremiah. So John Phillips Senior lost three members of his family to lightning in 1658 and 1666.

These deaths were ascribed to God's dispensation and the account reproduced herein, in most details, was contained in a communication from Rev. Samuel Arnold to Rev. Increase Mather of Boston.

Colonel Nathaniel, following the close of hostilities during which he had been actively engaged and had been promoted to Captain, continued his involvement in public affairs and resumed the practice of law. He was appointed head of the military establishment of Marshfield and was again frequently a selectman of the town and a deputy to the General Court of the colony.

A major turning point in Colonel Nathaniel's career occurred in the 1680's, one which would materially affect his own life and subsequent life of his family. He extended his law practice to the neighboring colony of Massachusetts Bay and the powerful interests centered in Boston. In furtherance of this he was admitted to the bar of the newly created Superior Court of Judicature in 1686 - one of the first to be sworn as an attorney. There was a new horizon now. Large challenges lay ahead, and opportunities for fresh victories.

His successful handling of final settlement of the estate of Captain Robert Keayne, wealthy benefactor of Boston and founder of The Ancient and Honorable Artillery Company, on behalf of Captain Nicholas Paige and his wife Madam Anna Paige, the "gay and worldly" and thrice-

Of Generations Past

married granddaughter and heiress of Captain Keayne, enhanced and broadened his professional standing and at the same time his social life and connections in Boston.

By the last decade of the century New Plymouth Colony, despite continuous efforts to maintain its individual and legal existence, came to an end. The colony was consolidated with Massachusetts and Maine under the Province Charter of 1691, its lands and its people becoming part of the Province of Massachusetts Bay. It was a royal settlement, with Massachusetts taking its place in the British Empire. The King would henceforth name its governor, a royal appointee, and the King could veto its laws. But the General Court or legislature of the Province could elect the Council, as it had under the colonial government.

In 1693 Colonel Nathaniel, to which rank he had acceded, was elected to the Council and was returned annually to that office until 1702. Likewise, under provisions of the new Charter, he was commissioned a justice of the peace and of the quorum in 1692 and in that year took his place on the bench of His Majesty's Inferior Court of Common Pleas and Quarter Sessions of the Peace for Plymouth County. After leaving the Governor's Council in 1702, Colonel Nathaniel was raised to the Chief Justiceship of the Common Pleas and was named also as Judge of Probate for Plymouth County. Then in 1712 the Council appointed Colonel Nathaniel to His Majesty's Superior Court of Judicature, the highest court of the Province. His successor on the Inferior Court of Common Pleas was his friend and neighbor, Isaac Winslow, the son of Josiah Winslow and grandson of Edward Winslow.

During the years Colonel Nathaniel sat on the Superior Court his associates were the Chief Justice Wait Winthrop, and Associate Justices Samuel Sewall (later Chief Justice), Jonathan Corwin, Benjamin Lynde, and Addington Davenport. Sewall was an inveterate keeper of a diary. He was articulate and perceptive, mirroring life in the Bay Colony. Among details of people and events, sittings of the Court, decisions of the justices, Sewall touched on aspects of his colleagues' personalities.

Early in 1715, for example, Justice Sewall rode to what is now Chelsea in the company of Paul Dudley, the Attorney General, to hold court. But he prefaces his diary entry with the comment: "Col. Thomas carrys Judith." It was no doubt in his calash - a light, low-wheeled carriage with a top - that seventy-two-year-old Mr. Justice Thomas escorted thirteen-year-old Judith Sewall, the daughter of his colleague on that ride on circuit.

The following year, a week after Justices Sewall and Thomas had set out for Kittery in Maine in the calash, Sewall had an "inkling" that two merchants had arrived there on that Sunday. If the rumor were true, then they had violated the Lord's Day law that prohibited travel on the Sabbath. After examining one of the merchants that night, he consulted Colonel Nathaniel. The Colonel, Sewall noted in his diary, was "inclin'd to admonish them as young, and strangers, and let them go." This sensible advice influenced Sewall, despite his reservation that he "consider'd Col. Thomas was not a Justice there" for Sewall viewed profanation of the Sabbath as very serious. If the merchants would acknowledge their transgressions, however, Sewall was prepared to let them go. Both travelers rejected the proffer "with some disdain" and tendered their fines.

Colonel Nathaniel Thomas continued to serve on His Majesty's Superior Court of Judicature for the Province of Massachusetts Bay until his death on October 22, 1718. With appropriate ceremony, he was interred on Tuesday, October 28, at Marshfield where lay his father, Captain Nathaniel Thomas, and his grandfather, William Thomas, Esq., "one of the Founders of New Plymouth Colony." It was in the burying ground on the land given by his grandfather to the town for such a use, a small parcel of land surrounded by the extensive acres of Thomas property, a rise on the edge of Green's Harbor River marsh where the 'salt sea air moaned softly through the branches of ancient gnarled cedars.' His gravestone bore a simple inscription, according him a title of high dignity in the Province: "Here Lyes Interred The Body of The Honorable Nathaniel Thomas Esqr..."

Colonel Nathaniel had possessed ability and energy and a vital interest in many things. He was constantly involved in the public service, from the age of twenty-two as a town constable to the age of seventy-five as a justice of the highest court in the Province. He was at various times and often at the same time a soldier and lawyer, town and county official, legislator, councilor, and judge. His personal life was no less full. He took the land left to him by his grandfather William Thomas and extended his holdings many times over. He acquired a house and lots in the town of Plymouth and nearly two thousand acres of land mostly in the towns of Marshfield, Pembroke, and Bridgewater, and other towns in Plymouth County. And not long before his death in 1718, upon the death

Of Generations Past

of his older brother William II earlier that year, he became possessed as the next eldest male heir of the more than one-thousand-acre farm theretofore occupied by his brother under the entail established by their grandfather.

At the time of his death Colonel Nathaniel Thomas, in addition to his land, possessed tangible personal property worth a thousand pounds. He was owed more than another thousand due on personal bonds and on account. By any measure, he was a wealthy man for his time.

Colonel Nathaniel maintained a country estate at Marshfield, where he customarily dispensed generous hospitality such as the "noble Treat" enjoyed by Justice Sewall and his colleagues, possessed a house in Plymouth, and spent much time in Boston where he was well acquainted. He was three times married - for the first time at the age of twenty-one and the last at the age of seventy - and sired ten children. He presented a fine appearance, carrying his "silver headed Rapier" or "Silver headed cane or Ivory headed Cane" and dressed in formal attire adorned with a "Sett of Gold Buttons."

Nathaniel Thomas, eldest son of Colonel Nathaniel Thomas, third of the name, and hereafter referred to as Judge Nathaniel, was born in 1664 at the Green's Harbor home of his family. In his tenth year, his grandfather Captain Nathaniel Thomas died, and the farm with the "house Commonly called the old house" near the Eagles Nest passed into Colonel Nathaniel's possession, and there the boy lived to manhood.

Colonel Nathaniel's professional career in the waning years of New Plymouth Colony and at the bar in Boston influenced his eldest son. By the time that Nathaniel Thomas, Jr., as he was then called to distinguish him from his father, married in 1694 at the age of thirty, he was already engaged in the practice of law. In June of that year he took as his wife Mary Appleton, daughter of Captain John Appleton of Ipswich in Essex County, and granddaughter of Colonel Samuel Appleton, a Councilor, and member of a Bay family of distinction. Their second child and eldest surviving son, John, was born October 21, 1696. Four other children followed, only two of whom lived to maturity.

Colonel Nathaniel Thomas had been a member of His Majesty's Inferior Court of Common Pleas and Quarter Sessions of the Peace for Plymouth County since that court's inception with the establishment of the Province of Massachusetts Bay in 1691. In 1702 he became its

Of Generations Past

Chief Justice. He continued so until elevated to the Superior Court in 1712. In 1702 he also became Judge of Probate of the county, and his son Nathaniel, later Judge, became Register of Probate of the county. Both father and son continued on in those offices after the Colonel had gone on the high court and the younger Nathaniel had been appointed to the Common Pleas lately presided over by his father.

Of Nathaniel and Mary *Appleton* Thomas's three sons, John was entered at the college in Cambridge, Harvard. At that time students were not ranked alphabetically in class listings but according to the civil offices held by their fathers, with due regard for the social standing of their families. Such placing or ranking was dependent, of course, on varying and often touchy considerations. Clearly the son of a Royal Governor, of a member of the Council, of a respected Judge, or of a distinguished divine would be destined, under ordinary circumstances, to a high place.

In John Thomas's Harvard class of 1715, he was placed or ranked eighth out of eighteen. Above him was Benning Wentworth of the powerful and propertied Wentworth family of New Hampshire that seemed to have a close hold on the royal governorship and other offices of that province. In first place was Samuel Danforth, scion of a leading family of Massachusetts that had furnished magistrates and ministers in the colonial and provincial governments and included a number of Harvard graduates.

John's extravagance while an undergraduate did not escape notice. "He distinguished himself by rolling up the largest bills for commons and sizings of any boy in his college generation." Commons was the daily fare supplied students at a fixed price; sizings were a definite quantity of bread, ale, or beer, and so forth, and entered as a "size" on the college buttery or kitchen books.

Along with this comment on his hearty eating and drinking habits, young John was the subject of only one entry in the college records: "The Meazels first broke out upon Thomas..." Three years later, he received his A.M. degree and for two more years preached as a candidate for the ministry and looked for a pastorate. But either his lack of success in finding a pulpit, or more likely, events of singular import in the life of his family caused him to abandon thoughts of a clerical career.

Of Generations Past

Shortly after John had received his degree, his grandfather, Colonel Nathaniel Thomas died. Earlier that year, 1718, Colonel Nathaniel's elder brother William II had also died. For more than half a century prior to 1718, William II had been the proprietor of the Marshfield property under the entail established by the will of their grandfather; and upon the latter's death that year, without having left children or other issue or a will, Colonel Nathaniel had taken possession as the next eldest male heir. When the Colonel died later that fall of 1718, his eldest son Nathaniel, third of the name and like his father a judge of the Inferior Court of Common Pleas of Plymouth County, succeeded to the estate. But then, his right to possession was challenged by his own family.

Nathaniel Matson, his first cousin and son of the late Colonel's sister Elizabeth, brought suit to recover possession of one quarter of "this great Estate," as counsel referred to the Marshfield property. Although claiming title as one of four co-heirs of his late childless and intestate uncle, William II, Matson had made no move to assert his claim prior to the death of Colonel Nathaniel. He may well have waited because of the Colonel's prominence and his position as a justice of the Superior Court. Or he may have waited until the Colonel's will was admitted to probate and its contents thereupon made a matter of public record, so that he could ascertain its provisions. But the Colonel acknowledged the entail established by his grandfather and the descent of the property to his eldest son, Judge Nathaniel Thomas. Such a view of the matter had the weight and authority of a Justice of the Superior Court of Judicature; and this, if nothing else, might have prompted Matson to take the extreme course of a legal proceeding as his only hope.

Matson was represented in the suit by Isaac Little of the Plymouth County Bar, first cousin of both Matson and Judge Nathaniel and son of the late Colonel Nathaniel's sister Bethiah. Neither Court, opposing counsel, the parties, or Isaac Little himself apparently saw any impropriety in his accepting a case in which he had a personal interest at stake in the outcome. For if his client Nathaniel Matson were to prevail, then he, Isaac Little, as one of the several co-heirs also of his late and childless uncle William II, would stand to recover part of the "great Estate." Conceivably, one wonders, was it a collusive lawsuit, with Matson and Little involved together in attempting to recover a portion, a quarter each, of their late uncle's estate?

The case came to trial before the Inferior Court of Plymouth County at March term, 1719. The Court, having taken the case under advisement

Of Generations Past

for a year, then delivered judgment for the plaintiff, Nathaniel Matson. The defendant, Judge Nathaniel Thomas, appealed to the Superior Court. Again, that Court took the case under advisement for a year until the April term, 1720.

The Matson case was of singular importance. It raised legal questions then confronting bench and bar of the Province, but there was a deeper, more serious matter of social import. In England entail and primogeniture had been a bulwark of the aristocracy. Old World concepts of social distinction, that with which the early colonists were familiar at home, survived in the New. There was a class structure in the colonies, not hereditary but indigenous. It was hierarchal, less rigid and more fluid but nevertheless pervasive. The social pattern of the local English communities from which most early settlers had come was ingrained, especially social deference. There were leading government officials, professional men of standing, substantial merchants, and large landed proprietors who, together, constituted the gentry. Those of rank were honored by the courtesy title of "Esquire" and often referred to informally by it, as "Esquire Thomas," and the gentry generally and customarily were accorded the title of "Gentlemen."

Then there was the great bulk of the people, the "middling sort," the yeomen. They were the minor officials and professional men, average and small farmers, small merchants, independent artisans, and shopkeepers. Often, however, prosperous yeomen with substantial freehold acreage rose to become members of the gentry. There was social mobility. Below that group were free men of little or no property and recognized as inferior by their dress and deportment, tenants, poor farmers and artisans, laborers, servants and hangers-on. At the bottom were indentured servants and indentured convicts, one held in servitude for a specified time, the other often for life. And finally, there were free blacks, and blacks and Indians kept in slavery.

Seventeenth- and early-eighteenth-century colonists knew that men were not equal, not in fact, not in theory, and certainly not by their mere creation. Theirs was not, initially, a democracy. This they accepted as part of the ordained scheme of life. But some questioned, nonetheless, the adoption of English law that would prefer the eldest male line of a family in the possession of that family's landed property to the exclusion of younger sons and of daughters and virtually in perpetuity. For, after all, the first settlers had risked the harsh Atlantic voyage, not only for

Of Generations Past

religious and political reasons but also and vitally significant to them, for the acquisition of land.

Would the Superior Court in the suit against Judge Nathaniel, by reversing the lower court, recognize and support with the weight of its authority entail and primogeniture? Entail and primogeniture favored the accumulation and retention of real property by the eldest male line of landed families from generation to generation, thus excluding younger sons and daughters, and the attendant concentration of wealth and power in the hands of the few. Or would the high court, by affirming the decision of the Common Pleas, thereby strike down the existence and course of descent of an entailed estate as contrary to the "Condition and Circumstances" of the people in the English colonies, to use words of counsel in the Matson case strikingly similar to a long line of later decisions of American courts?

At April term, 1720, when then Chief Justice Sewall noted that "swallows proclaim the Spring," His Majesty's Superior Court of Judicature convened in Plymouth. In his own behalf, Judge Nathaniel had stated in his written brief that "The notion of Estates Tayl is ancient Settled and known in the Collony of Plymouth..." Matson's counsel relied heavily on a Massachusetts statute of 1692 that permitted division of intestate's lands.

The Court rendered its opinion. It reversed the decision of the lower court and found in favor of the defendant, Judge Nathaniel Thomas. "We ply'd our business very close," Chief Justice Sewall commented, [and] "had great Actions."

The "great Estate" at Green's Harbor in Marshfield was now, by judicial decision, secure in the possession of Judge Nathaniel Thomas under the entail. With final determination of Nathaniel Matson's suit, the Judge and his family were able to give attention to other matters. The old Colonel had believed that his eldest son, the Judge, would indeed take possession of the entailed family property at his own death and he had left him additionally his farm near the Eagles Nest given him by his grandfather, the first William Thomas. So he made settlement of his other lands and money on his younger sons and daughters. He charged his executor, the Judge, with the duty and responsibility of carrying out his provisions for that settlement. This the Judge accomplished in February 1721.

Of Generations Past

The Judge's son, young John, frustrated in his search for a pulpit, took over management of the Green's Harbor property for his father. On October 8, 1724, four years after he had established himself on the family lands, John married. His bride was twenty-two-year-old Mary Ray of Block Island, his second cousin. She was the daughter of Captain Simon Ray and Judith Mainwaring of an ancient English family settled in Connecticut. Her grandmother was Mary Thomas, sister of Colonel Nathaniel, for whom she was named. Her grandfather, Simon Ray, was one of the original grantees of Block Island in the Rhode Island colony and a principal personage there. Mary Ray had come to Marshfield to visit her Thomas relations, and there met John Thomas.

During the next several years the young couple knew grief in considerable measure. In 1727 Judge Nathaniel's wife and John's mother died, "a Compleat Gentlewoman .. Beautified.. by her prudent, humble affable, peaceable, courteous and obliging temper and carriage.." She was laid to rest in the burying ground near her husband's father, the "Honorable Nathaniel Thomas Esqr." and his family's forbears, "where the salt sea air moaned softly through the branches of ancient gnarled cedars."

By 1730 John and Mary had buried three or four children, with only one child, a son William, left to them. The following year, 1731, their fifth and second surviving son was born on September 4, 1731. They gave him the name of Nathaniel Ray Thomas, honoring both their families.

IV

Young Ray

Nathaniel Ray Thomas was born in Marshfield. Among his first recollections were those of the house and yard on the farm, the "great Estate" which his father was managing, and then of the meadows and marshes beyond and of cattle grazing and horses cantering.

By the time young Ray, as he was familiarly called all his life, was five in 1736, his mother had borne two more children, sons, but neither lived much more than a year. Then, following the death of one of them, his older brother William, going on ten, died. Ray felt deeply the loss of a companion with whom he could play and yet to whom he could look up with a younger brother's admiration and a bit of awe. There was a sadness about the house. Death was common among children in those days, but the Lord's hand seemed especially heavy in the family of John and Mary Thomas. In a year's time there was final tragedy.

In March 1737 Mary Thomas's grandfather died in the 102nd year of his age. Simon Ray was a true patriarch among his people on Block Island. Less than a month later Mary Thomas gave birth to a son. His parents named him Simon in memory of his great-grandfather. On May 3, 1737, in the full beauty of spring, Mary *Ray* Thomas, wife of John Thomas and mother of Nathaniel Ray Thomas and Simon Thomas, passed away in her thirty-fifth year. She was laid to rest in the burying ground among her own and her husband's family "where the salt sea air moaned softly through the branches of the ancient gnarled cedars."

John Thomas had lost a wife still young even in an era of short life expectancy, particularly for child-bearing women. He had lost six of eight children, and Simon, only a few months old, already seemed alarmingly frail. He was himself only forty-one. On August 5, 1737, while in Plymouth, he made and executed his will. Two days later, August 7th, he was dead.

For young Ray it was sadness and sorrow beyond comprehension. He was six years old; but within a year he had lost two brothers, his mother, and now his father. His grandfather, Judge Nathaniel Thomas,

Young Ray

witnessing that year's events with deepening grief, resolutely continued his duties on the bench. With the resignation of the Chief Justice, Isaac Winslow, his lifelong friend and neighbor at Careswell and longtime associate, Judge Nathaniel succeeded him as head of the Court on July 8, 1738.

It was reassuring to the Judge that his second son, Nathaniel (hereafter referred to as Lt. Colonel Nathaniel), lived near him in Plymouth and that the deceased John had named Nathaniel executor of his estate and guardian of his two sons, Ray and Simon Thomas. But the Judge, worn down by sorrow over his family's afflictions and by a quarter century of dedicated service on the bench, was tiring fast. In late February 1739, Judge Nathaniel Thomas, Chief Justice of His Majesty's Inferior Court of Common Pleas and Quarter Sessions of the Peace for Plymouth County, died at the age of seventy-five. For the second time in two years, a funeral procession wound up Burial Hill in Plymouth and the Honorable Nathaniel Thomas was laid to rest beside Ray's father, John Thomas.

Upon his grandfather's death, Nathaniel Ray Thomas inherited the "great Estate" at Green's Harbor in Marshfield. Simon Thomas, frail from birth, had not long outlived his father, leaving Ray the sole survivor of eight children and the eldest male heir under the entail established by his great-great-great-grandfather, the first William Thomas, in 1651. But young Ray was then only eight years old. His uncle and guardian, Lt. Colonel Nathaniel Thomas, took over the management of the property and personal custody of the lad.

John Thomas, having recognized in his will that the entailed property in Marshfield would pass to his eldest son Ray if Ray survived his grandfather the Judge, directed that the boy "be brought up out of the income of my estate, until he arrives at the age of twenty-one years." And he had ordered that both Ray and Simon "be brought up to learning, if the income of what they shall be possesst of, will be sufficient to do it." In order to assure that the provisions of his will would be carried out, John Thomas authorized and empowered his brother Lt. Colonel Nathaniel to sell and dispose of personal property, including, John specified, his slaves.

During the ensuing few years Lt. Colonel Nathaniel Thomas discharged faithfully his trust as guardian, leasing out the Marshfield property and applying the income for the benefit of his ward. He took his nephew, young Ray, into his home in Plymouth where the lad found there his

Young Ray

cousin Hannah, a girl of about his own age. (Hannah was later to marry General John Thomas.) Three children were born to his Uncle Nathaniel and Aunt Elizabeth *Gardner* Thomas. One of whom, John Thomas, was named for Ray's father.

Lt. Colonel Nathaniel Thomas was much involved with military affairs. By the time war broke out between England and France, seven years after he had assumed the guardianship of Ray, he was lieutenant colonel and second in command of the Ninth Massachusetts Regiment. He accompanied his regiment when it was ordered to Cape Breton Island off Nova Scotia to join the expedition seeking to capture the great French fortress, Louisbourg. John Winslow, then proprietor of Careswell and lifelong friend of Lt. Colonel Nathaniel, was a captain also on the expedition. He had succeeded his father at Careswell upon the Chief Justice's death in 1738.

Following the capture of Louisbourg by the English and their occupation of it on garrison duty, Lt. Colonel Thomas - "a very worthy man" - died, probably of fever that raged among the men. As the nephew and ward of Lt. Colonel Nathaniel, young Ray had watched his uncle's preparations for the expedition to Louisbourg. Now, but a few months later, he was told of the Colonel's death. Ray was fourteen years old. Within that short lifetime his father and mother, four brothers, his grandfather, his great-grandfather, and his uncle had died. Two brothers and a sister had died before he was born. It was a grim toll.

Lt. Colonel Nathaniel, realistic as a soldier and knowledgeable as the son and grandson of lawyers and judges, quite probably arranged for the continuing guardianship of his nephew Ray if he himself should not return from the siege of Louisbourg. In any event, the Honorable John Cushing, Judge of Probate for Plymouth County, appointed John Thomas of Marshfield, a man with the same name as Ray's father but not related to the family, as the boy's guardian and administrator of Ray's father's estate. His appointment was effective November 11, 1745.

At the time of his appointment John Thomas was sixty-two years old, a man known for integrity and common sense, one who had performed responsible service for the town, for example. His grandfather had acquired a small property, described later as the "homestead farm" and of about fifty-nine acres, which lay between Edward Winslow's Careswell and William Thomas's Eagles Nest.

Young Ray

During the guardianship of Lt. Colonel Nathaniel Thomas, the lands at Green's Harbor had been leased and income applied for the benefit of his nephew and ward. Such an arrangement was continued by the Lt. Colonel's successor in that trust. Rent from the farm brought in £300 each year; expenses included such items as "Prizeing the Stock," "Ditching," and "two hundred of rails on the Farme." Ray's guardian had invested in bonds or promissory notes from which came some £40 in interest. And there were personal expenses involving Ray: boarding him at his guardian's, £60; clothing costing nearly £200 during the two previous years, including the purchase of such individual items as "one Beaver Hatt and Hatt Case," jacket, pumps, and stockings; making of shirts by Mary Bourne and Sarah and Bethiah Thomas, and the washing and mending of clothes.

Ray's father had directed in his will that he "be brought up to learning" if the income from what he had would permit it. John Thomas perhaps had some question about that, but after all, Ray's father had gone to Harvard and it had been virtually his dying wish that his son be educated. John Thomas decided that the boy should go to college. Preparations for that took nearly another £260, paid to Mr. Wiswall for "board and Schooling," to Mr. Ward for schooling, and to Master Harris, presumably for additional instruction, and to Ray himself for "Books and Expenses." It was early in August 1747. Ray was fifteen, going on sixteen. Harvard College would begin term in mid August.

Harvard was a larger and more imposing institution than it had been in his father's time, a generation before. There were now three red brick "colleges" forming three sides of an open quadrangle, with a low wall closing the fourth side and separating the buildings from the highway. A short distance away was a small brick chapel, on the east pediment of which was depicted in rich colors the family crest of its London donor. All of these structures were situated in what was then known as the "yards," the name deriving from ancient use of the site as a succession of fields known as Cowyard Row.

A typical day in the student life of Ray and his classmates began at five when they were wakened by the tolling of the first bell. They attended prayers at six and, after breakfast of bread and beer, went to classes at eight. Freshman courses included Latin, Greek, logic, rhetoric, and ethics. At twelve noon, with classes over for the day, students gathered in the dining hall for dinner. They sat at long tables covered with linen

Young Ray

and set with pewter plates and mugs. They were allotted a pound of meat and vegetables and a half-pint of beer or milk. After dinner the boys rushed to the playing field back of the college buildings and spent the rest of their free time until two o'clock playing football, rounders or bat-and-ball, and cricket. From two until six, when the bell rang for supper, all were supposed to go to their rooms and study. After supper, there was more study time until curfew call for lights out at nine.

Ray wrote to Marshfield dutifully. But his surviving letters, written to his guardian's younger son, Dr. John Thomas, Jr., suggest that he may have preferred indirect communication through someone more nearly his own age and not directly concerned with him as a ward. Of the two sons of Ray's guardian, Anthony Thomas and Dr. John Thomas, the latter was twenty-three years old during Ray's Freshman year. He had completed his medical education under Dr. Simon Tufts of Medford and, following two years of military service in Nova Scotia, had set up practice in Marshfield in January 1748. Not many weeks after that, he received a letter from Ray in answer to one of his. It was typical of the lad: a formal, polite, and not infrequently pompous communication - with a special plea or request slipped in at the end as a postscript.

"...I hope it is not long," Ray wrote, "before I Shall be among those Pleasant Shady Groves either to Spend my time in meditation or Something becoming my Most Sublime glory..." [P.S.] "Be Pleased to send me word whether you have any powder and Shot. I don't mean swan shot such as I shot the boar with..." His hope of returning to "those Pleasant Shady Groves" was realized early in April when the college went into vacation. On April 2nd, Dr. John Thomas noted in his journal, "Nath Ray Come from College."

Two days later he and Ray "went a Guning"; the Doctor added, "I Killed one Duck." Gunning was a favorite sport of the time; Harvard boys were no exception. On the 8th, "Nath Ray Killed one Goos etc. in the marshes"; the following day, the Doctor and Ray went "a Guning in the marshes" again. There were other activities. One afternoon they both "Botled Sider [cider] for Anthony," the Doctor's brother. Another day they dined at Joseph Kent's. Then on what apparently was the last day of Ray's vacation, he and the Doctor "went to Capt Foords A:M: and Dined at Uncle Winslows. Wee went with Mr. Hill to the Brant Rock etc.P:M:.."

Two months after Ray had returned to college, Edward Holyoke, President of Harvard, and the Tutors met on June 7, 1748 for their

Young Ray

annual ritual of "placing" the Freshmen. It was for the class of 1751. Just as students were ranked according to the civil offices held by their fathers, with due regard for the social standing of their families, in Ray's father's time a generation earlier, so were they placed in Ray's time. Nathaniel Ray Thomas was placed seventh in a class of thirty-one.

In the class of 1751 Joseph Dudley and Richard Saltonstall, both of families of ancient and distinguished lineage in Massachusetts Bay that had provided governor, assistants, councilors, and judges since the founding of the Colony, were obvious choices to lead the class. Samuel Epes was the stepson of the President of the College, but was placed third because of the civil positions held by his deceased father. William Cushing was known slightly to Ray. He was from Scituate, the town immediately north of Marshfield. His family had been prominent in the Old Colony, Plymouth, and had furnished not only members of the council of the Province but also a long line of judges, with some of whom Ray's grandfather and great-grandfather had served. Benjamin Greenleaf was the son of an incumbent Councilor; John Holyoke, the son of the President of the College. These then were above Ray in the order of precedence.

Immediately below Ray in the placing was Joseph Wanton, scion of a wealthy and prominent Rhode Island merchant family and son of the governor of that colony. Then came William Watson, Ray's cousin "Will," whose mother was a Thomas. Already boyhood friends, they saw much of each other at college and during vacations. Below "Will" was placed Mather Byles, who numbered among his forbears the Mather and Belcher families of Massachusetts Bay. The Mathers were long renowned and influential as clergymen; the Belchers, as civil servants, including a governor of the Province and members of the Council.

When Ray and his classmates arrived in August 1748 for the opening of term, he found that he would be rooming in room 24, Massachusetts Hall. The most recently constructed of the "colleges," it was one hundred feet long, three full stories high with a dormer-windowed half fourth story, and a clock high in the gable of the west end. There were thirty-two small, low ceilinged rooms with study dens or closets, one flanking the fireplace on either side. Two students occupied each room.

Ray was scheduled to room with John Wiswall, class of 1749, whose father, like Ray's, had been a Harvard graduate. (Roommates were not always classmates). That term Mather Byles occupied Massachusetts 1;

Young Ray

William Cushing, Massachusetts 3. On the second floor Richard Saltonstall roomed in Massachusetts 22, next door to Ray. He would remain neighbor and friend for their remaining three years as undergraduates. It was at the beginning of Ray's year as a Junior Sophister that he welcomed as a Freshman his third cousin and neighbor at Marshfield, Pelham Winslow, eldest son of John Winslow, proprietor of the Careswell estate and friend and fellow officer at Louisbourg of Ray's uncle, the late Lt. Colonel Nathaniel Thomas. Pelham, some years younger than Ray, was ranked second in the class of 1753 and was assigned to Massachusetts 6 in his first year.

That the placing of students was taken seriously by parents was evidenced by the concern of Pelham's father, then Captain Winslow, when that gentleman sought to impress upon President Holyoke his son's rightful claim to high rank. The Captain urged that, since the sons of New England were placed "according to the Degrees of their ancestors I have theretofore put in My Pretensions for my Son..." The Captain supplied his family genealogy and the record of his own military service. Swayed by this, Holyoke and the tutors placed Pelham second in his class behind the son of a councilor.

In late summer of 1748 young Ray got in his first scrape with the college authorities. Admittedly there were many opportunities for the "scholars" to run afoul of college rules and regulations. They were young - Mather Byles was only twelve and a half on admission; Ray, fifteen and three quarters - and they were energetic and spirited and fun-loving, however much their gentility and learning.

Harvard College laws were lengthy in number, specific in detail. They were forbidding, strict in their injunction, providing hard penalties for transgressions by young gentlemen. If there was a mandate impossible to follow - "All scholars shall behave themselves blamelessly" - there were many which it would be tempting to flaunt. Among the prohibitions and consequent fines were: swearing, lying, drunkenness, fighting - five shillings for each offence; making tumultuous or indecent noises in the college yard or in town - ten shillings; playing cards or dice - twenty shillings. Frequenting Cambridge taverns brought a fine of five shillings. And there was a requirement that young men seemed to find intolerable: that students should not go beyond the college fences without coat or gown.

Young Ray

For "drinking prohibited Liquors," Andrew Oliver, second-ranked student in the class of 1749 and member of a politically powerful Massachusetts Bay family, and Joseph Dudley, first-ranked in Ray's class, were among those fined. One student, for "singing in his chamber after midnight," paid twenty shillings as a penalty for his cheerfulness. John Wendell, class of 1750, transgressed the rules by "playing a flute in the Town at unseasonable hour of night." The minutes of the Tutors' meeting continued: "Also that Thomas, for not going to his Chamber, when order'd by a Tutor, be punish'd the Sum of twenty Shillings."

Word inevitably reached Marshfield of Ray's disgrace. It fell upon Dr. John Thomas to respond. He evidently wrote Ray a letter of severe reprimand to which the lad replied on September 21st. From this and the succeeding letters in the exchange that followed, there is a suggestion of other aspects of Ray's conduct that offended his guardian's family. Ray's letter of the 21st was, if nothing else, disingenuous; its postscript, strikingly brash. To anyone in his circumstances except apparently Ray himself, the letter would have seemed woefully undiplomatic. It was addressed to Dr. John Thomas at Marshfield:

> "Tis true," Ray wrote, "I am guilty to give you ground to think I have offended, but my offense is my misfortune rather than my fault. But sir, what if I appeal from your severe justice to your mercy? I know you're not inexorable nor did you suck the breasts of wolves and tigers. And since there is so much sweetness in your eyes, there needs must be some pity in your heart, at least so far as to forgive a poor repenting criminal. And since you [have?] such a bright idea of the author of all goodness you cannot but, like Him, delight in showing mercy to a criminal. I shall henceforth endeavor to be like Caesar's wife, not only free from guilt but free from suspicion, and further shall to expiate my offence always remain Your much afflicted servant, Nathl. Ray Thomas."

And then, in his postscript, he added: "I am in very low circumstances for Mr. [Taylor?] says that there is no need of my having anything but what is necessary for my chamber; therefore, I should be glad if you would send me some money so as not to let your father know of it."

John Thomas, doctor and soldier, was understandably furious upon receiving this brazen document. He seems to have taken it upon himself, though, to try to handle young Ray than to have his aging father burdened with worry and perplexity about the lad's attitude and behavior.

Young Ray

The Doctor may have sensed, despite the ignorance and disregard of his profession at that time for mental or emotional illness, that the tragic deaths of Ray's family when he was little more than a child, but a knowledgeable one; the sudden inheritance at an early age of extensive and valuable property; and the entry on his own into an aristocratic and sophisticated world of power and license may have warped the boy's perspective. That the boy was spoiled, there was no doubt - and by well-intentioned, kindly people at that who failed to see the need of a firm and disciplined hand. Dr. Thomas wrote Ray a strongly worded letter, yet one in which he was careful to preserve and extend the bond of friendship. That seemed all that he could do at the moment; for the future, he provided the opportunity for more. The letter was dated at Marshfield, October 4, 1748. John Thomas wrote in part:

> But since you have asked forgiveness, for my own part, in consideration of a reformation, I can sincerely forgive you and endeavor to forget such injury as I have taken from you and likewise pray God to forgive you. But as for my father's family who you have endeavored to your utmost for to defame and scandalize in every shape as much as lay in your power, as I can call several credible persons to witness this day, I say that family, the heads of which to my knowledge, have had a parental regard for you and, in witness thereof, have manifested it by their behavior towards you ever since you pretended to make this house your home, and the members of it I believe never were deficient in doing their part even beyond that was their duty.

The Doctor had some words of advice:

> Now if you are calm and unprejudiced in your mind, let me desire you to set down calmly in your study and reflect impartially on this past time and then I am sure you will see whether you will care to own it or not. I can't say that it is astonishing when no one of us that [illegible] there or remember of ever gave you a misbeholden word or offered anything of that shape that you should behave thus. When there has been so much more favor shown you beyond your merit or desert in this family, and I can't hear of or imagine that there was ever a misbeholden word spoken of you by any one of them before you was guilty of these many offenses, and was I now in your stead, I should be ashamed to show my guilty and un-grateful face...But I say for my part, if you are sorry you

Young Ray

> have offended, I can forgive you, although I hear daily of your unguarded folly and talk among those of your friends. But I hope you will not be such an idiot as to be frightened at a shadow or trodden under foot by the best of mortals. But notwithstanding these things, in your better behaviour, I shall be your friend...

From the Doctor's letter, young Ray, it seemed, had bandied about remarks concerning his guardian's family. They were thoughtless, no doubt critical, and quite probably patronizing. From his exalted station in life at Harvard, as he may have viewed it, he may have acted and talked in a condescending manner (or worse) about his guardian's family. Ray replied on October 25th from Harvard. In his own defense, however, he invoked the opinion of Cotton Tufts who, according to Ray, shared his own belief that he had not been "hypocritical," as Dr. Thomas had alleged. Tufts, two classes ahead of Ray at college, was the son of Dr. Simon Tufts of Medford, Dr. Thomas's teacher, and a close friend of Dr. John Thomas. This, Ray must have felt, would have exonerated him from fault.

Young Ray's troubles for that Sophomore year were not over, however. In the spring of 1749 "severl Scholars" were punished "for their absence from the College beyond the Time allow'd per law. This Absence consider'd as immediately after the Vacation and during the past Winter." Ray's fine of fifteen shillings seemed small when compared to the three pounds paid by two of his classmates and friends, William Cushing of Scituate and Cousin "Will" Watson of Plymouth.

With his roommate John Wiswall graduating in the spring of 1749 as well, Ray, now a Junior Sophister, was assigned another roommate for the college year 1749-1750. The lad was Thomas Malbone, member of a wealthy and cultivated Rhode Island family and fourth-ranked in the class of 1752. They continued to occupy Massachusetts 24. And both became involved in more and continuing difficulties with the college authorities. In March 1750, after winter vacation, young Ray was once again absent from college; only this time he was fined the sizable amount of four pounds, while William Cushing and Richard Saltonstall got by with ten shillings each.

Only ten days later both occupants of Massachusetts 24, together with Joseph Wanton, Ray's classmate and bosom companion, were chastised by the President and Tutors. For playing cards, Malbone was

Young Ray

fined ten shillings and required to admit his offence publicly in the chapel. But Thomas and Wanton, Junior Sophisters, were to be "severely punish'd... for playing Cards." The Faculty Records then recited what that punishment would be:

> "That they all who have gained by Gaming be directed to refund the Sevral Sums and other Things to those of whom they have won them and shall suffer as follows:
>
> 4. That Thomas and Wanton for often playing at Cards and frequently for large Sums of Money and other Things of considerable value be degraded, each of Them five places in the class, Thomas taking place hence forward between Willard and Russell..."

Having survived the vicissitudes of college life and their own misdoings, Ray and Tom Malbone returned to Harvard following the summer vacation of 1750. Both, however, were late in getting back, apparently an easily acquired habit. Ray was absent for three weeks and was fined twelve shillings; Malbone, a fortnight for which he was fined one pound, one shilling, one pence. Even in March 1751, as Senior Sophisters and not long before graduation, they straggled in after several days' unlawful absence.

Harvard Commencement, an ancient and colorful ceremony full of pomp and solemnity and attended by distinguished personages of the Province, proud parents and friends, and thankful Senior Sophisters of the graduating class, customarily took place on the second Wednesday of July in each year. In May 1751 Ray and Joseph Wanton, his chosen companion in hazardous pranks, risked serious consequences with a nocturnal escapade. The Faculty Records spelled out in detail exactly what had happened and the decision of the President and Tutors dictating their fate:

> Voted, That Thomas and Wanton for breaking open one of the Chamber Doors of the College, late at Night and making great Disturbance by the Noise, be punish'd the Sume of Twenty Shillings each, and make a public Confession of their Crime in the Chapel, besides making good all the Damage, which They have done the said Chamber. The above executed May the 4 1751 When Thomas and Wanton were called out of their Place order'd to Stand in the Chappel Alley, while the President [heard?] their Confessions.

Young Ray

There remained, however, the humiliating matter of their "degradation" in rank in their class. Two other Senior Sophisters shared their disgrace, Richard Saltonstall and William Parker. The four classmates, petitioning the President and Tutors for leniency, sought to be restored to their former places. The president and Tutors met again to consider the petition. The record revealed their final judgment:

> Upon the humble Confession of Saltonstall, Thomas, Wanton, and Parker, who now stand degraded according to vote,...as also the Petition to be restor'd to their original places in the class, Agreed that upon their being present and behaving Themselves with a proper Decency, then the said Confession shall be read in the Chapel... and according have their Names in that order in the Theses and Catalog to be printed this year.

What had prompted Ray and Wanton to such a violent burst of feeling only weeks before their graduation may have been uncontrollable exuberance of the desire for one final act of defiance. Or there could have been some other motive. But it had been risky business: the two boys had stood to lose a great deal. They had gambled and won.

Harvard Commencement 1751 took place as scheduled, on the second Wednesday in July. It was a glorious occasion. Crowds thronged Cambridge. Families and friends of the graduates were everywhere in evidence. Doctor John Thomas had come up from Marshfield, a young man still at twenty-seven, composed, thoughtful, and highly capable and well thought of. As the time for the Commencement exercises approached - eleven o'clock - people pushed into the meeting house across from Harvard Yard to take their seats. The great church bell, ringing for ten minutes, ceased.

Leading the procession into the church, the Senior Sophisters marched two by two according to their rank in class. They wore black gowns, they were bareheaded, their hair queued and powdered. Then, at an interval appropriate to his position, strode the President of Harvard, Edward Holyoke, a man of striking presence, and behind him the professors and tutors of the college. There was a moment of silence, the audience hushed - all looked to the front of the church. His Majesty's Governor of the Province of Massachusetts Bay, His Excellency William Shirley; His Majesty's Lieutenant Governor, His Honor Spencer Phips; members of His Majesty's Council; His Majesty's Chief Justice of the Superior Court

Young Ray

of Judicature, the Honorable Paul Dudley, and the Honorable, the Associate Justices; and other dignitaries, resplendent in crimson and gold lace, formally accoutered with swords and military boots, strode up the aisle of the church to take their places of honor.

After opening prayers and the commencement sermon, the Senior Sophisters, one by one, mounted the platform where President Holyoke waited to exchange a formal colloquy with each in Latin and to bestow the degree of Bachelor of Arts. Graduation, except for celebration and festivities, was over. Ray was now Nathaniel Ray Thomas, A.B. 1751. But his academic career was not yet over. For the next three years he studied for his second degree, the Master of Arts. In the spring of 1754 he took the affirmative side of the Quaestio, "An Submissio universalis Probabiliter majora Mala naturalia, quam Insurrectionis temporariae, cum Jura peculiaria, invaduntur?" [Whether universal submission probably brings about greater natural evils than temporary insurrections when rights characteristic of one person or group are invaded?] and received his Master of Arts.

The year following his graduation from Harvard with his Bachelor's, Ray Thomas became twenty-one years old. On September 4, 1752 he attained his majority, came into full possession of the Thomas property in Marshfield - the "great Estate" - and proceeded to settle accounts with his guardian, John Thomas. Efforts to accomplish such a settlement took several months. Finally, in March 1753, guardian and ward reached agreement and the latter executed the following:

> To all to whom these presents shall come: Know ye, that I, Nathaniel Ray Thomas, of Marshfield in the county of Plymouth, gentleman, have this day settled and adjusted accounts with my late guardian, Mr. John Thomas, of Marshfield aforesaid and also as he was the administrator of my late honored father, John Thomas, late of Plymouth, Esq., deceased, and have received of him this day in balance forty pounds which I acknowledge to be in full for what he received from the administrator of the late Nathaniel Thomas, Esq., of Plymouth aforesaid, deceased and of all other sums that the said John Thomas, guardian and administrator, received as rents and moveables, and hereby discharge him therefrom, as witness my hand and seal this nineteenth day of March, Anno Domini, 1753.

To all To Whome These Presents Shall Come Know
ye. That I Nath:ll Ray Thomas of Marshfield in
the County of Plymouth Gentlemen have This day
Settled & adjusted accompts with my Late
Gaurdian M:r John Thomas of Marshfield aforesd.
and also as he was Administrator to my Late Hon:d
Father John Thomas Late of Plymouth Esq:r Decd.
and have Recd. of it This Day in Bulleon Forty
Pounds which I acknowledge to be in Full for what
he Received From the Administrator of the Late
Nath:ll Thomas Esq:r of Plymouth aforesd. Due
of all other Sums that the s:d John Thomas Gaurdian
& administrator Recd. ents & Moveables, and here
by Discharge him. From as Witness my hand
& Seal this Nineteen March An: Domini 1753

Signed Sealed & Delivered
In Presence of
John Winslow
Anthony Thomas   Nath:ll Ray Thomas

Discharge by Nathaniel Ray Thomas of his guardian.
Collection Estate of William H.B. Thomas.

Young Ray

It was signed by Nathaniel Ray Thomas in a bold hand, with his seal affixed. It was witnessed by John Winslow of Careswell and Anthony Thomas, the Doctor's older brother.

Nathaniel Ray Thomas, gentleman, had come of age.

V

Marriage and Country Life

During his years in Cambridge as an undergraduate and later while studying for his Masters, Nathaniel Ray Thomas, as Harvard students have ever done, crossed the Charles River to Boston. He could take the ferry from Charlestown, on the Cambridge side of the river, across the half-mile expanse of water to Boston. Or he could cross on the "Great Bridge," for nearly a century spanning the river just down from the College, and, riding along the south bank, arrive at Boston by way of Boston Neck.

Ray had a personal reason for visiting Boston. His grandfather, Captain Simon Ray of Block Island, had married a second time. Of the four daughters of this marriage - Ray's aunts of the half-blood - the oldest, Judith and only five years his senior, was then living in Boston, the wife of Thomas Hubbard. During those last years at Harvard, Ray often crossed the Charles by bridge or ferry to visit the Hubbards.

Boston had just claim for her title as the "Metropolis of New England." With a population of more than 16,000 in 1743, she was larger by several thousand than either Philadelphia or New York. At mid-century Boston remained the "Metropolis"; and twenty years later, even after Philadelphia and New York had outgrown her, she was hailed as "the largest, most populous Town in the British Dominions in America." Pride died hard.

But the town was not well situated for further growth. It had been established on a roughly diamond-shaped, hilly peninsula extending out into Boston Harbor. Connecting the peninsula to the mainland was the Neck, a desolate mile-long stretch that provided the only approach by land. Ray, arriving by that route, would pass by the gallows and rock-marked graves of criminals and suicides before reaching the town gate. Ray might have seen, dangling from the gallows as a gruesome warning, a skeleton or a corpse hardly cold. Not far beyond was the gate constructed of brick, with one archway for those on foot and another for those on horseback, driving livestock, or tending wagons. There was a fortification commanding the gate. It was guarded day and night.

Marriage and Country Life

From the town gate to the Town House - where the courts, the Council, and the House of Representatives met - was one mile along the "High Street," which bore several names in succession. From the gate Ray rode first along Orange Street; then, in order, Newbury, soon Marlborough, and finally Cornhill as it passed the Town House. He would pass the Governor's or Province House, an elegant structure of brick, three stories high with a dormered attic and surmounted by an octagonal cupola, which faced Marlborough Street. The Town House was at the head of King Street which, running off Cornhill at nearly a right angle, extended down to the shore line and out on Long Wharf for some two thousand feet or almost a half mile. Here the largest sea-going vessels could tie up. Countless other wharves and docks, some quite substantial themselves, and the warehouses of prosperous merchants spread out along Boston's waterfront.

Nearby, Ray wandered about the North End, where narrow streets and tiny alleys, crooked and seemingly aimless in direction, added to the ancient flavor of the area. They bore names like Fish Street and Ship Street, Sun Court and Moon Street, Bell Alley and Governor's Alley, and Pudding Lane and Change Avenue. Wedged along and among these myriad ways were the unpretentious, often grimly dismal, dwellings of small craftsmen and artisans and shopkeepers; the more commodious two-story framed houses of the prosperous "middling sort"; and, here and there about town, Georgian mansions set in pleasant gardens of the mercantile and commercial gentry and royal officials. And now and again a sharply gabled, half-timbered, rough-plastered structure preserved a medieval touch in the midst of change.

What never failed to amaze Ray on his early trips into Boston was the bustle, the sounds, and the smells of the Provincial capital. Even the studied indifference carefully cultivated by young gentlemen from Harvard could not entirely mask reactions stemming from a country background. There seemed so much activity. People were hurrying about in every direction, on business or pleasure, to church or to court. Without the haven of sidewalks, pedestrians vied with other pedestrians and horsemen - cursing wagon drivers and their wagons, shrilly screaming boys pulling and pushing carts, men of the fire companies yelling "Fire!" as they rushed along with their leather water buckets - for use of the narrow, twisting streets, alleys, and lanes.

Marriage and Country Life

There were sounds of the streets. There were fish vendors calling out their wares, and oystermen too. There were the sounds of hammers and mauls in the shipyards by the water, the clap-clap of horses' hooves on cobblestones, the mournful cry of seagulls circling overhead, and in the quiet of night the town watch calling, "Ten o'clock, and all's well." And the bells of Boston tolled. They tolled for the dead and for the living; they tolled at the fearsome cry of "Fire!" and to open and close the markets; and to call the citizens to church service on God's appointed day of prayer and rest. Schoolbells, cowbells, and doorbells sounded their lighter tinkling rings. And there were the drums - the muffled cadence for the dead, and martial cadence for musters and for calling men to the Royal Standard.

Smells, too, were pervasive and varied. Always there was the smell of the sea that washed the wharves at water's edge, the salt sea air that came in fresh and strong when the east wind blew. There was the smell of people, those people milling about in the streets for whom washing meant a quick douse of water over the head and hands in the morning and, at best, a weekly going-over in a great copper tub. There was the smell of straining, steaming horses; of horse leather; and of horse dung. And there was the brisk, pleasant odor of wood smoke from chimneys near and far; and the heavy pungent smell from pots of boiling tar. Indeed, it was thought to have been "the carelessness of a boy in letting a pot of tar boil over" that started the fire in Boston which Ray Thomas reported to Dr. John Thomas in October 1748. Ray added the opinion that "if the tide had not have been up it would have burnt up half the town."

It may have been on one of those pleasant forays that Ray Thomas met Sarah Dering. A year younger than Ray, she was perhaps eighteen at the time. She was the daughter of Henry Dering and Elizabeth Packer, whose father, Colonel Thomas Packer, an Englishman, had become Judge of Probate and a Councilor of the Province of New Hampshire. Her other grandfather, the first Henry Dering, had been commissary general in the expedition of Sir William Phips against Acadia [Nova Scotia] in the late seventeenth century. He was a successful merchant, selectman of Boston and moderator of its town meetings, and a promoter of various civic projects. Both he and his wife died in 1717 and were buried in the same grave, a fact that elicited later comment. Mr. Justice Sewall and two members of the politically powerful Hutchinson family were among Henry Dering's pallbearers.

Nathaniel Ray Thomas. Courtesy of the Duxbury Rural and Historical Society.

Sarah Dering Thomas. Courtesy of the Duxbury Rural and Historical Society.

Marriage and Country Life

Sarah's father, the second Henry Dering, died in 1750. He was known as "a gentleman famous for 'Liberty and Property'." As the elder Dering had been before him, he was a successful merchant and a selectman of Boston. At his death he was possessed of an estate worth some £5,000, which included four houses and six lots in the vicinity of the Town House. One of the houses was occupied by the Dering family. It stood at the intersection of Cornhill and Queen Street, directly across from the Town House at the head of King Street, and faced on Queen Street. A short distance away on Cornhill, behind the Dering house, was the First Church in Boston, which sheltered a venerable congregation existing from the first years of settlement. In two other of his houses lived Henry Dering's daughters Elizabeth and Mary and their husbands, Samuel Wentworth of the powerful and proprietied Wentworth family of the Province of New Hampshire and John Gooch respectively. Both sons-in-law were merchants also. A third daughter, Ann, had married an Englishman bred to the law, James Monk, who, having served as an aide to William Pepperell at Louisbourg in 1745, became one of the earliest grantees of land in Halifax, Nova Scotia. All three girls were married by the time they were twenty; all three, by their first cousin, Reverend William Welsteed, in the Brick Church in the north end of town. Following Henry Dering's death in 1750 his other children - Thomas, Sarah, and Henry Packer - as yet unmarried, continued to live in the house at Dering's Corner.

Ray's introduction to the Dering family may indeed have come through his aunt, Judith *Ray* Hubbard, and her husband Thomas Hubbard. (A Thomas Hubbard was one of those who appraised Henry Dering's estate in 1750, which suggested a possible prior acquaintance.) However that may have been, Ray received a formal invitation to call upon Thomas Dering and his sister Sarah. Once in the house at Dering's Corner, Ray was immediately aware of the cultivated setting in which the Derings lived. The rooms were amply furnished; and there were distinctive touches for the time and place; curtains at the windows, rugs and carpets on the floors, tablecloths and napkins on the dining table. There was a "standing candlestick" and a "dumbwaiter," probably in the sense of a portable serving table or stand. There was a substantial array of "wrought plate," or worked silver, and Delft china. Seven pictures, at least, hung on the walls; a "Harpsacord" stood in the parlor.

There was at least one bookcase and some two hundred volumes. They were mostly religious or practical in nature to be sure, but they were seasoned with such historical and literary works as <u>England's Monarch</u>,

Marriage and Country Life

<u>The Life of Queen Mary</u>, <u>The Life of Oliver Cromwell</u>, <u>History of the Wars of New England</u>, and Nathaniel Morton's <u>New England Memorial</u>; and John Milton's <u>Paradise Lost</u> and <u>Paradise Regained</u>, the works of Vergil, <u>Winter Evening Entertainments</u>, <u>The Ladies Library</u>, <u>The Guardian</u>, <u>The Spector</u>, <u>The Humorist</u>, and <u>Hudibras</u>.

There were other items - personal accessories, for example - that a casual visitor would not have seen. Some eighteen rings, two lockets, one pair of earrings, two bloodstones, a sardonyx, and "a Gold Whistle" and "1 toothpick" were listed in Henry Dering's inventory of 1750.

Shortly after having made the acquaintance of Sarah Dering, Ray presented himself formally to Thomas Dering to ask permission to call upon his sister. Thus began a courtship that culminated in the publishing on November 7, 1754 of their intention of marriage. The wedding was set for December 3rd, plans were made, preparations begun.

Ray's Aunt Judith and her husband, Thomas Hubbard, lived in Boston with the latter's mother and her second husband, John Franklin, brother of the distinguished Dr. Benjamin Franklin. In the fall of 1754 Dr. Franklin visited Boston, his birthplace, on official business. While there, he put up at the house occupied by his brother and his wife and Thomas and Judith Hubbard. During those weeks of November before his wedding, Ray Thomas, one might suppose, called on the Hubbard-Franklin household to pay his respects to his Aunts Judith and Catherine, who had come up from Block Island for the wedding. Catherine Ray, or Caty as she liked to be called and Catherine as she preferred to spell the name, was twenty-three and only two months older than her nephew, Ray. She had a striking personality; she possessed wit and had a good mind as well; she was vivacious and enjoyed people. And people responded. Dr. Franklin, twice her age, was captivated.

If the Doctor had been in at the time of one of Ray's visits, one or another of the family would have presented Ray to their distinguished guest.

Those weeks of November finally did pass. On December 3rd Nathaniel Ray Thomas and Sarah Dering were married in the First Church on Cornhill, a short walk from the Dering house on the corner of Queen, with the Reverend Thomas Foxcroft officiating. Forty years after the wedding, Caty Ray, by then Caty Greene, could still picture "Sally Dering [as] a charming girl" and recall that the wedding guests had "sack posset

Marriage and Country Life

[milk curdled with white wine and laced with sugar and spices] and a beautiful drest plumb cake for supper."

Ray Thomas and Sarah Dering may have remained in Boston after their wedding, perhaps at Dering's Corner, until after Twelfth-night. One day they departed for Marshfield and home.

Country life in New England in the half century preceding the Revolution, particularly in the Province of Massachusetts Bay, possessed a "social vitality" increasingly evident and pervasive. With survival no longer a main preoccupation and Puritanism and the Puritan social order less of a somber influence in the older settled region, colonists could turn their attention to the fulfillment of varied aspirations. Profits from mercantile, maritime, and commercial activities that included importation of West Indies rum, privateering, and the slave trade as well as more routine business; and exploitation of natural resources that included fish, fur, and timber could not provide what colonists, thinking of themselves as Englishmen in America, could order from "home" or build or acquire as Englishmen built or acquired "at home." Just as the dream and apparent possibility of acquiring land in the New World had been a driving force for thousands of Englishmen to hazard the Atlantic crossing, so, too, the vision of a landed estate and of the status of a country gentleman was ever in the minds of an ambitious and energetic few. Merchants of Boston and other seaport towns, as their counterparts "at home," placed money garnered from trade into country places. By 1750 a people thinking of themselves as Britons and not yet as Americans, intensely loyal and warmly attached to the British Crown, brought over British culture, custom, and fashion; and what they could not import, they imitated as best they could. They retained the urge to reform the hierarchy of social classes. It was more flexible and less structured than that "at home," but it was still a class system. The landed gentry, indigenous to America as it may have been, commanded a great respect. It was only to be ranked in precedence by the principal officers of His Majesty's Government and such few titled personages as lived in the colonies.

Some of the gentry held their land by "ancient grant," as had been pleaded on behalf of Judge Nathaniel Thomas in <u>Matson</u> v. <u>Thomas</u>; some of them as the Court decided in that case, in fee tail and as the eldest male heir. Others held by "ancient grant" also, but in fee simple absolute. Those families of the gentry had been proprietors of their lands for at least a generation, and in some instances since the earliest days of settlement. Along with their inherited property, they recognized

Marriage and Country Life

their traditional obligation of service to the state and performed that service in notable ways and seemingly almost as a matter of right. They were colonial counterparts of county families in England; they possessed the prestige of family in New England. They were such families as those of Edward Winslow and William Thomas of Marshfield, who had acquired extensive properties more than a century earlier in the beginning years of settlement and who had themselves been associated in the magistracy of New Plymouth Colony; and their families in subsequent years, members of which had graduated from Harvard College, had furnished the Province of Massachusetts Bay with councilors, judges, and military officers.

Probably well before he and Sarah Dering returned to Marshfield as husband and wife, Nathaniel Ray Thomas, accepting as his proper due his status as a country gentleman, proposed to fulfill that role with exactitude particularly as to appearance and prerogative. Such an attitude was understandable considering the nature of his own personality, the tenor of his own life thus far, and the conventions and customs of his own time. There were, of course, positive aspects of the situation. Ray Thomas was well educated for his day, despite his transgressions at Harvard. He was well mannered and courteous in his social relations, certainly with those whom he considered of his own standing. He seems to have been well intentioned, determined to make every effort to make a success of his endeavors.

At twenty-three and twenty-two respectively, Ray Thomas and Sarah Dering were a personable couple. Sally was a "charming girl," brought up in a family of position, wealth, and culture; exposed to strong religious influences; and if, as girls of that day, not formally educated, at least trained by intelligent parents and surrounded in her youth by books, music, and art. Ray, as a likeness made in later life attests, possessed well-molded regular features, refined rather than distinctly handsome. That the two shared the romance and dreams of youth seems certain. That their marriage, despite insurmountable financial difficulties, dramatic political ruin, the peculiarly harsh scourge of civil war, and the poignant reality of starting life anew in a strange land, survived with a deep and even deepening affection is true. No letter from one to the other is thus far known to exist; but an extensive array of correspondence and documents, including many of their letters to others, bears out this conclusion.

Marriage and Country Life

Perhaps the first order of business to which Ray Thomas turned his attention upon resuming life in Marshfield in the early months of 1755 was the renovation and repair of his house there. What prompted him to this was very likely the desire to have a country house which he would consider appropriate to his station in life. Perhaps neither the "old house" near the Eagles Nest, which had been the home of his great-grandfather, the old Colonel, or the main house on the "great Estate" suited him. Perhaps one or both of those were in such disrepair as to make advisable such renovation and repair. Whatever his reason, Ray Thomas advised his brother-in-law Thomas Dering on February 24, 1755 of his "Carpenters beginning to work Monday next upon my House..."

In his letter of February 24th to Thomas Dering, Ray Thomas, along with news of the beginning of work on his house, enclosed a "Memorandum" of items he desired his brother-in-law to send him. These a tailor could fashion into clothes to enhance his wardrobe. The material he ordered included "Red Shalloon," a twilled worsted; "Buckram," a linen or cotton fabric; "Blue Mohair," a superior kind of fabric or "camlet" made of Angora-goat hair; and "Red Plush [silk, cotton, or wool material] enough for a pr Britches." In addition, he wanted "2 Dozn White Mettle Coat Buttons, 2 [Dozen] Jacket Buttons, 2 Hand [kerchiefs] 1 Silk the other Cotton, and 1 pr Worsted Stockings." And in a later letter he spoke of someone stealing his "Black leather Britches."

As so often in those days, letters were carried by hand from the sender to the recipient. Often that was a more certain, and less expensive, way to communicate than by using the postal system. In this instance, Ray Thomas acknowledged receipt of letters from his brother-in-law delivered to him by Lieutenant Colonel John Winslow. The Colonel, who as a captain had served with Ray's late uncle and guardian, Lieutenant Colonel Nathaniel Thomas at the siege of Louisbourg ten years before, was the proprietor of Careswell, the Winslow estate adjoining the Thomas property. Colonel Winslow was nearly thirty years Ray's senior; the younger man regarded him with respect and warmth, and at that particular time with interest and concern.

There was already a kinship between the Winslows and the Thomases. The Colonel had married some years before Mary Little, an older second cousin of Ray's. It was their son Pelham Winslow, who had been at Harvard in Ray's time. Now matters of serious import involved John Winslow. Once again, for him, the scene of action was Nova Scotia.

Marriage and Country Life

That island, connected to the mainland of New France, Canada, by the isthmus of Chignecto, had been acquired by England by the Treaty of Utrecht in 1713. The French, in order to prevent penetration of the mainland by the English, constructed Fort Beausejour to obstruct passage of the isthmus. As part of England's grand plan to defend the frontiers of her American colonies, the reduction of the French forts Beausejour, and further inland, Niagara, Crown Point, and Duquesne was deemed essential.

Governor William Shirley, acting in close concert with Governor Charles Lawrence of Nova Scotia and having received approval of the Massachusetts legislature, set about raising a regiment of New England troops for the expedition against Beausejour, to be known, out of courtesy, as Shirley's. The regiment was placed under the active command of Colonel the Honorable Robert Monckton and comprised two battalions, the 1st commanded by Lieutenant Colonel John Winslow; the 2nd, by Lieutenant Colonel George Scott. Among Winslow's more immediate duties was that of recruiting troops for the expedition against Beausejour. A close friend and frequent visitor to Careswell in recent years and in those first months of 1755 was the thirty-one-year-old country doctor John Thomas, who had seen military service and was then a militia officer. It took little persuasion on the Colonel's part to persuade his younger friend to join him on the expedition and equally little urging by the Colonel for Governor Shirley to issue a new commission. For John Thomas was already known to the governor as an able soldier. He was commissioned in His Majesty's service as Captain-Lieutenant of Winslow's own company, with the rank of lieutenant but with the command of the company. (Winslow himself could not hold both a regimental command and a company command.) Lieutenant Thomas also continued to act as assistant surgeon of the regiment.

Whatever the personal relationship of Dr. John Thomas, young country practitioner, and Nathaniel Ray Thomas, still younger country gentleman, may have been in those first few months of 1755 in the wake of strains sustained during Ray's college career, it does seem likely that they reached, at least, some understanding between themselves and a consequent exchange of courteous civilities. Ray Thomas would then have been interested in and concerned about the impending departure on active service of Colonel John Winslow, whom he may already have begun to look upon, consciously or not, as an older man taking the place of his own long-dead father or his soldier-uncle Colonel Nathaniel

Marriage and Country Life

Thomas; and of John Thomas, a considerably strong influence in his own younger days.

In what would prove to be a continuing exchange of correspondence during the remainder of the year 1755, Ray Thomas next wrote his brother-in-law on March 3rd. As to that correspondence, Ray commented, "Nothing gives me more Satisfaction than a Correspondence. I embrace the first oppty. of writing you in order that I might not be in arrears on that tho' in many things I shall think myself oblig'd beyond a Letter's Correspondence." He noted also that his carpenters had begun work that day on his house; he advised that "I'll tarry at Home till they have gone so far as to do without immediate inspection." He requested Thomas Dering to send him "some Spanish white," a finely powdered chalk useful both for coloring and for cleansing, and a quantity of "Blue Broad Cloth." Less than a week later, writing about the Spanish white and the broadcloth in answer to a letter from Dering, he remarked that he would have been earlier in answering "had not all communication Ceas'd Since the uncommon Snow Storm."

During the months of May and June, with work progressing on his house, but still demanding his attention, Ray Thomas found it necessary to consider the matter of his servants. Asher, who had been with the family for many years and may have accompanied Ray when he first set out for Harvard, was still on hand and well. But Mrs. Prior, possibly the cook, had been "Sick with a fever" during one of Ray's trips to Boston and, he reported on his return, "mends but slowly." Within a month or so, however, Mrs. Prior was talking of going to Boston with Bisby, apparently the captain of a vessel in the coastal trade often used for transporting goods to and from Boston for Ray Thomas. The latter, noting in a letter to his brother-in-law that she might visit him, added: "however you know her so won't need Say any thing of her impertinence." Despite this, Ray explained that, "from our present Circumstances," he thought best to engage Mrs. Prior and her daughter Betty for the season. Still concerned about Mrs. Prior, however, Ray hired "a Negro Man and Wife for a Month upon trial." He added: "She understands the Business we want her for; and Mrs. Prior is always complaining for want of help. However I hope we shall have Some body that will do better than she."

Matters other than the finishing of his home and his grappling with the servant problem preoccupied Ray or took time and effort. He became interested in heraldry and expressed to Thomas Dering his liking for a

Marriage and Country Life

certain emblazonment; but added, "I don't think the Rae arms to appertaine to my Mother So must leave it out." He was apparently endeavoring to marshal or combine the arms of his own and related families in an appropriate escutcheon. Horses were the subject of recurring comment. When his mare which he proposed to use for his chaise proved to be with foal, Ray had to find one "for the season in Town." Reminding his brother-in-law of his failure to mention anything about a horse in a recent letter, he advised Dering: "My Sadle Horse will go in Harness upon occasion..., tho' I had rather get one if I could Conveniently and not worry my Horse with a Harness." But another horse, which Ray either bought or borrowed from a friend, elicited the light-hearted comment: "Hir Horse is got very gay. I put him in my Chase to try the Lady and [she?] thought him full [of] Life enough."

Renovation and repair of Ray Thomas's house had progressed steadily during the late winter and spring of 1755. In that time he ordered additional boards, and brick, tile, and shingles from Boston; and, as the work neared completion, such items as locks for the doors of the various rooms, three with brass "rubs" or plates and six without, and a latch and a large lock for the front door. [The lock is now in possession of the Historic Winslow House Association] Ray's letters revealed a glimpse now and then of other details of the interior of the house. He noted that his carpenters had "found room Sufficient for two closets in my little Parlour each side of the chimney"; and in other letters he commented that "as to the paint for my Chamber it seems to me some other colour for Wainscoat would do better" and reported that "the Room is paper'd and paint'd" and the other would be finished that day. There was also mention of some items of furniture. He inquired of Dering "the bigness of the press Bedstead" - the framework of a bed which could be folded up into a press or cupboard and covered by a door; and in another letter he wrote of sending up "a Couple of Ruggs to put over the Chest of Drawers or what you and Mrs. Thomas thinks best." All of this was in preparation for shipping "our Furniture" by Captain Bisby and his coasting-vessel from Boston to Marshfield.

But despite the impending completion of the renovation and repair, Ray began to show the effect of care and work. "I'm Sick and tired with my House," he wrote to Dering on May 30th, "and every thing worries me and no one to unbend with in the Cares of Life makes it tedious." (Sarah Thomas was apparently spending this period with her brother at Dering's Corner in Boston.) "However," he continued, "I expect to finish so as to

Marriage and Country Life

be in town the beginning of the Week after next and hope to be ready soon after to embark for Marshfield."

Whether or not Ray made the trip to Boston in the interval, he wrote to his brother-in-law from Marshfield on June 8th. He was looking forward to the "pleasure of enjoying you and Our Friends mutually with Mistress Thomas at Marshfield, Oh Wish'd for Time!" But to that happy thought he added a melancholy postscript: "I wish there was a Man to be got to take off some of my care for I'm almost Dead, and wonder amongst so many Friends as I've got, can get none of 'em to [pronounce?]." On the 20th at long last, the homecoming at Marshfield was imminent. "I've wrote to Mrs. Thomas concerning our coming down," Ray advised his brother-in-law, "so you and she'll conclude to do as you think Fit." Sometime not long thereafter Sarah Thomas joined her husband in their newly refurbished house.

On July 24, 1755, not long after her arrival in Marshfield, Sarah wrote to her brother Thomas Dering. It touched on personal matters and provided a glimpse of the "social vitality" of country life in provincial Massachusetts. Ray Thomas, of course, also mentioned in his correspondence that spring, summer, and fall of 1755 various individuals by name, most in connection with business but some also as family members. Mr. Wentworth was Samuel Wentworth, prominent Boston merchant and husband of Sarah's sister Elizabeth; Mr. Green was probably Joseph Green, also a Boston merchant and husband of a cousin of Sarah's; Mr. Monk was presumably Judge James Monk of Halifax, Nova Scotia, and husband of Sarah's sister Ann; and "Aptp & S" were James Apthorp, son of the wealthy merchant Charles Apthorp of Boston and husband of Sarah's niece Sarah Wentworth, whose marriage was to take place a few days after Sarah wrote to her brother.

But Sarah's letter provided a more detailed, personal report on country life. After acknowledging her brother's "kinde and repeated invitation" to visit Boston (which she planned to do the following week) and expressing her pleasure at his being able to attend Harvard Commencement despite the "exstream hot weather" and the wedding of James Apthorp and Sarah Wentworth, she described events at Marshfield. "We have had Mr. Howard and Juge [Judge] Lightfoot to make us a visit," she wrote. "Thay ware very gay, and we spent our time very pleasantly. I wish'd for you hear, and did not forget you over our Glass, when we often wish you health, with the rest of our friends, Mr. Sheaf and Mr. Goldthwaite in perteculare, the former of which I forgot to

Marriage and Country Life

send my Compliments by you and return him many thanks for the Lemons he sent us. Theay Stud us in great sted while those Gentealmen ware hear... Doctr Stockbridge is to dine with us to day and it is time to dress..."

Mr. Sheafe and Mr. Goldthwaite were probably William Sheafe and Ezekiel Goldthwaite, both prominent merchants of Boston. Dr. Stockbridge was almost certainly Dr. Charles Stockbridge of Scituate, a warm friend and physician to the Thomas family. In the letter to her brother Sarah also mentioned Mr. and Mrs. Green, the merchant Joseph Green of Boston and his wife Anna, Sarah's first cousin. After Mr. Green's departure from Marshfield, the matter of Anna Green's return to Boston posed a problem for Sarah. She included in her letter to Thomas Dering a plea for help: "If you could get any body to come down without haveing it known, and bring Mrs. Green up by next friday week I should be glad, because I had rather be drove by Mr. Thomas, then by her, or a servant..." A solution presented itself when her sister Mrs. Gooch arrived. "Mrs. Gooch," Sarah added in a marginal postscript, "says you need not send any body to fetch Mrs. Green, for she will ride with her and I shall ride with Mr. Gooch or Mr. Hubbard [Thomas Hubbard, husband of Ray's Aunt Judith] one of which is to come for her. Fare you well for to night it is past eleven and I must be up early."

It may well have been that Sarah's reluctance to ride with anyone other than Ray was occasioned by her advanced stage of pregnancy and the birth of her first child. Two weeks later this occurred. Sarah was safely delivered of a son on August 5, 1755. Some three weeks later, on August 24th, the boy was baptized in the First Church in Boston, where his parents had been married. He was given the name Nathaniel Thomas for his father, a name borne also by a succession of his forbears. On that day as well Nathaniel Ray Thomas as an adult person, "publickly recognized the Baptismal Covenant."

In an era when one might have expected formal communication especially between military personnel on active duty, Colonel John Winslow, in Grand Pre, Nova Scotia as commander of the First Battalion of Shirley's Regiment, began a letter to Joshua Winslow, commissary of British forces in Nova Scotia, on September 19, 1755: "Dr.[Dear] Josh..." A few days later Joshua Winslow wrote John Winslow with a bit of local news gathered from Marshfield and forwarded by Thomas Dering. Dering spoke of "Mr. Thomas having a Son Born [Nathaniel, born

Marriage and Country Life

August 5, 1755]" Joshua added this comment: "So your Neighbour Ray has not been Delinquent in regard to a Son & Heir (as it may happen)..."

That fall of 1755 witnessed a series of earthquakes in the American Colonies and in Europe. There were at least two earthquakes in Marshfield, the first occurring on November 17th, which were described by both Ray and Sarah and for their safe deliverance from which both were devoutly thankful. "I think it an infinite Mercy of god," Ray wrote Thomas Dering, "that we Survive the last nights tremendous Shock which we have been most Sensible affect'd with, for one of my Parlour Chimneys was Shook down, the Noise of which upon the House and within the Rooms, Join'd to the Roaring of the Sea Greatly affec'd my Dr.[dear] Mrs. Thomas and Mrs. Gooch with the whole House, and very Justly too...Our House was really shaken the Tables and Chairs and evrything was Shooking..." He added in a postscript: "Mrs. Thomas would have wrote but has not yet Compos'd her Self." Ten days later Sarah did write her brother regarding the "grate shock" and another as "sevear." She commented soberly: "I joyn with you in thanks to almighty God for his grate goodness to us in preserving us in such an awfull time of danger...It would seem almoste as tho' we ware rise from the dead..."

By that late fall of 1755 the news from Nova Scotia, both of the reduction of Fort Beausejour and of the expulsion of the Acadians, who though British subjects had maintained their allegiance to France, reached Marshfield. Colonel John Winslow, commanding the First Battalion of the provincial regiment, and Lieutenant John Thomas, commanding Colonel Winslow's own company of that battalion, had been actively engaged in the Nova Scotia operations. Indeed, Colonel Winslow had been in immediate overall charge of the removal of the Acadians. Lieutenant Thomas, was one of the junior officers involved in rounding up the "French prisoners" as the Acadians had officially become, preparatory to their evacuation and in carrying out punitive measures against their property. Even after ships began to transport the displaced Acadians to New England and the southern colonies for resettlement, provincial troops continued to search out the French and to destroy or confiscate their property. Under date of November 17th Lieutenant John Thomas recorded a typical foray by the provincial troops: "we marched all Night very Bad Traviling Came to memoramcook about Break of Day we Soronded about 20 Houses but thay were all Deserted Except one house whare we found 9 women & Children but no man the most of them were sick we Burnt 30 Houses Brought away one woman 200 Hed of Neat Cattle 20 Horses we Came away about 10 a m..." Although the

Marriage and Country Life

British authorities justified the expulsion of the Acadians, who refused to take the oath of allegiance to the King on political and military grounds, many Provincial officers and men no doubt shared Colonel Winslow's sentiments: "This affair is more grievous to me than any service I was ever employed in."

That year of 1755 was memorable and long remembered. The opening of hostilities in The Great War for Empire - the Seven Years War in Europe, the French and Indian War in America - and the awesome natural catastrophe of earthquakes at home and abroad were portentous events that rhymesters celebrated or lamented in doggerel or folk verse or ballad recited and sung around many a family hearth. So the heroic deeds of war and the manifestations of God's wrath alike became traditions passed down from generation to generation in crude poetry or song. In a town some miles inland from Marshfield an unknown author composed a ballad that might then have been widely known:

> *We that did live in fifty five,*
> *That were preserved & kept alive,*
> *We may record what god has done*
> *Beneath the circuit of the sun.*
>
> *How he display'd his mighty power*
> *And passed before us in an hour,*
> *In various ways which he did take*
> *By thunder stormes and the Earthquake.*
>
> *First in the spring the wars begin.*
> *To punish men then for their sin;*
> *They beat their drums & so they cry,*
> *Who will unto the battle fly?*
>
> *They list a man with Courage bold*
> *Their armour bright & money told;*
> *The time comes on, they must not stay,*
> *But Quit their friends & go away.*
>
> *While husbands parting with their Dears,*
> *And mothers for their sons in tears,*
> *Not knowing but that they must die*
> *Or go into Captivity.*

Marriage and Country Life

> *They first arive at East-ward shores,*
> *Where drums beat and Cannon roar'*
> *A hero Spirit they retain;*
> *Which puts the french-men to great pain.*
>
> *They take their forts & so Possess*
> *Their pastures and their Wilderness.*
> *The Joyfull News spreads O'r the land*
> *That we have gain'd the upper hand.*

And so through twenty-three verses.

The relocation of the Acadians from Nova Scotia to the British colonies to the south gave Ray Thomas an apparent opportunity to improve his situation with regard to hired help, whether house servants or farm hands. For, with the beginning of 1756, that problem continued to vex Ray and Sarah. Ray wrote his brother-in-law about a man and woman whom Dering had suggested: "If you find they will suit us do let me know their price, etc...We want such a couple and if no material objection do let us know as we shall soon dismiss Tom and Mary." He wrote also concerning Asher, who had been with the family as a servant for a least a dozen years. "You may tell him," Ray advised Thomas Dering, "that if he will continue to serve me till this last December twelvemonths, I will give him his freedom signed before witnesses provided he will go out of the government, as I must give him more security than I choose if he continues here. I must pray you to let him know in full the bonds I shall be obliged to give, etc." Asher was very likely an indentured servant, whom Ray was willing to release from his indenture.

Some months later Sarah also requested help from Thomas Dering about the servant problem. "If I have not time to write to Heps [Hepsibah Small, a close friend of the Dering family], pray tell her she must look out for a maid for me, for Elizabeth is going away to be married in October and Asher's time is out in December and then I shall be quite destitute of servants. I think to complete my letter of wants I must say I wish you could get me a good negro woman, for, in short, I believe I shall have no steady help till I get one."

About that time an easing of the problem of hired help, at least as far as farm hands went, seemed likely in the form of the Acadians recently and forcibly removed from Nova Scotia. Many of the families were relocated in Massachusetts; some, in Plymouth County. Ray Thomas hired one

Marriage and Country Life

family of the "French Neutrals," as they were called, upon his giving bond to provide them with certain necessaries. The term of his agreement for their service was one year. But the arrangement did not work out well. At the end of the term the "French Neutrals" petitioned the Governor and Council. They claimed:

> Our whole Family, being hired to Mr. Rea Thomas of Marshfield on condition that he would give each Man a full suit of Working Cloths and another of Sabath cloths and to our Wives and Daughters the same...but your Petitioners having faithfully served him a full year according to Agreement he now means to give us nothing but the mean old duds on our Backs which is [all] we have had during our Years service but our Women are a great worse being almost naked.

Ray Thomas countered by alleging that the "French Neutrals" refused to work and were insolent to him and his family. He was released from his bond. So that solution for obtaining hired help proved illusory.

The problem of getting and keeping servants continued to be a vexatious one for Massachusetts families. Most families had servants, at least one, usually a house servant indentured for a specific term of years or for life or they had a Negro slave, brought to the American Colonies by a slave ship. Only by 1783 was the institution of slavery abolished by decision of the highest court in Massachusetts.

Until that time, large landowning families such as the Winslows and Thomases, or merchant families with extensive business or trading undertakings kept slaves or servants to meet their needs.

The Winslows, for example, had some servants known to us by name. There was Cato; an Indian woman named Nab Nowit; Jane; and one who was part of the household by 1747, named Briton Hammon, a Negro man and probably a house servant. Hammon had heard stories of distant and foreign shores from visitors to the Winslow house, and was fired up by them. He asked then Colonel Winslow if he might have permission to undertake just such a voyage. The Colonel agreed and on Christmas Day, 1747, Hammon went to Plymouth and signed up on a ship bound for Jamaica.

Thus began a voyage marked by harsh treatment and near disasters, until Briton Hammon returned to Boston, having found his former master

Marriage and Country Life

after thirteen years, General Winslow, in London. Hammon sailed home to Boston with the General after a harrowing voyage.

Briton Hammon's ship had been wrecked and the crew had been murdered by Indians in the Caves of Flanders. Hammon escaped and was captured by the Indians, who confined him for more than seven years in a "close dungeon." Later he escaped again and encountered a ship that took him to England where by amazing coincidence he met up with General Winslow, who treated him very kindly. Hammon shipped back to Boston with General Winslow and made his way to Marshfield in 1760 after thirteen years.

Colonel John Winslow, having executed his responsibility of expelling those Acadians from Nova Scotia in the late fall of 1755, returned to Marshfield in early 1756. But his stay there was short. Military duty called him back into active service. Governor William Shirley of Massachusetts, who had succeeded as commander-in-chief in America upon the death of General Edward Braddock at Fort Duquesne, proposed a several-pronged attack on the French. One would move against Fort Niagara on Lake Ontario; one, to try again to take Duquesne where Braddock failed; and the final effort, a feint, to ascend the Kennebec River toward Quebec. On February 18, 1756 Shirley appointed John Winslow a major general to command the campaign against Crown Point. Early in the summer Winslow was pushing his "raw and untrained" New England troops from Albany up the Hudson River toward Fort William Henry at the head of Lake George. Beyond, to the north, were the French at Crown Point and at Fort Carillon (soon to be known as Fort Ticonderoga) where Lake George emptied into Lake Champlain.

But that spring William Shirley, able and energetic (if sometimes too impetuous) governor of Massachusetts, was superseded in military command by John Campbell, Earl of Loudoun, and his senior subordinates Major Generals James Abercromby and Daniel Webb. At about the time of Lord Loudoun's arrival in New York in July, General John Winslow was at Fort William Henry with his New England and other colonial troops. Early in August the French general the Marquis de Montcalm captured Fort Oswego at the eastern end of Lake Ontario. By then Lord Loudoun had called off Shirley's plan to attack Crown Point with militia; and, with the fall of Oswego, he ordered Winslow to remain at Fort William Henry to contain the French in that area. After two months of skirmishing but of no significant moves on the part of either

Marriage and Country Life

British or French, the latter withdrew toward Canada and winter quarters. General John Winslow and his troops were ordered home, and the General retired from active military service.

Winslow's friend and subordinate in the Nova Scotia operations, Lieutenant John Thomas, was promoted to captain in 1756 and three years later was commissioned a colonel to command a regiment of Massachusetts troops. He was now a field-grade officer at the age of thirty-five. During the year following he was once again in Nova Scotia, with his regiment garrisoning Halifax and other points. Upon the expiration of that duty Colonel Thomas was ordered to Crown Point. He was senior colonel of the Massachusetts troops under the command of the British commander-in-chief in America, Major General Sir Jeffery Amherst. In the late summer of 1760 came the last assault on Canada. It was to be the attack on Montreal, the only remaining French stronghold following the capture in 1759 of Quebec by General Wolfe and of Crown Point and Ticonderoga by General Amherst. The plan of operations against Montreal provided for Sir Jeffery to lead the main British force down the St. Lawrence River from Fort Oswego on Lake Ontario; General James Murray to lead another up the river from Quebec; and Colonel William Haviland to proceed from Crown Point down Lake Champlain and the Richelieu River and reduce the French fort at Isle-aux-Noix on that river.

On August 11, 1760 Colonel Haviland left Crown Point with Colonel John Thomas, the senior officer in command of the Massachusetts troops. Their force, reaching Isle-aux-Noix, besieged the fort for twelve days with vigorous cannonading. On August 28th the French abandoned the fort. Colonel Haviland detached John Thomas and five hundred men to remain on the island and demolish the defenses, while he continued on to the juncture with Sir Jeffery Amherst and General Murray before Montreal. On September 8, 1760 the French surrendered that city and with it all of Canada. The Great War for the Empire was, but for some scattered fighting and a final peace treaty, over.

The Treaty of Paris in 1763 made England the strongest power in Europe, her King sovereign of the world's largest empire. But she was faced with intricate and perplexing problems in the administration of that empire, particularly in her relations with the American colonies; and she was saddled with an enormous war debt. The American colonies, on the other hand, were conscious of a differing sense of identity than before; their people now thought of themselves as Americans, no longer as

Marriage and Country Life

Englishmen transplanted from "home." They thought differently and acted differently, and they had differing values. They had come to realize, as a result of the war, that they could act in unison, and thereby more effectively. But when the young George III came to the throne in 1760, Americans greeted his accession with enthusiasm and warm devotion. His Majesty was still, after all, their liege lord.

VI

The Provincial Gentry

George III's accession to the throne of England in 1760 was acknowledged enthusiastically by his subjects at home and in America. The Great War for the Empire neared a victorious conclusion under the stern and inexorable guidance of William Pitt. James Wolfe, dying on the Plains of Abraham, had secured Quebec for his Sovereign in 1759. Sir Jeffery Amherst, leading a three-fold and successful attack on Montreal in 1760, had accepted the capitulation of all Canada on behalf of the Crown. England's far-flung conquests continued, reducing French positions in the West Indies and in India. With the signing of the Treaty of Paris in 1763, Great Britain became the strongest power in Europe and proprietor of a world-wide empire.

On October 25, 1760 King George II died. When the news reached Massachusetts, the great bells of the Province tolled in somber measured cadence; the Governor and Council went into mourning. On December 30th George III was proclaimed "by the Grace of God of Great Britain, France and Ireland, King, Defender of the Faith, &c." from the balcony of the Town House in Boston, the steps of county courthouses, and the pulpits of town churches. Now the bells rang in gratitude and joy. Now the people called out in unison: "Long live King George III! Long may he reign!" So in Marshfield from the pulpit of the First Church that faced the training field of His Majesty's militia was the new Monarch thus suitably honored.

By law and custom long established, commissions of civil officers appointed by and in the name of the Crown expired six months after the death of a sovereign. New commissions would be issued in the name of his successor. They might be to men previously in office or to men appointed for the first time. Among those officers of the Crown in the Province of Massachusetts Bay to whom commissions would issue following the death of George II were Justices of the Peace. Their office was one of ancient origin; their title, first bestowed in the time of Edward III in the fourteenth century; their duty, to act as "conservator" of the King's peace in their county. In time, their jurisdiction was extended over certain civil matters as well. Certain justices were designated as of the

The Provincial Gentry

Quorum, "because," as a contemporary legal treatise stated, "certain Matters of Importance cannot be done without the Presence of them, or One of them," as when the specified number of Justices held a court of General Sessions of the Peace for the County.

What sort of individuals received commissions as Justices of the Peace? That same contemporary legal treatise quoted with approval Michael Dalton's Country Justice, a manual for Justices of the Peace popular both in England and the Colonies, on appropriate qualifications:
> They must be Men of Substance and Ability of Body and Estate; of the best Reputation, good Governance, and Courage for the Truth; Men fearing God, not seeking the Place for Honour or Conveniency, but endeavoring to preserve the Peace and good Government of their County, wherein they ought to be resident; Lovers of Justice, judging the People equaly and impartially at all seasons, using Diligence in hearing and determining Causes, and not neglecting the Public Service for Private Emploiment, or Ease; of known Loialty to the King, not respecting Persons, but the Cause; and they ought to be Men of competent Knowledge in the Laws of their County, to enable them to execute their Office and Authority to the Advancement of Justice, the Benefit of the People, and without Reproach to themselves.

During the last months of 1761 and the first months of 1762, commissions were issued for the civil officers of the Province. Those for Plymouth County were as of January 28, 1762. At the head of the judiciary of the county was General John Winslow of Marshfield. He had been a Justice of the Peace since 1739; a new commission was issued appointing him also of the Quorum. At the same time General Winslow was named Chief Justice of the Inferior Court of Common Pleas and Quarter Sessions of the Peace for Plymouth County, a position once held by his father Isaac Winslow and by Ray Thomas's grandfather Judge Nathaniel Thomas and by his great-grandfather Colonel Nathaniel Thomas. Thirty-six persons received commissions as His Majesty's Justices of the Peace. Among them were Thomas Croade, grandson of Colonel Thomas and an older cousin of Ray's, who was also appointed of the Quorum and as a Special Justice of the Common Pleas; William Watson, cousin and Harvard classmate of Ray's; and Ray himself. His commission began: "George, by the Grace of God of Great Britain, France and Ireland, King, Defender of the Faith &c. To

The Provincial Gentry

Our Trusty and Welbeloved Nathaniel Ray Thomas, Esq..." Both Thomas Dering, Sarah's brother, and Samuel Wentworth, her sister Elizabeth's husband, were similarly commissioned for Suffolk County; and Ezekiel Goldthwaite, Ray's and Sarah's friend, was of the Quorum for that county.

Nathaniel Ray Thomas was thirty years old, well educated, and the senior representative of a family prominent in political and judicial positions in colony and Province since the time of his great-great-great grandfather William Thomas more than one hundred years before. In addition, he possessed a large estate - the "largest improved estate" he said - in Plymouth County; and, though he had friends and family in Boston, Plymouth, Newport, and elsewhere, Sarah commented twenty years after their marriage; "It is with very great difficulty he ever leaves the farm." He was indeed a countryman, even if as much by necessity as by choice; his family, a county family in true measure. As in England, "Justices of the Peace had administered and judged the English village and the English county, partly by virtue of their local importance as landlords, partly by virtue of their commissions as Justices granted them by the central government."

Ray had not been educated to the law nor had he formally read law under the eye of an experienced member of the bar. Indeed, there were still relatively few trained lawyers in the Province. But like most landed proprietors of his day he had a familiarity with numerous principles of law and their practical applicability. Particularly was this so in respect to land and, to a lesser degree, other property. As one who continuously had or tried to get hired help, either as house servants or farmhands, Ray had a working knowledge of the law pertaining to that relationship. Furthermore, as one who had frequent occasion to mingle among and observe the conduct of men and women of the countryside and who was aware of proceedings and procedures in both civil and criminal cases, he was knowledgeable about the administration of justice in the county. Among the books owned by his forebears and inherited by him there were probably law books of various sorts: compilations of statutes and manuals of practice and pleading and of the duties of Justices of the Peace and lesser officials of county and town - these almost certainly; and probably a treatise or two on conveyances or wills or other branch of law and possibly a set of reports of English cases. All of this - his experience and his own reading - could well have provided Ray Thomas at that time and place with what Dalton set forth as one of the qualifications of a Justice of the Peace; "competent Knowledge in the

The Provincial Gentry

Laws of their County, to enable them to execute their Office and Authority to the Advancement of Justice..."

"Of known Loialty to the King" - Nathaniel Ray Thomas attested to that when he took the oath required first of those holding commissions under the Crown, before they entered upon and acted in their offices. "I Nathaniel Ray Thomas do Sincerely Promise and Swear, That I will be faithful and bear true Allegiance to His Majesty King George. So help me God."

Following that were two oaths designed further to secure and strengthen the allegiance of loyal subjects to the House of Hanover and the Protestant Succession. By the Act of Settlement in 1701, the monarchy was wrested forever from the line of Roman Catholic pretenders to the Crown of England. There were resounding words of loyalty:

> I Nathaniel Ray Thomas do truly and sincerely Acknowledge, Profess, Testify and Declare in my Conscience before GOD and the World, that Our Sovereign Lord King GEORGE is lawful and rightful King of this Realm, and all other His Majesty's Dominions and Countries thereunto belonging...And I do Swear, That I will bear Faith and true Allegiance to His Majesty King GEORGE, and Him will Defend to the utmost of my Power against all Traiterous Conspiracies and Attempts whatsoever, which shall be made against His Person, Crown or Dignity. And I will do my utmost endeavour to Disclose and make known to His Majesty and His Successors, all Treasons and Traiterous Conspiracies which I shall know to be against Him, or any of them... And all these things I do plainly and sincerely Acknowledge and Swear according to these express words by me spoken, and according to the plain and common sense and understanding of the same words without any Equivocation, Mental Evasion, or secret Reservation whatsoever. And I do make this Recognition, Acknowledgment, Abjuration, Renunciation and Promise, heartily, willingly and truly upon the true Faith of a Christian. So help me God.

In the exercise of his office as His Majesty's Justice of the Peace, Nathaniel Ray Thomas had the power:

The Provincial Gentry

to cause to be Staid and Arrested all Affrayers, Rioters, Disturbers or breakers of the Peace, and such as shall Ride, or go Armed Offensively before any of His Majesty's Justices, or other of His Officers or Ministers doing their Office, or elsewhere, by Night or by Day, in Fear or Affray of His Majesty's Liege People; and such others as shall utter any Menaces or Threatning Speeches; And ... shall commit the Offender to Prison, until he find Sureties for Peace and good Behaviour; and seize and take away his Armour or Weapons, and shall cause them to be apprized and answered to the King as Forfeited; And may further punish the Breach of the Peace in any person that shall Smite or Strike another, by Fine to the King, not exceeding Twenty Shillings; and Require Bond with Sureties for the Peace; or Bind the Offender over to answer it at the next Sessions of the Peace, as the Nature or the Circumstances may be; and may make Enquiry of Forcible Entry and Detainer, and cause the same to be Removed; and make out Hue and Cries after Run-away Servants, Thieves and Other Criminals.

Where, in the breach of various criminal laws punishable only by fine, and those who broke the law had not money to pay, Thomas, as a Justice of the Peace having cognizance of the offence, had the power "to Punish breakers of the Peace, Prophaners of the Sabbath, and unlawful Gamesters, Drunkards, or prophan Swearers or Cursers, by setting in the Stocks, or putting into the Cage, not exceeding Three Hours, or Imprisonment Twenty-four Hours, or by Whipping, Ten Stripes; as the case may deserve, and where the Offender has not wherewithal to satisfy the Law in that case provided."

And in civil matters the law stated: "That all manner of Debts, Trespasses and other Matters, not exceeding the value of Forty Shillings (wherein the Title of Land is not concerned) shall and may be heard, tryed, adjudged and determined, by any of His Majesty's Justices of the Peace within this Province, in their respective Precincts..."

In the exercise of his office as a Justice of the Peace, therefore, Nathaniel Ray Thomas represented the Crown in those matters over which he had cognizance and brought to the people the power and authority of their Sovereign Lord the King. It was a somber responsibility.

The Provincial Gentry

For a century and a quarter Nathaniel Ray Thomas's ancestors had borne allegiance to the Crown of England and had sworn to serve their Sovereign in whatever duty they were commissioned. In 1642 the first William Thomas took the oath of an Assistant in New Plymouth Colony: "You shall all sweare to be truely Loyall to our Sovereigne Lord King Charles his heires and Successors. You shall faithfully truely and Justly according to the measure of deserning and descretion God hath given you bee Assistant to the Governor...according to the Nature of the office of an Assistant read unto you...Soe healp you God who is the God of truth and punisher of falsehood." In 1712 Colonel Nathaniel Thomas, grandson of William Thomas, took the oath of Justice of the Superior Court of Judicature of the Province of Massachusetts Bay: "You Swear, That well and truly You shall Serve Our Sovereigne Lord the King and his People in the Office of Justice of the Superiour Court of Judicature...So help you God." In 1715 Judge Nathaniel Thomas, the Colonel's son, took the oath of a Justice of the Inferior Court of Common Pleas and Quarter Sessions of the Peace of Plymouth County: "You Swear, that well and truly You shall Serve Our Sovereigne Lord the King and His People in the Office of Justice of the Inferiour Court of Common Pleas...So help you God." And in 1762 Nathaniel Ray Thomas, great-great-great-grandson of William Thomas, great-grandson of Colonel Nathaniel Thomas, and grandson of Judge Nathaniel Thomas, took the oath: "I Nathaniel Ray Thomas do sincerely Promise and Swear, That I will be faithful and bear true Allegiance to His Majesty King George. So help me God."; and then, the oath of a Justice of the Peace: "You Nathaniel Ray Thomas do Swear, that as Justice of the Peace in the County of Plymouth according to the Commission given you, You shall Dispense Justice equally and impartially in all Cases...So help you God."

Duty to the state, service to the King, as an obligation of privilege was taken seriously by the gentry of the colonies. It was a sense of responsibility that accompanied rank and station and the ownership of property. A country gentleman of the time would have accepted as his inherent obligation service as a Justice of the Peace or an officer in the militia, a selectman of the town or a representative to the General Court of the Province.

Not only was allegiance to the King and the obligation of service to the Crown deeply ingrained in Nathaniel Ray Thomas but also manifested for him in visible ways was the presence of royal authority and power. In no one among Ray Thomas's relatives and friends was that presence

The Provincial Gentry

personally more truly exemplified than General John Winslow of Marshfield, Chief Justice of His Majesty's Inferior Court of Common Pleas and Quarter Sessions of the Peace of Plymouth County. Young Elkanah Watson, grandson of the charming, thrice-married Priscilla Thomas and great-nephew of the General, described the latter as "a noble, generous and accomplished man, a distinguished officer in the French War... from the first of our Revolutionary difficulties, an asserter and defender of the rights and prerogatives of royalty..." Young Watson recalled Mr. Chief Justice Winslow "going in procession as a member of the Court, from his quarters to the Court-house. The Judges were clothed in robes of scarlet, and the clerk bore before them some formidable insignia of their power, the high sheriff with a drawn sword, and the deputies and constables with their staves, making up the escort." He added: "This was the pomp and etiquette, royalty reflected at that period upon every department of the colonial government."

John Winslow, it is certainly reasonable to suppose, had a considerable influence over Ray Thomas, whether consciously exerted or not. As an older man of the generation of Ray's father and uncle, he may well have taken their place for Ray as one to turn to for advice. He stood, as lawyers are fond of saying, in loco parentis, or, translated freely, "in the place of the parent." Ray was frequently "at the General's" or "gone to see the General." Nearing sixty at that time, John Winslow, after a distinguished military career in the service of the Crown, upheld royal authority and power on the bench. His Majesty's Chief Justice of the Common Pleas and Quarter Sessions of the Peace was staunchly loyal and, in himself, an impressive embodiment of British sovereignty.

There were others whose influence may have been felt by Ray Thomas at this time. One such individual would certainly have been Martin Howard, Jr. Born in England, he was brought by his father to Newport, Rhode Island, as a young child. He was some years older than Ray, who may have met him first through his mother's Rhode Island connections or possibly his Harvard College classmate and bosom companion in hazardous pranks, Joseph Wanton of Newport. Educated to the law and a member of the Newport bar, Howard had been entrusted by the Rhode Island Assembly with several responsible duties. He was cultured and, by some, considered brilliant. He had been a guest at Marshfield in 1755, among their earliest during Ray's and Sarah's first year of marriage, when all those present were "very gay." There may have been more visits during the next ten years; there was certainly correspondence between Martin Howard, Jr. and Ray Thomas. In

General John Winslow. Portrait by Joseph Blackburn. Courtesy of the Pilgrim Society, Plymouth, Massachusetts.

Judge Martin Howard, Jr., friend of Nathaniel Ray Thomas. Portrait by John Singleton Copley. Courtesy of the Fundacion Coleccion Thyssen-Bornemisza, Madrid, Spain.

The Provincial Gentry

December 1764 Sarah wrote of her husband's having received a letter from Howard in which he reported the death of his wife. By that time also Howard was known as firmly loyal to England and a strong supporter of royal government. Earlier that year he had written letters that were printed in the Newport press, urging the revocation of Rhode Island's charter permitting a popular form of government and the establishment of a royal government in its place. (Admittedly, the practices of government there were unlicensed.) To what extent his views may have had an influence on Ray Thomas is unknown; certainly Ray would have known of them. But one fact is clear: Ray Thomas gave such esteem to Martin Howard, Jr. as to name his sixth child and fourth son, Martin Howard Thomas.

General John Winslow, having retired from active military duty in the late fall of 1756, nevertheless followed, one might assume, the progress of British arms during the next several years of the French and Indian War. He certainly would have known that his younger friend, neighbor, and former subordinate John Thomas had received a colonel's commission in 1759; and that, after duty in Nova Scotia, Colonel Thomas had commanded the Massachusetts regiments in Sir Jeffery Amherst's reduction of Canada in 1760. Late that year or early in 1761 the Colonel had returned to Plymouth County and resumed the practice of medicine. It was about that same time that he married Hannah Thomas, Ray Thomas's first cousin and daughter of Lieutenant Colonel Nathaniel Thomas, General Winslow's companion in arms who died at the siege of Louisbourg in 1745. Now known as Dr. John Thomas again, he and his bride moved to Kingston, immediately north of Plymouth, where they resided permanently.

Despite growing tension between England and her American colonies, there were lighter moments as well for the members of the Winslow and Thomas families. In July 1752, Dr. John Thomas attended one of many pleasurable social events at the Winslows. "We had a Barbicued Hogg at Colonel Winslows. Much company from Plimoth. We Dined under the Shade of Trees." So the Doctor wrote in his diary. Later, on one occasion General Winslow and a group of friends had ridden on horseback out to Saquish Beach for a picnic. General Winslow fell asleep while there. Upon waking, he found that his companions had started to ride the fourteen miles back to Plymouth, and thinking that he would play a practical joke on those who had been with him, he swam his horse across Plymouth Harbor - a shorter route by far - and was

The Provincial Gentry

seated comfortably at the tavern where the party was headed when they finally arrived.

The families of General John Winslow, Nathaniel Ray Thomas, and Dr. John Thomas had settled on contiguous lands in Marshfield during the two decades of the seventeenth century from 1630 to 1650. Governor Edward Winslow and William Thomas, Esq., progenitors of two of those families, had each received grants in the name of the Crown of one thousand or more acres. John Thomas, the orphan taken under the care of Governor Winslow and the great-grandfather of Dr. John Thomas and Anthony Thomas, acquired the farm of about fifty-nine acres which the governor had given "for the better accommodation of a neighborhood," probably from his own lands. From that time until the 1760's, a century or more, the Winslow and William Thomas families had been closely associated politically, judicially, militarily, and socially, and in more recent years related by marriage as well. They were large landed proprietors, gentry, the "better sort." They were country gentlemen, their names distinguished by the title "Esquire" and in the instances when they held high office singled out as "Honorable." The family of John Thomas was, by contrast for most of that century, referred to as that of yeomen, men of respectable standing and owning their own property, but in the colonial social hierarchy of the eighteenth century not of the gentry, rather of the "middling sort."
But that social hierarchy was not as finite and fixed, nor as clearly defined in the New World as it was in the Old. It was far more fluid and flexible in the American colonies than in the Mother Country, England. A man could rise (and, of course, fall) as the result of his progress in life. The acquisition of land, the holding of political office, a distinguished military career, the successful practice of a profession or operation of a business - these could help a man in his upward aspirations. Blood and breeding, distinguished lineage, and extensive property fixed a man's position, but these were not the only assurances for high rank.

Samuel Thomas, son of the emigrant John and father of Mr. John Thomas, had prospered moderately. In his will probated in 1720, he described himself as "Inholder" [inn keeper] and made disposition of a number of pieces of land and some bequests of money. The "homestead farm" of his father, however, had been inherited by an older brother, but passed on that brother's death, to Samuel's son, Mr. John Thomas. The latter augmented his inheritance of land in Duxbury and Marshfield from his father and of the "homestead farm" from his uncle by the acquisition of other property. At the time of his death in 1770 he

The Provincial Gentry

owned upwards of two hundred acres; he had been well respected and had served in several capacities on the town's behalf; he was described on his gravestone as "Mr. John Thomas," a mark of his standing in the community.

Although the two Thomas families were not related, Ray Thomas had known Anthony Thomas and his younger brother Dr. John Thomas all his life and, intimately, during the seven years of their father's, Mr. John Thomas's, guardianship. From 1745 to 1752, except when away at Harvard, he lived in that household. The family occupied a small, probably a story-and-a-half, house with a center chimney on land described at the time as "the home meadow so called consisting of about twelve acres of salt marsh; and the homestead farm so called consisting of about forty two acres of upland and swampey land, with the buildings and fences standing and being on same, lying and being in Marshfield aforesaid, between the lands of Nathanl. Ray Thomas Esqr. and John Winslow Esq."

In his younger days Ray had not had occasion to become as well acquainted with Anthony Thomas as with his brother, the Doctor. During one of his Harvard vacations, Ray had helped to bottle cider for Anthony; and in 1753, at the time of execution of Ray's release of Mr. John Thomas as guardian, Ray's signing of the document was witnessed by General John Winslow and Anthony Thomas. At an earlier period the latter was in Boston, engaged perhaps in commercial and mercantile endeavors and in seafaring, possibly in the coastal trade, for he was described as "marriner." He was certainly engaged in farming and over the years had acquired substantial holdings of land. In the recitals in some of the conveyances to this property, however, he was referred to as "yeoman."

Against the background of the families of John Winslow, Nathaniel Ray Thomas, and Anthony and Dr. John Thomas, two contemporary documents recorded clearly, on the one hand, the social structure of the South Precinct of Marshfield - the town's first-settled and wealthiest section - and, on the other hand, the social fluidity of the time. These two documents originated during the decade immediately preceding the American Revolution, in 1769 and 1771 respectively. The first of these was an assessment of taxes - poll, real property, and personal property - for the South Precinct of Marshfield in 1769; the second was a deed of division of real property by the heirs of Mr. John Thomas and was dated April 16, 1771.

The Provincial Gentry

The assessment of taxes in 1769 listed one hundred and thirty names of individuals, five of whom were accorded the title of "Esqr": General John Winslow; his son Dr. Isaac Winslow, and his cousin Kenelm Winslow, a Justice of the Peace; Abijah White, also a Justice of the Peace; and Nathaniel Ray Thomas. Two men were called "Mr.": John Thomas and his son Anthony Thomas. Several were given their military or church titles. The remainder were simply listed by name only.

Real property tax assessments, indicative of the extent and value of the property itself, were significant because of the singular importance attributed to land economically, socially, and even to a degree politically. The relative amounts of the real property taxes paralleled substantially the social status of the individuals assessed, as shown by the titles accorded them in the same assessment. Those individuals with real property taxes of 12s or more were: Nathaniel Ray Thomas, Esq., £2-18-1-2; Mr. Anthony Thomas, £1-5-3-3; John Winslow, Esq. £1-3-5-1; Dr. Isaac Winslow, £1-3-5-1; Kenelm Winslow, Esq., £0-16-10-2; Abijah White, Esq., £0-14-3-0; Mr. John Thomas, £0-12-2-1. Three other individuals were assessed taxes in excess of 12s; Thomas Ford, Jr., £0-16-0-2; Deacon Nehemiah Thomas, cousin of Mr. John Thomas, £0-14-0-3; and "Widow" Lucea Bourn, £0-12-6-0. The remainder of the real property taxes assessed were, for the most part, well below 12s. The fact that General Winslow and his son Dr. Isaac Winslow were each assessed £1-3-5-1 suggests that the General may have conveyed one half of the Careswell estate to his son. In the aggregate, therefore, the combined taxes of the Winslows of £2-6-10-2 was only slightly less than Nathaniel Ray Thomas's, which bore out the similarity in size and value of the properties of the two families. What appears most striking about these figures, comparatively, is that Mr. Anthony Thomas was third in the assessment, only exceeded by Nathaniel Ray Thomas and the Winslows as combined. The personal property tax assessments followed substantially the real property assessments, and Mr. Anthony Thomas appeared again to have a comparatively high personal property tax assessment.

The deed of division of real property executed by the heirs of Mr. John Thomas in April 1771 exhibited clearly the status of members of the family and the social fluidity of the time. The opening recitals were:
> Know all men by these presents that we Anthony Thomas of Marshfield in the County of Plimouth and Province of Massachusetts Bay in New England

The Provincial Gentry

gentleman, John Thomas of Kingston in said county of Plimouth esqr. James Bradford of Plainfield in the county of Windham and government of Connecticut in New England yeoman and Zerviah his wife (in right of his wife) Joseph Kent of Marshfield in the county of Plimouth marriner and Lydia his wife (in right of his sd wife Lydia) Jeremiah Kinsman of Norwich in the county of New London and government of Connecticut aforesaid yeoman and Sarah his wife (in right of his said wife Sarah), the said Anthony, John, Zerviah, Lydia, and Sarah, being all the children and heirs of John Thomas late of Marshfield yeoman deceased...

The tax assessment and the division deed presented the social structure of a town, Marshfield, and the social structure of a family within that town, the family of Mr. John Thomas. General John Winslow and his son Dr. Isaac Winslow and Nathaniel Ray Thomas were clearly of the gentry, the "better sort," and their families had been so since the earliest days of settlement. Kenelm Winslow, cousin of the General and descended from a younger brother of Governor Edward Winslow, would have been included among the less conspicuous of the gentry and he was, moreover, a Justice of the Peace. Abijah White was of an old family, his great-great-great-grandmother Suzannah White, the second wife of Governor Edward Winslow; he also was a Justice of the Peace and so of the "better sort." He was also Representative to the General Court at about that time. John Thomas and his son Anthony Thomas were called "Mr." in the assessment, the former perhaps out of respect for his integrity and service to the town, the latter for his industry and effort by which he had acquired a substantial landed property. These were not hard-and-fast lines of demarcation in the social hierarchy of the town, except for the ancient acknowledged standing of General Winslow and Nathaniel Ray Thomas.

The deed of division revealed clearly the social structure of John Thomas's family. That John Thomas was described as "yeoman" in the recitals indicated that was probably how he thought of himself and possibly how the townspeople thought as well, and that the title "Mr." was indeed out of respect and courtesy. That Anthony Thomas and Dr. John Thomas were accorded the titles of "gentleman" and "esquire" respectively was, no doubt, the result of the former's acquisition of a considerable landed estate and the latter's distinguished military and professional career. Two of their sisters were married to men described

The Provincial Gentry

as "yeomen"; the third, to a "marriner." The rise in standing of Anthony Thomas from "marriner" to "yeoman" to "gentleman" - a member of the gentry and of the "better sort" - illustrated well the fluidity of the social hierarchy. In the long course of Anglo-American history, the old aristocracy has always been infused with the blood of "new" men. In the crucial years before the American Revolution, years of mounting tension and strife between England and the colonies, the emergence of "new" men would contribute largely to the shape of events.

Thus were constituted the Province gentry of the third quarter of the eighteenth century - that period of material prosperity, cultural enrichment, "social vitality," and political vigor which preceded the break with England.

During the first ten years of their marriage, from 1755 to 1765, Ray and Sarah extended frequent, if modest, hospitality at what Sarah called their "retired habitation" at Marshfield, "entertaining...in the best manner" of which they were capable - which Sarah invariably wished could be better. They were on intimate terms with their neighbors at Careswell, General John Winslow and his wife Mary, a cousin of Ray's, and their two sons Pelham, who had been two classes behind Ray at Harvard, and Isaac. It was the "General's lady" who offered to take a letter of Sarah's to Boston and then "was so unkind as to go and leave" it. A few months later Sarah would have sent a letter to Boston by twenty-year-old Pelham Winslow, "if he had been complaisant enough to have let me known of his going."

General John Winslow not only married a cousin of Ray's but also, as a man thirty years Ray's senior and a friend of Ray's father and of his late uncle and guardian Colonel Nathaniel Thomas, apparently stood in the position of an older family friend and one to whom Ray could turn for advice. Early in July 1757 Sarah, at the end of the letter the "General's lady" had forgotten, wrote that she was "so surprised with a shock of an earthquake we had about five and twenty moments after two this afternoon that it is not in my power to write, being scarce able to hold my pen to write even this. Mr. Thomas was gone to see the General when the shock came but he returned immediately." And, similarly, some years later, she wrote: "Mr. Thomas is this evening at the General's."

A friend and guest of both General Winslow and Nathaniel Ray Thomas was John Rowe, a leading and wealthy merchant of Boston: much involved with civic, charitable, and religious affairs; a convivial

The Provincial Gentry

gentleman, admired as a host and sought after as a guest; and, during his frequent forays into the country, an ardent and skillful fisherman. Not unlike Mr. Chief Justice Sewall of an earlier day, Rowe kept a detailed diary which recorded in engaging fashion the many facets of life in colonial and Revolutionary Boston and Massachusetts. As the editor of his diary has pointed out: "All the notable houses in the Province were open to Rowe..."

On May 1, 1765, on his way from Boston to Plymouth, Rowe "set out early this morning [from Hingham], reached Pembroke went fishing had bad luck, began to Rain which was much wanted. got to Duxbury Mills, went a fishing, had tolerable luck, dined at Mr. Nath Ray Thomas on a Mess of Trout. Spent the eve'ng & slept there." The next day Rowe went on to Plymouth where he "dined at Mr. Edwd Winslow's [the younger brother of General John Winslow] with him, Mrs. Winslow, Miss Penny & Miss Sally Winslow, Major Vassall, Jos. Loring, Edwd Winslow Jr. Mr. Walter, Mr. Calef & Mr. Pelham Winslow." And on May 3rd Rowe "went a fishing with Mr Wm Watson [Ray's cousin and Harvard classmate, Cousin Will], had very good sport." Rowe caught "one very large Trout & several other fine ones." Again in the spring, three years later, John Rowe was a guest of General John Winslow at Careswell in Marshfield. The next morning, as Rowe noted, "Mr. Pelham Winslow joyned us wee went a fishing had but poor Luck. Returned to Generalls & dined there with him Mrs. Winslow Miss Massy Little Miss Polly Little Wm Sever Esq & Daughter Mr Pelham Winslow Mr Nat Ray Thomas Mr Knights Mr Calef."

Often, guests at the Thomas's "retired habitation" were relations. In August 1758 Sarah's brother Thomas Dering and her sister Elizabeth Dering, and the latter's husband, Samuel Wentworth, were among the "Company" at Marshfield. Wentworth, member of the politically powerful and propertied New Hampshire family, was the son of Lieutenant Governor John Wentworth of that province. He was a merchant of Boston, one with whom Ray Thomas frequently dealt. On the 20th Sarah wrote her brother after his departure: "...wish I had bin a pertaker with you, in your fine dish of strawberrys but I doe asure you I was quite unneasy all day to think that I was so thoughtless as to neglect giveing you the Chease," which Thomas Dering was so taken with that he offered to pay Sarah for some of it, "and the wine and Tongue we talk'd so much about." But, she explained, "hope you will except the will for the dea'd [deed], as I took care to have a bottle fetched up and the other things rol'd up after you went to bead [bed], that they might be ready for

The Provincial Gentry

you in the morning but Mr. Thomas and you Plagued me so about speading [speeding] the going Guests that I forgot every thing else." She also thanked her brother for his care "in sending the Cover for my Chare, tho' its not the exzact Couller of the back, it does very well I have got it done and it looks very smart indeed."

Late in 1764 Sarah Thomas described "a visit this fall from Mr. Apthorp and wife. They have not been here this five years before. How it is I cannot say; some think he is reformed. I can only say they appeared to be very fond of each other here and never any man could behave better than he did all the while." James Apthorp, almost exactly Ray's age, was the third son of Charles Apthorp, reputed "the greatest and most noble merchant on this continent" and "a truly valuable member of society." Young Apthrop had married Sarah Wentworth, daughter of Sarah Thomas's sister Elizabeth *Dering* Wentworth and her husband Samuel Wentworth, in July 1755, upon which occasion Sarah Thomas had asked her brother to "tell them I wish them a great deal of Joy and happiness." But that there were problems in the relationship of James Apthorp and Sarah Wentworth, or perhaps more accurately about James himself, was evidenced by comments in letters of Ray and Sarah Thomas and others. Even before their marriage Ray had noted to Thomas Dering: "Am Surprised at what you write about Aptp & S but pray Let me hear of that..." and at about the same time he added: "Suggest but am Sorry for the Sake of the Family, but Mr AP acts from there indulgence so they have themselves to Blam for it." Something about James Apthorp's conduct, possibly financial irresponsibility may have been the cause.

The years from the Boston Massacre in 1770 to the Boston Tea Party in 1773 were relatively calm and uneventful in colonial relations. At the very end of 1773 there was, of course, the burning of the tea in Marshfield. It was in the year 1773 that Anna *Green* Winslow visited Sarah *Dering* and Ray Thomas. She was a cousin of Sarah's and the mother of Anna Green Winslow, whose diary during that period and while she was a schoolgirl in Boston has been published. It is from that diary that much is revealed about contemporary life, particularly in Boston. Mrs. Winslow, the mother, also kept a diary during the first half of 1773 while she was at the Thomas's. This provides an insight into life in Marshfield, especially among Tory families such as the Winslows and the Thomases. Among the entries are the following:

February 6, 1773. "This day Mr. Thomas carried Miss Dering & my daughter it being very pleasant weather, to visit Mrs. Johnson as a reward for their work the past week. Mr. Nathll [Nathaniel] went a fox hunting but caught none."

February 8, 1773. "In the afternoon Mr. Shaw & Mr. Wadsworth one of the tutors of Harvard Colledge drank tea with us. When they went away Mr. Thomas & his son Natt went with them to the generals.."

February 27, 1773. "Dr. Stockbridge & Dr. Winslow dined & drank tea with us - Mr. Thomas dined yesterday at the Doctors."

March 10, 1773. "Mr. Thomas dined at the generals went a guning but got nothing."

March 11, 1773. "Clear weather which induced me to walk with my children to the barn to see a young calf & lamb that came yesterday...the children mightily pleas'd with walking but the little one afraid of the creatures."

April 5, 1773. "Drank tea with Mr. Thomas & Miss Green and Miss Dering at the generals - the Drs. Wife & Daughter were there."

April 14, 1773. "Mr. Nathll returned from College in the morning brought letters from Mrs. Deming Mrs. Storer Mrs. Green and Jemmy - Afternoon Abraham Walker was here - Children all complaining."

April 20, 1773. "Mr. & Mrs. Shaw, Mr. & Mrs. Williams & Mrs. Kent at tea..."

April 24, 1773. "The young Ladies spent the afternoon with Miss Polly in Mrs. Goochs chamber & were treated with sweetmeats &c."

April 27, 1773. "Mr. Thomas at the generals my young Ladies & Master John at Cap Thomas's..."

May 5, 1773. "Mr. Thomas & the young Ladies drank tea at the generals."

May 10, 1773. "Mr. & Mrs. Shaw at dinner & tea."

May 11, 1773. "Dined with the family at the generals. Dr. Winslow & his wife there."

May 18, 1773. "We had a visit in the morning from Miss Barker & her sister - in the afternoon with Mrs. Thomas Mrs. Gooch & the children to Capt Anthony's return about sundown."

This is a glimpse of the social life of Marshfield, particularly among those who would soon become Tories. It is interesting to note, however, that

The Provincial Gentry

both Sarah Thomas and Anna *Green* Winslow, judging from the diary entries, were on good terms with the wife of such a Patriot leader as Anthony Thomas, later Colonel Anthony Thomas, leader of Marshfield's militia. Apparently Tories and Whigs, as the Patriots were known, were friendly and communicated with one another, except for the most intransigent, right until the outbreak of hostilities.

Tea and tea drinking were very popular with the American colonists. Anna Winslow's diary shows just how popular this was. It is true this diary reflects the tastes and customs of what we would call the "upper class" or the "better sort" or the "gentry," in the language of the day. But tea was nevertheless popular with all classes of people. From the diary it would seem that, just before the beginning of the war, well-to-do people, at least, daily either went to a friend's house for tea or had tea at home.

Humor must have had a place in the lives of people in those days. But there is a notable scarcity of it in the written record. There are bits of dry humor in the letters of Sarah Thomas. She wrote this to her brother in 1764:

> We have been unfortunate in our turkeys, lost nine fine ones by the foxes, killed all in one night. Mr. Thomas grieved so much I did not know but he would put on at least the fashionable mourning, which I suppose you have heard is nothing more now for a wife than a piece of crepe round the arm.

On another occasion she wrote:

> Mr. Winslow's [Joshua Winslow] famile is all well. He and his daughter [Anna Green Winslow, the young diarist] is just returned from Boston, and Sally [Mrs. Thomas's daughter, Sarah] as usual went to see them two days ago and I have never seen her since. I hope she will not spend the winter.

The winter of 1773 had been a severe one. Sarah commented that they had never been "so blocked up" since she had lived in the country. Mrs. Anna *Green* Winslow, Sarah's cousin and guest for part of the year 1773 kept a diary in which she made many observations about the weather. In one entry she noted: "I dont remember that I ever found it colder in my life than when riding over the hills" and in another entry remarked "I believe this has been the most extream cold day that has happen'd in many years. My bason of water froze on the hearth with as good a fire as we could make in the chimney." An even greater amount

The Provincial Gentry

of space in her diary was devoted to serious pious reflections. But she wrote at considerable length about what her family and friends were doing. On January 17, 1773 she wrote to her husband, Joshua Winslow, that she had "inclosed Nanny Greens journals and letters to her Aunt Deming." She refers to her thirteen-year-old daughter's diary which has been published as The Diary of Anna Green Winslow.

Sarah and Ray Thomas, in addition to Sally mentioned above, had other children: Nathaniel, familiarly known as Nat and then attending Harvard College; Henry Dering, then in the British Navy; Sarah, known as Sally, the thirteen-year-old eldest daughter; John, nine years old; Mary, seven years old; Martin Howard, five; Elizabeth Packer, three; and Charles, aged one, the baby. With the exception of Nat and Henry Dering, the children were all at home with their parents.

Even though in early 1774, Sarah said of her husband that "it is with very great difficulty he ever leaves the farm" and "as for my own part I have not been to Boston this four years and a half, nor at present cannot think of anything could carry me there," Ray Thomas did visit the Provincial capital on occasion. His friend John Rowe shared an evening with him in January 1765 at the lodgings of Boston's Collector of Customs in company with a number of gentlemen including Rowe's "old Friend" and Ray's brother-in-law Samuel Wentworth; Rowe's brother-in-law Ralph Inman of Cambridge, whose hospitality was elegant and sumptuous; Duncan Stewart, Collector of Customs at New London; John Robinson, Collector of Customs at Newport; the Comptroller of Halifax; and the Captain of His Majesty's Sloop of War Fortune. The evening was interrupted by the cry of "Fire!". Rowe, a member of one of the companies, rushed out to help and noted in his diary: "got myself much wet." And in the fall of 1770 Rowe reported that he "went on Board the Rose with Capt Caldwell from thence to the Cassell [Castle William, located on an island in Boston Harbor] and from thence on board the Romney and dined with Commn Hood [Commodore Samuel Hood] his Lady, his Son, Major Butler of the 60th, Major Powell of the 38th, Dr. Petersby, Mr. Thomas and Mr. West."

Among other social activities of the gentry in which Ray Thomas participated were the dinners and annual Forefathers' Day celebrations of the Old Colony Club in Plymouth. Composed of twelve members, several of whom were Harvard men and also cousins of Ray's, the Club was formed as a social group but soon, in addition, dedicated itself to honoring the Pilgrim Fathers. One of the seven founding members was

The Provincial Gentry

twenty-four-year-old John Thomas, Ray's first cousin and son of his late uncle and guardian Lieutenant Colonel Nathaniel Thomas. Of the Harvard class of 1765, John had been fined for "prophane cursing," breaking windows, and making a "tumultuous Noise." In his senior year he had roomed in Massachusetts 25, directly across the hall from Ray's old room, with Nathaniel Sparhawk, ranked first in their class and the grandson of the first Sir William Pepperell and brother of the second Sir William. Another of the founding members was Pelham Winslow, who in his time had also lived in Massachusetts Hall, Ray's third cousin and son of General John Winslow. Three other of the founders, Isaac Lothrop and his brother Thomas Lothrop and John Watson, were likewise related to Ray through the charming, thrice-married Priscilla Thomas. Finally, Edward Winslow, Jr., graduating with John Thomas in 1765 and nephew of General Winslow, was another who formed the Old Colony Club four years later. One of those afterwards invited to become a member was James Warren, nephew of General John Winslow and husband of Mercy Otis, James Otis, Jr.'s sister.

The Old Colony Club planned a hearty celebration for December 22, 1769 to commemorate the landing of the Pilgrim Fathers at Plymouth more than a century and a half before. Members of the Club descended from the Old Comers, as those on the Mayflower and other early ships were called, and usually from leaders of New Plymouth Colony. On the festive day, ceremonies began with the raising of an "elegant silk flag" over the Club's quarters bearing the words "Old Colony 1620." Members then proceeded in the early afternoon to a nearby tavern for dinner. Though the banquet table was "dressed in the plainest manner," the banquet was sumptuous. It consisted of a number of dishes of food known and savored in an earlier day. Set first before Club members was a large baked Indian whortle-berry pudding; then a dish of succotash, a dish of clams, a dish of oysters and a dish of codfish; next and the main course, a haunch of venison roasted by the first jack brought to the Colony, followed by a dish of sea fowl and a dish of frost-fish [a fish resembling cod, but smaller] and eels; and for dessert, an apple pie and a course of cranberry tarts and cherries.

At four o'clock in the afternoon, Club members, no doubt replete, formed a procession to return to their hall. Headed by the Club steward, Elkanah Cushman, who carried a folio volume of the Old Colony laws, they marched hand in hand through the streets to the accompaniment of cheers and the firing of small arms. Back at their quarters, with President Isaac Lothrop presiding from a "large and venerable chair,"

The Provincial Gentry

members and their guests extolled with a generous succession of toasts their ancestors and the worthies of the Old Colony and sentiments appropriate and timely. They drank to the same sentiments against arbitrary power as their ancestors had been endowed with; to the colonies being speedily delivered from oppressions now as then; to a lasting union between Great Britain and the colonies; and to the prosperity and happiness of the colonies. Following these expressions of hope and good wishes, the members and their guests talked long into the evening of the old days and the worthy character of those who were long gone. Finally, to end the day's celebrations at eleven o'clock, there was a firing of cannon and a resounding three cheers.

Old Colony Club members customarily invited guests to their dinners and Forefathers' Day celebrations. Many of those guests were gentlemen of property and position or of rising professional repute. Among the guests were General John Winslow and his son Dr. Isaac Winslow and Nathaniel Ray Thomas of Marshfield; General Winslow's brother Edward Winslow of Plymouth, father of the Club member of the same name; Dr. Charles Stockbridge of Scituate; John Adams and Robert Treat Paine, barristers-at-law, of Boston; Thomas Oliver; Richard Lechmere, British Naval Agent of Cambridge and Boston; and James Otis, Jr. and his brother Samuel Allyne Otis of Boston. Nathaniel Ray Thomas was a guest of the Club on May 17, 1769, together with General John Winslow, Dr. Isaac Winslow, and Dr. Charles Stockbridge; on January 2, 1771 with General John Winslow and his brother Edward Winslow; and on February 17, 1773, with Edward Winslow.

The gentry of the Province did indeed possess a "social vitality" that was evident in many facets of their way of life - in their "genteel" entertainments to use John Rowe's word, their dinners and dances, banquets and balls, country excursions and fishing parties; in their portraits by Joseph Blackburn and John Singleton Copley; and in the expression of their taste in architecture and the furniture and furnishings with which they surrounded themselves. Quite possibly no more evocative glimpse can be had of the Province gentry, the "old aristocracy" as it has been called, than that revealed in their likenesses as portrayed by Blackburn and Copley. During the third quarter of the eighteenth century they caught the spirit and feel of the world of the gentry of that day in depicting the features, the dress, and the poses of their sitters - government officials, clergy, military officers, merchants, landowners, men of leisure, and with them, their ladies. Their portraits convey a quiet elegance, an easy self-assurance: gentlemen in wigs, wearing shirts

The Provincial Gentry

with ruffled sleeves and neckcloths and expensive waistcoats revealed under casually parted outer coats; ladies in lustrous silks and satins, rich in color, with necklines often cut square and low to show the curve of bosom. Copley possessed a sense of "likeness," a realism of portrayal, that made his subjects remarkably believable and true to life; Blackburn had a fondness for more informal poses and lighthearted expression.

Of the family circle and close friends and associates of Nathaniel Ray and Sarah Thomas, quite a number sat for Blackburn and Copley or some other portraitist of the time. Ray and Sarah themselves were painted by some unknown artist in miniatures on ivory, probably at a later period. Such renderings were very popular. Thomas Dering sat for Joseph Blackburn shortly before 1760. The unknown artist indulged his bent for informal poses and lighthearted expression by depicting Mary Dering with a hat festooned with flowers in her left hand, a shepherd's crook in her right hand, and a white lamb at her feet. Sarah Thomas's niece Frances Wentworth, a young lady of outstanding beauty, married as her second husband her cousin John Wentworth, shortly to be appointed Governor of the province of New Hampshire. Copley painted the Wentworths: John in elegant formal attire, Frances in a low-cut gown of lustrous satin, rich in color, wearing a necklace of fine stones, seated at a table playing with a squirrel on a chain. She could well have been, as it was said, the "most beautiful woman in America."

Among Sarah's relatives visiting at Marshfield, in addition to her brother Thomas Dering and her sister Elizabeth Wentworth and her husband Samuel Wentworth, were Mr. and Mrs. Joseph Green, the latter Sarah's first cousin Anna *Pierce* Green. Mr. and Mrs. Green had several children, one of whom, Elizabeth, married Ebenezer Storer, a Boston merchant and later treasurer of Harvard College; and another of whom, Anna, married her cousin Joshua Winslow early in 1758. Both Storer and Winslow were truly close friends of the Thomases, as well as being Sarah's relatives, and both sat for John Singleton Copley. Moreover, Joshua and Anna *Green* Winslow's young daughter Anna Green Winslow was the subject of a likeness, a miniature, on ivory.

Another close friend, a relative by marriage, and member of a family intimately involved with that of Ray Thomas was General John Winslow, whose portrait was done by Joseph Blackburn. The General's son and Ray's third cousin, Dr. Isaac Winslow, also had his portrait painted. Another Marshfield figure who had a role in Ray Thomas's life was Dr. John Thomas, whose portrait was executed posthumously by Benjamin

The Provincial Gentry

Blyth. Martin Howard, Jr., (Ray's very dear friend) was painted by Copley in his robes as Chief Justice of the Province of North Carolina; and Peter Oliver, Chief Justice of the Province of Massachusetts Bay, a friend and one to whom Ray turned in later years, likewise sat for Copley.

In another area of their interest and activity, the Province gentry expressed themselves with vigor and distinction. This was architecture, whether of town house or of country seat. They built in an increasingly academic spirit, utilizing an academic architectural style that included the classic orders and emphasizing form rather than function. Many fine, large mansions appeared in the Province in the mid and late Georgian period before the Revolution. Houses less ornate in architectural detail but nevertheless notable, often the seats of leading families among the gentry, were likewise evident. General John Winslow of Marshfield added distinguished architectural refinements to his family home Careswell in the mid 1700's: a deep front portico with quoins at the corners of it and of the main structure; paneling, molding, wallpaper, and tiles edging fireplace openings in the house. A few years earlier Nathaniel Ray Thomas had renovated his residence; and then, probably about 1770, he decided to build a new house. It was completed in 1772 and in later years he would refer to it as his "New Mansion House."

When Ray Thomas came to considering a plan for his "New Mansion House," he was very likely influenced by the design of the house in Plymouth of his older friend and fellow guest of the Old Colony Club, Edward Winslow, brother of General John Winslow. Edward Winslow completed his house, built upon a commanding position overlooking Plymouth Harbor, in 1754. Both houses were framed and sheathed in wood, their exterior walls covered by clapboard siding; both were strikingly similar in dimension, plan, and architectural detail. Ray Thomas's "New Mansion House" measured fifty feet in length and forty-six in depth "at least," as he put it. It was comparable in size (if not in elegance of architectural detail) to Georgian mansions of the period, including, for example, that of John Vassall on "Tory Row" in Cambridge, later the home of Henry Wadsworth Longfellow, the poet, and known today as such. Its floor plan was typical: on the first floor, a transverse center hall, flanked by two rooms on either side; on the second floor, a center hall also flanked by two rooms on either side. A kitchen ell extended from the rear of the building.

The Provincial Gentry

In exterior appearance, the "New Mansion House" showed five bays [windows] across the front with a hip roof surmounting the whole. Two chimneys rose from the ridge at the peak of the roof slopes, providing for fireplaces in each of the eight rooms of the house. An architectural detail following closely the design of Edward Winslow's house in Plymouth was a clerestory capping the ridge line of the roof and extending across it from the outside of each chimney. The doorway treatment was probably recessed and paneled, framed by pilasters of one of the classical orders supporting an entablature with architrave, frieze, and cornice, and the door jamb itself topped by bulls'-eye lights. The windows were probably cased by a full architrave, their panes twelve in number, six over six. The "New Mansion House" was thus a commodious and architecturally, a modestly distinguished Georgian country house.

During that third quarter of the eighteenth century, the Province gentry pursued an energetic life in civic, business, commercial, maritime, and, as vigorous relaxation from all that, social activity. Boston merchant John Rowe, convivial gentleman, admired host, and sought-after guest, portrayed that life in candid, vivid detail. He described political doings (in which he often participated); he reported business transactions and commerce (as a merchant himself, the latter with concern); he noted the arrival and departure of ships (including his own). And Rowe took equal care to depict the social activities of his contemporaries and himself.

On July 16, 1772, the day after Harvard's Commencement, Rowe attended what he described as "the Genteelest Entertainment I ever saw" at the estate of his brother-in-law Ralph Inman in Cambridge. It was given to celebrate the latter's son George Inman taking his degree the previous day. Rowe noted: "... Three hundred forty seven Gentlemen & Ladies dined. Two hundred & Ten at one Table - amongst the Company The Govr & Family, The Lieut Governour & Family, The Admirall & Family & all the Remainder, Gentlemen & Ladies of Character & Reputation. The whole was conducted with much Ease & pleasure & all Joyned in making each other Happy - such an Entertainment has not been made in New England before on any Occasion." Later that evening Rowe "went to the Ball at the Town House, where most of the Company went to Dance - they were all very happy & Cheerful & the whole was conducted to the General Satisfaction of all present." If Ralph Inman's party honoring his son George was the "Genteelest Entertainment" Rowe ever witnessed, it was so in degree only. It was a social event typical of many that Rowe attended,

The Provincial Gentry

and recorded, during the years from 1759 to 1799 - which attested again to the "social vitality" of the Province gentry.

But not all was success and gayety in the life of the gentry. On September 12, 1766, John Rowe noted, "in the afternoon I went to the Funeral of my old Friend Saml Wentworth." Wentworth, Boston merchant, with whom Rowe was closely associated in business and social life, was the son of Lieutenant Governor John Wentworth of the Province of New Hampshire and had graduated at Harvard College in 1728. He married Elizabeth Dering, sister of Sarah (Dering) Thomas and Thomas Dering. The Wentworths, on one occasion, were guests of the Thomases at Marshfield at the same time as Dering. Samuel Wentworth also acted in business matters for Ray Thomas. Among the children of Samuel and Elizabeth Wentworth were Elizabeth who married John Gould, Jr., son of a Boston merchant and friend and relation of Rowe's; Sarah, who married James Apthorp; Mary, who married George Brinley of a prominent Boston family; Frances, who married her first cousin John Wentworth; and two sons, Benning and Samuel. Of the elder Samuel Wentworth, a personal glimpse was revealed in a short note dated April 25, 1763, possibly to Thomas Dering: "I send you part of what Seed I have hope they'l get safe to you ... providence has blessed you with a Country life [---] a fountain of pleasure, in it is Contained peace & plenty, three fourths of our wants in Such a life is Concealed, they progressively slip from our Memory & we never miss them, I hant time to give loose to my fancy now or I might give you an evenings entertainment..."

Then, little more than a year and a half later, on December 14, 1764, Sarah Thomas wrote to her brother Thomas Dering: "Poor Mr. Wentworth's family are to be pitied; indeed, a dark cloud seems to hang over them at present. I pray God to sanctify their afflictions..." And she added: "I had a letter after so long a time from our sister [Ann] Monk, where she mourns over our sister Wentworth..." Sarah Thomas's family, and Ray Thomas as well, had been concerned for years about the conduct of James Apthorp, married to Elizabeth (Dering) Wentworth's daughter Sarah. Now, Sarah Thomas expressed the dismay and sympathy of the family over the conduct of another Wentworth son-in-law, John Gould, Jr., husband of Elizabeth Wentworth. Gould, son of the Boston merchant whom John Rowe described as "my Old Friend" and a relation, "had failed and shut up" his business in June 1764. Yet it was not his failure in business - good men had gone bankrupt - that vexed the Wentworths and the Derings and others of his kin by blood and

The Provincial Gentry

marriage. It was his "bad and knavish actions," as Mrs. Hepsibah Edwards put it, that caused his disgrace.

In letters written in August, September, and October of 1764, Mrs. Edwards elaborated on her criticism of young Gould. She wrote in August: "Mr. Gould has gone off and he has been guilty of so many bad actions that it is thought he will never see his own country again." In September she continued: "Mrs. Gould is at Portsmouth yet and is much better but is not like ever to see her husband again. He has done so many bad and knavish actions were you to hear all you would hardly believe they could be true but he has sold his country for his wickedness." Then in October she declared: "Mrs. Gould looks like a dejected cretur. The small-pox has left her in a poor way and she that lived at the fountain head, must now with her 3 children go into some little house with one room and a kitchen and must never see her husband no more in this country, for he has proved such a knave that he must never show his head here again. Besides his plaguey whoring affairs there has not been an instance in any day of villany." John Gould, Jr. died in 1765, apparently out of the country. His widow, Elizabeth *Wentworth* Gould, then married in the fall of that year Nathaniel Rogers, of whom Mrs. Hepsibah Edwards wrote in a cheerier vein: "a charming husband everybody says." And Elizabeth herself could say: "I am in as happy a state as this life can afford which is far beyond my expectation..."

But, as Sarah Thomas had put it, "a dark cloud" seemed to "hang over" her sister Elizabeth Wentworth's family. On August 23, 1766 John Rowe, friend and business associate of Samuel Wentworth's, noted in his diary: "Mr. Wentworth lies dangerously ill at Roxbury"; and on September 12th: "...I went to the Funeral of my old Friend Saml Wentworth." Nathaniel Rogers, Wentworth's son-in-law, wrote to Thomas Dering in October: "Poor Mr. Wentworth died the 9th of last month after laboring under the complicated disorders of a dropsy and consumption and has left nothing for his family." This was a double tragedy for Mrs. Wentworth. Sarah Thomas's reference to "a dark cloud" seemed now more poignant than ever. For it had been but three years since Elizabeth Wentworth had said hopefully: "Mr. Wentworth's old luck has not entirely left him out, thank God. The war is now at an end, they [the military authorities] will take no more. They have had the last. Seven sail of vessels has he had taken and lost since the war came in."

The Provincial Gentry

Some months after Samuel Wentworth's death, his widow conveyed to her brother Thomas Dering details of her husband's affairs. It was a difficult letter for her.

> ...I have often taken up my pen to write and answer your letter, and laid it down again the tears that flow and the trembling hand that proceeded from a full heart continually prevented...Mr. Wentworth had it not in his power to leave me any thing, as all he had in the World belonged to Sir William Baker; no person, but myself and Sir William knew it, that those few debts he owed in Boston might be brought in and paid off. You will be much surprised when I tell you the goodness of that Gentleman. When the war [the French and Indian War] first broke out Mr. Wentworth was possest of five sail of vessels all his own, and in eighteen months stript of all, some taken others sunk the others cast away. He made me acquainted of it immediately, that he had sunk more than he was possessed in life. On which he wrote Sir William all his affairs, and told him the chiefs of all he owed in the world was to him; he was content to deliver up all he had, or keep it and work on while he lived and what left would be his at last. One of the kindest Letters he received in answer it was more like a Father then any thing else he bid him work on, that he knew his honest princepals, and if it was ever in his power he knew he would pay him, gave him leave to discharge all other debts and he remain the only creditor...He constantly kept the interest paid up to the last year but sickness prevented him doeing anything farther...But still my Brother, my Dear, forever dear, Mr. Wentworth is no more. What a Husband, friend, companion have I lost, left to mourn, forever mourn, in irreparrable ways. I think I may now be alowd to say he had few equals, and with my latest breath the World will see, the respect, love and honour I treat his memory with.

Of the Wentworth's two sons, Benning and Samuel, the latter attracted the attention of the family. The boy's brother-in-law Nathaniel Rogers, in his letter of October 1766 to Thomas Dering acquainting him of the elder Wentworth's death, commented: "Little Sam Wentworth is at Latin College and is soon to go to Oxford. Every body gives him the character of an uncommon genius. Jack Wentworth [John Wentworth, nephew of

The Provincial Gentry

the elder Samuel Wentworth] now in England is appointed Gov. in place of his Uncle [Gov. Benning Wentworth] who resigned, and has promised his care and countenance to Sam." Elizabeth *Dering* Wentworth, the boy's mother, wrote a few months later: "Governor [John] Wentworth is arrived at South Carolina. He intends to take me under his protection. He expresses the highest gratitude for the memory of his Uncle. He says his care of him in youth, and the instructions he has at all times received from him has been so great an advantage to him that he will never forsake his family. He had fixed my son [Samuel] at Oxford and provided for his support." The young man, having matriculated at Worcester College, Oxford in 1768, met and fell in love with a Miss Lane. Then, denied association and communication with each other by her parents, both committed suicide in 1769. It had been five years earlier that Sarah Thomas had said: "Poor Mr. Wentworth's family are to be pitied; indeed, a dark cloud seems to hang over them..."

Still, in the midst of the afflictions of the Wentworth family, Nathaniel Rogers had written: "We have had many melancholy scenes to go through...and yet thro' the goodness of God we can sing of many mercies as well as of judgment." His wife Elizabeth Wentworth, the former Mrs. Gould, could say despite the travail of her earlier marriage: "I am in as happy a state as this life can afford which is far beyond my expectations..." The Province gentry, not that far removed from Puritanism, accepted death and disaster as the will of God and an improvement in one's lot as the indulgence of divine Providence. Life did go on. Hepsibah Edwards, "Miss Hepsy," remained alert for news and gossip, good and bad and particularly about leading members of the gentry, delighting to pass it on to family and friends. Typically, she wrote to her kinsman Thomas Dering in December 1768: "Old Mr. Brinley is dead and now George [Brinley] is married to Molley Wentworth and live at Mr. Wentworth's...Jack Apthorp is published to Miss Greenleaf, Jack Nelson's mistress that was. Deacon Barriot's son, the widower with one child, is making his addresses to Sally Oliver and it is like to be a match; Judge Oliver's son to Miss Sally Hutchinson; Mrs. Gould to Nat Rogers and has got a charming husband everybody sayd. Poor Harry [Henry Packer Dering] has been down to Halifax I believe he got something by it he was gon a month is now returned. Left Mrs. Monk and family well. He is behind the meeting house yet with that creatur a second Betty, but talks of going to Jamaica, James Apthorp is as bad as ever. Old Mrs. Green thanks you for thinking of her, wonders you dont write to her. Sally Oliver says that you and Mrs. Dering must come to wedding. Polly says that she will put off the wedding if you will come in the Spring."

The Provincial Gentry

Nor was news of out-of-town family and friends overlooked. In his letter of October 1766 to Thomas Dering about Samuel Wentworth's death, Nathaniel Rogers made certain to include information about the former's sister Sarah Thomas and her family at Marshfield. "Mr. Winslow [Joshua Winslow, the Derings' cousin] has been up and has taken down with him and his wife Henry Dering Thomas, and has agreed to take care of him till he is 14 years old. Mrs. Thomas is now abed with a daughter [Mary Thomas, born September 17, 1766]. As few opportunities offer, I thought so particular an account of your friends would be pleasing to you."

VII

"Continual Uneasiness of Mind..."

Nathaniel Ray Thomas, in his Aunt Caty Greene's words, "was left rich; a farm that would cut 100 loads of salt hay, well stocked house, well furnished with everything. He was educated at Cambridge, and when he was of age it was all wasted but the land." More than fifty years later, following his death in 1787, he was "represented to be insolvent." And during that intervening half century he knew "continual uneasiness of mind" about money. So his wife Sarah expressed it; she shared that worry.

Whether or not Caty *Ray* Greene was correct in her assessment of a situation that prevailed long before she wrote, and one with which she could only have been slightly familiar, is uncertain. It was true, of course, that Ray, upon reaching his majority and settling accounts with his guardian, had received only forty pounds in balance, which the young man acknowledged to be in full for all revenues and assets of the guardianship estate. It was also true that he had been in possession of the family lands at Green's Harbor in Marshfield as tenant in tail since the death of his grandfather, Judge Nathaniel Thomas, in 1739; and that he could not have sold or encumbered those entailed lands.

When Ray's Aunt Caty remarked of his inheritance that "when he was of age it was all wasted but the land," she probably did not use the word <u>wasted</u> in a strict legal sense, as in the case, for example, of timber being cut down to the prejudice of the ultimate heir to the land on which it stood. (Mr. John Thomas did enter in his guardianship accounts to be sure, an amount for "Wood that Simmons fell down on the Farme.") She meant, no doubt, that the income from the Thomas property was almost entirely spent for Ray's upbringing until he reached twenty-one and for his education. But then, of course, his father had directed this in his will. In any event, as a consequence and at the outset of his adult life, Ray Thomas was faced with a critical shortage of ready cash money.

In a letter of May 7, 1755, Ray informed his brother-in-law Thomas Dering that "Mrs. Thomas [who was in Boston] will give you the Cash if necessary" for various items, while at the same time asking Dering to get

"Continual Uneasiness of Mind..."

him a quantity of boards "without cash." With a scarcity of cash often prevailing in the American colonies, landed proprietors bought on credit and relied on the sale of produce of their land to pay off resulting accounts and debts. In a poor year for crops and livestock, then, farmers - even large landowners - were hard pressed to meet their obligations. Indeed, almost always they experienced a shortage of ready money, theirs was a common woe. On August 30th, Ray wrote Thomas Dering: "Must desire you to Speak to Bell again as I want to Discharge some Particular Debts in Boston which his Buying my oxen will do to all whom I'm indebted to in Town." Of the oxen, he added that he had "ten to fifteen very good ones or more if wanted."

About a month later he wrote his brother-in-law a letter, the tenor of which suggests that Ray was casting about for any means by which he could realize cash to pay his obligations. As to his creditors in Boston, some of whom were apparently pressing for payment, Ray commented optimistically: "They shall have their moneys very soon." He went on to explain: "There has been four vessels sold in the admiralty. [The Admiralty Court at Halifax, Nova Scotia] this last week and is dayly some french Goods selling and I am in great hopes Mr Monk [his brother-in-law James Monk, a lawyer and judge in Nova Scotia and husband of Ann Dering] will be able amongst them to purchase some thing which will sell to a good advantage in Boston and make the payment of those debts something easeyer." And he concluded: "He would have bought a parsile of Casteel soap the other day but they run it up to six pence half penny. Had that gone Cheap it would have done to pay'd Patten but if any of those people inquir after me pray let them Know they shall have their money very soon. I am not unmindful of them." Other items which Ray was shipping to Boston by water included "8 or 10 Dozn of Geese...all Coop'd"; considerable quantities of wood on sloops unfortunately delayed in departure because of unfavorable winds; and "Hop Vines" destined for Mr. Green.

Even Sarah Thomas indulged in a somewhat whimsical effort to reap a bit of money. In January 1758, she wrote her brother: "...am oblig'd to you for your care of my Tickets, if it is not two much troble should be glad you would purchase three in the next Lottery for me, and mark one NT." Whether she or Ray ever won, their letters never revealed.

Nathaniel Ray Thomas was possessed of what he described as the "largest improved estate" in Plymouth County. It comprised about 1,100 acres of land, some 300 acres of which were salt marsh and valuable for

"Continual Uneasiness of Mind..."

the salt hay cut therefrom; and the remaining 800 acres of which were in pasture land, "English Meadow," arable or tillage land, orchards, and woodland. For its time and place it was, indeed, a "great Estate," as the property had also been called in <u>Matson</u> v. <u>Thomas</u> a quarter century earlier. Of his hay crop, harvested from the salt marsh and other lands, Ray Thomas estimated the annual yield at 300 tons. He raised clover, which could have been cut for hay or been grazed, and crops that included corn, wheat, rye, hemp, and hops. At one point he ordered twenty bushels of "Annapolis oats." He had orchards, which produced apples and other fruit. He raised or bought for resale livestock such as black cattle (of which he sometimes had 70 or 80 head), fat cattle for the market, oxen, horses, and hogs. At one point he was sending geese to Boston; all the time, without doubt, he kept turkeys and chickens. And from his woodland he cut wood which he regularly sent to Boston for sale.

Nathaniel Ray Thomas was a country gentleman "of a very good family," as his Aunt Caty said. He possessed extensive lands. But like most landed proprietors of his time, he was not a man of any considerable leisure. Managing a farm of the size and magnitude of operation as was his, took time and effort. There was the problem of getting and keeping hired help, ever present apparently, and the constant necessity of supervision. There was the remorseless toll inflicted by nature, which Ray took very seriously. After one violent storm that did much damage along the Massachusetts coast, he wrote: "And among the rest I am no small sufferer for it carried away my dyke and the land which is mostly clover is now overflowed with salt water, but hope it will be gone off enough to repair the breach; was ploughed for hemp.., which now damps my view." A short time later Sarah Thomas, congratulating her brother on his success with his poultry, commented: "We have been unfortunate in our turkeys, lost nine fine ones by the foxes, killed all in one night."

It was not merely the management of his farm that kept Ray preoccupied. He was actively involved in its operations. At one point, he wrote his brother-in-law in the summer of 1755, he could not "come to Town till this Day Sevennight if then" because he was "much Hurry'd at present with Hay Season." On another occasion, a year later, Sarah wrote her brother: "Mr. Thomas is just got home from his journey to Newport where he has bought a drove of fat cattle, but having not yet disposed of them should be glad if you will get me some few necessaries which we are in want of for the family." She added: "Mr.

"Continual Uneasiness of Mind..."

Thomas does not choose to send for anymore upon credit till he has discharged those accounts he has open, having a prospect of doing it in a short time, which is James's business in town at this time, to see about a market for the cattle...I suppose Mr. Green will write Mr. Thomas, but if he does not pray be so good as to speak to him about the cattle of Mr. Thomas's and let us know what he says."

In less than two years of marriage, Sarah Thomas understood clearly and sympathetically the difficulties her husband faced in the operations of the farm. She shared them, and the disappointments, and the discouragement. Not long after she had written her brother about a market for the fat cattle from Newport, she confided in him:

> The great friendship and regard you once professed for me emboldens me to write you as a friend the great straits I am in at present for many necessaries, which it is not in Mr. Thomas's power to get at this time and pay those people which he ought and must necessarily does...
>
> Some people think it is a very easy matter for Mr. Thomas to sell the produce of his farm, pay what he owes and have money to spare, never remembering that he has constant family expenses that we must have money going out for. As for his farm, it will not produce everything we want to expend in a family. Beside, he must find money to pay off his people every week that works on the farm, and glad to get them for there is none to be hired hardly since the last press of men [for military service]...
>
> I am sorry to give you so much trouble, but if it were not for hope, the heart would break.

Nearly twenty years later Sarah, writing to her brother on that same subject, reported the almost insurmountable difficulty confronting her husband in his farming operations. She said: "Mr. Thomas sends his kind love to you and says he has run behindhand too and has that to perplex him which you had not and that is, his farm in general is but poor land and takes a great deal of manure to make it produce anything worth while which makes it very expensive, and but little profit remains. And we have a large family to bring up and you are sensible it can take no small matter to maintain them in victuals and clothes..."

"Continual Uneasiness of Mind..."

In the spring of 1756 Sarah's brother Thomas Dering married. His bride was Mary Sylvester, daughter of Brinley Sylvester of Shelter Island, New York. On April 7th Sarah wrote her brother: "Pray return my proper regards to your lady and let her know, if she will do us the favor of a visit, we shall receive her with a great deal of pleasure and will do everything in our power to make our retired habitation as agreeable as possible to her."

A few months later, on July 23, 1756, Nathaniel Ray Thomas wrote a short note to Thomas Dering: "I understand by your sister you've removed. I wish you success in all your undertakings and hope the uninterruption of your new mansion will give you leisure to settle your father's estate, as your sister's portion will be of real service to your well wishing brother." Captain Henry Dering had died in 1750; Thomas Dering had been named his executor; six years had passed. Merely to express the hope then, that his brother-in-law would have time to devote to settling Captain Dering's estate would seem reasonable enough. But Thomas Dering did not take it that way.

Nearly a year of desultory correspondence ensued, and that mostly on the part of Sarah Thomas. Perplexed, she wrote her brother on June 25, 1757: "I received a few lines by James the meaning of which I cannot tell, for what should occasion your writing me that God knows whether you should see me at Marshfield again I can't devise. It is true God only knows whether we shall ever meet in this world again, but should our lives be spared I do not see why we might not meet at Marshfield as well as at Boston, if want of inclination does not prevent it..."

Letters from Sarah on July 17, 1757 and on September 28, 1757 revealed the misunderstanding and friction that had arisen. It was Ray's short note of July 23rd the previous year, apparently, that had upset Thomas Dering with its reference to the latter's settlement of Captain Dering's estate and to Sarah's portion being of "real service to your well wishing brother." After receiving a letter from her brother which she described as the longest from him "this year and a half past," she answered on July 17th:

> ...I would beg leave to tell you that would you but reflect calmly and impartially, you must allow you had no reason for so much blame to Mr. Thomas, for in answer to his pertecular behavouer, I would say I know of none. I am shure his Ideas of friendship are still the same. he has never don nor saide any thing more, nor so much, I may

Mary Sylvester Dering, wife of Thomas Dering. Portrait by unknown artist. Courtesy of the Metropoitan Museum of Art, New York.

Thomas Dering, brother of Sarah Dering Thomas. Portrait by Joseph Blackburn. Courtesy of the Metropolitan Museum of Art.

"Continual Uneasiness of Mind..."

> say, as he has saide to you yourself, and as to answering his ends, he had no ends to answer, but to ask you for what you could not but allow was right and just he should have, but for reasons only known to your self have sean fit to keep back...

And she continued:

> my dear Brother, you say you can see when you are inured [injured], forgive me this once if I speak my minde, and say I think it is you who have inured me; tho I must and doe think you have not done it designedly. had I bin there when my dear papa dyed, who I should have chose to have his affairs into their hands, there was no man upon the earth I should have nam'd before you...I know of no other thing upon the earth that has pas'd between Mr. Thomas or me, with you, that you possably could have taken offence at, if it is not at what has pass relaiting to settlement of my papa's estate...I never desier to menshon it more, have often saide and doe now say that I sincearly wish from my very soule that I had never the least prospect of receiving one penny from my father's estate, and then would hope ther had been nothing else to have maide the unhappy jar between two friends so nearly allyed to me as you and Mr. Thomas are. I only wish now I can saifly say that you would finnish the affair as sune as you can.
>
> You say you have reson to suspect Mr. Thomas friendship as you have not received a line from him since he came home nor the least invitation from him to make us a visit. it was not because he would have not bin very glad to have bin favour'd with a visit from you; but purely because he thought a letter from him would be dusagreeable to you as he had wrote you severall before we were last in town, but never receiv'd one line in answer from you, and so thought you ment it to let him know that you chose to drop your correspondence...
>
> ...beg leave to asure you once more that I am and hope ever shall be with the greatest sinsearity your most affectionate
> Sister Sarah Thomas

"Continual Uneasiness of Mind..."

Sarah's letter brought about a reconciliation, an easing of tension, between her brother and Ray Thomas. On September 17th the latter wrote to Thomas Dering in a vein somewhat more formal than had been his custom. Addressing his brother-in-law as "Dr [Dear] Sir," he informed him:

> Yr Compliments I recd by Mrs. Thomas Letters, and tho' there has been a long Silence I now let you Know that I don't Stand upon the Ceremony of a Lettr. for tho' you lay the Cuse to me, yet I say, there is no Crime in my desireing a Settlement as the Small Ballance would be of Service to me, and that is all which gave Suspicion; However I now let you know that my Sincere wishes attend you and yrs in all your pursuits, which I desire may put aside any heretofore Strangeness...

His letter was an overture, at least; but the matter of settlement of Captain Dering's estate still weighed on the family. Thomas Dering's letters to his sister and brother-in-law at that time, while reflecting an improvement in relations, nevertheless revealed a continuing touchiness. A few days after Ray's letter of the 17th, Sarah wrote to her brother:

> I am very glad to finde you take no acception to my last letter [perhaps her long, firm letter of July 17th], for I doe assure you I ment nothing amiss, only spoke my minde freely, as you youst [used] to give me leave to doe and as I hope you ever will to me, whenever you se anything in my conduct, which you can't readily account for.
>
> I am sorry you are like to finde so much dificulty in settling accounts with the famely, but it's no more than I expected. I wish it may be better than your fears and that you may not finde any puzell [puzzle] in making a division. But by what I learn by Mr. Henry thear will not be any great divison to be made. for my part, I am sorry there should be the least uneasiness about such a trifle as will be coming at last.
>
> As you have as near a relation yourself as Mr. Thomas is to me, you are the better able to judge how uneasy it must make you to have anybody take up a firm dislike to one so nearly allied and in a cause whear there was not

I take this opportunity to acknowledge the receit of your last letter by mr Clap, should have wrote you by mr Pelham Winslow of the best opportunity, although he have let me know of his going —

I am very glad to find you have not forgotten my last letter, for I doe assure you I ment nothing any ways to provoke my much Esteem'd Brother, and shall only speak my mind freely as you great offer for me to leave to live, and as I hope you will truly to me, when ever you see any thing in my Conduct which you cant readily account for —

I am sorry you are like to find so much difficulty in setling accounts with the family, but the more I then I respectly, I wish it may be better than your fears and, that you may not find any great difficulty in making a division, but hope what I can by no Means clear with out there should be the least inequity, abat—nch a trifle, only be coming at last —

As you have as near a relation your self, as mr Thomas is to me, you are the better like to judge how necessary it must make your to have any, any thing to keep a Correspondence, to see is always a joy and I am perswaded without there ever can out the least maintained by the time of gratitude but as we have lived in a family which the time has put all our days, I pray we may continue so to the end of them, it is not a love how to extend, with out ability is your but betwixt our to live in the dearest friendship with one an other, Considering it is so distant to content with one

enemys for our lives and libertys, which we seem to be awfully threatn'd to be deprived of in a short time

I am sorry to hear that you are still follow'd with your head ache, and as you think nothing but a journey will be of servis to you, I am sorry you have not favour'd us with a visit in all this pleasent season, I doe assure you n one would be more glad to have entertaind you in the best manner our situation would have afforided, and as it would have given us pleasure, should have don every thing in our power to have made it agreable to you while you tarred, and tho' the Country may not be so agreable now, still perhaps the journey may be of servis to you, if m:s Dering and you would take a ride now and make us a visit, as does mr Thomas joyns with me in, with best regards to m:s Dering and self, master Nat: duty to Uncle and aunt and Love to master Silvester, for I doe assure you he can speak his name very plain, Concludes me at present your most
affectionate Sister
Sarah Thomas

Marshfield Sep:r y:e 28 1757

Sarah Dering Thomas's letter to her brother Thomas Dering,
September 28, 1757.

"Continual Uneasiness of Mind..."

the least meaning to offend. But as we have bin a famely which has lived in peace all our days I pray we may continue so to the end. It is not a time now to contend with our friends for our right but behooves us to live in the strictest friendship with one another, considering it is suffishent to contend with our enemys for our lives and libertys, which we seam to be awfully threatened to be deprived of in a short time. [A reference, undoubtedly, to the French and Indian War in the colonies, in which the English had then been suffering severe reverses].

Finally, on October 22, 1757, in reply to Thomas Dering's complaint that he was the sufferer, Sarah may have put an end to further family discussion about settlement of her father's estate. She wrote: "I would much rather return it all [her portion of that estate] to you again, than you should ever be a sufferer by me, and that with thanks for past favours..." Nearly five years later Thomas Hutchinson, Esq., Judge of Probate of Suffolk County, Province of Massachusetts Bay, in the matter of Henry Dering, Esq., deceased, ordered a partition of division of his real estate into seven parts, the shares being allocated as Dering's will directed: two-sevenths to Thomas Dering and one-seventh each to Elizabeth *Dering* Wentworth, Mary *Dering* Gooch, Sarah *Dering* Thomas, and Henry Packer Dering, and the income from one-seventh part to Ann *Dering* Monk.

The protracted settlement of Captain Henry Dering's estate, extending as it did over a dozen-year period, was not unusual (though it might have seemed so to family members). That there were difficulties involved in working out the settlement again was not an unusual problem. When Sarah Thomas wrote her brother that she was sorry he found "so much difficulty in settling accounts with the family," she added: "But it's no more than I expected." What, then, had exacerbated the situation? What had happened that called forth such an outpouring of sentiment, a good deal of which was deeply felt?

Ray Thomas's short note of July 23, 1756 seems, indeed, to have initiated the estrangement. "I wish you success in all your undertakings," he had written, "and hope the uninterruption of your new mansion will give you leisure to settle your father's estate, as your sister's portion will be of real service to your well wishing brother." Thomas Dering may have taken this as implied criticism of his handling of the estate. He may have thought it presumptuous of Ray Thomas to inquire about Sarah's

"Continual Uneasiness of Mind..."

portion, although she herself reminded her brother that it was "right and just he should have." Or he may have considered, by then, that Ray was irresponsible about money and incapable of managing it properly, even that his brother-in-law had already called upon him too many times for financial assistance. Furthermore, Thomas Dering may not have been well during those years: his sister spoke solicitously several times about a headache or pain in his head that seemed to continue.

Whatever Ray may have felt about Thomas Dering's attitude, his letters to his brother-in-law, judging from those still extant, were to become noticeably less frequent and invariably more formal, bearing the salutation "Dear Sir:" instead of "Dear Brother." In the end, it was the twenty-five-year-old Sarah Thomas who, with understanding and practical good sense, brought to an end what she called the "unhappy jar between two friends so nearly allyed to me" - her brother and her husband.

For Sarah Thomas, in the late summer of 1758, there was continuing worry about money and the added affliction of losing a child and her own consequent illness. She wrote to her brother: "It is a greate disappointment to me Mrs. Wentworth being oblig'd to return before I am safe a bed but she cannot content her Self to tarry since she hear'd Benning [Elizabeth Wentworth's son, Benning Wentworth] was sick..." A month or so later, Sarah informed him: "I am sorry it has not bin in my power to send you the money I borrow'd when last in town, but hope you have not wanted it." She hoped to send it by James the following week or the week after. But then she had a miscarriage. On September 23, 1758 Ray Thomas told his brother-in-law that Sarah was "upon the recovery," but revealed just how serious her condition had been when he reported that "the Doctr. Said he never Set down with more horror of fear than [now?]." Ten days later Ray advised Thomas Dering that "Mrs. is mending."

Five years later Sarah Thomas was sick again, with what "the Dockter says...is a dissorder in my Liver." On July 27, 1763 she wrote her brother:

> I have bin very ill. I never remember to have bin in so poor a state of health before in my live. I was taken the first of April, after a complaining winter with a numness and general destress as tho all my Blood was Stagnated. after that went a littell over it seem'd to settell in a constant violent destress and oppression? at my Stom-

"Continual Uneasiness of Mind..."

ach. The Dockter says it is a dissorder in my Liver; it is a discouraging disorder and without attention may be attended with bad surcumstances but if I will attend to his proscription and not be wery and give out with the length of time, he sees nothing but I may doe Well at last. I have taken severall Hundred of Pills and am still taking. I am advised to ride for my health and believe if I live till winter shall take a Journey to Boston after I have weaned my littell one...We have a fine prospect for a plentifull Harvest. we have Beas'n [bees in] the new Boxes. I wish you could se them. I know you would think them entertaining and pritty. We have had a visit from Heps and her Husband in heigh sperits.

Three years earlier Thomas Dering and his family had moved from Boston to Shelter Island, New York, where his wife had inherited land from her father, Brinley Sylvester. The move in no way diminished the flow of letters from Sarah to her brother and later to her sister-in-law and her nephew Sylvester Dering. But, she told her brother, "I must confess, when I have endeavored to lay aside every care and lay a scheme to visit you, that the thoughts of crossing the water has been too much for me, even though I should have only to cross from New London, for I am a poor coward."

During those ten years from 1755 to 1765, Ray and Sarah had four children: Nathaniel, born August 5, 1755, whom his mother called "the bantling," or infant, who would "not admit me to write a long letter for he takes too much of my time up yet"; Henry Dering, born November 19, 1760 and named for Sarah's father; Sarah Dering, born October 8, 1762 and named for Sarah; and John, born August 30, 1764 and named for Ray's father, whose awakening one evening when three months old caused Sarah hastily to conclude a letter.

Probably sometime following the birth of his son John in August 1764, Ray's "continual uneasiness of mind" about money caused him to consider seriously, though hardly for the first time, what he could do to improve matters. He had, it was true, a substantial landed estate, the bulk of it his "patrimony" in Marshfield as he expressed it, and smaller pieces of property in the neighboring town of Pembroke, in the town of Londonderry, New Hampshire (in right of his wife), and on Block Island devised to him by his grandfather Captain Simon Ray. But there seemed no way to make his farm in Marshfield realize more income; Sarah had

"Continual Uneasiness of Mind..."

accurately described it: "his farm in general is but poor land and takes a great deal of manure to make it produce anything worth while which makes it very expensive, and but little profit remains." And she added: "We have a large family to bring up..."

Ray Thomas was then thirty-four, Sarah thirty-three. There was a likely possibility of more children. He was faced not only with the absolute necessity of feeding and clothing his wife and children and of providing for them in the event of illness, but also with the hope and expectation of educating his children and, ultimately, of making a reasonable settlement on them as a start in life. He had the desire, as well, to furnish his wife with some of the luxuries she had gone so long without. And there was the further realization that his "patrimony" would pass in its entirety to his eldest son Nathaniel under the terms of the entail established by Ray's great-great-great-grandfather William Thomas in 1651, more than one hundred years earlier. Under the law pertaining to estates tail, Ray could not sell or devise any part of that property. It could well have been the birth of his third son, John, that prompted Ray to a course of action that was available to him. He could terminate or "dock" the entail on the property, thereby enabling him to sell or devise some or all of it.

Such a procedure was frequently resorted to by landowners during the colonial period, in order to devise land among several children or to sell land to relieve financial burdens. To accomplish such a termination or "docking" of the entail were a number of methods, one of which - the common recovery - was frequently utilized. This involved a fictitious and prearranged lawsuit, not an adversary proceeding. A tenant in tail, such as Nathaniel Ray Thomas, seeking to terminate the entail, would agree with another person for the latter to bring suit under claim of rightful possession of the land in question. The court, in effect, would decide title to the property and, based upon a fictitious default, would give title to the complainant in fee simple absolute, for and on behalf of the original tenant in tail. Thus, the entail would be docked or cut off. In his "continual uneasiness of mind," Ray Thomas may well have consulted General John Winslow. The General was then Chief Justice of the Inferior Court of Common Pleas and Quarter Sessions of the Peace of Plymouth County, over which both the General's father Isaac Winslow and Ray's grandfather Nathaniel and his great-grandfather Colonel Nathaniel had presided also. The General would have been familiar, of course, with the entail on the Thomas lands. Ray may have asked the General's advice about docking the entail or possibly the General

*Nathaniel Ray Thomas's house built about 1772.
Courtesy of the Duxbury Rural and Historical Society.*

Nathaniel Ray Thomas's house with later additions by Daniel Webster. Courtesy of the Duxbury Rural and Historical Society.

"Continual Uneasiness of Mind..."

himself may have suggested it. It may also have been that the General's eldest son Pelham Winslow - Ray's cousin, Harvard friend, and fellow occupant of Massachusetts Hall - was asked to join any discussion of the matter. He was already a member of the bar. When Ray did decide to go forward with docking the entail, he retained his cousin Pelham Winslow to act as his attorney. As demandant for title to the Thomas lands, either Ray or one of the Winslows procured the assistance of Dr. Charles Stockbridge of Scituate, friend and physician to both families and whose sister Elizabeth would soon be courted by Pelham's brother Isaac.

Late in the summer of 1765, the preliminary instrument for docking the entail was drawn up, executed and recorded. The recitals stated:

> This Indenture made this thirteenth day of September Anno Domini one thousand seven hundred & sixty five between Nathaniel Ray Thomas of Marshfield in the County of Plymouth Esqr. on the one part and Charles Stockbridge of Scituate in the same County Physician on the other part WITNESSETH that for the better Assurance & Settlement of the Messuage & Lands &c hereafter named & the Appurtenances to the Uses hereafter by these Presents declared & in Consideration of the sum of five shillings by the said Nathaniel Ray Thomas to the said Charles Stockbridge before the ensealing hereof well & truly paid it is COVENANTED by the Partys aforenamed that the said Charles Stockbridge shall before the next Inferior Court of Common Pleas to be holden at Plymouth in & for the County of Plymouth purchase & sue forth against the said Nathaniel Ray Thomas a Writ of entry sur Disseizin in the post, returnable before his Majesty's Justices of said Court of Common Pleas at Plymouth at the Cost & Charge of the said Nathaniel Ray Thomas and shall thereby demand against the said Nathaniel Ray Thomas a Messuage & Tract of Land & salt Marsh lying in Marshfield aforesaid & some small part thereof in Duxborough in the same County Containing about one thousand & fifty acres...And it is further COVENANTED by the Partys aforenamed that the said Recovery of all and singular the Premises & Appurtenances in this Indenture mentioned & described shall immediately after said Recovery thereof and Execution had thereof be & enure

"Continual Uneasiness of Mind..."

> to and that the said Charles Stockbridge shall be and stand seized thereof to and for the only proper use, Benifit and Behoof of the said Nathaniel Ray Thomas his Heirs & Assigns forever. In Testimony whereof the Partys aforenamed have hereunto set their hands & Seals the day & year aforewritten.
>
> Signed Sealed and delivered in presence of us
>
> John Winslow N Ray Thomas
> Isaac Winslow Chas Stockbridge

On October I, 1765, "at his Majesties Inferiour Court of Common Pleas begun and held at Plymouth within and for the County of Plymouth...Nathaniel Ray Thomas of Marshfield in the County of Plymouth Esqr. was Summoned to appear...and Answer Charles Stockbridge of Scituate in the same County Physician In a plea of Land..." The Inferior Court of Common Pleas was composed of John Winslow, Chief Justice; and Thomas Clapp, Thomas Foster, and Gamaliel Bradford, Justices.

As for the disposition of the proceedings by the Inferior Court, Robert Treat Paine, Barrister at Law, who had prosecuted "to final Judgment & Execution a Common Recovery on Account of and to the Use of Nathaniel Ray Thomas of Marshfield in the same County of Plymouth," later testified and deposed that "thereby the Estate in Tail which the said Nathaniel Ray Thomas before that time had in the said Premises, was docked & became Seized of an Estate in Fee Simple to him & his Heirs in the same Premises." By the Court's action, Ray Thomas now owned absolutely and outright his "Patrimony" in Marshfield to mortgage, sell, or devise as he saw fit. Nearly ten years later, just before his life was to be forever altered by the onrush of patriotic fervor in the American colonies, Sarah urged him: "I tell him he had better sell some of his land and pay everybody off, and then he will have more left than he can well improve and not live in a continual uneasiness of mind as he now is." But Nathaniel Ray Thomas kept his land.

VIII

The Storm Breaks

In the spring of 1775, exactly 10 years after the docking of the entail on his estate, Ray Thomas's Eagles Nest was occupied by British troops. Ray, of course, had fled Marshfield that previous September. He had intervened on behalf of that town's inhabitants in their request for troops to protect them.

The stationing of British troops at Marshfield, at the behest of inhabitants under the influence of Ray Thomas and the Winslow family, "remarkable high Tories" as John Andrews mildly reproved them, continued to draw comment. Frederick Mackenzie of the Boston garrison routinely noted through the months of January, February, and March that pay and provisions were sent to Captain Balfour's detachment once a fortnight. To make certain that he and his officers would have an agreeable tour of duty, Balfour arranged to have a wine cellar constructed in the cellar of Ray's house.

Although it was said almost immediately upon their arrival that "the King's Troops" were "very comfortably accommodated, and preserve the most exact discipline," the subsequent conduct of the soldiers belied that remark. They harassed the inhabitants, farmers particularly and while at work in the fields or about their barns. They traveled about the countryside, even into neighboring Duxbury where they bothered parishioners of the First Church at their worship service and their mere presence about town terrified the women. One of Balfour's soldiers, a local story persists, apprehended when drunk, was lashed to the elm at the east end of Ray's house and thoroughly flogged.

Emboldened by the continued presence of the British troops in Marshfield, the Tories there dominated a town meeting held on February 20, 1775. They chose Dr. Isaac Winslow to chair the meeting as Moderator. Three items made up the order of business. First, "the vote was put to know the mind of the town, whether they will adhere to and abide by the resolves and recommendations of the Continental & Provincial Congress or any illegal assemblies whatsoever, and it passed in the negative. Second, "the vote was put to know the mind of the town

The Storm Breaks

whether they will return their thanks to Gen. Gage and Admiral Graves for their ready and kind interposition, assistance and protection from further insults and abuses with which we are continually threatened, and it passed in the afirmative."

The third matter on the agenda was the choice of a committee to draw up and send a resolution of thanks to General Gage and Admiral Graves. The committee consisted of the following men: Abijah White, Esq., (the town's representative to the General Court), Dr. Isaac Winslow, William Stevens, John Baker, Ephraim Little, Elisha Ford, Seth Bryant, Deacon John Tilden, Captain Amos Rogers, Captain Daniel White, Captain Nathaniel Phillips, Seth Ewell, Paul White, Thomas Little, Elisha Sherman, Simeon Keene, Captain Cornelius White, Abraham Walker, William Macomber, Lemuel Little, Abijah Thomas, Abner Wright, and Job Winslow. The first several members of that committee, excepting Abijah White, the Representative - Dr. Isaac Winslow, William Stevens, John Baker, Ephraim Little, Elisha Ford, and Seth Bryant - were, with Ray Thomas, the committee that had prepared the town's resolutions denouncing the Boston Tea Party the year before.

In all probability, these were the most active Tories left in Marshfield now that Ray Thomas had fled to Boston. Minutes of the town meeting on the 20th were kept by Nehemiah Thomas, Clerk. Not only did he head his entry, "At a legal Town Meeting...," but also did he note following it: "This Town Meeting was held agreeable to an Act of Parliament, entitled 'An Act for the better regulating the Province of Massachusetts Bay,' &c., passed in the last session of Parliament."

The address to General Gage seemed, indeed, to possess "the colouring which the Tories never fail to bestow on every thing that turns in their favour," as the Whigs shortly were to claim. It was fulsome:
> We, the Inhabitants of Marshfield, in legal Town Meeting assembled, this 20th day of February, 1775, beg leave to return your Excellency our most grateful acknowledgments for your seasonable assistance and protection, in sending a detachment of his Majesty's Troops to secure and defend the loyal people of this Town, from the threats and violence of an infatuated and misguided people. We assure your Excellency (whatever may have been surmised to the contrary) that there be sufficient grounds and reasons for making application; and we are fully convinced that this movement has preserved and

The Storm Breaks

> promoted, not only the peace and tranquility of this Town in particular, but of the County in general; owing, in great degree, to the prudence, firmness, and good conduct of Captain Balfour, who, with pleasure as well as justice we say it, has done every thing in his power to obtain those laudable ends and purposes.

The committee was not only expressing the appreciation of the town for the assistance and protection provided by General Gage, but also was putting on record, as it were, the justification for the request. It was diplomatic as well to go a bit further and praise Balfour too. In the next paragraph the committee was effusive in commending Gage:

> Thankfully we acknowledge our obligations to our Sovereign for his great goodness and wisdom, in placing at the head of affairs in this Province, in this day of difficulty, confusion, and discord, a gentleman of your Excellency's well known humanity, moderation, capacity and intrepidity, and shall constantly implore the Supreme Governour of the universe to assist and direct you in the faithful discharge of the various functions of your exalted station, with fidelity to your King, with honour to yourself, and with happiness to the people committed to your charge.

In the last two paragraphs of their address, the committee strongly stated their opposition to factions in rebellion against the constitution and government of Great Britain and voiced vigorously their loyalty and support of the Crown:

> With pleasure we embrace this opportunity of expressing our detestation and abhorrence of all assemblies and combinations of men (by whatever specious name they may call themselves) who have or shall rebelliously attempt to alter or oppose the wise Constitution and Government of Great Britain.
> Furthermore, we beg leave to inform your Excellency, that in the most critical and dangerous times, we have always manifested and preserved our loyalty to the King, and obedience to his laws; carefully avoiding all constitutional covenants and engagements whatsoever, that might warp us from our duty to our God, our King, and country; and as we are determined to persevere in the same course, we flatter ourselves that our

The Storm Breaks

> endeavours and exertions will meet with our most gracious Sovereign's approbation, as well as your Excellency's, and that under his and your gentle and humane government and kind protection, we may peaceably and quietly sit under our vines and fig trees and have none to molest or make us afraid.

The address was signed by Isaac Winslow, Chairman of the Committee.

A declaration of the town's sentiments similar in purpose but somewhat less effusive was dispatched to the Honorable Samuel Graves, Esq., Vice-Admiral of the Blue:

> We, the Inhabitants of Marshfield, in Town Meeting legally assembled the 20th of February, A.D. 1775, penetrated with the highest sense of gratitude, present our sincere and hearty thanks to you, sir, for your ready compliance with a request of a number of our inhabitants, in ordering an armed Vessel to protect and defend us from the lawless insults and abuses with which we were threatened by numbers of seditious and evil-minded people, for no other reason (that we can conceive) but our loyalty to the best of Kings, and firm adherence to the laws of Government. With hearts replete with gratitude, we contemplate the paternal care and goodness of our most gracious Sovereign, in the appointment of a gentleman to command his Navy in America, at this critical juncture, whose duty, inclination, and abilities, so happily coincide to answer the good purposes of his department.
>
> Permit us to acquaint your Honour, that we have always endeavoured to comport ourselves, and regulate our conduct agreeable to the laws of England and this country; that we have not been guilty of any riots or illegal assemblies, or adopted or subscribed any unconstitutional resolves, covenants, or combinations whatsoever, but have constantly and uniformly borne our testimony against such measures and proceedings; that it is our serious intention and firm resolution to respect the English Constitution and demean ourselves like true, loyal and obedient subjects, by doing which we apprehend we shall entitle ourselves to the continued protection of our most gracious King, your Honour, and every friend to peace and good Government.

The Storm Breaks

The Marshfield Whigs, incensed at the action of the Tories in promoting adoption of these latest resolutions, protested. Sixty-four inhabitants subscribed to the protest against the proceedings of the February 20th town meeting. "Being greatly aggrieved at the conduct of the said Town...and sensible of the high colouring which the Tories never fail to bestow on every thing that turns in their favour," the subscribers felt it their duty to their King, their country, themselves, and their posterity to remonstrate.

Their first objection was that the Selectmen intentionally relied on a statute that increased the number of voters of Tory persuasion over those of Whig partisanship so that, "in the choice of a Moderator, who happened to be a Tory, there appeared about twenty-six or twenty-seven more Tory than Whig voters." The second and fifth objections were likewise somewhat procedural in nature. The second was that the Selectmen and others had petitioned the Governor, in accordance with the Massachusetts Government Act, for leave to hold a town meeting (by the Act otherwise confined to one session a year for the election of officials.) Such action by the Tories, it was claimed, was "without the knowledge or advice of many in this Town." The fifth was that the Selectmen had given but a single day's notice of the meeting, that it was to be held "in a part of the Town where a Town Meeting was never before had," and that no information concerning the purpose of the meeting was given in the notice.

The third and fourth points made by the Whigs were directed to matters of more substance. The third complained that "the vote which passed in the negative, whether the Town will adhere to, and abide by the Resolves of the Continental and Provincial Congresses, or any illegal assemblies whatsoever...was craftily drawn, and put as if these Congresses were Illegal, when we suppose the present situation of our publick affairs makes them both legal and necessary." That vote had the effect, of course, of putting the town on record of having rejected the Continental Association in particular. The fourth concern of the Whigs centered on the town's vote to express its thanks to General Gage and Admiral Graves for their protection against "further insults and abuses" and claimed the Whigs neither knew nor believed "that any of the inhabitants of this Town" were "threatened with insults and abuses." This latest statement in the ebb and flow of Whig-Tory agitation in Marshfield appeared in the Boston press shortly after the February 20th town meeting.

The Storm Breaks

On the same day the Tories adopted the resolutions that so exercised the Whig faction in Marshfield, James Warren wrote John Adams. In his letter dated at Plymouth, Warren remarked that "we have no arrivals, no news. Our military Gentry remain in statu quo, at the Councillor's Mansion House at Marshfield. No body but the Tories here and there take any notice of them..." But notice was taken in other quarters. The Boston Gazette on January 30th had printed an item which scoffed at the stationing of troops and Ray Thomas's part in it: "Card players are said to be no Oeconomists. If the Troops at Marshfield do not pay Barrack-Money for the Houses they occupy there, yet when they fright a Wife and Children from Home into a Neighbour's House, Pence may be saved, and thus Simple Sapling may be called an Oeconomist." Correspondence printed in the Massachusetts Spy in February was sarcastic:

> Could Mr. Counsellor Sapling be so unacquainted with the temper and spirit of the people in the county of Plymouth, as to imagine that the appearance of a hundred regular troops, though ever so well dressed, powdered and disciplined, would throw them into such an amazing consternation, as to make them desist from the most trifling enterprize. If he could, he must be simple indeed, simple beyond belief. But ignorant as he is, he knew the order and tranquility, which reign among all ranks of men in that county, and in every part of the province, notwithstanding the complication of oppression, insult and injury, which inflame their minds.

Mercy Warren herself wrote to Abigail Adams about the troops in a vein somewhat surprising considering her comments on the matter as spoken by characters in her play, The Group. "You have doubtless heard," she remarked to Abigail, "that there is a detachment from headquarters stationed in the neighborhood of Plymouth. People here are much at a loss, what can be the design of this ridiculous movement; probably it is with intention to provoke, till some rashness shall give a pretext, to the beginning of hostilities." What Mercy Warren was saying quite plainly represented a favorite Whig rationalization: the British in their zeal not to coerce the colonists, were conniving, in the stationing of troops in Marshfield, to provoke the Whigs into some rash act which would justify commencing hostilities. Patriots, even some of their leaders, were aware of this possibility and cautioned against hasty action.

The Storm Breaks

The Boston Committee of Correspondence after all, in their alert to the Plymouth Committee of the dispatching of troops to Marshfield, had indicated their concern that such a maneuver was intended "to precipitate" the colonists "into a conflict with Great Britain." This advice was consonant with that of the "Grand Congress," the Continental Congress, that all "should act upon the defensive." The Boston merchant John Andrews had expressed the hope that people would be "prudent enough not to meddle with the soldiers." Ezra Stiles was aware of the Boston Committee's warning to Plymouth and the adjacent towns, "beseeching them," as he put it, "not to take fire & withhold all Violence. It being resolved to keep still & bear all Insults till news from Parliament."

While the Whigs, on the one hand, were convinced of a British ministerial conspiracy to force the colonies into submission - "the Marshfield affair" being viewed as a pretext to bring on hostilities by the British - the Tories, on the other hand, were justifiably concerned about their lives and property. They had had ample opportunity to know first-hand, harassment, personal insult and indignity. As Lord Dartmouth had correctly assessed the situation, "affairs of the Province" were "indeed in a very dangerous & critical situation." Certainly this had been true of Marshfield for some time past; tensions now, however, had intensified because of the continued presence of Captain Balfour and his troops.

As the situation deteriorated, events in England accelerated toward a showdown. In February 1775, Lord North managed through both Houses of Parliament a joint address to the King which unequivocally stated that "a rebellion at this time actually exists in Massachusetts." Parliament pledged both lives and properties of its members in support of its own rights and that of the Crown. Next North succeeded in getting through a bill restraining trade and commerce of New England. Specifically the bill prohibited New Englanders from fishing in their coastal waters, except for the men of Scituate and Marshfield who, for their loyalty, were permitted to fish in their home waters.

In the Province of Massachusetts Bay, as in other colonies, organized militia had existed since the earliest days. That institution, often recruited by way of draft, had as officers usually the leading men of a community. More often than not they were related by blood or marriage to one or more in their commands. In Marshfield lived Anthony Thomas, boyhood acquaintance of Ray Thomas and whose father had been young Ray's guardian. In that spring of 1775 Anthony Thomas was Colonel of Plymouth County's Second Regiment of militia. His brother Dr. John

The Storm Breaks

Thomas, who had had a distinguished career in the French and Indian War, had also been a friend of Ray's when the former was a student at Harvard. More importantly, in that spring of 1775 John Thomas was a general officer in the army organized by the Massachusetts Provincial Congress in anticipation of probable hostilities with the Mother Country.

That enlistment of soldiers was under way that spring is shown by a letter written to "Coll. Anthony Thomas Esqr." on March 20th by William Turner, an officer in the Third Company of Foot in Scituate in Colonel Thomas's regiment. Turner reported that he was enrolling men for another company. The letter revealed the informality of the recruiting system, for, when only a few men turned up at Turner's call, he and other officers decided to enlist them as minutemen instead of the more regularly constituted militia. They were to be called the Scituate Rangers also under Colonel Thomas's command. This was, according to Turner, "in Order to make one more Tryal further" to raise more troops and "save our Credit at this alarming Day."

In accordance with orders from the Provincial Congress, Concord had been chosen as the site for the storing of arms and ammunition. General Thomas Gage, acting under orders from London granting him discretion to proceed as he saw fit in the critical situation then developing, determined to send out troops to capture the military stores at Concord. Alerted by Paul Revere and William Dawes who had ridden out from Boston upon discovery of the British plans, minutemen and militia engaged the regulars at Lexington and Concord on April 19, 1775. Word of the fighting spread fast and far. The morning of the 20th a messenger, having ridden all night, arrived in Marshfield with the news that fighting had begun. Captain William Thomas ("Capt. Willie,") immediately climbed Ward's Hill near the Training Field and fired three warning shots, while a companion beat his drum, the prearranged signal that war had started.

General John Thomas started immediately for Cambridge, arriving there probably on the 20th. He left behind two regiments of Plymouth County militia men under the command of Colonels Bailey and Cotton with orders to move on Balfour's detachment in Marshfield and capture it.

Those two regiments of minutemen General Thomas hoped - but from his own experience probably did not expect - would move on the British with alacrity. It was indeed so. On the 20th Colonel Cotton had reached Duxbury and encamped that night at Major Bradford's; Colonel Bailey

General John Thomas by Benjamin Blyth. Courtesy of the Massachusetts Historical Society.

House of Colonel Anthony Thomas. Still standing at the intersection of Parsonage and Moraine Streets. Courtesy of Gerald McCluskey.

The Storm Breaks

had decided to take position between Ray Thomas's and White's Ferry in Marshfield where a British armed vessel was rumored to be. Captain Balfour likewise had the news. He put his command in readiness, sending out scouts to feel out the Whigs, to ascertain any moves they might try to make. The evening of the 20th they made contact. "Last night a Party of Belfars [Balfour's] Troops fired on a Centry of our Men killed one Jacob Dingley & wounded one Other," the Whigs tersely, but erroneously, reported the next day. Dingley did not die.

Along with word that hostilities had commenced, Nesbitt Balfour received communication from General Gage that ships were being sent to take off his detachment, and any Marshfield people desiring to flee. With fighting having started, Gage knew he could not send armed relief by land to Balfour and that officer knew he could neither elude nor break through the unnumbered hostile Patriot forces between Marshfield and Boston. Relief by water was the only chance.

At Colonel Anthony Thomas's house, about a mile and a quarter west of the British position at Ray Thomas's, during the day of the 20th, men gathered, armed with muskets and other weapons of their own, singly and in companies in some semblance of order. Colonel Cotton, with part of his regiment joined Colonel Bailey and his regiment at Colonel Thomas's, the agreed upon rendezvous. One of Colonel Bailey's officers, a first lieutenant in Captain Turner's company, was Briggs Thomas, Colonel Anthony Thomas's son. Another son, Waterman Thomas, seems to have acted as a clerk, for he wrote letters to his uncle, General John Thomas, commanding the wing of the American army holding Roxbury outside of Boston.

During that day the colonels present held a council of war. They prepared a letter to General Thomas at Roxbury, sent doubtless by horse courier. After describing the clash between Balfour's men and their own the previous night and the movements of Cotton's and Bailey's regiments, the letter made a strong appeal to the General:
> Colonels Request us to write that your Attendance is judged necessary as your Knowledge of the Ground Experience in the Art of War might be Advantageous. It is Reported that Said Belfar has a Number of Cannon and a Certain Piece of Ground advantageous for Playing them - they [the colonels] do not Chuse to Act without your Presence or on Express Orders.

The Storm Breaks

Seldom during the eighteenth century was the reputation of average militia considered good. George Washington, who had had experience with them, had little regard either for their military ability or their military training and discipline. General John Thomas, who also had had such personal experience, may have shared Washington's scorn, at least to some extent. Yet he realized that militia facing British regulars for the first time might be intimidated and hence cautious. His duties, as the siege of Boston began, prevented him going to Marshfield to take command. He would reinforce his colonels. He sent down "Eleven Hundred Brave Men with Canon," a formidable force which, together with the militia on hand, could completely dominate the British.

Probably as soon as the 19th, Gage's attempt to rescue Balfour began with Admiral Graves sending a schooner, the Hope, and two sloops to Marshfield. The ships hove to and anchored off Brant Rock to await Balfour's contingent and any Tories anxious to quit the town. During the council of war on the 21st at Colonel Thomas's house where the neighboring militia were gathering, Captain Peleg Wadsworth became impatient at the delay and started his Kingston men on the march to Ray Thomas's and the British garrison. His company was outnumbered, but his effort encouraged the colonels to order an assault on the British. The entire body of militiamen moved off from Colonel Thomas's, crossed the upper reaches of Green Harbor River on Solomon's Dam, up over the rise of Black Mount, and down through the fields toward Ray Thomas's house. Alerted to this movement of the Whig forces, Captain Balfour ordered his men into small boats in Green Harbor River, which ferried them out to the naval vessels waiting off Brant Rock. With the troops went a number of Tories.

Thus the British made good their escape. A young lad of Duxbury, he who had followed along behind the cart carrying Jesse Dunbar in the belly of the slaughtered ox to Ray Thomas's the year before, later recalled that had the militia been marched to the British position, the Whigs might have taken Balfour and his men "prisoners without a drop of blood being shed, as their captain afterwards was heard to say that he should not have thought of making resistance to so formidable a force." In fact, there had been blood shed in Marshfield - not British blood to be sure, but of Marshfield men. It was insignificant action at the beginning of a conflict of long duration and large consequence. Yet immediate notice was taken.

The Storm Breaks

On the 25th General Thomas's nephew Waterman reported to his uncle details of the last few days:
> I have the unhappy news to acquaint you of the Regulars getting clear from Marshfield, and part of the Tories. But part of them are taken, who were yesterday had under examination before the officers. Who they saw fit to put under close guard were Amos Rogers, Wm. Macomber, Luke Hall, Tobias Oakman, Samuel Trount, Joshua Chase, Calvin Lewis, Jedidah Eames, and they dismissed John White, James Lewis, Lemuel Little, Benjamin Eames, Francis Crocker, Jonathan Sylvester, Elisha Sherman, Lemuel Ford and David Thomas, on conditions that they should not be seen no two of them together nor be seen off their enclosure, and have caught several more today who are now under guard. They have disarmed all the Tories that they can find. Among Patriot troops involved were some from Middleboro. "The first company of militia and the second and third company of minutemen marched to Marshfield in consequence of the Lexington plan to surpress what was feared might be a rising of tories to whom Governor Gage had sent one hundred standard of arms. After two days' service they returned to their home."

Young Thomas revealed in his next words of his letter the hesitancy and inexperience and disorganization of the ordinary militia. "The Colonel want[s] particular order[s] from you in writing. There is none but Col. Bailey's regiment here; Col. Cotton's are all dismissed, who are most all at home about their business." A postscript added: "My Father desires you would send him particular orders, for Col. Bailey's regiment is most beat out and are uneasy that Col. Cotton does nothing and are a thought of going home unless orders from you." He referred here to the general custom prevalent at the time of civilian soldiers leaving their posts, with or without orders, to pursue their own affairs, often tending to their crops and stock. After all, most soldiers, officers and men, were farmers. Waterman Thomas ended his letter with a personal note: "I believe your family is all well and friends are well here, only very much confused..."

In the immediate aftermath of the "Marshfield affair," comments by several persons aware of what had gone on reveal other details of the incident. Ezra Stiles noted in his diary as soon as April 22nd:

The Storm Breaks

> We do indeed hear that Gen. Gage having sent a Vessel to take off his 100 Men sent to Marshfield, the Minute Men of the neighboring Towns assembled to prevent & secure the Soldiers from being carried off. And that a great Light was seen from Providence in the direction of Marshfield, which is 60 Miles off, supposed to be the firing of that Town. But this I do not credit. [This was a fire in Sandwich Woods.] But Marshfield is a dispersed Settlement. The supposition is in no wise credible. Tho probably the Party is secured - for Things are becoming more & more serious every day.

Two days later, Stiles made his final entry about what he had originally called the "Marshfield affair." He made this entry: "Gen. Gage sent 2 Transports on Wednesday last to take off the Troops at Marshfield. And it is said that they embarked on friday Noon." That young lad of Duxbury, Seth Sprague, reminiscing many years later, remembered vividly: "The Torys of Marshfield who had taken an open and active part in favor of the oppressive acts of the British Government went off to the British at Boston, others that had been less active remained at home, but the Whigs of Duxbury searched every house in Marshfield that was thought to be inhabited by a Tory and took all the fire arms they could find."

IX

War

When the storm broke - at Lexington and Concord with the fighting on April 19th and in Marshfield with the brush between Nesbitt Balfour's troops and local militia on April 20th - Ray Thomas had been in Boston for seven months. During that time General Gage, as governor, had avoided assembling the Council "as much as possible." When Ray learned in mid-January, however, of the threats against the Marshfield Loyalists made by those whom he called the "factious demagogues," as a member of the Council he had approached Gage urgently supporting the request for troops for the protection of those Loyalists.

Word from the country, from Marshfield, had filtered in to Ray that fall. News had become increasingly disquieting, worrisome. Ray was concerned about Sarah and the children. When his eldest son Nat, "young Simple Sapling" the Whig press derisively called him, had come posthaste from the Marshfield Loyalists with the petition to Gage seeking protection, Ray learned firsthand of affairs at home. Knowing that he could speak from experience of the temper of the Whigs and aware of the favorable impression he had made by his own conduct as a firm member of the Council, he felt certain General Gage would send the troops requested.

Preparations for garrisoning Balfour's troops at Ray Thomas's in Marshfield involved, of course, the removal of his family - Sarah and their children and Sarah's sister Mrs. Mary Gooch - to other quarters. Sarah's cousins and neighbors in Marshfield, Anna *Green* Winslow and her husband Joshua Winslow, took them in. When Ray had reached Boston that last September after his precipitous departure from Marshfield, it would have been natural for him to lodge at the home of Ebenezer Storer. Storer's wife was Elizabeth *Green* Storer, Anna Winslow's sister and another cousin of Sarah Thomas's. Storer himself had graduated from Harvard the same year that Ray had entered. Storer's house was on Sudbury Street, a few blocks from the Town House and Dering's Corner. Storer, following his father as a wealthy merchant and prominent townsman, had an extensive and elegant residence, the drawing and dining rooms wainscoted and panelled and embellished with furniture of carved mahogany, the library lined with bookshelves, and the walls hung with portraits and engravings. One post that he particularly cherished was that of Treasurer of Harvard College. Many years later a daughter of Ray's and Sarah's, writing to her brother, could call the Winslows and the Storers, in truth, "our parents' intimate friends."

Nat Thomas, having brought up the Marshfield petition for troop protection, apparently joined his father at Ebenezer Storer's and remained there, for Sarah wrote her brother later that year that Nat was in Boston as her cousin could inform him. Sarah herself may have visited Boston toward the end of January of 1775. A letter from her sister Elizabeth Wentworth, dated February 2nd, was addressed to her at Boston. It was a short note, written from Portsmouth with the news that Sarah's niece Frances, wife of Governor John Wentworth, had given birth to a son. The event had happened about the time the British troops were preparing to go to Marshfield, and "had a young prince been born there could not have been more rejoicing. The ships fired their guns. All the gentlemen of the town and from the King's ships came, the next day, to pay their compliments...and for one week, there were cake and caudle wine, etc., passing."

Sarah Thomas was in Marshfield before the outbreak of hostilities, before Captain Balfour and his troops were forced to retire to Boston. Early in April Dr. Isaac Winslow, in a letter to an old friend, concluded with wishing a lady well on her recent marriage:

"Mrs. Winslow, our daughter and the ladies of Mr. Thomas's family (who are now with us) join me in compliments of congratulations to her." Dr. Winslow pictured a somber situation in the Province:
>...discord and contention seem to have spread their banners, far and wide, and I am at times too ready to fear, that desolation is at their heels and just upon the eve of taking place amongst us. God only knows what great overtures may befall this land within the course of the ensuing summer; but very great ones, we have sufficient reason to apprehend. At present we have neither form nor order amongst us. No courts in the province, either legislative or executive, civil or criminal, the probate and admiralty excepted, which is a situation we cannot long continue in without the utmost confusion.

Lieutenant Joshua Winslow. Portrait by John Singleton Copley. Courtesy of Santa Barbara Museum of Art. Gift of Mrs. Sterling Morton for the Preston Morton Collection.

Ebenezer Storer by John Singleton Copley. "Now owned by Mrs. Lewis C. Popham," from *Diary of Anna Green Winslow.* Reprinted by Applewood Books, Bedford, Massachusetts.

War

Dr. Winslow's prediction came true, indeed very shortly. The storm broke. Two weeks after fighting between minutemen and Regulars flared at Lexington and Concord, a brief but deadly encounter between them erupted at Marshfield. As soon as practicable after Balfour and his men had abandoned their quarters at Ray Thomas's, Sarah and her family returned. Her sister Mary Gooch, that lady's maid, and Polly, as Mary Thomas was familiarly known, remained at Joshua Winslow's. All pitched in to set right the damage incurred by the British troops' occupancy - Sarah, the older children, and the servants.

The opening of hostilities brought quick response throughout Massachusetts and indeed all of New England. Men flocked to the environs of Boston, singly and in units, but units themselves disorganized and scattered, particularly those which had been in action on the 19th. John Thomas, hastening to the scene from Kingston immediately on learning of the fighting, arrived in Cambridge on the 20th, as did his superior, General Artemas Ward of Shrewsbury. Between these two men the makeshift army was divided; General Thomas taking command at Roxbury of the right wing of the army while Ward maintained his headquarters in Cambridge. For the moment Ward and Thomas were the two military leaders immediately responsible for the conduct of colonial war preparation. Above the generals in authority was the Committee of Safety, sitting at Cambridge, and its parent body and in supreme command, the Provincial Congress at Watertown but a few miles away.

Marshfield was not far behind other towns, nearer the scene of action, which were engaged in active preparation for war. A town meeting early in May chose Benjamin White, that ardent Whig who had been a leader in both the burning of the tea and removal of the town's ammunition, to represent the town in the Provincial Congress to be convened at Watertown on May 31st. In July another town meeting determined the necessity of a guard being kept on the shore for protection, and adopted a plan prepared shortly before by the Committee of Correspondence, Inspection and Safety to govern that operation. Apparently, a Committee of Correspondence, Inspection and Safety had been established since the deployment of Balfour's troops to Marshfield the preceding January.

It had been during the British presence in Marshfield that John Bourne, aged sixteen, and his neighbors heard wafting across the fields and marshes, the cry of the British sentries at Nathaniel Ray Thomas's "twelve o'clock and all's well." This so stirred the young Bourne that he ran away and joined the Patriot army besieging Boston. He continued in

War

the service till the end of hostilities, which occurred when he was in New York state. He walked the entire distance home and lived to be one hundred years old.

During the weeks from the battles of Lexington and Concord, and the skirmish at Marshfield in April to the battle of Bunker Hill in June, preparations for war, in the countryside outside Boston, as in Marshfield, continued unabated. But in Boston itself, the capital of the Province, the situation was increasingly confused. To be sure, in the first days of the siege, hostilities had not yet enveloped the civilian population of the town. Communication continued between those within the British lines and those in the surrounding towns and even in the more remote counties. This was true for both those of Whig and Tory persuasion. But the state of affairs worsened, and it would not be long before contact between Boston and the Massachusetts countryside would be almost completely ended.

Mrs. Sarah *Winslow* Deming in a very explicit letter, in the form of a daily log, to her niece, young Anna *Green* Winslow, gives a first-hand account of her feelings of fear, apprehension and entrapment and those of her household and neighbors as they live through news of the Lexington-Concord battles and the subsequent blockade of Boston. Mrs. Deming illustrates graphically the problems that beset would-be escapees wishing to leave Boston:

> I engag'd to give you, & by you your papa, & mamma some account of my peregrinations with the reasons therefore. The <u>cause</u> is too well known, to need a word upon it.
>
> I was very unquiet from the moment I was inform'd that <u>more troops</u> were coming to Boston. 'Tis true that those who had winter'd there, had not given as <u>much molestation</u> - but, <u>an additional</u> strength. I dreaded & determined if possible to git out of their reach, & to take with me as much of my little intrest as I could. Your unkle D.[eming] was very far from being of my mind, from which has proceeded those difficulties which peculiarly related to myself - but I now say not a word of this to him; we are joint suferers, & no doubt it is Gods will it should be so.
>
> Many a time have I tho't that could I be out of Boston, to go then with my family & friends, I could be content with

War

> the meanest fare & slenderest accomodations. Out of Boston, out of Boston at almost any rate - away as far as possible from the infection of small pox and the din of drums & martial musick as its called, & horrors of war - but my distress is not to be describ'd - I attemet [attempt] not to describe it....

She continued:

> We had not resolve'd where to go - in that respect we resembled Abraham & I ardently wish'd for a portion of his faith. We had got out of ye [the] city of destruction; such I lookt upon Boston to be, yet I could not but lift up my desires to God that he would have mercy upon, & spare the many thousands of poor creatures I had left behind...On Roxbury hills we met little parties, old, young & middle aged, some with fife and drum, perhaps not an hundred in ye whole; a kind of pleasant sedateness on all their countenances. We met such parties all the way which gave me the idea of sheep going to the slaughter...
>
> While we stop'd to refresh the horses at Dedham one told us that he had been with others on a high hill & discernd in the line of Marshfield the smoke wch [which] they concluded was that town on fire. I had heard before I left ye plain [Jamaica Plain] that our people had taken Genl Gages men that had been quarter'd there for the winter, & was therefore affraid there might be truth in ye conjecture...

Mrs. Deming was concerned about the Marshfield relatives of the Winslows:

> There was a light observ'd all the evening which ye people said was ye town of Marshfield on fire, wch for obvious reasons, I knew could not be, tho' the people of the house where we put up said also, that the light was in the line of Marshfield. I was affraid however that the houses there might have been fired & also the woods, wch might possibly be the light that continued so long. My brother liv'd in Genl Winslow's house - Genl Winslow sons were obnoxious to ye people - Lord preserve my brother & all his, was my constant prayer, tho' I spoke only in my heart...

War

..... when several men came in & told us that our people had kill'd (mythinks they should have said slaughter'd) every soldier, & every tory in the town of Marshfield. I said I hop'd it was a false report...But the Plymouth & Marshfield new's was happily contradicted before night...
Nothing very material respecting myself happend this day till towards evening. I was visited & consoled by numbers of fr'ds [friends]. I saw Capt Collins several times & he was contriving for me but the Assembly were siting & he was of the counsel. A number of families were preparing to move into the Southern governments, & four did go the next day. All was bustle - but no shocking news was brought us that day...
We got to Vollintown in Conectticutt that night. I might have said we left Providence at 1/2 past 10 o'clock AM. The next day about 11 o'clock we all arriv'd safe at Canterbury it being <u>Wednesday</u> April 26 - the 7th day of my journeying.

One of the problems that beset Boston civilians and British regulars alike was that of procuring food and other provisions. It was true that Gage received some supplies by sea but he did have need for hay to feed such livestock as his army possessed in the town. The Boston people also needed food, their dwindling supplies augmented by modest addition from the countryside. There were forays by both sides, consequently, to those islands in Boston Harbor which provided grazing for stock and hay for winter fodder. In late May the Provincials had moved against both Noddle's and Hog Islands, the largest in the harbor, to remove stock and destroy hay. (Ray Thomas had four horses on Noddle's.) The British intervened, skirmishing ensued, and both sides retrieved some stores and provisions and destroyed both livestock and hay.

Toward the middle of July, Abigail Adams, writing to John at the Second Continental Congress in Philadelphia, described an expedition of the provincial forces to garner stock and destroy hay on one of the islands in Boston Harbor. This was Long Island, off Dorchester, one of the larger islands somewhat south of the main shipping lanes into the inner harbor and Boston docks. After noting that several attempts to get on the island had been frustrated by the presence of British men-of-war and small patrol boats, she was pleased to report that "three hundred volunteers...came on Monday evening and took the boats, went on, and

War

brought off seventy odd sheep, fifteen head of cattle, and sixteen prisoners, thirteen of whom were sent by (Simple Sapling) to mow the hay, which were badly executed. They were taken all asleep in the house and barn. When they were taken, there were three women with them." No doubt Abigail took satisfaction that Ray Thomas's efforts to participate in relieving Boston's supply shortage was thus thwarted. A second foray to the island resulted in the firing of the barn and the hay.

The affair on Long Island came to the attention of General George Washington shortly after his taking command of the Continental Army. On the 14th of July Washington wrote to the President of Congress:

> ...The great Scarcecity of Fresh Provisions in their [the British] Army, has led me to take every precaution to prevent a Supply: For this purpose I have ordered all the Cattle and Sheep to be drove from the Low Grounds and Farms Within their Reach. A Detachment from General [John] Thomas's Camp on Wednesday Night, went over to Long Island and brought from thence 20 cattle and a Number of Sheep, with about 15 labourers who had been put on by a Mr. Ray Thomas, in order to cut Hay &c. By some Accident, they omitted burning the Hay and returned the next day to complete it, which they effected amidst the firing of the Shipping with the Loss of one man killed and another Wounded.

On June 17, 1775 the battle of Bunker Hill occurred. For the Loyalists in Boston, the outcome seemed a portent of ultimate disaster unless Providence intervened in their favor. A month later Mary Cheseborough, also a relative by marriage to Thomas and Mary Dering, wrote to them from Newport, Rhode Island, that "it is a fact that Grate Numbers has bin slan and the town of Charlestown is Lade in ashes and all most a Continuel Cannonading on both Sids and the small Pox's on Boston." Such an account, even more detailed perhaps, would have reached Sarah in Marshfield more quickly. She would have worried about the well-being of Ray and Nat. The difficulty of getting any news, let alone accurate news, from Boston was becoming increasingly more evident.

On July 17th, exactly one month after the battle, General Gage called a meeting of the Mandamus Council. This may have been, in fact, the first Council meeting since the previous August when members had been sworn in, for Gage had advised Dartmouth in December that he was refraining from holding a meeting "as much as possible" because of the

War

tense political atmosphere. But with the outset of hostilities, and particularly in the aftermath of Bunker Hill, the governor evidently thought it expedient to call the Council together.

The significance of the meeting impressed Gage. His presence seemed appropriate, indeed prudent. The roll call of the meeting read: "His Exellency the Governor, His Honor the Lieut. Governor, Chief Justice Oliver, Mr. Gray, Mr. Flucker, Brigr Ruggles, Judge Hutchinson, Judge Brown, Col. Edson, Col. Murray, Mr. Boutineau, Mr. Lechmere, Col. Erving, Col. Willard, Mr. Thomas, Col. Leonard, Mr. Loring, Sir Wm Pepperell, Col. Hatch, Mr. G. Erving." The Council requested that the governor give it the opportunity "to testify their Loyalty to their Gracious Sovereign and attachment to his Government in Humble Address..." General Gage agreed and appointed the Lieutenant Governor, Thomas Oliver; Chief Justice Peter Oliver; Treasurer Harrison Gray; Brigadier Timothy Ruggles; and Judge William Browne to prepare the address and report it to the Council. The meeting was then adjourned.

Three days later, when the Council reconvened, every member was present. The committee named to prepare the address to the Crown reported. The address was read and unanimously accepted. The Council expressed its will that the governor be requested to transmit the address to the Earl of Dartmouth to be laid before the King. "The Humble Address of the Council of the Province of Massachusetts Bay To the King's Most Excellent Majesty" was the last official expression of allegiance to the Crown of England by the government of Massachusetts Bay. All members of the Council, including Nathaniel Ray Thomas, were present when the address was read and unanimously accepted. It may be said, then, that it represented Ray's personal views and feelings quite eloquently and quite in line with his individual statements that have survived.

The address reveals the position of the Tory leadership, so very different and far removed in sentiment from that of the Whigs. It was and is a statement of belief in an existing order, loyal, conservative, and unaware, or perhaps unheeding, of forces at work far more deep seated and fundamental than any that they could imagine. Yet to understand the Tory point of view, particularly that of the Tory leadership, it is an instructive document:

> Most Gracious Sovereign [the address began],
> At a time when a most unnatural Rebellion is raging in this Province, we Your Majesty's Council of the

Massachusetts Bay, animated with the warmest affection for your Sacred Person, the most entire confidence in the wisdom and benignity of your Government, and the strongest attachment to the British Constitution, beg leave in humble Address to approach the Throne.

While we lament the disorders and confusions of Your Majestie's Colonies in America, we are constrained to express our abhorrence and detestation of those flagitious machinations of a number of evil men, who uninfluenced by the lenity and clemency of your Government, and unawed by the dread of your displeasure, have seduced the unwary and undiscerning multitudes to adopt their Principles and promote their destructive purposes.

With that humble satisfaction which arises from conscious integrity, we beg permission to assure Your Majesty, that notwithstanding the Resolves of Congress and the Obloquy we have been loaded with, the dangers we have encountered and the evils we have suffered; yet, supported by a sense of our duty, and the hopes of your most gracious approbation, we have steadily adhered to that cause, which from principle we are engaged in.

Regardless of those efforts to degrade us, we have ever been ready to discharge the trust reposed in us, chearfully acquiesing in the wisdom and goodness of Parliament, and acknowledging its Authority to bind us in all cases whatsoever.

It is with concern and indignation we see the honor of our King and the Authority of the Supreme Legislature injured and affronted; tho' with tenderness we contemplate that punitive Justice which the dignity of our Sovereign, the Authority of a British Parliament, and the security and welfare of an August Empire, Require to be exercised upon a refractory People.

We consider our connection with & dependence upon Great Britain as the surest basis of lasting peace, and prosperity to this Province. We think it our indispensable duty to contribute our utmost exertions to perpetuate, as well as our highest felicity to enjoy its blessings; and most ardently wish it may be established, under the

happy auspices of your Majesty and your illustrious family, to the latest Posterity.
In the name of and on behalf of the Council
                                    Thomas Oliver, President

Along with a reverence thought appropriate and duly obsequious for an address to the Throne, the Council set forth a position familiar to and much relied upon by the Tories. It was that Provincials, naive and uninformed, had been seduced into rebellious and democratic ways by "evil men," the leaders of the Whigs such as James Otis, Samuel Adams, and quite probably included also, John Adams. The Council went on to shrug off the edicts of the Continental Congress, the abuse with which its members had been charged, and the dangers and evils which they had suffered. There was no doubt that allegiance to and dependence upon Great Britain was, in the Council's mind, "the surest basis of lasting peace, and prosperity" for the Province of Massachusetts Bay. The address clearly and unequivocally marked the gulf between Tory and Whig.

Along with the Council's address to the King, General Gage forwarded to Lord Dartmouth a list of Council members, as required by the Colonial Secretary, and also the names of some twenty other individuals. Appended to the lists of Councilors and others was a note. It read: "The foregoing Persons, both Counsellors and others have suffered exceedingly in their property, for their attachment to government, by a Resolve of the Provincial Congress, and a total stop to all kinds of business." Three days later Gage followed these official communications with a letter to Dartmouth marked "Private."

"I am sorry to acquaint Your Lordship," the general wrote in part, "that many of the Friends of Government and even several of the Council who have sought Protection in this Town, begin to feel distress, the money they brought with them being expended, and the Rebels preventing their receiving any profits from their estates." Ray Thomas may have been one who was in that predicament, although Ebenezer Storer would have done all he could to help out. Gage went on to elaborate. "Some of the most respectable of the Council have applyed to me for assistance; we have no publick money, nor could I dispose of it in that channel if we had."

In his capacity as head of the civil government, Gage did what he could. "...I have been obliged to divide with them the little cash remaining of my

War

own. We shall all soon be in the same situation, till cash is sent to us by our Agents, for by a Decree of the Congress no officer's Bill is to be taken, and there is not a merchant, even in New York, who now dares to send us money for our draughts..."

Even before the Colonial secretary could have received that "Private" message from Gage, Dartmouth had written to the governor. His Lordship, known for looking sympathetically on the American position, expressed his concern that, if the British were forced to abandon Boston, "the Officers and friends of Government be not left exposed to the rage and insults of Rebels who set no bounds to their barbarity." As for members of the Council, Lord Dartmouth relayed the information that "His Majesty is graciously pleased, upon a representation made to him of the distress to which the Members of your present Council are exposed, to direct that you do, from time to time, give them such relief and make them such allowance as you shall judge necessary, and include the expence in your Contingent Accounts." Unfortunately the Secretary's letter would have reached Gage only shortly before the general, recalled by the home authorities, sailed for England on October 10th.

Glimpses of the sort of business transacted by and brought by Council, much of it routine in nature, some of it out of the ordinary, survive in contemporary records. There were individual efforts of Council members, also, as when Ray Thomas placed men on Long Island in a frustrated attempt to cut and take off hay. As might have been expected, committees of the Council had been established to deal with various aspects of its business. Ray served on one of these, at least, for on September 25, 1775 he, John Erving, Jr. and Colonel Nathaniel Hatch signed, as such a committee, a fishing pass directed to the "Commanding officer of the Main Guard," permitting William Collfleet and two other men to pass the guard - probably that on Boston Neck. A more unusual, and doubtless considered quite serious, matter came to the attention of the governor on October 4th. It was "a Theft...committed on the Province," in Gage's word: removal from the Council Chamber of the official seals of the Province. The governor referred the matter to the Council on the 6th.

On the 9th the Council met and appointed a committee composed of His Honor the Lieutenant Governor, the Chief Justice, the Treasurer, Judge Browne, and Mr. Lechmere to wait on Governor Gage with their answer. Despite a strict inquiry and examination under oath of all persons having

War

had access to the Council Chamber during the preceding month, no trace was discovered concerning the "Publick Seals."

General Gage acknowledged his recall on September 30th. Between then and October 10th, the day of his departure, the general received addresses from the Gentlemen and Principal Inhabitants of Boston, The Members of his Majesty's Council, and The Gentlemen who were driven from their Habitations in the Country. At Boston, on October 6th, Nathaniel Ray Thomas addressed "His Excellency General Gage:"

> "May it please Your Excellency, as His Majesty in his great wisdom has thought proper, for the present, to recall Your Excellency from the command of this province to receive the reward of a good and faithful servant, suffer me, for myself and for and in the name of my good and loyal town of Marshfield, to return Your Excellency most sincere and hearty thanks for Your Excellency's seasonable care and protection of that most loyal town; which through a ten year's political struggle and warfare never deviated from but has uniformly and invariably preserved and maintained its integrity and loyalty..."

Marshfield was very much on Ray's mind, rather more than his own situation. He went on to extol the town:

> "a town, the only one in New England, that in spite of the threats and intimidations of surrounding towns, counties and provinces has dared publicly and collectively to own and acknowledge their allegiance and the supremacy of the British legislature; a town, whose principal inhabitants were so firmly fixed and established in their principles of loyalty and in support of Government, that when there was a necessity of recalling the troops from that town and they were no longer able to support themselves against their enraged and infatuated countrymen, rather than ever tacitly submit to or countenance their rebellious measure and proceedings, readily quitted their farms, habitations and estates in the country to place themselves under Your Excellency's protection..."

The Marshfield Loyalists, Ray assured Gage,

> "have since done everything in their power, when called upon or employed, to promote His Majesty's service, as

War

> Your Excellency may observe by the enclosed list which I assure Your Excellency would been much greater had not the friends of Government been prevented from coming here by their rebellious countrymen. Some of the Loyalists are imprisoned, others laid under heavy bonds, and every species of artifice, insult and abuse that enthusiastic rage and malice can invent or exert are made use of to intimidate, divert and warp them from their duty to the best of kings and his government - amongst whom are a great many loyal inhabitants of the town of Scituate, who by these means have been prevented from more explicitly exhibiting their loyalty and firm attachment to Government, a list of a few that have been thus imprisoned, insulted and abused I beg leave to subjoin."

The communication to General Gage was docketed: "Mr. Thomas, Councillor of Massachusetts Bay, on the subject of the loyal inhabitants of Marshfield." This was evidenced by Ray's concluding paragraph in which he stated that, being one of His Majesty's Council, he submitted the plight of Marshfield Loyalists to the general with the request that Gage

> "would fully and strenuously represent them to our most gracious Sovereign, that these staunch friends of Government may in due season receive a just reward and recompense for the many hardships, difficulties, troubles and losses that they have suffered and endured, in being thus driven and separated from their friends, families and estates."

Immediately after General Gage departed for England on October 10th, Thomas Oliver, the lieutenant governor and president of the Council, waited on General Howe and Admiral Graves. Oliver assured them of his readiness to do all in his power "to promote the good of His Majesty's service," and offering his assistance, "and that of the Council, in any thing that might in the least degree contribute thereto." On the 25th, at the Council Chamber, Oliver appeared before Council and took the oaths required of his office, subscribed the Test, and swore that "he would faithfully perform the duties of Lieutenant Governor & Commander in Chief of the Province, according to his best skill and judgment." A majority of the Council, including Ray Thomas, were present for the ceremony.

War

Immediately after Oliver's swearing in and at the same meeting of Council, that Board took under consideration a message from the lieutenant governor. Oliver stated that Major General Howe, now the commander in chief of British forces in America, proposed to issue a proclamation recommending "an Association for the preservation of internal Order and good Government." This would "give an opportunity to the loyal subjects under his protection, to distinguish themselves from those who are disaffected to the King's Government, and at the same time to establish a Military Watch or Patrols for the better maintaining the Police and internal security of the Town." As an inducement to serve under such an arrangement, Howe offered such of the inhabitants as were healthy and strong, despite the scarcity of food and fuel, an allowance to those needing it of fuel and provisions "equal to what is issued to His Majesty's troops within the Garrison." The opinion and advice of the Council was that the lieutenant governor recommend to General Howe such persons to regulate the Association "that peace and good order & the safety of His Majesty's Loyal Subjects may be secured & established."

Later that October there came before Council the problem of stopping the spread of smallpox, which had broken out in several parts of the town. General Howe thought it should be stopped "for the benefit of the service, which induced Council to order that Richard Lechmere, John Erving and Nathaniel Hatch Esqrs be a Committee to prepare a Hospital to receive the several infected persons, and to take proper steps for their removal thereto." This seems to have been the last recorded official act of Council.

As Ray Thomas and his son Nat in Boston were beginning to feel the effects of dwindling supplies of food and other provisions and of fuel, Sarah Thomas in Marshfield was herself having a difficult time that fall. With her husband and two eldest sons absent, the responsibility for her younger children and for her ailing sister Mary Gooch was hers alone. Fortunately, her oldest daughter, named for her mother Sarah Dering Thomas, was thirteen years old and of welcome assistance with younger children ranging downward in age from eleven to three. She was thus able to tend Mrs. Gooch from time to time.

On October 14th Sarah Thomas wrote her brother Thomas, with news of their family and also of her own. Their sister Elizabeth Wentworth had been comfortably situated with Governor and Mrs. Wentworth, her daughter and son-in-law, at Portsmouth, Sarah noted, until a short while before, when, because of Whig protests the governor had moved the family to Boston. The word, Sarah had, was that both the Wentworth and Perkins families intended to sail for England. Of her own family Sarah reported that Nat was in Boston and Henry Dering, she believed, was in England. He had sailed from Portsmouth in a "Mast Ship in order to se if he should like to follow the Sea...but it is now three years and he has not returned yet, so you se how unhappily I am seperrated from one and another of my famely, who how ever dissagreeable to others must be very near and Dear to me..." She continued in that vein. "...but I forbare, tho I would hope should I inlarge it might not be so dissagreeable to your ears to hear the name of some of those who ought to be near to me, so detestable as they are to some of my near relations." In the growing passions of the moment, Sarah Thomas was well aware that some of her relations thought ill of Ray and his outspoken Loyalist view.

Not only did family concerns weigh on Sarah's mind. She had no communication at all with Boston, and so no word of Ray and Nat. "I have so many attentions indoores and out that I can Scarcely sit a moment without some interuption and Farming Business being till of late quite out of my Province, I am some times grately perplext, but I have reson to Bless a kinde Providence who has protected & provided for me all nesesarys for the Coming winter, and I humbly hope will carry me safe thro it...I cannot but have my Glumey hours when I have so unpleasing a prospect before me..."

In the past year since Ray's departure from Marshfield, Sarah had had to take over responsibility for the farm. That alone, if there had been nothing else to concern her, would have been a sobering task. For what Ray called his "Patrimony" was a farm of more than one thousand acres, some eight hundred acres of which were of arable land and woodland and three or four hundred acres of marsh and wetland. Upon Ray's departure there were some seventy or eighty head of cattle and numbers of sheep and swine. The livestock had to be fed and fattened for market. There were crops - corn and grains - to be planted, tilled and harvested. There was hay to be cut from the upland meadows and salt marshes, which annually amounted to some three hundred tons of hay, and this had to be stacked or stored in the two large barns on the farm. There were, of course hands to help with the farm work, but as time went on and tensions grew, even this assistance for Sarah became more and more difficult to obtain and to count on. Still Sarah had assured her brother that she had "all nesesarys for the Coming winter..."

War

The winter of 1775-1776 promised continuing hardship for the people of Boston, Tories and Whigs alike. In October 1775 Lieutenant Governor Oliver, in presenting to Council General Howe's proposal for an Association for preserving order and "good Government," had noted "the present scarcity of provisions and fuel" among "many loyal good subjects here." Early in July it was reported that there were about sixty-five hundred civilians left in Boston, two-thirds of whom were believed to be Whigs. By January 1776, when Lieutenant Governor Oliver described to Lord Dartmouth "the state of this Town" Boston, he estimated that the population was reduced to about thirty-five hundred of which one thousand were males. Of the latter number, Oliver had no doubt but that five hundred were "truly loyal subjects, and such as have exhibited the strongest proofs of their attachment to government." Altogether, with women and children, he guessed that about two thousand constituted "the Loyal and their connections." During the blockade of Boston, he added, "these people have generally subsisted themselves by their own means & industry. The difficulties they have undergone have been great and pressing."

The possibility of an evacuation of Boston by the British by now seemed real. For the loyalists trapped in that town loomed the problem, the disquieting question, of what would happen to them if Boston were abandoned. Would they be abandoned with it? In his communication to Lord Dartmouth, Lieutenant Governor Oliver recognized the reality of possible evacuation. If Boston were to be maintained as a military post or at least as the site of a garrison, the lieutenant governor noted, then certain steps regarding civil government might seem to be in order. "But if this Place should be abandoned & the army remove to any other part of the Continent," Oliver queried, "I beg leave to be directed how I shall dispose of the Council and other Civil Officers. To carry them with the army would perhaps be a clog to the Service: to leave them behind, would be to expose many of them to destruction." Oliver elaborated: "There are I suppose sixty or seventy Persons, with their families, who could never make their peace with the Rebels, and who would be unable to subsist themselves by any means when deprived of their Property."

That the British, in fact, were contemplating evacuation was true. The ministry had given General Howe permission to leave; it was sending ships to Boston to provide transport for both Howe's army and the Loyalists.

War

The Whigs of Boston, those too indifferent or too poor to have gotten out before the siege or those fewer in number of a respectable class who chose to stay for whatever reason, also suffered. John Andrews, the Boston merchant and close observer of that town's events, in a later account pictured the life of a Whig in moderately good circumstances. One can only surmise what the less fortunate had to endure:

> I am well in health, thank God [Andrews recounted], and have been so the whole of the time, but have liv'd at the rate of six or seven hundred sterling a year - for I was determin'd to eat fresh provissions, while it was to be got, let it cost what it would; that since October [1775] I have eat three meals of salt meat, but supply'd my family with fresh at the rate of one shilling and sixpence sterling the pound. What wood was to be got, was oblig'd to give at the rate of twenty dollars a cord, and coals, though government had a plenty, I could not procure (not being an addressor or an associator) though I offer'd so high as fifty dollars for a chaldron, and that a season, when Nabby and John, the only help I had, were under inoculation for the small pox, that if you'll believe, Bill, I was necessitated to burn horse dung. Many were the instances of the inhabitants being confin'd to the Provost for purchasing fuel of the Soldiers, when no other means offer'd to keep them from perishing with cold - Yet such was the inhumanity of our masters, that they were even deny'd the privilege of buying the surplusage of the soldier's rations. Though you may think we had plenty of cheese and porter, yet we oblig'd to give from fifteen pence to two shillings a pound for all we eat of the former, and a loaf of bread of the size we formerly gave three pence for, thought ourselves well off to get for a shilling. Butter at two shillings. Milk, for months without tasting any. Potatoes, from nine shillings to ten shillings sixpence [a] bushel, and every thing else in the same strain. Notwithstanding which, Bill, I can safely say that I never suffer'd the least depression of spirits, other than on account of not having heard from Ruthy [his wife], in one season, for near five months - for a perswasion, that my country would eventually prevail, kept up spirits, and never suffer'd my hopes to fail.

Scarcity of provisions and fuel was serious enough; inflated prices compounded the problem.

War

With the coming of George Washington as commander-in-chief of the American army besieging Boston, that army was reorganized by his order of July 22, 1775. Earlier, immediately after the news of Lexington and Concord, John Thomas had hurried from Kingston to the camps of the besiegers of Boston. Already commissioned a general in the Massachusetts forces by the Provincial Congress, Thomas took command of the troops at Roxbury that made up the right wing of the army. By Washington's order of July 22nd, General Thomas, commissioned by the Continental Congress as a brigadier general of the Continental Line, remained at Roxbury immediately subordinate to Major General Artemas Ward.

Prior to General Washington's arrival in Cambridge, Massachusetts, to take command of the American Army, Congress was endeavoring to issue commissions for the other general officers. When it came to the commission of brigadier generals, it failed to name General John Thomas as senior brigadier to which position he was entitled. Men that previously he commanded now outranked him. General Thomas was miffed and promptly threatened to resign from the service. Letters poured in, pleading with him to reconsider his decision. George Washington himself added his view to the outcry. To Congress he wrote:

> "General Thomas is much esteemed and most earnestly desired to continue in the service and as far as my opportunities have enabled me to judge, I must join the general opinion that he is an able, good officer, and his resignation would be a public loss."

But it was a personal letter from Washington that induced General Thomas to reconsider his decision. A new commission was issued to him making him the senior ranking brigadier of the army. Subsequently, he was appointed Major General to take command in Canada.

Immediately after his first commission as brigadier general, General Thomas was ordered by the Committee of Safety to seize the papers of Thomas Hutchinson, late Royal governor of the province of Massachusetts Bay. This he had proceeded to do with dispatch.

Early in September Washington, impatient to attack the British in Boston, proposed a plan to his generals, requesting their opinion whether it was possible "to make a successful attack upon the Troops in Boston, by means of Boats, co-operated by an attempt upon their lines

War

at Roxbury." There were reasonable grounds for such an attempt: the approach of winter, the attrition of the army, the increasing scarcity of powder. But the generals unanimously advised Washington that "it was not expedient to make the attempt at present," at least. Under the circumstances, considering the strength of the British position, this was prudent. Again in October the Commander-in-chief laid his plan before a council of war of his generals. All opposed it once more, some conditionally, most, including John Thomas, "at present." And then in January 1776, for a third time but then most forcefully, Washington emphasized "the indispensible neccessiaty of making a Bold attempt to Conquer the Ministerial Troops in Boston, before they can be reinforced in the spring." Once again the council of war was opposed.

Washington was, despite delay, active in planning for an attack on the British. One of his imperative needs was that of large cannon, sufficient to defend against British attack on the one hand and powerful enough to bombard his enemy on the other, particularly to screen his own activities. There were such ordnance at Ticonderoga in New York. To get these, hopefully across the winter snow on sledges, Washington picked Henry Knox, shortly to be named colonel of artillery. Knox succeeded in his grueling task.

Washington was at last ready for a move against the British. What the Commander-in-chief now contemplated was not a new concept. Both sides had early recognized the strategic importance of Dorchester Heights, which projected out toward Boston from the Roxbury lines. From the Heights artillery could command the British fleet, the Castle, and could enfilade the British lines on Boston Neck. Based upon a realization of this, a suggestion was made to General Gage to seize the Heights, which, on the fateful day of Lexington and Concord, he rejected. A few weeks later, on the rumor of a proposed attack by the British, General John Thomas at Roxbury marched his men round and round their hill camp to give the illusion of a force much larger than he actually had. There was little more he could do than that to forestall the British, without more troops and artillery. There were other supposed threats by the British to take Dorchester even up to the battle of Bunker Hill, but nothing transpired.

At this juncture, General John Thomas, commanding that wing of the American army about to fortify Dorchester Heights, had his headquarters in a house which still stands in Roxbury. It is known today as the Dillaway-Thomas House and has been restored.

War

General Thomas's young son John, aged 10, ran away from his servant Oakley in Roxbury. His father informed his wife: "Your son John is well and in high spirits. He ran away from Oakley privately; on Tuesday morning got by the sentries and came to me on Dorchester Hills, where he has been most of the time since."

In June, shortly before Washington assumed command, there had been plans by the Americans to take Dorchester but these were abandoned when their enemies looked at Charlestown. Now in February, 1776 the commanding general broached a plan to take and fortify Dorchester Heights. His generals agreed. Yet that effort had to be accomplished quickly in one night's time, and how to do it posed a real problem with ground frozen hard. An engineer officer came up with a solution. Rather than attempt to dig and throw up the earthworks, he suggested, prepare breastworks made up of bundles of sticks held in place by frames to be placed on top of the frozen ground.

The night of March 4th was selected for the maneuver, appropriate because the next day was the anniversary of the Boston Massacre, a date calculated to animate every soldier to fight hard. To carry out Washington's overall concept, he placed Artemas Ward in immediate command and left the execution of the attempt to General John Thomas. The Roxbury forces were reinforced by militia from the surrounding towns; large numbers of carts, teamsters, entrenching tools and quantities of marsh hay were gathered for the night's work. On the three nights preceding the actual move on the Heights cannonading from the heavy artillery was designed to screen the actual activities of the Americans. The British returned the fire, and the noise that resulted - Abigail Adams in Braintree called it "of the true species of the sublime" - muffled all sounds from Dorchester. The night was mild and clear, with a bright moon.

Ahead of the main body of soldiers went a covering party to watch the town for any British action. Then came the working party under General Thomas, twelve hundred men strong, followed by three hundred and sixty ox teams. According to General Thomas, he began his march to the Heights about seven o'clock in the evening leading some three thousand picked men including teamsters, artillerymen, and five companies of riflemen. All the men knew their duties, those raising the breastworks, those laboriously digging and shoveling earth to strengthen them, those felling trees to place in the way of advancing foot soldiers.

War

John Thomas pushed his men so hard, that by ten o'clock in the evening when the General pulled out his watch, they had built two forts strong enough to withstand fire from small arms and grapeshot from cannon. At three o'clock in the morning three thousand fresh men relieved those working on the fortifications and manning the works.

At daylight on the fifth of March, civilians and soldiers alike in Boston viewed with complete surprise the works of the Americans on Dorchester Heights. General Howe was reported to have said, "The rebels have done more in one night, than my whole army could have done in months." And it was evident the forts could command with their fire the shipping in the harbor and at the wharves and, most significantly, the town of Boston itself. There was now no alternative for Howe but to dislodge the Americans or abandon Boston.

The British commander ordered preparations for an assault on Dorchester Heights. Troops were gathered, but no attack was set in motion. On the Heights General Washington had arrived to inspect the defenses erected so expeditiously during the preceding night. Generals Ward and Thomas joined him. All were waiting. By evening it seemed certain that Howe would not attack that day. The British were planning a move under cover of darkness and with a favorable tide. But then a fierce storm arose. In the morning Howe issued orders that "the intended expedition of last Night was unavoidably put off by the badness of the Weather." In actuality, because his council of war had advised the evacuation of Boston, General Howe had used the storm as an excuse to call off the attack and to reconsider his next move. In fact, he personally seems to have favored an evacuation but felt that an attack would preserve his honor and that of the army.

Howe's decision to embark - taken in stride by his soldiers who, from general officers down to privates, were impressed into salvaging all that they could of arms, ordnance, and stores of every description - came as a devastating blow to the Loyalists. So long as Crown troops patrolled the streets and manned the fortifications, the Loyalists felt some sense of security. Now that world was about to crumble around them. With the immediacy of departure very real, time was crucial. What and how much could these harried people take with them? In what places, in what ships could they be assured of berths? Preparations for the evacuation began on the morning of March 6th.

War

Several days later, on March 10th, Lieutenant Governor Thomas Oliver sent one of his last communications from Boston to the Colonial Secretary, the Earl of Dartmouth. "...I am now preparing to embark for Halifax," Oliver informed Dartmouth, "with the Council, and such of the inhabitants as dare not trust themselves to the violence of the People...General has been so kind as to provide us ships, but as our removal is sudden and the means of transportation rather confined, we are obliged to content ourselves with taking only such necessaries as will barely suffice for the passage. The remainder of our effects we must leave behind..."

There was enough shipping to have transported army stores, Loyalist household goods, and much merchandise as well. But there was not time. Lieutenant John Barker of the 4th Regiment, the King's Own, who had reported the move of Balfour's troops to Marshfield over a year before, described the scene now in Boston as "nothing but hurry and confusion." One of that town's Selectmen, a Whig, reported exactly the same. "The town all hurry and commotion," he observed. But the Loyalists saved but little. It was said that pieces of mahogany furniture were found floating near the docks or washed up on nearby beaches.

A month later from Halifax, Nova Scotia, Lieutenant Governor Oliver informed the Colonial Secretary, Lord George Germain: "The Honble Major General Howe having determined on the 6th of March to evacuate the Town of Boston, made me acquainted with his intentions, & desired I would with the greatest expedition prepare the Council and such of the Inhabitants as choose to leave the Town, for embarking with the Army. Accordingly the short time allowed for that purpose was employed in making the necessary preparations; and on the Tenth of March...we embarked on board five transports allotted for that purpose. The very hasty manner of our embarkation, as well as the crowded condition of the ships, prevented our taking with us any thing more than our private Papers, Plate, and Sea Stores."

It was a tumultuous and emotional time for the saddened, bewildered, occasionally embittered, sometime stubbornly courageous Massachusetts Tories. They came from all classes of society: the colonial officialdom, the wealthy and propertied, the better educated; the supporters of taste and culture; the small merchants; the farmers; the artisans; the "middling" and the "meaner" sort. More than half of the living graduates of Harvard College and much of the old aristocracy, as it was viewed, left on the evacuation - never to return. And with them

War

went wives and children, and other dependents, a pitiful but loyal group, at last unable to do anything else. One observer noted, "The Torys that went with the enemy Carry'd death in their Faces..." One evacuee graphically pictured the scene on the crowded vessels: "Men, women, and children; parents, masters, and mistresses, obliged to pig together on the floor, there being no berths."

Of the some eleven hundred Loyalist refugees who sought protection with Howe's departing troops and hopefully deliverance in some distant haven, eighty-five comprised the lieutenant governor and members of the Council and their families. Ray Thomas and his son Nat were among them, sailing in a schooner that belonged to Ray. Because it had been commandeered, they left behind property that included household furniture, such merchandise as 1200 bushels of salt and 3 tons of iron, and a "Coasting Sloop" of about 80 tons burthen. Poignantly, however, they left behind relations and friends, such as Ebenezer Storer and his family who had steadfastly remained close, and, of course, most dear of all, Sarah Thomas and the younger children in Marshfield.

By the morning of the 17th of March, Saint Patrick's Day, General Howe embarked his remaining troops and the last of the British quitted Boston. The ships carrying the Loyalists were already down the harbor, ready for the convoy to form and put out to sea. Their passengers must have crowded the rails in an effort to catch a last wistful look at the shores of their native land. It was a fine day, with a fair breeze. The sails of Howe's fleet, white dots filled out in that breeze, marked the more than one hundred ships leaving Nantasket Roads.

On Dorchester Heights, now but a rise on the horizon, were the troops of General Thomas's command, those who had done such good work on the night of March 4th. The General himself was still there, and had been, in fact, constantly since that night. Of soldierly deportment, John Thomas was reserved by nature, not given to thoughts that strayed too far from the matter at hand. But it would have been only human if he viewed with satisfaction the scene before him. Departing with the enemy fleet was his wife's first cousin, his one-time boyhood friend - Nathaniel Ray Thomas whose pronounced Tory sentiments would carry him to a destiny apart. The irony of it all could not have been lost on John Thomas.

X

Years of Separation

General John Thomas watched the last of the British ships, hull down on the horizon, disappear from sight. But Sarah Thomas in Marshfield would not know of the fate of Ray and Nat for several days. Then, from Boston, word came of the departure of Howe's army and of the Loyalists. With relief at the prospect of her husband and son free of the confines of the siege, came Sarah's concern at their ultimate destination.

On March 29th Howe and his ships put in to Halifax, "a cursed, cold wintry place, even yet," as one of his officers found the provincial capital. Mercy Otis Warren, articulate and highly partisan Whig observer of the Revolutionary scene, commented on the evacuation of the Tories and their arrival in Halifax. To the wife of the President of the Continental Congress she wrote: "Your compassionate heart heaves a sigh of pity for the miserable group indiscriminately hurried on shipboard to escape the just resentment of their affronted, injured country. Do you think there was ever a more sudden reverse of hopes and expectations than these poor creatures suffer?" To John Adams at the Congress, she described their condition in Halifax as "a panic struck multitude, huddled into fishing boats, or Royal barks, unhappy wretches lately transported from Boston..." In both letters Mercy Warren, hinting at commiseration and compassion for the Tories and their plight, nevertheless depicted them as usual objects of contempt.

During his stay in Boston, Ray had started assisting Colonel Samuel Cleaveland in the ordnance department of the British Army. After finding modest accommodations for himself and Nat in Halifax, Ray continued his service with Colonel Cleaveland. But this was of short duration, for early in June General Howe began to ship out his troops to New York. With them went Ray and Nat, among other civilians providing aid to the British forces. When Sarah learned of the shift to New York, she could well have surmised that her husband and son had accompanied the army. Certainly word would have reached her, in the public press at least, of the British troops' impending arrival. Once in New York Ray Thomas kept on with his efforts for Cleaveland's ordnance department.

Years of Separation

In Massachusetts, with the departure of the British, the Whigs, controlling the situation, were ever more vociferous in their views and demands. On June 19, 1776, as Howe's army was on its way to New York, a town meeting was held at the First Church, or the South Meeting House as it was generally known in Marshfield. At that meeting those present voted a set of instructions to be sent to Nehemiah Thomas, Esq., the town's representative to the General Court then sitting at Watertown. Those instructions were couched in strong language. They were prefaced: "Your constituents not doubting of your patriotism, now in legal town meeting assembled, think it necessary to instruct you touching the Independence of America."

> To the amazement of your constituents, the King of Great Britain is become a tyrant. He has wantonly destroyed the property of the Americans, and wickedly spilled their blood. He has assented to Acts of Parliament, calculated to subjugate the Colonies unparalleled by the worst of tyrants. Our petitions he has rejected, and instead of Peace he has sent the sword. Every barbarous nation whom he could influence he has courted for the destruction of the colonies.
>
> Once we would have expended life & fortune in defence of his crown and dignity, but now we are alienated, and conscience forbids us to support a tyrant whose tyranny is without refinement.
>
> Alliance with him is now almost Treason to our country, but we wait patiently till Congress, in whose counsels we confide, shall declare those colonies Independent of Great Britain. The inhabitants of this town, therefore, unanimously instruct & direct you that if the Continental Congress should think it necessary for the safety of these United Colonies to declare them Independent of Great Britain, that the inhabitants of this town, with their lives & fortune, will most heartily support them in the measure.

Along with this strong show of support for independence, the town concerned itself with other pressing matters relating to the inception of hostilities. Already in 1775 the townspeople had voted to keep a guard on the town's seashore, which the following year comprised six men to be paid according to agreement. The Committee of Correspondence, Inspection and Safety was likewise that year enlarged in membership. For those who had borrowed powder, balls and flints from the town's stock, it was ordered that payment be made. More ammunition was

Years of Separation

purchased. Upon adoption of the Declaration of Independence in July 1776 and upon order of the General Court, a copy of the Declaration was sent to all ministers and directed to be read to their congregations after "Divine Service...in the aftenoon on the Lord's day..."

Before the Declaration and earlier in 1776, there appeared in a Philadelphia newspaper an epic poem said to be perhaps the most popular such effort in eighteenth-century America. This was <u>M'Fingal: A Modern Epic Poem</u> written by the poet John Trumbull. The poem's setting is a town meeting somewhere outside of Boston. Protagonists, one representing the Whig's side of the political crisis with Britain and the other, M'Fingal, the Tory position, oppose each other in debate. It is a sprightly piece, virtually a burlesque, with whimsical and often satirical asides on persons and events.

As in Mercy Warren's <u>The Group</u>, members of the Massachusetts Mandamus Council and other governmental figures come in for their share of ridicule and caricature. In a long diatribe by Honorius, the Whig, thought by some to represent John Adams, appear the following lines:

Did heav'n appoint our chief judge, Oliver
Fill that high bench with ignoramus,
Or has it councils by mandamus?
Who made that wit of water-gruel,
A judge of admiralty, Sewall?
And were they not mere earthly struggles,
That rais'd up Murray, say, and Ruggles.
Did Heav'n send down, our pains to medicine,
That old simplicity of Edson,
Or by election pick out from us,
That Marshfield blund'rer, Nat. Ray Thomas;
Or had it any hand in serving
A Loring, Pepp'rell, Browne, or Erving?

Later in <u>M'Fingal</u>, Abijah White, Marshfield's representative to the General Court in 1774, shares in the satire:

Or as Abijah White, when sent
Our Marshfield friends to represent,
Himself while dread array involves,
Commissions, pistols, swords, resolves,
In awful pomp descending down,

Years of Separation

Bore terror on the factious town.

A footnote explains about Abijah White: "He was a representative of Marshfield, and employed to carry their famous town resolves to Boston. He armed himself in as ridiculous military array, as another Hudibras, pretending he was afraid he should be robbed of them."

Early in 1777 the Selectmen and Committee of Correspondence of Marshfield, according to an act of the General Court "to prevent monopoly and oppression" with respect to prices of enumerated commodities and services, set prices for farm produce and work, clothing, cider and tobacco, and numerous other items, and provided fines for overpricing of goods and services. Colonel Anthony Thomas and Captain Thomas Waterman were members of a committee to raise money for a bounty "as an encouragement to the soldiers to enlist into the service of the Continental Army."

On the 8th of August 1777 Sarah Thomas wrote to her nephew Sylvester Dering, to whom it was obvious she was becoming increasingly attached. She wrote to him in Middletown, Connecticut, to which place the Derings had removed from the New York area because of the British occupation. Young Sylvester and his sister Betsy had visited in Boston that summer, and when he returned to Middletown Betsy and Charles Storer, Ebenezer's son, journeyed to Marshfield to pay a visit to Sarah and her children. Charles, who was courting Betsy (or Sarah at least reported so to Sylvester), evidently enjoyed himself thoroughly. Sarah informed her nephew: "I must not inlarge for I have yet to write your Papa, and Charles goes by Brake of Day tomorrow, besides he and the Girls Keep such a clacking I hardly know what I write."

Sarah did add a request relating to farm business. "If you Should git Horses or any stock that you can conveniently transport to me I shall esteam it as a grate pleasure to let them run upon the Farm and will take all the care in my power, of them till you shall call for them again or have an oppertunity to dispose of them to your mind." It may well have been that Sarah, having sold off her own stock, wanted animals to graze her pastures and keep the grass down till she could get some of her own. And she expressed the hope that Sylvester would visit her and the children often: "as every visit more and more indears you to me I shall ever be wishing to se you."

Years of Separation

A month later Betsy Dering was still in Marshfield with her Aunt Thomas and her family. On September 20th Sarah Dering Thomas, Sally to her family and friends, Ray's and Sarah's eldest daughter, aged fifteen, wrote to Sylvester in Middletown. "...the occasion of my writeing to you," Sally told her cousin, "it is to ask the favor of you to get me two pair of white kid mittins and one pair of Gloves dont get them too Small my Cozn Betsys Gloves fit me for bigness but not in lenth I Should be Glad to have them longer then hers I should be obliged to you if you will not send but await till you favor us with a visit and then I will thank you to bring them." From what Sally next requested of Sylvester, it was apparent that the Derings in Middletown were intermediaries, as it were, in forwarding letters to and from Ray Thomas in New York for his family in Marshfield. "I have wrote to my Papa and I Shall take it as a perticular favor if you will forward it as soon as possible, and if he sends any thing to Middletown for my mama or me I will beg the favor of you to take care of it and forward it as soon as possable. I Shall depend upon you my Cozn as I have no other Friend that way to ask such a favor of."

Communication between Loyalists finding themselves in British-held territory and their families in countryside almost completely Whig-controlled posed continual uncertainty and often ended in failure. Five days after Sally had written her cousin, her mother wrote to Sylvester. She, too, was concerned about letters to and from Ray. "I am much obliged to you my dear for attending to my request and take it as a grate favoure that you would give your selfe the troble to write to your Uncle as I know it will give him grate pleasure to hear so direct from us I shall make grate dependance upon a letter throw your hands and hope not to be dissopointed." And Sarah sent to Sylvester a letter of her own to Ray. "I have inclosed you a Letter for your Uncle thinking you might have some such oppertunity I have wrote nothing that will doe either you or me any hurt shuld it be thought proper to be opened..."

Sarah felt keenly the separation from various members of her family. She repeatedly expressed her feeling. "I long much to se you," she wrote this time, "...and I shall evr think my selfe happy in doeing every thing in my power to make our retierment agreable to you. I pray you would leve your Business in such order as not to run home as you usaly doe but make us a good long visit." Betsy Dering was still at Marshfield and Sarah directed her next remarks to Sylvester about her niece. "I cannot consent that you should take your sister home with you if you come that is except you finde she cannot Content herself with us. then we must give up our Gratification to hers but we shall be quite

Years of Separation

Lonesome this winter without her. She has many admierers for two Gentalmen we heard of Last Evening which were smitten Last Sunday. I doe not know but that we Shall have a duel fought about her at last."

As for herself, Sarah acknowledged: "You will observe I recon my selfe amongst the young folks, but that is no matter, thay are obliged to have me amongst them some times for want of some body that is younger for such frolicks as the two Girls have some times is better for you to Conceive then for me to write." She expressed the wish that Sylvester might find someone to attract him that they might see more of him, but then such a pleasure might prevent them from seeing as much of him as they did then. In any event, Sarah wished her nephew enjoyment should he find a companion of his choice to marry.

Some two weeks after the American victory over General Burgoyne at Saratoga in October 1777, Sarah wrote again to Sylvester. "Had you not bin a Gentealman of so much Propriety and Polightness as not to omit one Tittell of Mr. Burgoins extensive Titell," she chided Sylvester whimsically, "which filled up the greatest part of your Letter, I suppose you would have mentioned your Sister in it...I shall not troble her with my scrible by this oppertunity so pray you to present my kinde Love to her and tell her I mis her much. I long to hear her musickel Voice, which ever put joye into all around her."

Sylvester's aunt Mrs. Gooch, Sarah informed him, was worse. "She has not one moments peace of her life..." Sarah then referred to her greatniece, Grizzell Apthorp, daughter of Sarah *Wentworth* Apthorp, who was then visiting her Apthorp relations in New York. "As you ware so kinde as to menshon my sending a message to Grizey I should be much obliged to you if she is not gon to tell her I should take it kinde of her if it be praticable to make it a point to desier Mr. Thomas or Nat to send a pound of opium by the same Vessell she goes in if it returns amedately or by the first that comes that it is likely it will come safe to your hands or Direct it to Mr. Storrer. I suppose it will not be much more expencive then an ounce would be hear, but that I doe not minde. For she takes it in such quantitees that an ounce is sune gone and if I could procure a quantitie it would at least ease her minde and I beleive her Body, and Wish to give her all the ease I can the short time she has to tarry in this worlde."

Returning to thoughts of Grizzell Apthorp, Sarah added: "Pray give my Love to Grizzey tell her I wish her a happy meating of her friends, to

Years of Separation

remember me to all my dear friends and let her Uncle Thomas know I begin to think he has allmost forgot me - it is so long since I heared a word about him or the Chilldren."

Not long before Christmas 1777 Sarah wrote again to Sylvester. Her nephew apparently had mistaken a remark in a recent letter of hers, thinking it reflected on him for not noticing her. What prompted that, probably, was the expression in her letter of early November of regret that Sylvester and his sister did not visit her on their recent trip to Boston, "your being so near." And that was followed by a seldom-expressed sense of self-pity in the reference to herself as "your poor old forsaken and almost forgoton Aunt." But in her letter of December 8th she had recovered her customary equanimity and reassured Sylvester that her remark, far from what he thought, referred to "the common Friendship of the World which you will say is not worth my notis."

Sarah then indulged in an early and one of the few emotional reactions she expressed about the attitude of those once seemingly friendly but with the advent of hostilities and the taking of sides, now estranged and scornful. Acknowledging that "the common Friendship of the World" might not be worth her notice, she observed that "Humain Nature cannot help some times reflecting when they se those who once Courted and Corest [caressed, in the sense of flattery or cajolery] there acquaintance, now neglect and despize them." But she reassured Sylvester once again that "I will endevouer to keep up my sperits overlook all these things and despise them [the attitudes of others] in my minde now and should Providence bless me with an oppertunity, with pleasure return good for evil."

Much of the character and personality of Sarah Thomas was revealed in her numerous letters to her family and friends. Her warm attachment to them, her love for those closest and dearest to her, her compassion and understanding, her careful reticence, her human and normal occasional outbursts of anger and distress, and withal, her flashes of simple and kind wit, still attest to the woman she was. It is not surprising that there survive personal tributes to Sarah from those who knew her. Her name was perpetuated in the family until the last "Sarah Dering" died in the 1900's.

In that same letter to Sylvester Dering, she gave him news of the family. There was the unfortunate news that Hepsibah Edwards was in deep melancholy over Mr. Edwards' serious illness and that his Aunt Gooch

Years of Separation

was so badly off that Sarah had to be up with her almost every night. Yet Mary Gooch, despairing of her life, was "led out every day into the parlour to dine." There was happier news. "The Children all, boath grate and small, desier to be rembered to you," their mother dutifully reported, "and Charles says I must write you he has got a Coat and wastecoat and can dress himself and I beleive never was one better pleased or thought themselves more of a man then he does at present." She added: "Mr. Winslows [Joshua Winslow's] famely is all well. he and his Daughter is just returned from Boston and Sally as usual went to se them two days ago and I have never sean her since. I hope she will not spend the winter."

When Sarah had written her brother Thomas Dering in October 1775, she mentioned that their sister Elizabeth Wentworth had been comfortably situated with Governor Wentworth and her daughter Frances but that he had moved the family from Portsmouth, New Hampshire, to Boston because of the Whig unrest. Further, there was word that the Wentworths might go to England. In January 1776 the governor sent Frances and her young son Charles-Mary to England and then or shortly thereafter Mrs. Elizabeth Wentworth sailed as well. Upon the evacuation of Boston in March, Governor Wentworth went to Halifax and in June, with General Howe and the army, to New York. In the spring of 1778, following the British defeat at Saratoga and after obtaining permission from the British government, he himself departed for London.

Preceding him to England were not only his wife and son and mother-in-law, Sarah Thomas's sister, but also Nathaniel Ray Thomas. In the late fall of 1777 Ray, his health deteriorating perhaps from his efforts to assist Cleaveland's ordnance department in New York, decided also to seek refuge in London. He sailed presumably in early or mid November, for on January 1, 1778 former Governor Thomas Hutchinson, welcomed him at his London residence on St. James's Street. "Mr. Thomas, one of the Massachusetts Council, arrived last night from N. York, last from Ireland, called on me," Hutchinson noted in his diary. Ray would have thought this an understandable visit, since the former governor was the leading figure among the Tory exiles then in England. Hutchinson also had had much to do with securing Ray's appointment to the Mandamus Council. But now the situation seemed bleak for British arms. In his diary entry the next day Hutchinson, referring to Ray's arrival, decried: "Affairs never looked so dark."

Years of Separation

Governor John Wentworth had distinguished friends in England. The Marquis of Rockingham, who had been Prime Minister at the time of repeal of the Stamp Act but was then out of office, was a distant relation of John's and some years earlier the two had become close friends. Another of the Wentworth blood, Paul Wentworth, had come from New Hampshire and was called by the governor, "my kinsman," although the exact relationship is not clear. In New Hampshire Paul Wentworth had been appointed a member of the Council in 1770 but had never been sworn in and he was also an important contributor to Dartmouth College, which later conferred a degree of LL.D. on him. He had an extensive estate in Surinam, but he spent most of his time in England and on the continent. Governor Wentworth referred to Paul Wentworth as his "dearest friend and Relative" as late as 1784.

It was not surprising, therefore, that John Wentworth, reunited with his wife, son, and mother-in-law, was invited to make his and his family's home with Paul Wentworth in the spring of 1778. A worldly man, possessed of considerable wealth and ever greedy for more, Paul Wentworth was adroit and experienced in the stock market, a manipulator, some said. He was also an agent of the British government, a master spy he has been called. He organized and directed an espionage network in Paris, a principal object of which was to undermine the American efforts in Paris to negotiate and carry out a treaty with the French government for military aid against Britain. He was not successful, despite much ingenious maneuvering.

Paul Wentworth lived at Brandenburgh or Hammersmith House at Hammersmith, some four miles outside of London. It was an elegant house, suitable for its occupant's luxurious way of living. To this delightful rendezvous, Paul Wentworth invited Elizabeth Wentworth, Sarah's sister; and the governor; Frances and little Charles-Mary, who bore the first names of the Marquis and Marchioness of Rockingham; and, as a close relation by marriage of the Wentworth coterie, Nathaniel Ray Thomas. Thus began a strange alliance between Governor Wentworth and Ray Thomas, and Paul Wentworth, which, commencing in trust, would end in disillusionment and financial disaster for Paul Wentworth and Ray Thomas.

Back at home in America, feelings about the Loyalists, or more commonly and disparagingly called the Tories by revolutionary Americans, had intensified with passage of the Coercive Acts by Parliament in 1774. Particularly offensive was the Act for better regulating the Government of the Province

Years of Separation

of the Massachusetts Bay in New England, which established the Mandamus Council. Those named in the Act were viewed with scorn and hostility. Every kind of persuasion, intimidation, abuse - both personal and threatened - was brought to bear to force them not to accept seats on the Council or, if they had accepted, to resign. Those who did accept were objects of particular vilification and harassment.

But Tory leaders and government officials were not the only individuals singled out on suspicion of being inimical to the colonial cause. Even before the outbreak of hostilities, committees of correspondence were active in scrutinizing local affairs. Such committees expanded to become committees of inspection, investigating and enforcing agencies for the Continental Association, and finally committees of safety with overall supervision of town and county activities. These committees, whatever their names, looked into, with great care, the political sentiments and sympathies of people suspected even on the slightest evidence or rumor of being "enemies."

In Marshfield, "that most loyal Town" as Ray Thomas had characterized it, many of those with pro-British sympathies were clearly known, and not in that town alone. Early in 1775 the Whig merchant John Andrews in Boston had described "a number of the inhabitants of Marshfield" as "under the influence of Ray Thomas, and the Winslow family, who are likewise remarkable high Tories..." When Ray sought refuge in Boston in 1774, almost two hundred loyal inhabitants of Marshfield followed him, according to contemporary sworn testimony. A list of Loyalists from Plymouth County contains the names of more than seventy from Marshfield, headed by Nathaniel Ray Thomas.

At the time of the evacuation of Boston, a vessel with twelve Marshfield Loyalists aboard, apparently intended to accompany Howe's fleet to Halifax. After "lurking about the Bay" from March 7th to May 2nd they put back into Marshfield. Local authorities arrested them and jailed them in Plymouth. They petitioned the General Court for their release, claiming that fear and their "timid Minds" caused their disloyal actions. The local committee of correspondence supported their petition, influencing the General Court to be lenient and to order them to be confined to their homes.

At a Marshfield town meeting the following year it was ordered that "a list of townsmen who had opposed the war and taken the part of tories" be published. In fact, the town took considerable pains to ferret out those

Years of Separation

suspected of being loyal to the Crown. Seven men were imprisoned in the jail at Plymouth for their "toryism" and released in October 1776 upon their paying the expenses of proceedings against them and upon condition that they would remain on their properties except for attending worship on the Sabbath. Others were seized and carted to the Liberty Pole and required to sign a recantation and statement of allegiance. Still others were proscribed and banished. One William James of Scituate, writing in 1777, noted: "we have Corts Very thick to try the torreys & condemning those that prove Enemies to the United States [in] Marshfield they Condemd one Who was a Hatch..."

Such was the attitude and treatment of those believed loyal to England. But immediately after the outbreak of hostilities at Lexington and Concord, many Tory women, at least, stayed on their husband's properties. On May 14, 1775 the Committee of Safety of the Provincial Congress had enacted a considerate measure: "...wives and children of such persons who shall choose to remain in Boston with General Gage, may and ought to be treated with humanity and tenderness in the Several Towns they may go to dwell in, during the present troubles, and by no means to suffer the least injury, or meet with the smallest mark of disrespect upon account of their husbands and fathers." This gesture was early in the war, of course, and severe restrictions were to follow. Initially, Sarah Thomas and her children at Marshfield were reasonably secure. There were difficulties quite naturally, but the course of their life was much as before. Family and personal news filled Sarah's letters.

But then in October 1778 the Massachusetts legislature, the General Court, enacted a measure of somber import. This was the Banishment Act, by the terms of which more than three hundred named individuals were proscribed and forever banished from Massachusetts, punishable for attempting to return by deportation for a first offense, by death for a second offense. Heading the list of those named were "certain notorious conspirators against the government and liberties" of Massachusetts, including former royal governors, members of the Mandamus Council, and other lesser officials. It must have seemed like a chilling indictment to Sarah Thomas. Ray would not be able to return to Massachusetts, but what then?

Early in March 1779 Sarah wrote to Sylvester Dering that she had received a letter from his "coz Nat," delivered by Mrs. Coffin. That lady had seen Nat in New York, reporting that he was very well and that she understood he kept a store. Sarah then noted she would have a good

Years of Separation

opportunity for writing, since Miss Sally Winslow of Plymouth planned to go with her father to Narragansett Bay in Rhode Island to see his son before the younger Edward went to England. Since both Winslows had held office under the Crown before the war (from which they had been removed) and were known for their Loyalist sentiment, the elder Winslow had had to petition for leave to make the trip. He had been born in Marshfield, the brother of General John Winslow and uncle of Dr. Isaac Winslow. Both father and son were close friends of Ray Thomas and his family.

Father and son, and Miss Sally, did meet under a flag of truce. It was an emotional, poignant meeting, described by Edward Winslow, Jr. in a letter. It was dramatic, all the more so because newspapers, of which the father had a copy, had reported his son as dead. Edward Winslow, Jr. described the scene: "There were present rebel officers and rebel soldiers, King's officers and King's soldiers, sailors of both denominations and negroes - not a heart among them that did not melt. All the formalities usual with flags were forgotten, every man turned from us, walked different ways, and were profoundly silent...The old man declared he was happy and when we parted he only shook his head and pronounced 'God bless my son.'" It was a war that separated families not only with opposing views but with also similar views, each situation in its way heart-rending.

Five years later, in 1784, Edward Winslow Sr. died in Halifax, Nova Scotia where he had gone after joining the British forces in New York. He was a gentleman of fine presence and his funeral was attended by many dignitaries of the Province.

His son Edward Jr. carried the Royal Coat of Arms of Britain from the Council Chamber in Boston to Halifax, Nova Scotia upon the evacuation of Boston. Later he returned to New York where he was appointed Muster-Master-General of the British forces with the rank of Lieutenant Colonel. At the close of the war, he was made Military Secretary to the Commander-in-chief of British forces in Nova Scotia. Later he was appointed a judge of the Supreme Court of New Brunswick. He died in 1815. He was "a good son, an affectionate Husband and Father and a True Friend."

Sarah continued her letter to Sylvester with the news that Joshua Winslow, "our Friend," is going to Boston to bring "Coz Anna home I suppose to pack up for a removall. I am grieved to think she is going

Years of Separation

...what shall we have to grace Marshfield when you come again..." Sarah was further concerned about what she saw around her. "O the dayly mortifications i meat with, but all is for the best I hope. how littell are those things when compaired to many others who are pinched for want of Bread the [decay?] is grate around us, trobles on every side no one is exemt." For herself she wrote, "amongst my grate trobles I recon Mr. Ws going, who is indead a grate friend to me whenever I want assistance or advice which way to turne."

As for difficulties, Sarah added: "but what can we say, it is the fortune of War. May God in his providence hasten the time We shall again have peace in our once happy land and the P[e]ople which are imployd in destorying one another spend there time in Cultivating the ground that these poor unhappy famelys may have bread to eat..." This may well have been the period during the war described as the "direful `dearth of bread'" when Sarah fed those same people from whom she had suffered many indignities at the height of party feeling.

Sometime during the last two weeks of May or the first ten days of June 1779, Mrs. Mary Gooch died. Hers had been a long and painful last illness, probably cancer, the severity of which Sarah had done her best to alleviate during the past four years. Reporting her sister's death to Sylvester early in June, she commented that, though not unexpected, her death was "destressing when it came to the last parting sean." By her will Mary left several specific legacies. To her "beloved sister, Mrs. Sarah Thomas," she gave her horse and chaise, gold watch, long cloth riding hood, and a suit of black "Padusey" [paduasoy, a rich corded silk], which had belonged to her mother, Elizabeth *Packer* Dering. To her niece, Sarah Dering Thomas, she left her other suit of black "padusey" and also a set of "Pencil China Ware." To her niece, Elizabeth *Packer* Thomas, she gave a "large burnt China Dish and a dozen Burnt China Plates." To her "beloved Brother, Thomas Dering Esqr." she left five guineas; and to two friends, a like sum to each. And to Joshua Winslow of Marshfield, Mary's and Sarah's intimate friend and cousin, she gave "whatever may be due and coming unto me, by virtue of a note or obligations, from Nathaniel Ray Thomas (late of Marshfield, Esqr.)" Any such sums were to be disposed of by Winslow according to her desire, as expressed in a separate writing executed that same day.

All the remainder of her estate, real or personal and wherever found, Mary Gooch gave and bequeathed to her niece, Mary Thomas, or "your Coz Polly" as Sarah called her in a letter to Sylvester Dering detailing

Years of Separation

Mary's death and her will. Sarah's sister constituted and appointed Joshua Winslow and Ebenezer Storer of Boston executors of her will. Witnesses to the will included Dr. Isaac Winslow and young Anna Green Winslow. Whatever thankfulness Sarah must have felt that her sister was spared her pain and suffering, she must also have realized sadly that her remaining sisters and her brother lived far from her - in Connecticut and Long Island, and in Canada and England.

Shortly before Mary Gooch's death, the Massachusetts General Court enacted a law that dealt with particular severity with "certain notorious conspirators against the government and liberties of the late province, now state, of Massachusetts Bay." Already proscribed and banished, these individuals were singled out as the worst offenders. They had been the leaders of the royal oligarchy. They were twenty-nine in number, of the some four hundred male Loyalists who left with Howe's fleet on the evacuation of Boston in March 1776. About eleven hundred altogether departed then; others fled at other times; some never left, undisturbed because of their moderate views. Some who did leave returned. Toward the end of the war, and certainly afterwards, there was increasing amnesty toward Loyalists. But, despite all of that, the twenty-nine "notorious conspirators" would never have been permitted to return.

Those twenty-nine were specifically named in the Confiscation Act. They were: Sir Francis Bernard and Thomas Hutchinson, Esq., governors of the Province of Massachusetts Bay; Thomas Oliver, Esq., lieutenant governor; Harrison Gray, treasurer; Thomas Flucker, Esq., secretary; Peter Oliver, Esq., chief justice; Foster Hutchinson, John Erving, Jr., George Erving, Sir William Pepperell, James Boutineau, Joshua Loring, Nathaniel Hatch, William Browne, Richard Lechmere, Josiah Edson, Nathaniel [Ray] Thomas, Timothy Ruggles, John Murray, Abijah Willard, and Daniel Leonard, Esqs., mandamus councilors; William Burch, Henry Hulton, Charles Paxton, and Benjamin Hallowell, Esq., commissioners of the customs; Robert Auchmuty, Esq., judge of the vice-admiralty court; Jonathan Sewall, Esq., attorney general; Samuel Quincy, solicitor general; and Samuel Fitch, Esq., solicitor or councilor-at-law to the board of commissioners. Already the Provincial Congress of Massachusetts had decreed that the names of the mandamus councilors, including Nathaniel Ray Thomas, be published in the daily newspapers that they "may be sent down to posterity... with the infamy they deserve..."

Years of Separation

Those persons were deemed to have "justly incurred the forfeiture of all their property" and "shall be held, taken, deemed and adjudged to have renounced and lost all civil and political relation to this and the other United States of America, and be considered as aliens." And the second section of the Act declared that "all the goods and chattels rights and credits, lands, tenements, and hereditaments of every kind, of which any of the persons herein named and described, were seized or possessed...shall escheat, enure and accrue to the sole use and benefit of the government and the people of this state, and are accordingly hereby declared so to escheat, enure and accrue..." But it was provided also that the wives of such persons, resident in the state, should be entitled to have their dower right in such land thus subject to escheat.

This latest evidence of harassment, of retaliation really, by the new state government Sarah accepted grimly. As she expressed in a letter to Sylvester in February 1780, her problems involved both "Publick as well as private matters." Confiscation of private property was based on the exercise of sovereign power for the overriding good of the public. Even in those times of intense party feeling, procedures were established to carry out such confiscation. Agents were named and authorized to investigate the details of Loyalist properties preparatory to action being taken. Joshua Thomas, Esq. of Plymouth, a young Whig lawyer, was named "Agent on the Estate of Nathl Ray Thomas, Esqr (an Absentee)..." He was also a third cousin of Ray's, their respective grandfathers having been brothers.

Exactly six months after the April 30th effective date of the Confiscation Act, Joshua Thomas appeared before Joseph Cushing, Judge of Probate of Plymouth County. He made oath that the inventory he presented to the Court contained all the estate of Nathaniel Ray Thomas, Esq., ("an Absentee"), both real and personal, of which he was "Seized and possessed, at the Time of his departure from this State." The inventory was taken by Joseph Tolman, William Turner, and Robert L. Eells, and was dated at Hanover, November 30, 1779. The inventory and appraisal listed the following:
2 Looking Glasses @ £8 and 1 round broken Table @ £6
1 old Table @ £8 one tea ditto 2 36/ 1 old Desk @18
2 old Chairs with Leather bottoms @ £28 3 pair andirons 2 £4
2 Fire shovels & Tongs £4 & 4 Trammels @ 4 14
1 Iron Tea Kettle @ 18/ 2 Skillets one Iron & one bellmeattle @ 4/
6 pewter Dishes @ £6 6 12 ditto plates @ £4
4/ 1 Tin Trammel @ 6/

Years of Separation

1 Cullinder [colander] @ 12/ 1 Quart pot @ 6/
2 Tin Candle Sticks @ 6/
2 Brass Candle Sticks @ 30/ 1 dripping pan @ 24
3 Flat Irons @ 24/ 2 Iron potts @ 4 16 1 Iron Kettle @ 2 8
1 Bake pan @ 12/ 1 Flesh Fork @ 6/ 1 Iron Skinner @ 36/
1 Brass Kettle @ £4 3 Beds @ £135 3 Bedsteads 21 8
3 Blankets @ £10 6 pair of Sheets @ £19 4/
3 Counterpins @ 12 1 suit of green paniteen Curtins @ £32
2 old Beds for Servants @ £15 1 Common Table @ 12/
1 old Case of Drawers 2£3 1 old Chair & round about @ 30/
10 yellow earthen plates @ £3 6 Coffe Cupps @ 12/
4 Stone Saucers 6 Stone Cups @ 6 Stone Cups @ 9/
1 yellow earthen Dish @ 12/
1 Black Stone Tea Pot @ 4/ 1 earthen Bowl @ 5/
1 yellow Mug @ 3/ 1 old Chaise @ £50 1 Gundalo @ £15
1 Plow @ £15 1 Harrow @ £15 1 Cart @ £75 1 Chain @ £3
2 Yoaks @ £3 4/ 2 Axes @ 2 8/ 2 Hoes & spade @ £1 12/
4 Oxen @ £415 1 fat ox @ £150 4 Cows @ £300
2 Heifers @ £50 3 Calves @ £60 1 horse @ £20
10 Sheep @ £75 4 Hoggs @ 196 1 Shoat @ £25
6 Table Cloaths @ £9 12/ 1 Chamber Table @ £5
6 Kitchen Chairs & large Kitchen Table @ £3

Inventory Continued Sum brought forward: £1844 17

30 Bushels of Corn @ £126 6 ditto of Rye @ £34 4
3 Bushels of Wheat @ £27 12 Bushels of Potatoes @ £14 8/
5 Bushels of Turnips @ £6 6 Tons of Hay @ £108
[Sub Total: .... £2160 9]

Homestead, containing 300 acres of Salt meadow @ £22,500 and 800 Acres of Pasture, wood & arable Land, with the Buildings thereon @ £40,000

Total....................... £64660 9
Hanover November 30th 1779

NB
The 300 Acres of   '/s/Joseph Tolman
salt meadow is   '/s/Wm Turner
under mortgage   '/s/Robert Eells

Years of Separation

Hanover, ss: Novbr. the 30th, 1779

Then Joshua Thomas Esqr, Agent on the estate of Nathl Ray Thomas Esqr. (an Absentee) made Oath that the foregoing Inventory Contains all the Estate of said Absentee that Come to his Knowledge & if hereafter he Should know of any Other he'l Render an Acct. of it the Appraisers being Also under Oath.
Before Jos. Cushing Judge Probt.

Joshua Thomas was approaching thirty years of age at the time. Although he and Ray were of the same family, relatively close cousins as such things were reckoned, Joshua, his father, and three brothers had served in the Continental Army; Joshua himself had been military aide to General John Thomas. When he presented under oath the inventory of the estate, both real and personal, of which Ray had been "seized and possessed, at the Time of his departure from this State," Joshua undoubtedly realized that it did not, could not in fact, have reflected completely the entirety of Ray's property at that point. He was well aware, indeed, of Ray's reputation for living well. And three and a half years had passed since the evacuation. Recognizing the hardships suffered by Loyalists' wives and children who were left behind, the young lawyer quite correctly assumed that Sarah Thomas, as with so many others, had had to sell what she could, in her case, furniture and silver plate, in order to provide for herself and children.

Joshua's assumption was, in fact, correct. But the most valuable part of Ray's property, the "largest improved estate in Plymouth County" as Ray alleged, was still intact and available for confiscation and conversion into ready money. As agent in charge of liquidating Ray's estate as advantageously as he could for the state, he accepted reality. Furthermore he was apprised of Sarah's reputation for excellent character. That Joshua Thomas may have brought a genuine sympathy to Sarah's situation seemed at least to be suggested by a comment in her letter of February 2, 1780 a month after the filing of the inventory with the Court. "...I expect my Agent next week to dispose of the Stock etc. - when I shall be better able in May next to informe you how far his generosity went..."

"I have bin dayly hoping amidst Publick trobles," Sarah added, "I should have the private satisfaction of a letter from New York, but no inteligence from there so long it seams as tho my friends were all dead. Pray let me

Years of Separation

know whether you can learn if Mr. Thomas has ever returned from England or if Nat is still in New York." Knowing only that Ray had departed New York for England and that Nat had been in New York, Sarah became increasingly anxious to find out where and how they were. Later, in June 1780, she hoped to learn from Charles Storer, just returning from a trip to London, about Ray and particularly about Nat and Henry, "what business thay are in and how my sons behave in life," as she put it. That she was greatly concerned about her absent sons was evident from her remark: "why should I please myself with the thought that I am happy in my Children when perhaps all the while thay may be the most profligate fellows in the world...I pray God forbid that to be the case."

There were other worries of a family nature that spring of 1780. Early in the year the twenty-year-old daughter of Sarah's cousins and intimate friends Joshua and Anna *Green* Winslow, who lived nearby in Marshfield, became seriously ill. Young Anna Green Winslow, the diarist who portrayed people and events in her family circle with engaging candor, was stricken apparently with consumption. Mrs. Winslow and her daughter had gone to Boston for medical advice and from there the mother wrote Sarah. Recounting all of this to Sylvester Dering, Sarah wrote: "...Coz was much worse then when she left us a fournight ago so febel she could not walk four houses of[f] from Mr. Storer's without fainting to a nurse which she was advised two by Doct Bulfinch, as being the most speady way of geathering strength by Brest Milk she being two week to make use of Medison."

Sarah was saddened by the news. She lamented: "O what seans of sickness and death are we call'd to meat with one year after another in our House...what terible tydings must it be to her Father I sinsearly pray the means may be blest for her recovery but it seams to be the last resort when a person is reduced to Brest Milk, it may norish for a Seson but I fear will not perform a cure..." It was not a cure. Young Anna died within weeks. "Mrs. Winslow...upon the hole behaves to admiration and seams much more composed than I could possable have expected," Sarah observed sympathetically and with thoughtful insight, "but the worst I conceive is not yet come...her mind is at present much ingaged about many things that she can only say now often times that she has no Child, but when the hurry of makeing her morning and setling funeral charges puting up her poor Childs Close overlooking her paper &c is don then she will have nothing more to doe but to sit down and realize

Years of Separation

the Fact, that she is Childless indeed O that God may support her under this sore trial..."

That Sarah Thomas had the mature faculty of not dwelling unduly on tragic or unfortunate circumstances was demonstrated by remarks in the letter describing Mrs. Winslow's sad bereavement. Following that description, she suggested to Sylvester that he visit Marshfield on a planned trip to Boston and return to Middletown. "...suppose you should return home by the way of Marshfeild and if Charles should be returnd from N Yorke time enough before your Business is don in Boston or Portsmouth what if, you persuaded him to take a ride down with you, my thinks you might make a sort of party with some of them. poor Aunt Edwards I hear is very sick and wants to come to se us, why cannot she borrow Mr Storers Chaise, or sume friends and so come down with you and if Charles or Gorge would come on Horse back, thay could take the Chaise back and leave Aunt Edwards with us and you go from hear on your journey homeward, if you like'd." Sarah then added: "doe not think by the above skeam I only wish you to come by way of convaying other friends to se us, but be assured you are the dear object alone we are so ancious to se."

During the late summer of 1780 Sarah and her family had numerous guests, "tho' we are deprived," as Sarah admitted, "of those means which we once had, of showing our Hospitable Friendship to our friends..." The evening after Sylvester Dering left from his recent visit to Marshfield, Sarah wrote on September 2nd that she had been "engaged with Company ever since." That evening the Miss Barkers came with Mr. Blake. Two days after her two sisters with a Nephew of theirs came and has bin with us ever since, besides Mr Winslow and wife with Mrs. Watson of Plimouth have spent two Nights with us and Mrs Pelham Winslow one night and Mr Apthorp and Wife spent a week with us, but are all return'd except two Miss Barkers and thay with your Coz Sally are gon to see a Neighbor of ours and Mrs Winslow another..."

Eighteen-year-old "Coz Sally" wrote to Sylvester that same day her own version of the family's social activities. Apologizing for not having written before, she explained: "...but I really could not steal one hour for that agreeable purpos, to say the truth my time has been taken up with a number of agreeable Friends from Hingham, viz. Miss Sally Barker your favorite, and Mr. Blake..." There was more: "...I went to Plymouth with them and spent a very agreeable day and night...when we return'd From Plymouth we din'd and drank Tea with my dear Miss Sever...Miss Sally

Years of Separation

Barker has left me but her sister Debby and my Friend Bethiah is with me - and beleav me Cozn I have left them to write this scrawl and dont be too vain at the idea." Apparently word of French intervention on the American side had reached Marshfield, for Sally commented with seeming sarcasm: "in answer to the News you wrote me I say, French A-L-I-E-S and the beauties of your I-N-D-I-P-E-N-D-A-N-C-E."

It may have been during this busy period of entertaining that, at last, Sarah heard long-awaited, welcome news from Ray. The latter, still in England, had directed a box and letters through the good offices of a Mr. Smith apparently to Ebenezer Storer to be forwarded to Sarah. This Sarah learned from Sylvester, an acquaintance of Smith. The box arrived safely, but the letters miscarried. Sarah was concerned about the letters, as she wrote in her September 2nd letter. "I look upon my self perticularly unfortunate in being deprived of my letters, which you neads think would have bin a grate gratification from a friend so nearly coonect'd and who improved every oppertunity by sume indearing [proffer?] to convince me the length of way nor long and tedious seperation has lessened his tender afections for his family." She requested Sylvester to tell Mr. Smith that the box came safe to hand, that she was much obliged to him, and that she would appreciate it if Mr. Smith would tell Sylvester if he knew what business Mr. Thomas was engaged in, where and with whom he lived and whether he enjoyed his health.

Sarah was pleased, indeed, to receive such welcome items as the box contained, for she and her family suffered in those days of scarcity and high cost of even the simplest things. It was with a warm sense of thanks and, for Sarah as well as the children crowding around, happy excitement. As Sarah lifted out carefully each of the contents, cries of pleasure and wonder echoed back and forth. There were "silk and worsted shoes and Cotton stockings" particularly directed to Sarah and her daughters; "silk and worsted knit patterns for wastecotes one of each sort to each of my sons"; for eight-year-old Charles, "a cloth collered bever Hat shagd I beleive you call them and a few silk and some lining Hancerchifs and silk stockings, old ones which he menshons on a card as put in to fill up the Box."

Sarah was perturbed about the mislaid letters from Ray. As she noted to Sylvester: "I hope to hear to night by the News carryer whether Mr Storer is likely to recover the other things. it will be a sad dissopointment to me if he does not, for I shall not know how to turn for sume nesesarys, but

Years of Separation

the people hear Gentel and simple all seams to think they are in bad hands that is to say men of no feeling where there intrest is concerned what ever professions they make to the conterary, but I hope justis will be made to take plase in that and all other cases."

Later that fall of 1780 Sarah received distressing news. She learned from young Charles Storer on his return from New York that her son Nat had gotten into an "indolent way and neglected his business." But, as Sarah wrote to Sylvester, "I cannot help entertaining a hope that it may arise from sume misfortune in his business and that he really does not know what to doe till he hears from his Father." For, Sarah rationalized, she had heard from someone else from New York that "his father had left him in business and the cair [care] of Vessells to the amount of 500, sterling when he went away but he had imprudently improved them in such a manner that he had met with misfortunes...So you se my dear I cannot help puting the best construcshun on his conduct," Sarah admitted, particularly since Charles Storer had not mentioned any certain vice. Nat himself, indeed, had written her that he was not then in business but expected to be that fall upon his father's anticipated return to New York.

Particularly devastating was news of the death of her son Henry, Henry Dering Thomas who, at the age of fourteen had sailed in a "Mast Ship in order to se if he should like to folow the Sea..." For six years Sarah had not seen him. Now he was dead. "O my dear Nephew," Sarah wrote to Sylvester, "I have long bin habituated to misfortunes but thay seam dayly to increase and fall with grater weight...I desier to submit to God's will conserning me in all things but O, my dear, you will not wonder when I tell you the Heart of a Fond Parent cannot help wishing to have at least lent the assistance of a tender hand to have smouthed [smoothed] the bed of Death..." At twenty Henry was the first of her children to die. "It was the will of the Lord and I ought to be content with whatever seameath good in his sight."

Sarah learned this unhappy news in a letter from her niece Sarah Apthorp, whose mother Elizabeth *Dering* Wentworth had forwarded the intelligence from London. But there was welcome word from Elizabeth Wentworth as well. Ray Thomas, with the Wentworths at Hammersmith House, had been well the previous spring though in low spirits over the death of his son. Then there was the heart-warming message from Elizabeth that Sarah shared with Sylvester: "But I will endeavor not to look wholly upon the dark side but remember the same pen informed me

Hammersmith House (also known as Brandenburgh House) where Nathaniel Ray Thomas lived while in England. Courtesy of Alderman Library, University of Virginia, Charlottesville, Virginia.

Years of Separation

of Mr Thomas's health and add[ed] that if I could but know half the regard and anxiety he has for me and his family I should pronounce him one of the best men in the world..."

Sarah's concern for her son Nat in New York lessened during 1781 for she heard more frequently from and about him. Sylvester Dering was, as usual, the intermediary. To him she wrote, when she learned to her sorrow that Nat was not in business: "...I rejoyce to know he is retierd from those who live a life of dissipation wholly." She inquired with interest: "I presume if he spends so much time in reading he must be upon sume Study. pray inquier whether it be not the study of Law he is upon. Does he not inform you of his intention to make us a visit in a Cartal [cartel, literally, a written agreement for the exchange of prisoners]. I wonder he thinks of it except he could first obtain leave from hear, which by the way I beleive he never can...Surly thay must have very different ideas about our mannagement hear from what thay realy are, or thay would not speak of a visit as tho it was not much difficuly to obtain. You will very readyly beleive me when I say I long to se him but still I doe not know what to say to him about coming." Sarah had little expectation of Nat's being able to get home.

In March 1781 Sarah learned of the destruction by fire of General John Thomas's house in Kingston. General Thomas, friend and companion of Ray's thirty or more years before, had married Hannah, daughter of Ray's uncle and one-time guardian, Lieutenant Colonel Nathaniel Thomas. As Ray's first cousin and his guardian's daughter, Hannah was well known to Sarah and her children. On the 30th of the month Sarah wrote to Hannah, sympathizing with her in the "mellancoly Providence." But she went on to say: "...I shall be [ac]aceiding glad if you or any of your famely will [occ]upy a part of my House and we shall be happy [to] make it agreable to one or all of your famely - at [le]ast I should esteam it as a favour if Mr Willis or [su]me friend can make it convenient to bring my Coz Hannah over to tarry till you can acomidate your self [mo]re agreably...If I can git a Horse will send my own Chaise over."

Whether or not Hannah accepted Sarah's invitation to stay with her, that invitation did indicate the normalizing of emotions following the war.

During the summer and fall of 1781 the sale of Ray Thomas's real estate at Marshfield under the Confiscation Act of 1779 and subsequent statutory power of sale took place. Various local people - "our Neibour Kent," Tom Ford, Esaph Waterman, and Paul Sampson - were purchas-

Years of Separation

ers at the public auction. Of the buildings on the farm only the corn house was sold, but this, Sarah complained, "put me to grate Inconveniency by obliging me to remove my Grain into the House." On the 13th of October, pursuant to warrant, Sarah's friend and neighbor Dr. Isaac Winslow and Nathaniel Little and Joseph Kent assigned and set off to Sarah her dower in Ray's Marshfield land, a half century earlier called the great Estate, and by the family the Eagles Nest, even then. What had been withheld from confiscation and preserved for Sarah embraced several hundred acres of land, the buildings on the property including Ray's "New Mansion House," and, apparently as an afterthought or overlooked, "the pew in the meeting-house." By statute, wives and widows of those proscribed were entitled to retain their dower right or one- third, of the landed property of absentee Loyalists.

Early in November Sarah wrote to Sylvester news of the sales of the farm land and assignment to her of her "thirds." During that fall her son John and one of her daughters, possibly Mary or Maria as she was sometimes called, visited the Derings at Middletown, Connecticut. While Sarah had agreed to their visit, now she thought that both should return home. "For this is a changeable world we live in and what may turn up between this and spring we know not." In her letter Sarah turned once again to Sylvester for help with one of her children. "I shall think myself much obliged to you to bestow a few hours upon your cousin John and advise him to attend a little more to his own behaviour...it is not one of my smaller trobles but one of my greatest mortifications that he at this age does not make sume appearance in Life not to say a shining one." Sarah was concerned that John, at the age of seventeen, showed little polish or manners. "I wish him for his own sake and appearance to others that he would treat me with a littel more duty and respect, espeshaly before the Servants more than for my own sake, for I can safely say, my foyble if I know myself, does not lay in that others should treat me with any great respect more than common Civility." Caught up in her own feelings, Sarah confessed: "How happy should I think myself had I the pleasing prospect in my sons that I think your Father has in his."

Before the year was out the same court-appointed men who had inventoried and appraised Ray Thomas's real and personal estate heard, examined and passed on claims against his estate which had been due before April 19, 1775. Claims totalling one thousand two hundred nine pounds, seven shillings, and two and one quarter pence were allowed. The largest single claim, some two hundred ninety-four pounds,

Years of Separation

was owing to Ezekiel Goldthwaite of Boston, one-time guest of Ray's and Sarah's at Marshfield. Thomas Dering, Sarah's brother, was owed over a hundred pounds. Two acquaintances of Ray's, one still friendly and the other a friend only in their youth, Dr. Isaac Winslow and Col. Anthony Thomas, were also owed money. "Cousin Will" Watson and James Warren of Plymouth were also listed among Ray's creditors. Even Sarah herself was included for debts she had paid off for Ray since his departure. The appraisers had acted carefully and impartially, so they swore under oath, but the magnitude of Ray's debts, even though they were to be satisfied by the sale of the land, was a sobering reality for Sara.

XI

Reunion

Early in the new year, 1782, Sarah received from Ebenezer Storer a letter written to him from Ray Thomas at Hammersmith House, London. Ray's customary method of attempting to furnish the wants of Sarah and the children was to have Sarah draw bills upon London, but this he learned was costly. Fortunately, Storer's young son, traveling in England, agreed to forward a trunk to his father's care in Boston. The latter would transmit the contents to Sarah with any balance of funds left after costs. Apparently Ray had used this method at least once before the previous summer when he had sent "a large case of sundreys for the family in general." Ray was trying to meet the needs of his family.

He wrote Ebenezer Storer thanking him for his assistance in the following letter of January 20, 1782:

> I am informed my Dear Sir, by Mrs. Thomas's letters, what her family are otherwise sufficiently sensible of by the comfortable effects; that you have invariably exercised a most kind, generous, and benevolent attention to her, and their, destitute and painful situation, during my long and tedious <u>exile</u> - permit me to add, that this can only proceed from a mind that rightly understands and applys that great and comprihensive gospel Virtue, Charity, which is reason made perfect by Grace: It is a beneficence, which arises from a contemplation of the world, from a knowledge of the Great Creator, and the relation we bear to him and to our fellow creatures. It is that reason into which all other duties owing from man to man, are ultimately resolved; and to say in a word, what is the character, the temper, or the duty of a disciple of the gospel. Charity is the only word that can express my meaning, and the recompence of the just, its only adequate and sure reward.
> Their is no good office therefore which you have not a just right to claim at my hands: as there is none which I shall not at all times be most warmly and joyfully ready to return.

Reunion

> Our friend Mr Winslow has informed me of the great loss that must attend Mrs T. drawing Bills upon London, as I have frequently desired her to furnish her servants that way. My young <u>friend</u>, your amiable son, has undertaken to forward a Trunk to your care. A Bill of parcels you have here inclosed of the contents. must pray you to forward the articles for Mrs T. (having sent her via Nyk last summer a large case of sundrys for the family in general) have only put a Dozn pr shoes 1 pr. silk marked and directed; and pray Mrs Storer, to accept the silk directed for her, from an absent friend, and Miss Storer, a pr of the silk embroidered shoes from the same.
>
> And when the person shall have finished the sale of the sundrys, and payed his commission & (whom your Judgement shall direct;) you will be as good as to pay the balance to Mrs T.
>
> God Bless you my Dear Sir! I shall ever think of your many civilities with great gratitude, and hope for a continuance of them to my family. yes, and with them my most friendly wishes, for all you wish in this world.

The trunk young Storer was to forward, it seems, was the subject of a letter from Ray himself to Sarah in the summer of 1782. He advised her, Sarah wrote to her brother Thomas Dering, to petition the Governor and Council "for leave to receive the artecles sent for the support of the famely, convinced that their enlarged and liberal minds would not suffer the rule of Police to supersede the reason of Justice and equity in my partecular case and circumstances." Sarah's reaction was abrupt and sarcastic, another one of her very few outbursts. "Poor man he is gratly mistaken, about there inlarged minds. He will finde thay are - excuse me I will forbare." In a postscript, Sarah added that Ray had said that God "has sean fit to wean his foolish heart from this vain world and shew him how littell the persutes of earthly objects avail to happyness, and many parrigrafts of the same import."

Sarah had also received letters from her sisters Elizabeth Wentworth and Ann Monk. In Elizabeth's from London there were words that Sarah found pleasing, "pleasing after so long an absent to be informed from another pen as well as his own, that she thinks it must afford me grate consolation that she can assure me, if it is possable Mr. Thomases affections is rather heightened for me and his family then when he left us, and she thinks it must give me a sensable pleasure to be assured

Reunion

from her pen that he is much estameed [esteemed] by every body as well as his pertecular friends."

By early fall of 1782 the war was grinding down. On November 30, 1782 a preliminary peace treaty was signed. Two months later the final treaty was executed. On March 30, 1783 Ray Thomas wrote to Ebenezer Storer, rejoicing with him that the war had ceased. "The happy effects may we both soon realize in the restoration of that most valuable happiness of men in this world, that which arises to them from domestic relations." But well aware that the state of Massachusetts had proscribed and banished him and confiscated his Marshfield property as one of "certain notorious conspirators against the government," Ray was uncertain of his status. "I find myself obliged, contrary indeed to my wishes and expectations, to tarry in this country another year," he informed Storer, "to wait the result of that article of the peace, relative to persons of my description." Then he appealed to Storer: "Will you therefore, Give me leave to expect your answer in particular and General on that subject. As their is no person whose Judgment I so safely rely upon, it will determine in degree my future measures." He was warned by Storer that a Loyalist as prominent as he would never be welcome in Massachusetts again.

In the spring of 1783 John Wentworth was named Surveyor General of the Woods for Nova Scotia and sailed for Halifax. But before leaving Hammersmith House, he presumably advised Ray Thomas to emigrate to Nova Scotia where Sarah and the children could join him. On May 20th Ray wrote Sarah, therefore, that he thought Nova Scotia would be the asylum for absentees. That brought from Sarah once again one of her infrequent outbursts: "...hard Loyns indeed for those at my time of life to set out in setling a new country because the unfergiving sperit still reigns with all its force as at the beginning of the War. Mallace, Hatred, an[d] revenge forbids those absent friends to return not only to there own estates but to there Country again which might could thay be admited make me in sume measure forgit the very many difficulys I have had to incounter throw [through] the last nine years."

After that outburst, Sarah regained her composure and reported in that same letter to her brother Thomas: "I have had pleasing accounts from Mr T of his grate attachment to me and his famely, that all tho he is surrounded with every Comfort, he findes no sattisacktion so long as he has not his famely around him. May God direct him to sume comfortable retreat from all his Enemies but more espeshaly guard him from

Reunion

adversary of souls." Then, having learned from Mrs. Winslow of a friend's being married again two months after burying his wife, Sarah remarked: "Daugt Sally says she beleives it is a part of the good peoples religion, for she observed thay which are remarkable serious all marry by the time there first Wifes are Cold..." And she closed her letter with an expression of her unalterable affection "whether in the retierment of Marshfield or Bannished to the Deserts of Nova Scotia."

Toward the end of August that summer Ray Thomas had indeed decided to go out to Nova Scotia. Charles Storer, Ebenezer's son, was in London at the time and reported that John Wentworth's wife, Frances, was about to sail for Halifax with Mr. Thomas to join her husband. Ray visited young Storer in London as well. Ray apparently left Mrs. Wentworth in New York and proceeded on to Nova Scotia where he arrived at Halifax shortly before the fourth of November. On that date he wrote Ebenezer Storer that he had had a safe arrival, "though somewhat exhausted from a tedious passage of 9 weeks," and that he had written Sarah "four lines to acquaint her of my arrival."

Whether or not, that fall of 1783, Sarah had reconciled herself to the idea of Nova Scotia as a haven for her and her family, she accepted that idea as a foregone conclusion when she received Ray's "four lines" announcing his arrival in Halifax. Presumably, also that fall, she had learned from her son Nat in New York that he planned to go to Nova Scotia as well. With the cessation of hostilities at Yorktown and commencement of peace negotiations, many New York Loyalists were among "those, who for their attachment to Government, and after numberless fatigues in supporting the Royal cause - have been Obliged to quit their All and take refuge within the King's lines." Encouraged by Sir Guy Carleton, the newly appointed British commander-in-chief in America and stationed in New York, hundreds of those Loyalists now looked to Nova Scotia as their haven. Under Sir Guy's good offices, land for settlement on Nova Scotia's southwest shore presented itself. This was at and around Port Roseway and in the fall of 1782 the Port Roseway Association of carefully screened Loyalists was formed in New York. Among the Associates was Nathaniel (Nat) Thomas, listed as "farmer, Marshfield, Massachusetts." On Sir Guy Carleton's recommendation, the Associates formed themselves into a militia composed of companies consisting of one captain, two lieutenants, four sergeants and thirty-six rank and file. The captains were authorized to act as magistrates until the Nova Scotia government named others in their places. In the fall of 1783 Sir Guy Carleton commissioned Nat Thomas

Reunion

one of the captains to embark with his company in the fall sailing and final evacuation of New York. Port Roseway, by then renamed Shelburne, was their destination. On November 12, 1783, apparently unaware that his father had already arrived at Halifax, Nat wrote to John Wentworth, advising him that he had just arrived at Shelburne and requesting from Wentworth, Surveyor General of His Majesty's Woods, an appointment as one of his deputies. Nat represented that his present situation, "by means of several Misfortunes during the late unhappy war," was rather disagreeable.

Nat's father Ray Thomas, accommodated at the Governor's house in Halifax since his arrival, dispatched a somber letter to Paul Wentworth, his friend and host at Hammersmith House for the past five years. Ray found the country "gloomy" and contrary to his expectations. Practically all of the improved land was held by the first proprietors, the settlers who had gone from New England to Nova Scotia in the 1750's, and had greatly increased in price, some farms in good order had sold for five thousand pounds sterling to wealthy New Yorkers. He lamented his situation, that of one "destined to cultivate the soil of a wilderness and that in a most inhospitable climate," which he had not had the foresight to discern. "What remains! A conscious satisfaction of having at all times exerted a zeal superior and with such effect as to convince the world at large that I desired the preservation of the tranquility of my country." Ray Thomas could always come back to that consolation.

In that letter to Paul Wentworth of early November, Ray advised him: "I have wrote to Mrs. Thomas to employ proper persons to make an estimate, prior to 1774, of my losses, consulting and submitting the form and vouchers to Mr. Morton's [discretion?]." Perez Morton, a young attorney of considerable reputation, had married Sarah Wentworth Apthorp, daughter of Sarah Thomas's niece Sarah Apthorp, two years earlier. Ray closed his letter to Paul Wentworth with the observation: "It is unnecessary for me to inform you what comfort and satisfaction of mind I must receive from being enabled to remove my family, after more than nine years' separation, to a country where I may once more enjoy the greatest happiness in this life, viz, that which arises to a man from the society of a wife and children."

Halifax, with its splendid harbor, was a metropolis important in the imperial scheme of things. Yet its population not many months before Ray Thomas's arrival was only about fifteen hundred. Then the influx of countless Loyalists and former soldiers mustered out of service swelled

Reunion

its numbers several thousandfold. Many of these souls were bereft of the most basic needs. Housing was in particularly short supply. Public buildings, warehouses, and churches were appropriated for shelter. Disbanded soldiers and their families were accommodated with tents on the slopes of Citadel Hill. Private lodgings were at a premium. Still, important buildings stood out above the rest: Government House, the Citadel, St. Paul's Church, and a few others. These provided an air of dignity to the overcrowded town.

Writing to Thomas Dering just before the end of the year 1783, Sarah expressed her feelings over the news of Ray's arrival in Nova Scotia. "With a mixture of pain and pleasure I have to acquaint you my dear Brother that I have accounts of Mr Thomas's arival at Halifax where he hopes to meat me with his family the next Spring. Might it bin the will of Providence I could have wished to have sean him hear rather then bin obliged to quit my native Country." She added that she had received "a very polite letter from Govr. Wentworth and Major Monk offering me their servises." The former was John Wentworth, one-time governor of New Hampshire and ever after known as "Governor" and then Surveyor General of the King's Woods, and the latter, George Henry Monk, son of Sarah's sister Ann *Dering* Monk. Both men were, of course, in Nova Scotia.

Sarah then added: "I cannot bare the thought of leaving the Country without seeing you." But, she elaborated, "I have so much business on my hands I know not where to begin such as procuring an estimate of this Estate giting it apprized again have the paper to take out of the Probit offis [office] attested, Coppys to take Duplicates &c to send to Mr Thomas and settell accounts with Pople Provide for my voige [voyage] and so many things of various sorts that added to the perplexity of my own thoughts seams sometimes two much for me. The prospect of crossing the water is very distressing to me indead but I desire to put my trust in him who alone can protect me boath by sea and land and remember that as a sparrow doath not fall to the ground without his knowlige so nither doath those things befall me without his amediate direction."

Sarah Thomas's letter bore eloquent testimony to the problems she faced that winter and spring of 1783-1784. She was obviously upset with the thought of leaving America without seeing her brother Thomas and his family. But on the other hand she was deeply involved in gathering documents, in forwarding information to Ray about his estate in order to

Reunion

support his claims for his losses, and in the often disheartening and sometimes impossible matter of settling accounts with those whom Ray had, and she even then, owed money. Not the least of her concerns was her worry about the sea voyage to Nova Scotia. But as always her faith in the Lord supported her.

The effect of knowing of their impending departure from Marshfield and unimaginable trip across the water to an unknown land both excited and alarmed the children. With Nat, the oldest, already away from home for nearly ten years and Henry Dering now dead, Sarah was left with six children under her protection. Ever since Ray's abrupt escape from the Whig mob in 1774, she had felt keenly her sole responsibility for them. Her oldest daughter and eldest child with her, Sarah Dering (Sally), was nearly twenty-two and a stalwart and affectionate helper, particularly with her younger brothers and sisters. John, approaching twenty, had manners that still bothered his mother but he was her oldest son then with her. Mary, Maria or Polly as she was sometimes called, was eighteen. Martin Howard, named for his father's good friend Judge Martin Howard, was about sixteen, while Elizabeth Packer, named for Sarah's mother, was fourteen. Charles, the youngest, was twelve.

For the children, only three of whom - Sally, John and Mary - had been as far away from home as Boston or to the Derings at Middletown, Connecticut, it was a dramatic time. Good-bys to be said to nearby friends, farewell notes to distant relations, insistent beseeching and strident haggling over who should be allowed to take what, tears and laughter - all marked the last months at Marshfield. Elizabeth Packer rushed to complete a sampler which she had begun some years before. (This sampler now hangs in the Isaac Winslow House in Marshfield, Massachusetts.) For Sarah, the mother, there seemed so much to do that there was not time to mull over their situation, to worry or be depressed. She had her own good-bys - to servants, friends, and, of course, to special people whom she might be seeing for the last time and so leaving forever. Of the latter there were few, but they were very special. Dr. Isaac Winslow and his wife Elizabeth, and Reverend William Shaw, Sarah's minister, were particularly hard to leave.

In Nova Scotia Ray Thomas was endeavoring to locate property on which to settle his family. On the fifteenth of March 1783 he entered a memorial with the government for a grant of twelve hundred acres of land on St. Lewis Bay. Three days later this was approved for one thousand acres on Plaister Cove near the entrance of the River

Reunion

Antigonish and St. Lewis Bay. Whether or not this grant ever issued is not clear. But later in March, probably at the suggestion of George Henry Monk and his brother-in-law George Deschamps, both of whom were involved in arranging for the settlement of Loyalist families particularly in the area of Windsor, Ray looked at Windsor himself. On March 31, 1784 a land speculator and entrepreneur, Joshua Mauger, conveyed something over three hundred acres in Windsor, Hants County, to Nathaniel Ray Thomas, George Deschamps, and George H. Monk. Two weeks later Ray Thomas apparently bought the others out, executing a purchase money mortgage in their favor. Then, in June of that year, Deschamps and Monk quitclaimed their interest to Ray, which left him with title to the property at that time or shortly thereafter known as Prospect Place Farm.

With Windsor, Nova Scotia, now certain to be their destination, Sarah and her children hurried their final preparations for the journey. They wrote last letters to distant friends, they exchanged last farewells to nearby friends, they gathered last items to take along. On May 20th Sarah wrote to her niece Elizabeth *Dering* Gardiner: "Tho just on the point of sailing as it were I cannot let my Niece go without a line to thank you for your kind letter. I could have rather have wished you to have accompanyd your brot and visited us once more at Marshfield...nothing would give me grater plesure then to see you boath at my habitation in Winsor where I can venter to promise you a kinde reception to whatever our fair may be."

To provide passage to Windsor from Marshfield for Sarah, the children, and several servants, Ray had borrowed £133. Arrangements were made for a coasting vessel to put in to White's Ferry on the North River and take aboard the family and servants. As the day approached for departure, Sarah became increasingly quiet. As she looked about the house and farm, she remembered the day thirty years before when she and Ray had returned home from Boston after their wedding. They had shared happy times: the birth of their children, the entertaining of family and friends. They had known difficult times: financial reverses, harsh quarrels with close relatives, bitter political opposition. The last ten years had been especially hard for Sarah. Left alone with the children after Ray's abrupt departure, Sarah had had the full responsibility for their well being. She had had to face Whig enmity, suffer humiliation from neighbors once considered friends. She had had to endure separation from Ray for a decade, often hearing nothing from him or about him for months on end. She had had to sell hers and Ray's silver and furniture

Reunion

from the house and stock from the farm in order to survive. And, finally, she had had to stand helplessly by as most of Ray's ancestral land was confiscated by the state and sold at public auction.

Departure from Marshfield was scheduled for June 15th. Sarah, the children, and the servants left the farm for White's Ferry; Sarah somber, the children excited and awed at the unknown that lay ahead. They were, quite possibly, escorted to the ship waiting at the ferry by their long-time personal friend and adviser, Dr. Isaac Winslow, whose family association with the Thomases stretched back to the earliest days of settlement. Then, at the ferry, with all aboard, the last good-bys said, the ship slipped her moorings and put out to sea.

"As I know you must be desirous to hear an account of our voyage," Sarah later wrote to Thomas Dering from Nova Scotia, "I will endeavor to recollect though I was so unwell as to be unable to keep any journal." Despite her condition, she recounted her story with vivid description. "The 15th of June we left Marshfield came to sail with a small gale. In the after part of the day was becalmed. The next morning a pleasant gail prevailed till the afternoon. When the wind dyed away the Captian saw a fogge off, and thought best to come to ancer [anchor] in a harbor that night where we lay very quiet. Tho I should have told you, the first night we were becalmed we were all taken very sick but my son Charles who suffered no inconvenience throu the voyage. Son Martin soon got over his sickness but daughter Sally and myself were very sick. But to proceed."

"The next night and day we had a fine fresh breeze and sailed at the rate of 8 nots. In the midst of this fine wind the Captain thought fit to put up a long river to put out some of his own laden [lading] at Machias by which means we lost our wind. I should have told you when we harbored before at Mount Desert and it appeared to be well so named. I unfortunately was taken with the fever and ague which together with my sea sickness brought me very low so that when we went on shore at Machias I was led between two into a house near the water side where I met with kind treatment. The family all dined on fine fresh salmon but I lay on the bed and ate my plumb oatmeal gruel."

Sarah accepted her unfortunate condition with stoicism. Her children, relieved momentarily of the constraints of the ship, wandered about with curiosity and with considerable excitement reported to their mother what they had seen and heard. "We all laid on shore that night which was

Reunion

Saturday (we sailed on Tuesday). The next morning the children went to meeting, heard one Mr Lion preach serious sermon. I was too unwell. They saw some smart people at worship but the land looked barren. There was saw mills and vessels loading with lumber which made it look like a place of business."

"In the afternoon the wind was fair and we came to sail, passed by many places Cranberry Island, Cape Blow me down, Cape Split &c. The latter appeared like a huge great rock split in halves. Someplaces we passed looked like a wilderness here and there a hut. Some had the appearance of fine farms handsome buildings and houses, fine large barns and other out houses orchards &c...At one harbor we were making the wind suddenly dyed away and the tide had liked have cast us on a rock they called the bar, but having recourse to their oars we through the protection of a kind Providence safely harbored without my knowing the danger till it was past."

"On the whole," Sarah continued, "if I had not been sick we saw so many vessels of various sizes passing to and fro saw so many pleasant prospects harbored almost every night sailed along the shore lost sight of land not more than twice had no bad weather no high winds or boisterous waves not even in the Bay of Fundy which I had such formidable accounts of but found no more inconvenience there than elsewhere till we came in sight of Windsor, where the Captain being unacquainted with the harbor came to ancur in a wrong place where the tide left us that we could not get up to town that night."

Sarah and the children were almost at their destination, their journey almost over. But they experienced one more worrisome moment. "...When all the sailors were gone to rest, not one to keep watch, the children were up and I lay sick in my cabin with the weakness the ague and fever had brought on me, we suddenly heard a great rush of water and noise like thunder which the children thought it was, but I told them it must be something that struck the vessel for she trembled like a leaf. I called the Capt. who answered what is that? He turned out and went to bed no more that night, but found by ancuring in the wrong place his vessel had stuck in the quick sand, which tho his vessel was somewhat in danger did no harm." In reality, the vessel was struck by a "tidal bore," the noisy rush of the incoming tide.

With the vessel at last anchored in the right place, Sarah continued her account. "In the morning Major Monk which is Henry by name, with

Reunion

Betsey's son John [Dr. John Gould, son of Elizabeth *Wentworth* Perkins and brother-in-law of George Henry Monk] came on board to let me know that Mr Thomas was at the farm and they had sent him word the vessel was arrived." The ten-year separation of Ray and Sarah and their children at last was about ended. Sarah recalled the moment. "He [Ray] soon came and looked around the cabin saw me and took my hand but can you believe me my brother when I tell you that I was so weak and ill that I felt no emotion either of joy or sorrow but lay like a dead log. Saw Mr Thomas take his son Charles in his arms, who burst into a flood of tears which I wondered much to see, as he had not wished to see his Papa as much as the other children not having any remembrance of him but he now likes him and thinks him a pretty clever man."

Nor was Charles alone in sharing in the warm embrace of his father. All were affectionately greeted. If Ray was pleasantly impressed by their grown-up appearance, he must have been particularly so with that of Sarah Dering, his oldest daughter and at twenty-two now of age. But for all it was a joyful reunion. The family, accompanied by Major Monk and Dr. Gould, went ashore and made their way to the farm. The servants followed.

Prospect Place, as it was familiarly called, occupied the highest point in Windsor. It overlooked meadow, cropland, and, beyond marshes, the rivers St. Croix and Avon which, joining, emptied into Minas Basin and so the Bay of Fundy. The house on Prospect Place was small, one-and-one-half stories in height, of frame construction, and shingled on the exterior. The rooms were low-ceilinged with chair-rails and fireplace mantels with simple pilasters and mantel shelves.

Sarah continued her story of the voyage and arrival at Windsor: "...by the help of a puke and the bark, I have quite recovered from my complaints. What I have sean of the country appears very pleasant. The mountains at a distance appear to be covered with woods quite in a state of nature, but there is rides they tell me quite level for fifteen miles as plain as a house floor not a stick or stone. All around me appears quite clear good land, fine large fields on each side the roade with herds grass red clover and fine white honeysuckle appear like a fine field that has been sown just ready to mow, the grass very high with uncommon large heads. Even in some places on the sides where the dyke meadow is appears to be lodged it is so thick and they tell me there never was a seed sown there, and I see in some back fields where the woods and underbrush stands uncultivated this same mixture of

Prospect Place, Windsor, Nova Scotia, home of Nathaniel Ray Thomas and family. No longer standing. Photograph by William H.B. Thomas.

grass is all amongst it and if cleared of the underbrush would be just the same."

"There are wheat, barley, oats, potatoes growing in fine abundance. Many gardens I see belonging to private families where they have fine peas, beans, and every vegetable as in my native land, some orchards cherry trees, plums, currants in great abundance, and strawberries, blackberries, and raspberries. Fine Mutton lamb and without any exception the finest grass fed beef I ever ate we have now brought to market, and I see go by good poultry of many sort, but that is excessive dear. We waite till our own poultry is in eating. We have fine cod fish, salmon, shad, salmon trout, trout, asparagus &c."

Sarah assured Thomas Dering: "You see I have been very particular, my brother, because I thought you would like to know how I fared in life and I have endeavoured not to exagerate but to write you the real truth. I suppose I see the country in its glory though they tell me it was not so cold the last winter as in my native land. It was a very moderate winter hear and a very severe one with us, as I suppose it was with you."

Sarah concluded her account of the voyage and arrival, as she often was in the habit of doing, with news of their family. She informed Thomas that their sister Ann *Dering* Monk was in "tolerable good health" and "trips about and seems to be in fine spirits." Their niece, Ann's daughter Nancy, was married to George Deschamps and, though complaining of many disorders, looked "like the picture of health" and, Sarah added, "you would not suppose anything ailed her." Their nephew, George Henry Monk, and his wife the former Polly Gould were well. Sarah closed her lengthy and detailed letter: "I have only room to add Mr T and the children join in love with your affectionate sister."

Perhaps by the time she finished her letter, Sarah had achieved what she had lamented at the letter's beginning: "I inroll it among the gratest trials of my life that I could not visit you before I left my native land but it was not the will of Providence. Therefore, I desire to be content..." Perhaps, indeed, in the writing of the letter itself and in the "happy issue out of all their affliction," Sarah was content at last.

XII

Refuge

A month after Sarah had written Thomas Dering of the family's safe arrival in Windsor, she, Ray, and the children were established at Prospect Place. All of the children, that is, except Nat and John. John had apparently come with the rest to Windsor, stayed a short time and then had returned to Marshfield. Hepsibah Edwards, writing to Thomas Dering in the middle of August 1784, elaborated: "We have heard from Mrs. Thomas. She is got safe with her family. They are much pleased with their new prospects. Poor things, I wish it may be well with them all."

As for John, Mrs. Edwards wrote: "Poor John is at Marshfield. I know not what will become of him, hope he will doe well. Mr. Shaw has been up, says he does well as yet but they are afraid he will marry a girl that they don't like. (I hear that his Father wants him to come to him to work on his new farm and help bring it [too] for him) but I think," Mrs. Edwards commented, "if John will keep his Mother's right and be a good husband he may doe better where he is for they all like him at Marshfield, but what any of them will doe I cant tell."

Late that fall Benjamin Marston, whose mother was a Winslow of Marshfield, General John Winslow's sister, was traveling to the new province of New Brunswick to take up a position as a Deputy Surveyor of the King's Woods. He stopped at Windsor and there visited the Thomases at Prospect Place. In his journal Marston wrote: "I spent a very agreeable evening with N.R. Thomas Esq. Find him very well brought up after nine years tossing about, much to his and his family's satisfaction. They are in a comfortable warm house." Marston's assessment was not wholly shared, however, by the family at Windsor.

For, despite the family's thankfulness at being reunited and Sarah's initial enthusiasm at what she saw in and around Windsor, there were serious problems confronting them. As Sarah was later to write of that time, the farm, Prospect Place, was not paid for, there was no livestock on it, and there were debts not yet satisfied. And it was winter, in an unfamiliar land. There was more trouble to come.

Refuge

That winter, Sarah advised her brother Thomas, "that much dreded destemper the small Pox" struck her and her family. Sarah was inoculated that December with no great difficulty. But the servants did not fare so well. Sarah's servant girl was left with an inflammation of the eye that kept her from her duties until spring. The man servant ran a nail through his foot the night after he was inoculated and, even as Sarah wrote, he was in danger of losing his foot, probably due to infection. Still, "Hapyly we have all recovered."

About the time that Sarah dispatched this information to her brother Thomas, she received the sad news that her sister Elizabeth Wentworth had died in London; and only a few months later the even more shocking word that Thomas, "my dear and only Brother," had passed away. She immediately wrote his son Sylvester to express her condolences and her own "smart in the loss of so kinde and affectionate [a] Brother."

Knowing that her nephew, in common with all of her distant relations, would want to know about her own family, Sarah recounted her news. "...we have sean our famely all once more together. Your Cos. Nat, is still with us. Will spend the winter at least, and as he has the carrecter of being a rather indolent person in business, I have the pleasure to acquaint you he is of grate servis to his Father very attentive in keeping his men at work and what is more is very diligent, in working with his own hands." On this cautiously optimistic note, Sarah continued: "I wish it may continue for his own sake, that should he leave us he may have habituated himself so much to business that it will be a pleasure to continue in the practis of it."

What Hepsibah Edwards in the late summer of 1784 had had to say about Sarah's son John had probably been shared with or sent straight to his mother in Windsor. Sarah learned that John might be marrying a girl Marshfield people did not like. Yet Hepsibah Edwards was of the opinion that if John were to get and keep his mother's dower right (which had been assigned to her) and be a good husband he might do better where he was "for they all like him at Marshfield." She was aware, of course, that Ray wanted John to come to work on "his new farm," Prospect Place, in Windsor.

But John, remaining in Marshfield, decided to make an effort, at least, to recover some part of his family's land. In November 1785 Sarah Thomas, writing to her nephew Sylvester Dering, mentioned that "your Coz John is a-bout petitioning to have the thirds of Marshfield revert to

Refuge

him. If so, wishes to tarry upon it; if not, will return to Winsor in the spring." It seems probable that Perez Morton, then a rising young attorney of Boston married to Sarah *Dering* Thomas's great-niece Sarah Wentworth *Apthorp*, assisted John Thomas in his quest for the land.

A petition on behalf of John Thomas of Marshfield, signed by him, was presented to the Senate and House of Representatives of the Commonwealth of Massachusetts in October 1785. The wording and thrust of the petition seems to have reflected the professional experience of Perez Morton, for the petition clearly appealed to the compassion of the legislature at a time when feelings toward former Loyalists and their families had softened.

The petition began with a recital of facts:
> That your Petitioner's fathers Estate lying in said Marshfield was, during the late War, confiscated to the Use of the Government, and the Use and Improvement of one third part thereof was by due course of Law assigned & set off to your Petitioner's mother; That she is since gone to Nova-scotia to reside with her husband:- That your Petitioner from his Infancy to this period has dwelt with his Parents in said Marshfield, and bestowed all the labour & exertion of his Youth upon their Estate for their Use, without any further compensation than the future hopes of enjoying a Part of their Estate in reversion & he has accordingly remained on said Estate to this day improving for the support of his mother, such part thereof as, since the Confiscation, has been assigned to her as Dower.

Having set forth the background of John's case, the petition continued on a more immediately personal note:
> He flatters himself he has in the whole course of his Conduct acquitted himself as a faithful & good subject of the State, and politically demeaned himself as a friend to his Country, & in every other respect to the general satisfaction & approbation of his Neighbours & Fellow townsmen, as will appear by the annexed Certificate.

Attached to John's petition was a statement certified by the Selectmen of Marshfield and signed by more than sixty of John's neighbors and fellow townspeople. Those signing attested that they had "the highest

Refuge

Opinion of said John Thomas, as a good Citizen and friend to his Country, that he is an industrious & valuable Member of Society, and are desirous that he may obtain the Prayer of his Petition..."

Furthermore, the petition alleged that, because of his, John's, dependence on enjoying some part of his father's estate for his means of support, should he be disappointed in this expectation, he would have to leave the state to seek a livelihood elsewhere, no matter how attached he might be to his native country and its "happy Constitution." All of the preliminaries in the petition led up to John's ultimate request that the legislature grant him in fee simple "that part of his Father's Estate...assigned and set off to his mother, during her residence here [in Marshfield], and which since her departure from this Government, he supposes is vested in the Commonwealth..."

John's petition came before and was acted upon by the House of Representatives on November 23, 1785. It was approved, with an amendment that John should pay any claims against his father's estate remaining after the application of the proceeds of the sales of his father's land to his debts. It was then sent up to the Senate for concurrence and signed into law by the governor, James Bowdoin, on February 23, 1786. Having paid the remainder of the debts against his father's estate, John Thomas, not long after his twenty-first birthday, came into full and complete possession of his mother's dower right in the family lands that had been assigned to her.

When Benjamin Marston visited Ray Thomas and his family in Windsor in late 1784, he had reported in his journal that he found Ray "very well brought up after nine years tossing about." But Ray continued to be haunted by his son John's refusal to accompany the family in their flight to Nova Scotia to join him and by his apparent allegiance to the American cause. When it became clear that John not only had attempted to get back some portion of the family's ancestral estate, but actually had persuaded the Massachusetts legislature to convey to him his mother's dower right in the Marshfield property, Ray was deeply upset.

In a letter written May 21, 1787 to his friend Paul Wentworth in London, Ray commented bitterly that Sarah's dower had been granted by the legislature of the State of Massachusetts to John Thomas of Marshfield. "He was a fine Boy of about ten years of age, having no Parent whose Authority he regarded. He imbibed the ruling principle of his Country,

Refuge

and his Parents earnest intreaties had no effect to obtain his residence in N. Scotia, so that he has married in that Country and become an alien, to my no small sorrow."

Four months later Ray wrote again to Paul Wentworth about his son John, among other matters. Ray stated:

> My son John was a very fine spirited Boy, 10 years of age when I was obliged to leave my home 1774 in August. Mrs. Thomas [was in] charge of a numerous family, provision to be made for them by her improving the Farm which was sequestered soon after, & Mrs. T. obliged to pay rent, prevented her paying that attention to the Government of her children; so as to keep him from imbibing the reigning principle of that day, that he could not be prevailed on to come with the family to N. Scotia And hes now become an Alien, but forsaken his family & marri'd in that Country, a Person who has never seen any other Spot then that on which they were born, has the strongest predelection for the same, and he has found means to make the Legislature of that State his friend;...This can never in justice be admitted in bar of my claim...

Young John's attitude and course of action, hurting Ray deeply and causing much bitterness, was one of several trials that faced the family at Prospect Place soon after their arrival.

Late in the spring of 1786 Ray wrote to John Wentworth, the former Royal governor of New Hampshire married to Sarah's niece Frances and then Surveyor General of the King's Woods. Responding to Wentworth's friendly offer to help a friend "in real distress," Ray described his present situation:

> Accustomed to polished society, I dreaded at the Eve of life to settle in the Wilderness of N. S. I therefore purchased the Farm on which I now reside, and by the goodness of my creditor yet subsist upon, overwhelm'd in the common calamity by the Dikes being broken, I had 22 Bushell Corn sown on that land, the produce of every kind lost for 2 years, my quota, which is to be furnish'd next week, & on, till the repairs are completed is Seven Teams, sixteen men &c. per day, by Judge Deschamps calculation, 'twill exceed £200, to your friend. My only

consolation has been that, I was to receive some degree of compensation this Autumn, but, if that prospect ceases, I must from my present feeble habit of Body, I fear, sink under the weight of disappointments, which has been my Lot for the last 12 years...Nothing now remains my Dear Sir, but to through [throw] [myself] my all, and that of my families on the Commissioners Compassion, that which regards myself is the smallest part of my sufferings. I have involved an affectionate Wife, and seven innocent children to share distresses, painful to relate.

The "Commissioners Compassion" to which Ray referred was that of The Lord's Commissioners of His Majesty's Treasury. For some time prior to his death, Ray had communicated with the Commissioners concerning his claim for compensation. The Commissioners, now sitting as a body in Canada, were charged by the Crown to examine and either approve or disapprove the claims for losses suffered by Loyalists whose property, land and personal belongings had been seized and confiscated by the Patriots during the war. In Ray's case he also had been deprived of his compensation as a member of the Mandamus Council. Ray apparently had been receiving an allowance of £200 a month for sitting on the Council. But his claim for loss and damage to property in the amount of £48,000 was disallowed. Nevertheless he appealed that decision and after his death his wife and daughter Sally added their entreaties for compensation by writing to the Commissioners. Ray's friend Paul Wentworth joined in several petitions or memorials on Ray's behalf.

A month or so later George Henry Monk, Sarah's nephew who had greeted them on the family's arrival in Windsor, wrote also to John Wentworth. "Poor Uncle Thomas has been lately very much indisposed," Monk advised Wentworth, "which, added to the misfortune of Inundations that ruin his marsh Land, and continued Drought that parches his Upland, has made him very low Spirited indeed, and with very great reason." He then alluded to the rest of the family, and, pointedly to John. "Aunt Thomas and the rest of the Family are in tolerable Health and Spirits, and my Cousin Nat is vain of being industrious, which, if it continues, will make him a comfort to his Family, and make the Loss of his Brother John much less felt."

Refuge

By the beginning of 1787 it became evident that Nathaniel Ray Thomas was seriously ill. There was other sad news as well. Sarah Thomas wrote to her sister-in-law Mary Dering in March the distressing news. "We have bin visited with sickness and death ever since the last of janr. Mr. Thomas has layed dangerously Ill with a fever, a servant man in the House sick all winter in a Consumption and, in this destresst situation, my dear Childe Martin Howard was taken Ill at Halifax; the two latter are now numbered with the dead, and Mr. thomas still remains so week as not to determin him out of danger."

Not long after his mother's letter, Nat wrote to Mrs. Elizabeth *Stockbridge* Winslow, the wife of Dr. Isaac Winslow of Marshfield, in reply to a letter from that lady. "It made me happy to know that your family were in health," Nat began. "It would be a further addition to that happiness to in return tell you that ours were so, but that is far from being the case. My dear Father has been very ill ever since the middle of January and, although a little recovered, it is with difficulty he can sit up three hours in a day. Upward of five weeks he was confined entirely to his bed and, when first seized with his illness, I did not imagine he would live five minutes."

Nat then spoke of his mother. "My Mother, you know her attention, never left his room for a month and now is not absent from him ten minutes a day. It has almost made her sick and I wonder it has not killed her. Added to these afflictions, judge of her distress at receiving an account of the death of my poor brother Martin. Indeed, my friend, it was almost too much for her." With warmth and sadness he spoke of his brother. "Dear youth, happy for him that he is relieved from the distresses of this world. Alas, how delusive are all earthly hopes. At a time when he enjoyed a far greater share of health than had fallen to his lot for many years and was in a way, had he lived, of being a comfort to his friends from his assuidity and attention to business, he was summoned to take that journey whence no traveler returns." Finally, Nat wrote of John: "Receive my thanks for the mention you make of my brother John. It gives me pleasure to hear he is so happy. May he long continue so and prosper."

Ray Thomas's illness that spring of 1787 alternated in severity. From the moment he was taken ill, when his son Nat declared "I did not imagine he would live five minutes," Ray rallied from time to time to the point where his daughter Sally could report on September 13th that "he has been much better," though then "again relapsed and become so weak

Nathaniel Ray Thomas's gravestone, Windsor, Nova Scotia. Photograph by William H.B. Thomas, 1989

as not to help himself." Sally had prefaced her comments by noting that "the last Ten months of my life have been one series of sickness, melancholy, and Death. I fear it is to be continue'd through the year..." Referring again to her father, she said: "He has two watchers, and as many of us as possible about him all day. My mother is worn with fatigue and I wonder how she keeps off the bed. Papa will not allow any person but his wife or Daughter to lift or assist him."

It was evident to the family who hovered by his bedside that Ray was near his end. Sarah, worn down herself by the long and constant solicitude over Ray, described his last hours to her brother Thomas's widow not long after Ray's death:

> ...a week before his death he apprehending himself to be drawing near the close of life, he with more composure and resignation then I can with my penn discribe, toled us that he had not a desire to live, nor one uneasy thought on his own account, and his familey he could trust in the hands of a good God who had promissed to be the Widows God and Husband, and he trusted would be the Father of his Fatherless Children. He knew in whome he had believed and that his Redeemer lived to make intersession for him He admonished and advised his familey and Children, took every precausion to prevent any difficuly arising to his familey after his death, then took leave of us all, told us not to be uneasy; it was the will of providence and we ought to submit, remembering one day we must all experience the same he then did. He felt his Limbs stifning and growing cold which they must doe till a period was put to his Life. He then saide, "Lay me down in the hands of my God." and never spoke more in this World...

Nathaniel Ray Thomas died on September 20, 1787. That previous June 8th he had made his will, probably with the guidance of George Henry Monk, who was one of the attesting witnesses and also, of course, Sarah Thomas's nephew and an attorney. Some two weeks after Ray's death, his will was presented for probate upon the oaths of the subscribing witnesses, Michael Head, George Deschamps, and Major Monk, and admitted to record.

The provisions of Ray Thomas's will were straightforward. Of outright pecuniary bequests, he gave his son Nathaniel fifty pounds and his son

Refuge

John five pounds. Of the residue of his personal estate, he gave all of it "includeing all and whatsoever, Sum and Sums of money, that may be allowed, due payable or comeing to me, Upon the Report or Reports of the Commissioners for examining the Claims of suffering Loyalists or that may be found due and allowed to me, as compensation for my losses and Services, by the Commissioners appointed by act of Parliament..., in consequence of their Loyalty to his Majesty and attachment to the British Government..., to my ever dear and Esteemed Wife Sarah Thomas." He also named Sarah sole executrix.

All his lands he devised also to Sarah for her life and after her death to Sally, Mary, Elizabeth, and Charles, or their issue, in equal shares. The provisions of the will may indeed have been straightforward, but they were virtually of no effect. For Nathaniel Ray Thomas was described at the time of his death as "insolvent." Some months later Hepsibah Edwards ventured a shrewd appraisal: "I dont know how Mr. Thomas has left her but I fear but poorly."

Mrs. Edwards also described for Sylvester Dering's information more details of their relations in Nova Scotia and those left in Marshfield. Young Polly Storer, Ebenezer's daughter, had spent the winter since Ray's death with Sarah Thomas, "Aunt Thomas," as many in the family called her. "Polly" (Mary Thomas) was expected to return with her cousin, Polly Storer, to Boston for a visit. Mary Thomas's sister Sally "has gone to Quebec to Aunt Anna [Green] Winslow, who has sent for her. I don't like Quebec for so fine a girl as Sally Thomas, but I know not what their poor Mother can do with them all. I wish it were in my power to help them..."

Her comments about John Thomas were doubtless well intentioned but hardly encouraging. "Poor John is married and a poor thing it seems he's got. She is a quiet country girl with, I fear, but little faculty. He, I fear, is unhappy. He goes to see nobody and nobody goes to see him. Mrs. Apthorp went down to see him and by her account he has got a poor 'do-little.' He works like a horse. I wish I could write something more agreeable to you about our family, but so it is and I know no help for it."

A problem that perplexed and bothered Sarah was the education of her youngest son Charles. That year, 1790, he was eighteen. Sarah was very pleased when an Academy was established in Windsor at the instigation of the Lieutenant Governor of Nova Scotia. "I am so happy,"

Refuge

she wrote, "as to be situated in a Town where we have an Academy well founded and attended two, and a Prospect of sune having a Collige Built about a mile from my own House. With stone, it is to be Built & there is a Grant from Parliament of a Thousand Pounds to begin with..." Sarah referred to what shortly became known as King's College School, today King's-Edgehill School, in Windsor. The School was divided into two departments, the Latin School and the English and Mathematics School. The aim was to provide a classical education. "But alas want of Ability deprives me of the advantage I might otherwise reape from them & by not having it in my power to Educate your Coz Charles at them, for I am now obliged to take him from the Acadamey to Labour upon the Farm this summer, which indead destresses me very much as you who know the valew of a liberal Education, must know..."

As for Charles, his mother continued: "how Erepairable the loss must be to him at this time of life, but what can a poor unfortunate Widowed Parent doe for a Son deprived of the advantage of having a kinde Father ambitious of introducing his Children into life, in a way that they might make a figure in the Worlde by keeping up the name of their father and reaping advantage to themselves." And Sarah lamented: "and that at a time when he seams to stand the moste in nead of a hand to introduce him into sume way to provide for himself in life."

In another letter, written at the same time, Sarah repeated her news about Charles. "I have bin obliged to take my son Charles from his schools to Labour on the farm this summer, but I hope to have it in my power to send him to school in the winter a little while but it destresses me much to know what Business he will fix himself in without money or friends to take him by the hand..."

Before Ray's death, Sarah had had difficulty financially in caring for her family. Since his death, the situation had worsened. Writing to Sylvester Dering, she remarked at this time: "Every day [I] feal my loss in your Uncle." Young Sally Thomas, writing also to Sylvester, put it more bluntly: "... you know not (and I pray never may) what it is to be reduced as my family are." When Sarah's cousin, Mrs. Anna *Green* Winslow, heard of Ray's death and correctly guessing that his family would be hard put to survive, she asked that Sally be allowed to come to her and her husband, Joshua Winslow, in Quebec whence they had fled. It was not the first time that the Winslows had taken in some one or more of Ray Thomas's family. Nearly twenty years before they had welcomed Ray's and Sarah's son Henry Dering Thomas into their home; and not

Refuge

long thereafter, when the British troops under Captain Balfour had occupied the Thomas residence in Marshfield as barracks, once again the Winslows opened their doors to Sarah and her children.

In fact, Sylvester's sister Elizabeth [Dering] apparently invited her cousin, Elizabeth Packer Thomas, to stay with her and her husband, Dr. Gardiner. But Sally opposed the idea. "Mrs. Gardiner is all goodness, but I really believe if Eliza was to quit her Mother, it would shorten that life so precious to us her children. Mama was but too deeply wounded by her removal, and to part with another in the same way might prove too much for her."

As for her own course of action Sally informed Sylvester: "To you I will say that but for my fond Mother's sake I would never be a burden on any mortal. My health is good and I am able to support myself, which I would have done in preference to being a weight on my friends had I not known my Mother would have been greatly hurt thereby. For her I sacrifice my choice and view it my duty to do so."

Then Sally switched her recital to tell of her brother Charles. She hoped he would get some employment in Halifax. "If our Boston friends were able to assist him, I should imagine they [would] do something for a certain namesake of him who seems to be quite a rover. This only is for your ear my Cousin." Sally undoubtedly referred to Ebenezer Storer and his family and, in particular, to Charles Storer, who, not too many years before, had been traveling about Europe.

That Sally herself merited a warm appraisal from the Winslows was evident in the words of Anna *Green* Winslow in a letter to Sylvester Dering of June 9, 1792: "Indeed, she is a most attentive worthy good girl, and what I should do if she should accept the offers that have been made to her to join hands in the matrimonial line...Her sister Mary I hear is about to try that change of state." Mary Thomas, in fact, was married to Benjamin Gerrish Gray, the son of a Loyalist, that December of 1792.

In the early summer of 1793, Mary *Thomas* Gray wrote her brother John Thomas in Marshfield. She rejoiced, she told John, that their mother had received recent letters from him. As for herself, Mary went on, "I have now the cares of a family and want of help, and yet I would sometimes taken an hour to write a letter to a friend that I know would be rejoiced to hear from me. I mean to write your Lucy [John's wife], and she is not very good in the writing way either. So you have three girls - I dare say I

Refuge

should love them all. But my Sally [John's eldest daughter, Sarah Dering Thomas, named for her grandmother] carries the day, dear lovely creature. I am very glad she has not forgotten me; I charge you not to let her."

Mary also mentioned that their sister Eliza [Elizabeth Packer Thomas] was about to follow hers and John's example and get married, "not choosing to follow our eldest brother and sister [Nat and Sally], for they are quite out of our row and mean to content themselves with loving our children." Mary went on about Eliza: "She, I trust, has made choice of a good man [Richard Cunningham] and if she has, my brother, he has a pretty fortune for her and she may shortly live at her ease. I suppose even if Heaven should smile on you and me we shall never be worth one quarter as much, both put together, but perhaps we may be just as happy. Tho I really think she has a very clever man. It is very pleasant her living in Windsor so near our good Mother."

Richard Cunningham came from a family with considerable land holdings in and around Windsor. On one of these tracts, Saulsbrook, Richard established himself about 1785. The property was not far outside of Windsor. It was at about this time also that he made the acquaintance of the Thomas family.

By then, Sarah Thomas, deciding to sell Prospect Place Farm, had moved into the town of Windsor. Since Ray's death, she had mortgaged the farm to a family friend, the merchant John Lawson, of Halifax and with the proceeds had paid off the mortgage Ray had placed on the property. In May of 1793, then, apparently in order to retire the Lawson debt, she determined or may have been forced to sell Prospect Place. The sale was consummated on June 22, 1793, the purchaser one Colin Campbell. If the family were distressed at parting with their home of nearly ten years, their surviving correspondence fails to reveal it. If anything, there seemed an element of relief.

Richard Cunningham and Eliza, living at Saulsbrook, were close to her mother now that Sarah had moved into Windsor. The Cunninghams soon had a child, a son, "the quietest child," his grandmother said. Eliza's new situation moved her mother to report to Sylvester Dering in the summer of 1795: "She [Eliza] makes a very attentive, good mother and though a wild girl is become quite the grave matron, never better pleased than when she is employed in tending her child and her husband sitting beside her, which is not as often as she wishes for he is an active man, lives on a fine farm consisting of 1000 acres about two miles from my habitation."

"An active man," Richard Cunningham became one of Nova Scotia's large landowners and was active in developing the Province's gypsum industry. Tradition survives that Cunningham was a "heavy-handed" man, whose name was associated with an unpleasant murder case. However the truth of that charge may be, the Cunninghams remained at Saulsbrook. Two more children were born to them, Eliza Dering Boyd and Frances Sarah Wentworth.

Referring to the fact that several of her children and grandchildren were near her, and her satisfaction at that, Sarah described to Sylvester Dering her feelings about her son John:

> ...I cannot help feeling the same love and longing desire to see my son John, although he so sadly neglects me in the writing way. I am, like a fond parent, ready to make every excuse for him and do consider he has his time much taken up on the farm which subjects him to fatigue by day and drowsiness by night, that he cannot afford to keep necessary help and unfortunately for him his little family consists of four girls when I last heard from him. For I have not received a word for four years at least, I think it is, though Mr. Gray has paid him a visit in the time by whom I have endeavored to offer him every little proof of my affection for him and his family. But nothing can ever force a line from him, though from other I hear that he expresses a great attachment to me and his family of brothers and sisters.
>
> The last letter I had from him he wrote very particularly of everything, even down to what number of chickens he had, and gave me a particular account of his children's dispositions and everything I could wish, and with the greatest affection begged me not suppose he ever should forget me because he did not write me so often as he could wish. But alas, I cannot feel that satisfaction to an anxious parent who wishes to feel for and with a child in every joy and sorrow.

In reply to Sylvester's invitation to Sarah to visit her native country, she declined. "It is true I have but a small family," she wrote, "and but little

Refuge

left to call for my attention, but that little is my all.. I feel a something that still draws me toward the ashes of a dear departed friend, as though they spoke in tender strains of affection and said, 'Do not leave me. 'Tis but a few days and we shall again lie down together.'"

As always Sarah worried about the future of her children, particularly her youngest child Charles. With two of her daughters already married and her son Nat apparently settled down in business, she had been concerned about what occupation Charles might be able to find for himself. When the possibilities of bookkeeping seemed to elude him, he had turned to the military service and found a position through the good offices of John Wentworth, by then governor of Nova Scotia.

In her lengthy letter written in the summer of 1795, after informing Sylvester about John's situation, Sarah spoke of Charles;

> I suppose ere this you have heard that Gov. Wentworth received the honor of being made a baronet, so now it is Sir John and Lady Wentworth. They still continue their friendship to my son Charles, who by a most rapid promotion occasioned by Prince Edward [Duke of Kent, son of King George III and commander of British forces in Nova Scotia and New Brunswick] having troops sent over from England in answer to his request for raising a second battalion has made such changes through his first, that my son stands a great chance of being promoted to Captain within two years, being the third lieutenant and the two above him being men of fortune who intend to purchase a company immediately, so that he comes on, of course, next in command.

She went on:

> He is now indulged with the pay of a company for one that is absent, in addition to his pay, and, a lieutenant told me yesterday, was a lucky fellow (to use his expression) being in much favor and esteemed by the Prince, to which he was pleased to add 'He richly deserved it,' for he was an attentive, good officer, well disposed and guilty of no ill conduct, which is flattering to hear...I have reason to bless God that he is placed in so exemplary a regiment of officers who are noted for not being guilty of any open crime, and I pray God to deliver his soul from secret sin.

Refuge

Sarah had reservations about Charles going into the military, which she shared with Sylvester:

> I join with you in saying I would not have made choice of the military life for him, but it appeared at the time to be the way for him to provide for himself. Providence seemed to point out that as the only way to promote him and take him from the humbling station of a common laborer who worked very hard for his daily bread. But I trust in the Almighty. There will be some way pointed out for him (as I believe is his wish) to settle him down with a family and enjoy the fruits of the toil of his youth some future day.

Sarah reflected on what she had written and added:

> For the Prince is a very strict, though a good, officer, and while he leaves not any time for idleness or dissipation in his officers, they have no cause to complain, as he is the first himself both early and late to exert himself in attention to the works going on in Halifax, as well as by constant and daily attendance to his duty on parade to a moment.

In a postscript Sarah included that "Sir John and Lady Wentworth have passed through this town last week in their chariot and four horses on their way to Annapolis to see the country, and are so very urgent to take me home with them in the carriage that I fear, though unfit at my time of life to show myself in public at Government House, I shall be obliged to go with them or give offense, which will not do while I live for children's sake who are so dependent...I hope this will not get into the post office as if it should it will cost much more than it is worth."

Two years later, in the summer of 1797, Sarah was visiting her daughter Eliza Cunningham at Saulsbrook near Windsor. Her other married daughter, Mary Gray, living near Preston, was expecting her second child, and her sister Sally was with her. Sarah took the opportunity, while at Saulsbrook, to write to her son John at Marshfield. She reported that she was about to leave Eliza the next week "when I shall return home for your brother [Nat] is keeping Bachelors Hall with only one servant in the house." But she wished John would write to his brother Nat, "as he wishes much you would and it would please him to hear that you have a school for your children and that my namesake can

Refuge

write so well...Oh what a blessing I should esteem it could I show my affection by assisting you with a few hundreds, but it has not pleased God to give me the pleasure. I dare not murmur or complain at my small allowance; it is better than being entirely dependent or being reduced to beggary." She ended her letter to John: "You will not omit my best love to your wife and children, tho the poor little creatures do not know who sends it to them. Be assured they have it, altho I have never seen them."

Sarah returned to her home in Windsor. It was now the middle of August 1797. On Thursday, the 17th of that month, the garrison at Halifax was alerted to the disappearance of several private soldiers. Prince Edward immediately dispatched an officer and an armed guard to search out, seize, and return the deserters. Shortly, when the Prince was riding along Barrington Street, he came upon two officers of his command walking together. The officers were Lieutenant Brenton Halliburton and Lieutenant Charles Thomas of His Majesty's Royal Fusilier Regiment. The Prince informed the two that he had already dispatched Lieutenant Robinson with an armed guard to apprehend the deserters and that Robinson had expressed the wish that Charles Thomas might accompany him, to which the Prince assented, and now the Prince ordered Thomas in pursuit also.

Having heard that soldiers had been seen in some woods near St. Margaret's Bay Road, Robinson led the search party in that direction. The group soon came upon the deserters who, finding themselves surrounded by armed troops, gave themselves up without a struggle. Returning to Halifax and when about eight miles from the city, the two officers decided to halt the return march for rest and refreshment. They themselves undertook to put up at a nearby inn.

Preparing to lie down for a short rest, one of the officers remarked that they should check their pistols to see that they were in order in the event the deserters should try to rise up against them or to escape. Whereupon Lieutenant Robinson, picking up his, noted that it was just as well they check for his had no powder in the pan. He laid the pistol on a table and it accidentally fired, the ball passing through the chest of Charles Thomas.

His fellow officer, Robinson, emotionally unnerved by shock and grief, snatched up his other pistol with the intent to kill himself. But Charles, though seriously wounded, called out for help to restrain Robinson. That officer was bound with ropes, but told the men who thus secured and were ordered to watch him that he would not rest until he had killed himself.

Refuge

Robinson, in fact, broke loose from the ropes that bound him and jumped off a steep cliff, suffering severe bruises though not fulfilling his intention to kill himself.

Prince Edward, having learned that the search party had apprehended the deserters but that Lieutenant Thomas was wounded, had ridden out from Halifax with an attending doctor to meet the returning group. Shocked to find Charles Thomas indeed seriously, if not mortally wounded, the Prince had the doctor bleed the stricken officer and ordered the party to carry him to Government House in Halifax, the official residence of Sir John and Lady Wentworth. Lady Wentworth was, of course, Sarah Thomas' s niece and young Charles Thomas's first cousin, which may well have prompted the Prince to direct that the wounded man be taken to Government House.

By all accounts the Prince was deeply distressed at his young officer's condition. He summoned all the surgeons of the garrison to attend Charles. But it became quickly apparent that medical attention would be to no avail. The Prince immediately sent expresses to Windsor to summon Charles's mother and to Preston to his sister Sally, whom Charles particularly wished to see.

Sarah was too frail to attempt the trip to Halifax, but Sally arrived in time to embrace Charles while he still remained conscious. Charles Thomas, aged twenty-four, died in the arms of Lady Wentworth about four o'clock that same afternoon of August 17, 1797.

Immediately following Charles' death, Prince Edward had the news sent to Sarah at Windsor by means of the telegraph, a system of semaphore signals sent from hilltop to hilltop. The Prince himself had been distraught, weeping over his young officer and personal friend. Seeing this, Charles exclaimed to those around him, "Let all that love me, love Prince Edward."

Nor did Charles forget his mother. Praying for her well being and that she should receive every consolation, he said, "Poor old lady, I fear this shock will be too much for her." Writing to Charles's brother John in Marshfield somewhat later, Sarah admitted one might suppose it would have been too much for her, "was it not for more than human aid that supports one under such severe trials...But", she went on, "what affords me the greatest consolation is, he never could have left the world with a more unblemished character...In short, though he was my son and your brother, in justice to him I ought to say he left as good a moral character as ever any young man did..."

Lieutenant Charles Thomas, 7th Regiment of Royal Fusiliers. Son of Nathaniel Ray Thomas. Courtesy of The Duxbury Rural and Historical Society.

Refuge

Charles Thomas had died and his body was carried from St. Paul's Church to the cemetery, "surrounded with all the honors of war..., attended by every mark of respect that could be shown by the Army, Navy and by the inhabitants, making the greatest procession that was ever seen in Halifax, at which the Prince and Sir John [Wentworth] attended with every mark of respect and distinguishing appearance of distress and grief."

On Tuesday, August 22nd, the <u>Halifax Gazette</u> carried the following news item:
> Last Thursday [August 17th] died at the Government House, Lieutenant Charles Thomas, of His Majesty's 7th Regiment of Royal Fusiliers, cousin to his Excellency Sir John and Lady Wentworth in the 25th year of his age. The zeal and talents he evinced in the service of his profession promised future usefulness in the service, to which he was attached, and the uniform amiable character he supported in private life justly endeared him to his numerous friends, who with heartfelt sincerity lament his loss; and Saturday his remains were interred with full military Honours.

Then, sometime later, a flat stone was placed over Charles's grave in St. Paul's Cemetery, with an inscription which recited, in part, that the stone was "placed as a Testimony of/High Friendship Esteem/by/Lieut. General His Royal Highness/Prince Edward/his Colonel."

> Together with these tributes to her son, one at least for all succeeding generations to read, there were other expressions of sympathy and praise. Sarah had received, as she wrote to John Thomas, "such friendly letters of condolence from Prince Edward and Lady Wentworth I could wish you could have the perusal of them." She lamented that grief prevented her: "from taking that consolation which I ought to do, when Prince Edward has condescended to write me with his own hand that he mourns for the loss of my son Charles not only as a man and one of his best officers but as a sincere friend, for he loved him with the tenderest affection and valued him as highly as was possible in life for one friend to regard and esteem another, and must feel his loss most sensibly for he should regret him till the last day of his existence...This from the hand of one of the

Refuge

> Royal Family could never have been once thought would have been offered to me..."

Added to the expressions of figures close to this tragic affair and of the press were other outpourings of sentiment about Charles Thomas's death. In a postscript to a letter from Sally Thomas to her brother John in September 1798, she wrote: "Time will not allow me to write those pieces composed on the death of our dear departed Brother Charles, but I will send them to you ere long." At least two pieces of poetry survive.

One of the poems, almost certainly in the handwriting of Sally Thomas and sent to John, may have been her own composition or possibly a copy of someone else's. It was, indeed, an elegy, and several of its lines reflect its mournful tenor:

> ...when the hidden shaft, the sudden blow,
> Like lightning's fatal flash strikes, and lays low,
> Youth! beauty! Honor! worth! and manly grace!
> Goodness of heart depicted on the face,
> With rising honors, ev'ry wish enjoy'd
> We see in one dread moment all destroy'd,
> Torn from our grasp and ravish'd from our eyes!

And there was recognition of the family grief shared by Sir John and Lady Wentworth, the latter, of course, Charles's first cousin.

> Thy worthy patron, relative and friend
> And his lov'd partner wrung with sorrow bend
> When first the dread alarm assail'd their ears,
> Aroused their terror, Waken'd all their fear.
> Haste, bring him to our arms, our hearts, they said,
> Hither, oh hither, let him be conveyed!
> Blest in their pow'r, with eager haste they strove
> Their efforts equal'd only by their love,
> Heard thy last sigh, receiv'd thy parting breath,
> And thought thee lovely in the arms of death.
> Drop'd o'er thy corpse the agonizing tear
> And pour'd parental fondness o'er thy bier.

Finally, the author, whether Sally or another, paid homage to Prince Edward and his solicitude for his fallen officer and his family.

Lady Frances Wentworth, niece of Sarah Dering Thomas. Portrait by John Singleton Copley. Collection of the New York Public Library; Astor, Lenox, and Tilden Foundations.

John Briggs Thomas, great-grandson of Nathaniel Ray Thomas the Tory and Colonel Anthony Thomas the Patriot. Great-grandfather of the author.

Refuge

> *Still more, oh Thomas! numbered with the dead,*
> *What precious hallow'd tears for thee are shed,*
> *Thy noble-minded Prince benignly deigns*
> *To pay this tribute to thy dear remains.*
> *He calls thee friend! and hastens to impart*
> *Sweet comfort to thy woe-fraught mother's heart.*

The other poem, appearing in a Yarmouth, Nova Scotia, newspaper over the name of a Mrs. Fletcher of Yarmouth, lamented the death of Lieutenant Charles Thomas, "accidentally shot by his most intimate friend at Shelburne." One stanza set the scene for the elegy:

> *The Martial arm with sable crape entwined,*
> *The drum deep muffled, and the inverted spear.*
> *The mournful dirge that floats upon the wind,*
> *And strikes in plaintive sounds in pensive air.*

And the last stanza called to mind Prince Edward's compassion:

> *A nobler meed, was thine, - a nobler fame -*
> *Think not, ye friends, his destiny,*
> *Whose valour, virtue, and whose fate could claim*
> *From Royal Edward's eye th' impassioned tear.*

Charles's death had devastated the family. His mother, in particular, had suffered through the deaths of her second son Henry Dering years after he had gone to sea with the British Navy, of her fourth son Martin Howard in Halifax even before that of his father, and the decision of her son John to remain in Marshfield and not to remove to Nova Scotia with the rest of the family. But as always, faced with grief or disaster, Sarah Thomas calmly accepted all as God's will in His infinite wisdom.

XIII

A New Century

With the turn of the century, Sarah Thomas interested herself even more, if possible, in her family. She was now sixty-eight years old. The remembrance of her son Charles was ever present, but the particular tragedy of his death, the manner in which it occurred, the suddenness of it, was by then at least softened. One particular wish, a special desire on Sarah's part, was uppermost in her mind as the new century came in.

On the 29th of January 1800 Sarah wrote to her son John in Marshfield. She spelled out a plan that matured in her mind:

> You led me to hope, my son, that should God spare our lives, you would hope to pay me a visit when the pleasant season came on. I need not tell you how glad I should be to see you, for surely you cannot doubt the happiness it must afford to an affectionate parent, as you have so long been one yourself.

and she went on, pressing her point:

> And I hope after all I have frequently said to you, neither you nor your wife will doubt my sincerity if I again tell you I should be rejoiced to see your wife with you, but should you plead that impossible from her grave fear of crossing the water, as you before told me, adding that you could not both leave your house and family together, allow me to make one request more, that you will bring with you my namesake [twelve-year-old Sarah Dering Thomas, her granddaughter], with your wife's leave and consent, to be left with me for six or ten months, if she finds she can content herself after she comes to remain with me for that space of time or longer.

From the tenor of Sarah's letter it was apparent that she had already, and probably for some time, been contemplating the idea of a visit to Nova Scotia by John and especially her granddaughter and namesake. In fact, she had doubtless talked of it with her children. Indeed, not more than a month after Charles's "sudden and awful death" as Sally Thomas put it,

A New Century

she wrote her brother John in Marshfield: "I wish my dear John you could pay us a visit in the Spring; it would raise my parents spirits and gratify all your attach'd relations in Nova Scotia."

Almost exactly a year later, Sally wrote again to John with news of their mother and of his possible visit. "Our good mother is wonderfully well considering the many trials of her life; every grandchild adds at least two years to her number for they amuse and delight her, so her married children keep up her spirits and Old Sarah takes care of her health and family." Then, whimsically, Sally went on: "...I feel as if I did as much good as you mighty married people who think we cannot be anything without joining your social group. Indeed, Brother, you made me laugh by the alarm your pen expressed for my age and lonely situation." [Sally was then thirty-six.] "It is true I have counted myself in the list of Old Maids near six years, still I am as happy as many younger women and if you will come to Windsor can laugh with you at my want of charm to captivate Gentlemen."

But, she continued seriously, "it delights me to find you think of visiting us. I beg you to fulfill your promise as the seeing you will enliven us all, particularly your dear parent who lives but in her children's society...Pray bring one of your daughters when you come and compare them with our two sisters' little pets that you may resolve which is to gain the greatest applause...The money I gave Mr. Gray to give you was a trifle but I thought it might serve to remember me by. I gave a guinea for you out of which I desired my namesake, your daughter, might have a pair of red shoes..."

Sarah Thomas, Sally's mother, continued her letter to John:
> I will take care to provide for her, and her aunts will instruct her in anything that she has not already made herself mistress of, and she shall be carefully [taught] while she remains with me, not to forget her reading, writing and ciphering.

And Sarah reassured her son:
> And they will join with me in promising, should I be called away, to see her safely returned with some careful person to her parents again... I hope it will not be long before I shall hear from you that you are all well and happy, and I shall flatter myself you will let me know you will consent to comply with my request in allowing your daughter to come visit me...Sally bids me say nothing shall be wanting on her part, of care and affection for her

A New Century

namesake, and that she can even teach her to spin if she has occasion for it...I beg your children's pardon, as many of them may think it is wrong to call them 'little ones' now.

Later that spring Sally wrote to her brother John regarding the hoped-for visit of her niece and namesake. "My mother tells me she has wrote to request you will allow your daughter Sarah to spend a few months with her. I hope it will be agreeable to you and her mother that she should come, as my mother will be lonely when I leave her and she will be highly delighted with her granddaughter's society. You have so many friends that you might lend one for a little while for the comfort of an old lady who will take every care of her."

Sally's reference to leaving her mother was to her, Sally's, forthcoming marriage. In a light vein she wrote John: "As you sometime since wrote our valuable Mother that you thought I was old enough to marry if I ever meant to enter social life, I have taken the hint and have consented to join your order of beings some time in the course of this year. I write to say that I shall be particularly gratified if my Sister Thomas and you would come to be present at my wedding. You might come if you only believe you could. I have not fixed any particular time for it to take place...Do be good humored and come to Windsor in August before Indian corn harvest that you may be back in time to gather that for your winter's comfort."

Sally told her brother about the man she intended to marry. "The gentleman who I have consented to give my heart is Mr. James B. Francklin, brother to the young lady who came to Windsor with our family. It is probable you may remember him; at any rate I wish you to know him...Our dear Mother is blessed with perfect health and looks charmingly for one at her time of life. Our two sisters are also well. Mary has only two boys, Eliza Packer one boy and two girls...Brother Nat is in Halifax on a visit to his friends."

But Mary Gray soon became seriously ill and for two years declined in health. She received, as her mother said, the best medical advice that could be obtained. All who knew her strove to provide every comfort. Her husband, Benjamin Gerrish Gray, did his best "to procure her everything she could want." Indeed, he moved his whole family, his ill wife Mary and their two sons, back to Windsor to be near her mother Sarah and her brother Nat and sisters Eliza and Sally. For Sarah Thomas, it was a

A New Century

familiar trial and burden to bear: first, her son Henry Dering's death; then her son Martin Howard, passing on in 1787 before Ray's own death; then, and grievous to bear, her dear son Charles's untimely end.

Sarah described to her son John the last two months of Mary's life. "...for the last two month of her life I did not leave her night or day, by her own and Mr. Gray's request and never to her last breath heard her utter a groan, though she said, 'Oh Mamma, it is impossible for me to tell you the distress I feel. I think I can suffer nothing more than I have except the last agony. Do not grieve too much for me, Mama. It will not be long before we meet again.'" And Sarah wrote of her last moments: "Her dear little boys were called to take their leave of their fond mother. She looked steadily at her husband who was kneeling by her as he had often done, lifted up her poor feeble hand and stroked his cheek. Then the struggle she had expected took place for a few moments, and she took her flight from all her sufferings to the blest abodes of rest."

Writing to her brother John on June 27, 1802, Sally, now Sarah Dering *Thomas* Francklin, noted that Mary's death on the twelfth of May had occurred at half past four in the afternoon, "the very time in the day our good Brother Charles died." Mary Gray was thirty six. "Our excellent Mother," Sally went on, "does on this as she has on every trying event through life conduct with great calmness and becoming submission to the Decree of heaven, yet she shakes under the affliction and is at present not very well."

Sally also advised John that Mary had directed that a lock of her hair be given to all her near relations, including one to be sent to him. This she was now inclosing. In addition, Sally informed John that Mary had said she left him "the miniature pictures of your Father and Mother because she thought you would value them...I believe my Mother has them to send by the first safe conveyance." These miniatures of Nathaniel Ray Thomas and Sarah *Dering* Thomas were probably executed prior to the former's leaving Boston with the British in March of 1776, and are now in the Gershom Bradford House in Duxbury, Massachusetts.

A year passed. Sarah Thomas wrote to her son John in May 1803 about "a fine large English ram" that Richard Cunningham wished to present to him. It was apparently the offspring of English sheep that Prince Edward, now more commonly known by his title, the Duke of Kent, gave to the Agricultural Society before he left Nova Scotia. Sarah was concerned about arrangements John could make for getting the animal

A New Century

from Boston to Marshfield after it had been sent from Windsor. She urged John to answer her request as soon as possible. Three months later Nat Thomas advised John that he had shipped the ram to Boston, "directed to be left near the 'Boston Stone.'" It was a Cotswold or Southdown bred ram, Nat wrote John, "of a very fine breed for mutton...Their wool is fine, but not much in quantity, but the excellency of the breed is that they are fat, and though from short legs they do not appear to make a show, yet they weigh heavy and are easily kept, having much flesh and little bone."

Sarah was, as usual, preoccupied with her family that spring of 1803. She had gone on a visit to her niece, Lady Wentworth, in Halifax, where she was detained all winter "for want of snow to take me home [by sleigh], " and when at last she could leave, she was "obliged in the month of March to travel in the Governor's close wheel carriage over very bad roads, my anxiety was so great to get home to your sister Francklin." Sally was, indeed "very complaining and distressed with a fever." Sarah needed little urging to stay with her daughter and remained with the Francklins for six weeks until all were relieved when Sally gave birth to a "fine stout daughter," whose Father gave the child its mother's maiden name, Sarah Thomas Francklin. At this happy event, Sarah marveled: "...that I should live to have ten grandchildren, and the one your sister C. [Cunningham] lost made eleven."

Of those grandchildren, she went on, her late daughter Mary's husband, Benjamin Gerrish Gray, had "two fine sons, the youngest still in petticoats, the picture of his dear Mother, and that same earnest manner of speaking that she had, with sparkling black eyes... I long to see your dear family of children. I often think of and converse about them, and though I never see them, they share in my affection as well as those I have around me."

In Nat's letter to John telling about the dispatch of the ram to Boston, the ram from Richard Cunningham, he noted that "vessels go constantly between this place [Windsor] and Boston. Three have arrived this week in four days passage, and some have arrived this season in sixty hours from Long Wharf." Reverting to family news, Nat added: "your Mother enjoys her health remarkably well for a person of her age, keeps her good looks and is active and smart, more than she was some years ago. She will be seventy-one years old in November next."

A New Century

About their sisters, Nat reported virtually what his mother had written John. "Your sister Francklin has a fine hearty girl, being quite fat and stout, with excellent health and very well and happily married. Your sister Cunningham has been for two months past very ill after lying in, in consequence of taking cold during some very hot weather, and then, while warm, exposing herself to the air. We have been very much alarmed about her, lest she would never recover, but by the blessing of God, we have within two or three days past some hopes, as she seems to be a little better."

"I sincerely hope your wife and family are in good health," Nat continued, "and that you may long continue so. I desire to be kindly remembered to them all, and to Dr. Winslow, Mr. Shaw, and all my old friends in Marshfield and elsewhere when you see them... My own health has been very precarious for two years past in consequence of a violent fatigue from hard riding. It had nearly killed me. The weather was extremely hot, and I rode to Halifax on horseback in six hours and back in the same time." World news brought a comment as well. "You have no doubt heard that Great Britain and France are again at war, which could not be avoided as the French wish to subdue the world, but this, I trust, with God's assistance to England they will never effect while her 'Wooden Walls' (the British Navy) last."

With the first of the new year, 1804, Nat married. His mother informed his brother John in a letter of March 1804. "Perhaps you as well as the rest of the family," Sarah wrote, "may be surprised when I tell you that your brother has at last taken to himself a wife, and the first of January this year was married to the eldest daughter [Sarah Hersey Otis DeWolf] of Mr. Benjamin DeWolf, whose house you may remember dining at when you were in Nova Scotia." With Nat married, Sarah realized that it would be best for her to make other living arrangements. She had been living with Nat. It was now time to make a change. "As I found I was illy able to attend to my own family, I should be less able to attend it when increased, and, recollecting young people and old might not always agree in judgment, I thought best, as your sisters are so frequently wishing me to spend some of my time with them and your poor sister's health calls me to be much with her, to give up the care of the family and agree to keep a room to retire to as my home, and allow them an acknowledgment for the time I should be with them out of my small income."

A New Century

Sarah continued: "Your brother is now paying off what little I am in debt, and should I have anything left, more than to bury me, I shall leave it as my desire that you shall have your share, though it be but a dollar apiece. Providence has not seen fit to gratify my wish to have sufficient to give a proof of my affection to my children as I have ever wished, so they must accept my best wishes that God would reward them with every blessing. Remember, no children ever possessed a larger share of their parent's tender affection than my children can boast of. I have written thus only to convince you that you are never forgotten by me. Although out of sight, you are never out of mind. I hope before I die to get sufficient allowance from the King's pension to put me decently in the ground."

Finally, Sarah brought herself to tell John about his sister's health. "My heart aches to tell you that your sister Cunningham appears to be fast following her sister. Her cough still remains and pain in her side that wears her flesh, with loss of appetite and sleepless nights, makes me dread the warm weather weakening her daily. I trust it will please the Almighty to prepare her and all concerned for His holy will concerning her."

In the spring of 1804 Mrs. Anna *Green* Winslow paid a visit to Marshfield from Quebec. She paid a call on John Thomas and met his wife and children, writing to Sarah that she was impressed with the sight of John's wife Lucy with their children "sitting around her, so neatly drest, each one employed with their work, that she knew it would be pleasing for me to hear..." Anna met John also at Dr. Winslow's whither he had gone to meet her. Sarah was particularly pleased because, as she wrote John in June, "she had been so long a resident in our family and you was obliged to her for your first insight into your reading and writing when a child..." Anna informed Sarah also that she was well received by some of their old neighbors and dined and lodged and drank tea with them.

There was the seemingly inevitable news about the family's health. John's sister Sarah Francklin had been in great danger of losing her little girl and, if the child lived, her mother worried lest she should lose one or both eyes from a "violent inflammation in them caused by teething." Eliza Cunningham also was in poor health. "She has talked of paying you a visit, thinking the change of air might be beneficial, and she would have the pleasure of seeing you too, but as she is very sick at sea, the Doctor thinks it would be better to take a journey, so she has altered her plans

A New Century

and is going to Annapolis in a few days, although she, no more than myself, has much expectation of her ever getting benefit from sea or land. We cannot help watching the changes come on just as they did on your poor sister Gray."

Sad times, it seems, confronted all of Sarah's family. In far-off Marshfield, John Thomas and his children suffered a loss that struck hard. Lucy *Baker* Thomas, John's wife died in August 1804 at the age of 40. She and John had been married in the spring of 1786, a short time after he had recovered his mother's dower right in the Marshfield property by grant of the Massachusetts legislature. Their first child, and Sarah's granddaughter and namesake, Sarah Dering Thomas, was born in 1788. At the age of sixteen when her mother died, young Sarah took over the management of her father's household and looked after her brother and sisters, ranging downward in age from fourteen to two.

As usual, John's family shared his loss. Sarah *Thomas* Francklin wrote her brother that she sincerely sympathized with him and his children over their "very melancholy bereavement." She deeply lamented the death of her late sister-in-law, whom she had hoped one day to see. Sarah Thomas wrote her son about the same time, a few months after Lucy Thomas's death, but her letters were not forwarded to Marshfield until some six months afterward. By then, John Thomas had secured a housekeeper whom Sarah hoped would be faithful to his interests. Even so, she felt for his children, who Sarah knew, would "mourn their worthy mother's care and attention to them... We seem to be a mournful family. One passes off after another. May the Lord prepare us all to meet that blessed world above where there is no change. God bless you, my dear child."

Despite illness that must have seemed always near - Eliza Cunningham was declining with what was felt to be consumption and Sarah Francklin's daughter was "in a very weak state of health" - Sarah Thomas followed her children's and grandchildren's lives with love and attention. She was pleased that Nat had a son, a fine little fellow of whom his father who loved little children was deeply fond. She had written her granddaughter and namesake Sarah that she was sending her a "set of quillwork boxes" and a pair of earrings. The earrings she enclosed in a tablecloth, together with a silver porringer, to be forwarded to John Thomas in Marshfield through the good offices of Mrs. Storer. The porringer, one of several which had once belonged to Sarah's father, Henry Dering of Boston, was for John to be given to the latter's

A New Century

son when his father thought appropriate. Sarah had already given a porringer to each of her children as they married. As Sarah wrote to John: "I send it [the porringer] to you that you may know that though out of sight, you are never out of my mind, and though but the widow's mite, I wish you all to share equally in any little I may have..."

In the late summer of 1805 Sarah Francklin and her husband James Boutineau Francklin lost their two and one-half-year old daughter Sarah. An "uncommon stout and healthy" child, like her aunts Mary Gray and now Eliza Cunningham, she was stricken with consumption. Her grandmother described to John Thomas in Marshfield his little niece's final hours.

The child's parents took her on a short trip, thinking a change of air would do her good. But on the trip she became worse, and the Francklins set out for home. They stopped at an inn on the way. But despite all their efforts to keep her warm, to love her, to reassure her they were going home, the little girl died. "They brought her fifteen miles, across their laps, home (a Great trial it must have been to them, I said to your sister) but she answered she wished to have her near them as long as she could." As for herself, Sarah added cheerfully: "My own health is as well as I could expect, but pains of old age remind me that I am but tottering to the grave."

In the late fall of 1805, on November 5th, Sarah wrote a letter to her seventeen-year-old granddaughter (Sarah casually addressed the girl, "my dear niece"), her son John's first-born named for her, Sarah Dering Thomas. Young Sarah had written her grandmother that the family in Marshfield were all in good health. This reassured Sarah, who feared that some of John's family might have been very sick from something in a letter from Dr. Winslow's wife. Thankful, she began a letter to her grandchild: "I am very happy, my dear," Sarah wrote, "to find from the purport of your letter that you feel such a sense of the dispensations of Providence towards you...And by reflecting upon the good counsel you received from your deceased mother, be led to follow her steps and be able to say, it was good for me that I was afflicted in the days of my youth."

"I am much pleased to hear," Sarah continued, "you are able to conduct the affairs of your father's family so well as to have the commendation of many of your and my friends. I hope and doubt not you will by your constant attention and affection for your <u>only</u> parent increase his love for

A New Century

you all daily, and, in a proper time, will not only merit but obtain a worthy companion for your own comfort and satisfaction through life." Sarah added: "I am sorry you did not get the quil boxes, but glad the other things got safe...I will try, if I live this winter, to get another set that will do for your sister, if you get those I sent before and like them."

John's family, in particular, his children, were never far from Sarah's thoughts and feelings. In the spring of 1806 she wrote John: "It is with more pleasure than I can express to you what I feel from the particular account Mrs. Winslow has given me of each one of them when she visited you at Marshfield; and sums up all by saying they appeared not to be wanting, in their good behavior, of anything, and that you had much merit in your parental attention to them... I have not heard, my dear son, whether you have ever given them up in baptism, to the protection of their Heavenly Father, but I trust you have. If not, pray make no delay, but remember it is a command and a duty incumbent upon you."

Finally Sarah commented: "It is indeed a long time, my dear son, since I got a line from you. It would gratify me exceedingly, as it does to think, that your children are willing to give so much pleasure sometimes to an old Grandmother that they never saw, but sincerely loves them not only from the near relation they stand in to me, but also from the very good accounts I hear of them from others."

Sometime later, Sarah, relaying to John the news that his brother Nat had lost his only son at fifteen months of age, "a most pleasant time, as you know, in our little ones' lives," remarked: "There seems to be a dark cloud hanging over our family, the gloomy prospect of sickness and death ever before us. My feet from age must be tottering on the brink of the grave.." She brightened up: "I thank God I am not become a useless member of society, as some at my advanced age are..."

John and his children were also very much on the mind of John's sister Sarah Francklin. That same spring of 1806 she wrote to her brother. "...I send six boxes made of birch bark by the Indians who are about this part of the world. They are for your Daughters if they will accept them as a small token of their Aunt Francklin's love." She went on: "In one of them I have put two necklaces, one red beads and the other white, which I beg my two oldest nieces to keep for my sake. They are fashionable here, and I hope will be pleasing to them. In the same box is a little red leather purse containing a guinea that pray give your son with my love

A New Century

and tell him I trust he will at all times find as much in the purse when he wants money to do a good action with...Aunt Winslow mentions your family with high approbation and seems quite delighted with her visit at your house. I take an affectionate interest in your children, to whom I wish every possible blessing."

Sarah Francklin also had observations about farming that she thought might interest John. "Our farming would make you laugh. We raise about half a bushel of Indian corn and between thirty and forty bushels of potatoes very good. Cut ten tons of prime hay, such as would make your cows laugh to look on in the winter, and it really keeps our cows in good beef. I have a cow that is a descendant of one we brought from Marshfield with us, so you see I like to keep a remembrance of my native country. Pray mention me in terms of regard to Doctor Winslow and his wife, also to my old friends who remember your affectionate sister."

In the spring of 1806 John Thomas married again. His second wife was Lucy Turner, who seems to have been living in Dr. Isaac Winslow's household for some time. Sarah Francklin congratulated both John and Lucy in separate letters written on June 10, 1806. A few months before, Eliza Cunningham had died of consumption after a several-years illness, leaving three small children who Richard Cunningham put out to board. Cunningham himself remained alone at Saulsbrook with only two servants. Although both he and her son Nat wanted Sarah to stay with one or another of them, she felt that she should go to Sarah Francklin's, whom she had not been much with during Eliza Cunningham's illness.

In her many letters to Marshfield, Sarah almost never failed to send her regards to Dr. Winslow and his family. After all, the Winslows, near neighbors in Marshfield, had long been intimate friends of the Thomas family. The two families, in fact, had been friends since the first settlements. Immediately upon receiving a letter from Dr. Winslow, Sarah sat down to answer. In the early summer of 1807, she would say: "...since I had the pleasure of a letter from you, I have never heard so much about the place or people I left in my own country, and believe me, however I may from absence be forgotten by many, length of time or distance has not lessened my friendship for those I loved in my own country. The sympathy of a friend affords much comfort to one in affliction, and as you well remark, I have drank deep of the bitter cup, but God is merciful and while he smites with one hand, supports with the

A New Century

other...it has pleased the Almighty to spare me to an advanced age, while he has called off many of my children I hope to himself."

Sarah was gratified to learn more about John's new and second wife, Lucy, from Dr. Winslow. "Allow me to thank you sincerely for the particular account you gave me of my son's second connection. It is with much pleasure I hear from several friends how deserving a woman he has made choice of, but I am more happy from what you relate to me than anyone else, as you have been so long acquainted with her, and must know her to be possessed of all the good qualities you name to me...my own health is as well as I can expect at my age, tho not free from the complaints that attend old age. My greatest worry at present, I am told, is a boil that distresses my stomach very much at times, makes me feel sick and ends for awhile in pain. I often wish I had you, my friend, by me to advise with, that I might not feel such a worry at my stomach, but I must not complain while I am able to go about and visit my children without being a trouble to them or myself...I have great cause for thankfulness that it has pleased God I should have two of my children so comfortably settled with me that seems to vie with each other which shall accommodate me best...I have often named your bright example for your acknowledgment of all the mercies you have partaken of in this world, which very few ever think to name, only misfortunes being thought of...Who would have thought Duxbury would be such a thriving place? I seem never to know when to quit my pen, my friend, when writing to you....You remain the same man, I find, by what you say of your daughter Sarah, but pray tell her from me that she is not so old as my daughter, her namesake was, and if she gets as good a husband she will think him worth waiting for, and I doubt not she will in good time...I subscribe myself your much obliged and sincere friend..."

The following fall Sarah wrote John in Marshfield, congratulating him on the birth of a son, Charles, a name she was much pleased with. The boy's whole name was Charles Henry Thomas, for the two brothers John had lost, Charles who had been mortally wounded while serving in the British Army and Henry who had died while aboard a British ship in preparation for a British naval career. She advised John she was sending him another sheep to replace the one Richard Cunningham had sent and which had died. She assured him also that the family in Nova Scotia were well, his sister Sarah's new baby of two months doing well and his brother Nat's second child, a girl, walking by holding onto a finger.

A New Century

It was about that time that John Thomas had financial difficulties, or so it seemed, and his mother wrote: "Altho you had been a little embarrassed, you had a good advisor in Dr. Winslow and had extricated yourself and now was quite easy in your affairs." To ease her son's possible concern lest John worry about the effect of this news, Sarah added: "This intelligence, my dear son, as I trust you do not think my affection is lessened by long absence, you can but believe gave me the greatest joy and satisfaction, tho I felt much for your embarrassment, but there is no happiness in this world without some alloy."

This prompted Sarah to assure John: "Happy should I be if I could at this moment afford you even a small token of my lasting tender affection, but my income you know is but small and is subject to a tax since the war, and while I have anything to depend upon, I cannot think of imposing myself ever upon my own children." Even residing with her children who wished her to do so, she was determined to compensate them for her board. And she reassured John again that she counted him as one of her children and if she could spare anything, he could receive it "as the widow's mite."

Sarah went on to remind John that Sir John Wentworth was being superseded as governor, the King having "thought it proper in the present state of affairs, supposing us to be so soon to be engaged in war, to have the Civil and Military joined in one man, and for Sir John to retire upon a pension." The Wentworths were to sail for England as soon as Lady Wentworth was sufficiently recovered from an illness to make the trip. Even so, Frances Wentworth was seriously ill and thought likely to die any day.

"Your sister Francklin," John's mother continued, "has been this two days past from home to visit her Ladyship and take a last farewell of her...She [Lady Wentworth] has been remarkably kind to your poor departed sisters in their last sickness, and her attention to your poor brother Charles, even to nursing him herself is more than I can tell you. Could I think myself able to undertake to drive as far as The Lodge [the Wentworth's residence outside of Halifax] without hurting myself, gratitude as well as the near relation I stand in to her would lead me to think of going to take my last farewell of her..."

Wistfully, Sarah concluded her letter with a familiar request. "Give them [her grandchildren] my tender love, and when either of them can spare time from better business or pleasing amusements amongst themselves

A New Century

or with their young friends, to let me hear how the family health is and give me some account of the neighborhood where I once resided. It will gratify an old grandmother...Pray offer my regards to Dr. Winslow and Mr. Shaw [the Pastor of the First Church in Marshfield, which the family had always attended]..."

Sometime late in the fall of 1808, Sarah Francklin and her husband James Boutineau Francklin moved to a large house in Windsor not far from her brother Nat's, and Sarah Thomas, of course, accompanied them. This had made it easier for Nat to visit his mother every day that winter, during which she had been very ill. Sarah had had pleurisy, followed by a bout of shortness of breath. For sometime she had wanted to send John a few dollars. Soon she expected to have a safe opportunity to do so, and wrote John that she would send "a few dollars as a token of sincere love and affection..."

In the early summer of 1809, while Sarah was even then recovering from her illness of the past winter, she wrote to her "very dear granddaughters." "I thank you, my children, for your friendly expressions in your letters, where you say you will take any advice of mine in friendship. Upon that promise, as I feel both for your spiritual as well as temporal welfare, allow me to beg of you to remember your Creator in the days of your youth, and remember that though the old must die, the young may die...and I trust in the mercies of our Redeemer, though we are separated here, we shall meet together in the Eternal World...where no affliction, sorrow, sickness can come."

Sarah was conscious of her own frailty. She continued her letter. "After several attempts I have made out a pretty lengthy letter, but I must to add a little more; and say, I heard some long time since that my namesake was going to be married, but could never hear anything further about it. I suppose, as she has never given me the least hint or her Father about it, I must apply to her sister Ruth and ask if it is so, and spare her blushes in answering me....accept my most affectionate wishes for every blessing both through time and eternity, and all in good time I hope you will be settled with some good character as a companion, who is most worthy of your regards and with whom you will spend your days in mutual affection is the sincere prayer of your aged grandparent from whom perhaps may never be able to write you again. Should it prove the last, accept the blessings both of you, from your affectionate grandparent, Sarah Thomas." The letter was addressed to Miss Sarah D. Thomas, Marshfield. It was, indeed, the last letter, at least

A New Century

that has survived, from Sarah Thomas to her namesake and her sister, Sarah's "very dear granddaughters."

Nat Thomas wrote also to John at about the same time as did his mother to John's daughters. He enclosed her letter with his. In his own, Nat spoke of their mother. "Our dear Mother has been extremely ill during the last winter, but is now much recovered and looks better than you can suppose, at her period of life, being now near seventy-seven years old. She is as perfectly upright as ever she was, and cheerful. You should write her as it will afford her much happiness to hear from you, and it pleases us all to hear how things go on in your part of the world."

Nat reported also on their sister Sarah Francklin. She was in good health and lived "in the next street to my house, about as far distant as from your house to the pond." She had what Nat described as a "fine little daughter about two years old," named Elizabeth Gould Francklin. Nat also spoke of Eliza Cunninghams' children, a son and two daughters, and his own, a daughter, Sarah about two-and- a-half years old and a son named Nathaniel Charles Wentworth, about six months. "Your late sister Gray's children are fine boys. The eldest is at Bermuda with his uncle, and about sixteen years old, doing well. The youngest is at college [School of King's College] in this town." As was the custom of his mother, Nat sent his regards to Dr. Winslow and Mr. Shaw.

It was about that same time in the summer of 1809 that Richard Cunningham, the late Eliza Thomas's husband, was married at Sir John Wentworth and Lady Wentworth's residence, The Lodge, outside of Halifax. His bride was Sarah *Apthorp* Morton, described in the newspaper notice of the wedding as "grand-niece of Lady Wentworth." The Rev. Benjamin Gerrish Gray, husband of the late Mary Thomas and thus recently brother-in-law of Richard Cunningham officiated at the service. The new Mrs. Cunningham was related and known to Sarah Thomas also, since her great-grandmother Elizabeth *Dering* Wentworth had been Sarah's sister. Sarah Thomas commented: "Mr. Cunningham seems quite happy in his second choice of a wife."

When Sarah Thomas received a letter from John in Marshfield in the spring of 1810, she was particularly pleased. "I cannot tell you what a cordial it was to my drooping spirit to hear from your own hand that you and your family were all in good health and that you had married your daughter so much to your satisfaction...They have my best wishes for every blessing that is to be enjoyed in the married state." It had been on January 11, 1810 that young Sarah Dering Thomas, Sarah's eldest

House of Major Briggs Thomas and family at Rexhame, Marshfield, where the author spent his youth.

A New Century

granddaughter and her namesake, married Waterman Thomas. Waterman Thomas, twenty-six, was the son of Major Briggs Thomas and grandson of Colonel Anthony Thomas, former representative to the Great and General Court and principal military leader of Marshfield's militia in the early years of the American Revolution. Their marriage united the two Thomas families of Marshfield, one Patriot and one Tory. Their first-born child, a boy, was named for his respective grandfathers, John Briggs Thomas. The writer is the great-grandson of John Briggs Thomas and remembers seeing his great-grandfather's portrait at the Rexhame farm each summer of his childhood. The portrait now hangs in the writer's study.

In a postscript to her letter to John, his mother, thinking of her granddaughter, added: "It gave me pleasure to hear my niece [granddaughter] was settled on the Neck. I remember it to be a pleasant place and a good farm. Pray did not Mr. Briggs Thomas marry a daughter of Deacon [Nehemiah] Thomas? I often think of Mr. Waterman Thomas [young Waterman's uncle] Do he and his wife still live at the eastward? I conclude as Mr. Briggs Thomas has given the Neck farm to his son he lives himself in his father's house."

Major Briggs Thomas remained on the Neck farm with his son Waterman and daughter-in-law Sarah, and it was at this farm that an event took place during the War of 1812 which provided a story handed down through the family to the writer.

On the Massachusetts coast, fronting on the open ocean between the ports of Boston and Plymouth, was the farm of Major Briggs Thomas at Marshfield. The farmhouse, situated on a broad hill, overlooked pastures laid off with walls long since built of stones dug from the very fields they enclosed, pastures which sloped away to the east toward sand dunes and the beach beyond and a wide sweep of the ever-changing sea. To the west, below the hill, were salt marshes through which the South River curved on its way to a union with the North River at the upper end of the farm, and there the latter flowed into the ocean. Ships were built on the North River, and its broad and deep outlet enabled coastwise packets to come and go, carrying their cargo and passengers.

During the War of 1812 between England and the United States of America ships of the English Navy patrolled the coast of Massachusetts. They formed a blockade - to keep American fighting ships bottled up in harbors such as Boston and to prevent trading vessels from entering or

A New Century

leaving any port. One of the English men-of-war was His Majesty's Ship Shannon, a full-rigged, three-masted frigate, rated at 38 guns - a good ship, it was said, commanded by an able captain, Philip Broke.

It was springtime. The pastures were green again and flowers bloomed around the farmhouse. It was an old house even then, with a massive center chimney of brick and a long sloping rear roof which seemed indeed to reach for the ground. There was, about it all, the fresh beauty of May.

At that time the war could have seemed quite remote to Major Thomas, his son Waterman and his daughter-in-law Sally [John Thomas's daughter, Sarah Dering Thomas]. But the Major well remembered the troubles with England which led to the Revolution in which he had been a young officer. And those troubles and that conflict perhaps also were recalled for him, even if unwittingly, by the fact that Sally's grandfather, Nathaniel Ray Thomas, had been the leader in Marshfield of those loyal to England, a Tory, a nearby landed proprietor whose stubborn adherence to the Crown was rewarded with a seat on His Majesty's Council of the Province of Massachusetts Bay, but at the same time cost him the loss of all his property and a final, precipitous departure forever from Massachusetts.

On the particular morning of this story, therefore, Major Thomas may well have gone to the village or elsewhere, for it can be questioned whether what was about to take place could ever have happened or at least might have happened in the way it did, if the strong-willed old officer had been at home. That morning, a ship of a size not usually seen making land thereabouts eased into the mouth of the North River and hove to. From the farmhouse those who watched could not tell at first what she was - the river mouth was about a mile away - but the Major's telescope shortly revealed her identity. The ship was a British frigate. And this, as might be expected, caused much excitement and concern at the farmhouse. In a short while a group of figures, obviously a landing party from the enemy vessel, came into sight as it began to make its way across the sandy stretches and toward the meadows, quite certainly headed for Major Thomas's. This was not surprising, if anyone had thought about it, since the Major's was the only house clearly in view from the ships's anchorage. The group, disappearing now and again behind sand dunes, came into the open of the meadows. By then, the Major's glass revealed handsomely-uniformed officers leading a small body of sailors. From time to time they were hidden by rising

A New Century

ground, but when they came into sight again they were continuing their march directly to the farmhouse.

It is not difficult to imagine the mounting excitement and concern at the Major's. Those watching could easily have imagined a raiding party of the enemy planning to plunder house and farm buildings, destroying cherished possessions and valued livestock, and leaving behind nothing but smoldering ruins. And then too, what would happen to the family?

Those at the farmhouse, fully aware of the possibilities, took hasty precautions. Such of the stock as could be were locked in the barn. A musket and pistol, if futile armament, bolstered spirits. Word was dispatched to the village to alert neighbors and townspeople and to call out the militia. And then there was nothing to do but wait.

The British officers and men reached the farmhouse, and their glances about the place and their murmured conversation seemed foreboding indeed. The leader of the party - obviously the senior officer, though tradition does not say whether it was Captain Broke - introduced himself and his fellow officers of H.M.S. Shannon. He then posted guards well down the road leading to the farm, warning that no effort should be made to resist or call for help, or he would be forced to take stern measures, exactly what he may have left to the imagination of the others. The militia, perhaps fortunately, did not appear. Next he ordered an officer and several men to search the farm buildings and to report forthwith what they found, and he undertook to go through the farmhouse himself.

It was at this moment that young Sally Thomas, perhaps heedlessly, perhaps schemingly, chose to invite the officers to dinner. They accepted. In the low-ceilinged parlor of the farmhouse, with its wainscoting and paneling over the fireplace, the British officers were entertained; while in the kitchen with its immense hearth large enough for logs three feet through which would burn for days, holding a fire that rarely went out, and its massive hand-hewn beams overhead darkened by the smoke of a century-and-a-quarter past, a bountiful meal was prepared.

When dinner was over the officers excused themselves and went outside, yet remained clearly in sight through the windows. They appeared to be discussing something but in apparent disagreement, looking at the house and outbuildings, the barn and other farm buildings,

A New Century

pointing and gesturing as they talked. For those in the farmhouse, watching with renewed apprehension, there could have been but one question: What would the British do? Then, the senior officer who had listened but had not said much ended the discussion with an order. The officers returned inside.

"Madam," the British officer's next words have not been handed down, but he may well have addressed himself to Sally, "we appreciate your kind hospitality and your excellent dinner. I have decided what we shall do," and he paused, perhaps smiling slightly, "and that is...only to take with us three little calves."

Thereupon the British officers and men left Major Thomas's, leading the three little calves, and in due course H.M.S. Shannon sailed away, her great billowing sails at last disappearing from sight as the ship made her way to the northward, toward Boston, and to an imminent and victorious, though bloody, naval duel with an American ship, the Chesapeake.

It was in this engagement that the stirring words which have been a rallying cry of the United States Navy ever since were uttered by the dying captain of the Chesapeake, James Lawrence - "Don't give up the ship!" Major Thomas's family long remembered and often spoke of the visit - a raid, they had feared - by the British officers and men from H.M.S. Shannon, and the story of the three little calves has been handed down from them.

Sarah Thomas was surprised to learn from John's letter written in the spring of 1810 that he was a member of what she called the "House of Assembly," really, of course, the Great and General Court or legislature. Then she commented: "...as you can find time from your farming to engage in public business, I trust that for the short time I have to remain in life, I shall find you can spare a few moments to gratify your old mother with a line more frequently...I heartily wish you may have wisdom from above granted you to direct you in the right way of duty both in public and private affairs." Happily, the next letter from John to his mother, written in June, arrived at the end of that month.

It was in August 1810 that Sarah Thomas wrote to her son John Thomas what seems to have been her last letter to him. "...I shall send you five eagles - all I can make out at present. I have been lying by a dollar at a time as I could to ask your acceptance of them as a small token of my regard. I wish I could send you something more worthy of

A New Century

your acceptance, but my small pension has been repeatedly taxed that has reduced it, small as it was at first, that what with paying for my bread, clothing, doctor's bill and medicine and other things I can but just make out with my only income. Therefore, you must accept the will for the deed. It may serve to remind you that, though you are out of sight, neither time nor distance has or ever will erase you from my affectionate remembrance."

Sarah was concerned when she learned that John's situation had been much affected by the drought, just as farmers in Nova Scotia had been. Then she remarked: "I wish I had it in my power to put Eagle's Nest in the order that your brother says he could, if in your situation, so as to produce you double the profit, but where money and labor is wanting there is little to be done, I know well." Sarah called the Marshfield farm Eagle's Nest, which seems to have been the name by which the family knew it. The name may, indeed, have had its origin in the wording of the original grant of the property to William Thomas in 1641, in which the General Court of Plymouth Colony referred to "a point of upland called the Eagle's Nest."

Sarah closed her letter very much as she had so many ones previously. "Pray remember me affectionately to them all [her grandchildren]. I love them for your sake as well as for the praises of others, though I have never seen them. I greatly rejoice to hear how much they merit the esteem of all that know them...Pray for me, my dear son, that I may be prepared for the great and last change which hastens so fast upon me. Your tenderly affectionate parent, Sarah Thomas." Sometime before October 9, 1810 Sarah died. Of the death of her cousin and long-time intimate friend, Anna *Green* Winslow wrote that December that it would be to her "very grievous, only for the hope that she is free from sin, sorrow, and pain."

As her son Nat wrote, Sarah died, "lamented by all who knew her..." Her thirty-year-old great-great-niece and Richard Cunningham's second wife, Sarah *Apthorp* Morton Cunningham, composed "Lines to the Memory of Mrs Sarah Thomas who...completed a life which had been filled with virtues, followed by respect and surrounded by affection." Sarah Cunningham evidently wrote the poem at the time of Sarah's death, October 1810 at Saulsbrook, her residence outside of Windsor.

A New Century

The poem, consisting of nine stanzas in manuscript, was signed with the initials "SAC", Sarah *Apthorp* Cunningham. Several of the stanzas have recognizable allusions. They are:

> *Still flashed the Eye, and sparking played*
> *More, than could lips express,*
> *And still, the melting smile betrayed*
> *A soul of tenderness;*
>
> *Thy Life by sense, and judgement, moved*
> *By virtue's self inspired*
> *Through every changing scene beloved*
> *In every part admired,*
>
> *Though at thy Heart so off were driven*
> *The arrows of despair,*
> *Thy tearful Eyes were raised to Heaven,*
> *And shielding Faith was there.*
>
> *Blest shade forgive these feeble strains*
> *Affections duteous part*
> *For the same blood, that warmed thy veins*
> *Is mingled in this Heart.*
>
> *And <u>he</u> whose <u>feelings all are mine</u>*
> *Whose will, my soul reveres,*
> *Bent, over thy being's last decline*
> *With more than filial tears;*

Of the foregoing stanzas, the first three clearly relate to Sarah Thomas. They speak of her tenderness, of the love and admiration bestowed on her, and of her faith when beset by despair.

The fourth stanza reveals that the author, Sarah *Apthorp* Cunningham, is of the same blood as the lady she eulogizes, Sarah *Dering* Thomas. She was, of course, related through the Derings, her great-grandmother Elizabeth *Dering* Wentworth having been Sarah Thomas's sister. And finally, the fifth stanza brings in Sarah Cunningham's husband, Richard Cunningham, who had married as his first wife, Elizabeth Packer Thomas, Sarah Thomas's daughter.

A New Century

Appended to the eulogy were several lines of poetry by Mrs. Tonge, a lady of a prominent family in Windsor, Nova Scotia. She refers to Sarah Thomas as her "sainted friend," and compliments the author Sarah Cunningham by saying that, while her pencil only gives the face, "Thy sweeter power, the Soul can blend."

But Nat Thomas summed up everyone's feeling, simply and with few words: "She lived beloved..."

XIV

Aftermath

Months after Sarah Thomas's death, her daughter Sarah Francklin spoke of her mother sadly but with pride and warmth. Writing to her cousin Sylvester Dering early in 1812, she commented: "Could you have seen my blessed Mother prior to her death it would have delighted her, as she retained all that warmth of attachment to her family and friends which marked her life till the close of her earthly journey."

Sarah Thomas had frequently expressed her love for her family, her children and grandchildren, and the wish that she could give them more tangible evidence of her feeling. But her pension provided for little beyond her personal daily needs, which she always insisted on paying herself as she often reminded her children. She was firm about this, though acknowledging the desire, the eagerness, of Nat, Sally Francklin, and even Richard Cunningham, to take her in and care for her.

If not money to leave her children, Sarah Thomas had carefully preserved a few personal belongings that she had brought from Marshfield. Nor in the disposition of those few items had she forgotten her son John in Marshfield, whom she had never forgotten and for whom she had felt deep affection. So, among her limited bequests, were those things she had intended for John. Together with a modest gift of money, Sarah Francklin advised John, he was to receive his mother's watch and "a pair of silver candlesticks's washed with gold" that had worn off, however, through constant use. In addition, his mother had left John a small mahogany table, which, with the pair of silver candlesticks, Richard Cunningham and his wife, Sarah *Apthorp* Cunningham, intended to carry to John upon their proposed trip to Marshfield.

In the early summer of 1817 Sarah *Thomas* Francklin, her husband James Boutineau Francklin, and their daughter, ten-year-old Elizabeth Gould Francklin, arrived in Boston for a visit that was planned to include Marshfield and her brother John and his family. On their arrival Sarah and her family were staying in Boston with Mrs. Storer, "our excellent, wonderful, and amiable friend." Sarah wrote John that "we propose visiting you at Marshfield where you will please treat us as part of yourselves. The

Aftermath

harder you allow us to sleep the more we shall feel at home as our place of rest there is always a mattress."

The Francklins spent "three very happy weeks...at your mansion of comfort in Marshfield," Sarah wrote her brother on July 28, 1817. She had not acknowledged the extreme kindness of John and his wife Lucy before, "because we have been so constantly visited by my old friends as to occupy every hour since our arrival in Boston..." She reflected: "...I feel that time has not lessened my affection for those that I loved in early life nor has it so blunted my powers that I am prevented from admiring the virtues and attaching to the persons of the amiable relations and dear friends who have been added to my family and acquaintance during an absence of more than thirty years."

Sarah remembered John and his family in particular. "My heart expands with gratitude to Heaven, my dear brother, who has blessed you with such a numerous circle of charming children and I hope that they may live long to comfort you and to enjoy every happiness in their own lovely children. Pray assure my married nieces and their deserving husbands of my affectionate regard. Embrace their children for me, who must be taught to remember their old Aunt Francklin who loves them truly. To Betsey, Ann and the boys give my best love, in which Mr. Francklin and Elizabeth join." John and Lucy Thomas had Elizabeth Packer and her half-sister Ann and her half-brothers Charles Henry and young five-year-old Nathaniel Ray Thomas still living at home.

Sarah Francklin and her husband hoped that the weather had been as good as John could have wished for his hay and that he had got most of it "secured in 'Hyson tea order.'" She reported that "Elizabeth felt leaving Marshfield so much that but for meeting her cousin Mary [Mary Gray Thomas, married to Daniel Bassett] at Hingham I really think she might have been ill...We have spent an afternoon at Mr. Quincy's and seen the wonderful cow and every improvement upon that seat of enchantment, which is graced by his accomplished wife and his beautiful family of children. They asked after you both with much kindness. Indeed, there has been a vast number of inquiries about your health from all the friends whom I have seen."

By the middle of August the Francklins were back home in Halifax. Before they left Boston they had the pleasure of a three-day visit from Sarah's first cousin Sylvester Dering, as she wrote to John at Marshfield. She and her family, remembering their "happy visit at Marshfield with

Aftermath

great pleasure," sent their love and best wishes to all their dear relations and kind acquaintances there, "not forgetting Dr. and Mrs. Winslow."

Isaac Winslow would not be forgotten. In the summer of 1819, at a time when the Doctor, at the age of eighty, was obviously failing, Sarah Francklin wrote Lucy Thomas: "Whenever Dr. Winslow may depart this world, you will feel it a loss. Indeed, since brother John and myself can remember anything, the Doctor's present mansion has been the residence of an intimate friend of our family, and these friends of our parents and of our own childhood take deep hold on our affections." Sarah asked that she and James be remembered, "with friendly respect and gratitude to Dr. Winslow, indeed to your circle of friends who were so kind to us."

In the spring of 1820 Richard Cunningham, his wife and his family, including his two daughters by his first wife, Elizabeth Packer Thomas, planned a long visit to Boston. Sarah Francklin, in fact, seemed to think that the Cunningham's arrangements suggested that they did not intend to return to Nova Scotia to live. She wrote John that should her niece Frances S. W. Cunningham accompany her family, Sarah hoped that Frances would be able to visit her Uncle John Thomas and all her relations in Marshfield. She described her niece, the daughter of Eliza [Elizabeth Packer Thomas] Cunningham, as "a gentle fine-tempered young woman" and gave Frances a letter to her Uncle John and urged Richard Cunningham to take her to visit in Marshfield.

In October of 1820 Sarah Francklin wrote to John's wife Lucy that Frances Cunningham had had "a delightful visit" to Marshfield. "She only laments that she should have lived so long without knowing her amiable relations there...She was much gratified with her visit and says her uncle kept her laughing all the time."

Apparently Richard Cunningham suggested to John Thomas when the former visited Marshfield that John consider moving to Nova Scotia with his family and seems to have had a particular property in mind for him to settle on. During the winter of 1820 Lucy Thomas, John's wife, wrote to Sarah Francklin asking her opinion about John moving to Nova Scotia. Sarah replied: "The subject is important and, while I should rejoice in my brother and his amiable family living near me, I would not venture to say 'Come' until my brother had seen for himself. At all events pray urge my brother to come and judge for himself. You could accompany him and see how you like Nova Scotia. I beg you to think seriously of it next

Aftermath

Spring. Do coax my brother to slip here and see for himself the place Mr. Cunningham wants him to fix on."

Sarah Francklin's attention shifted from her brother John's possible move to Nova Scotia to other family matters. In a letter to her brother, Sarah reported on their niece Sarah Thomas, daughter of their brother Nat. "I have no doubt that Mrs. Thomas told you that Sarah was a great belle, and she is certainly much admired, and is a showy fine girl, but her friends look so high for her in consequence of her cousin having married a Colonel of high rank and family, that she may not be married as soon as might otherwise."

Sarah mentioned her own daughter, Elizabeth. "Your niece Elizabeth has not been brought up to look high (though she is very proud) but I trust she will not (even if she should have an opportunity) marry above her own station in life, as those alliances are not the most likely to make anyone happy, in my judgment. Indeed, Elizabeth seems to think little about marriage. She is very fond of reading, is constantly employed about something, and seems very happy." About that time, as a matter of fact, Sarah Thomas, Nat's daughter was spending some weeks with the Francklins on a visit. According to her aunt, Sarah was "pretty and a very fine girl, tall for her age, and very interesting."

In the late summer of 1821 a ship from Massachusetts, from the Marshfield area, arrived at Windsor, Capt. Baker commanding. Sarah Francklin wrote her sister-in-law Lucy Thomas that "Mr. Francklin says as you and my brother did not come in Capt. Baker's vessel to visit us, he will not go to see you anymore and that brother John shall have the office of selectman taken away from him." This from Sarah was, of course, a whimsical remark. She went on in a more serious vein. "Mr. Cunningham and all his family came to Halifax three weeks ago tomorrow and were with us two weeks. Mrs. C. is still here with her youngest son, waiting until her head shall be well enough to go to Windsor with Mr. Francklin, who will drive her and John to their home."

Then Sarah observed about the Cunninghams: "Mrs. C. loves the States and her friends there so much and thinks so little of Nova Scotia, that it seems a mistake her having married a man whose property is here under a government that she hates."

A June 22, 1822 letter from Sarah Francklin to her sister-in-law in Marshfield comments on some of the family happenings. There was

Aftermath

news that John Thomas's daughter, Lucy Baker Thomas who had married Peleg Ford, was returning home to live following the death of her husband. Sarah Francklin had also raised the question of John Winslow, Dr. Isaac Winslow's son, living in what Sarah called the "Mansion House," after the death of Dr. Winslow. She wondered how John Winslow could live in the house "when he could not live near the sea in his fathers lifetime." And finally Sarah Francklin reported that her niece Frances Cunningham was with the Francklins on a visit, "as amiable as ever. If we should be happy in visiting you again, we will, if possible, take dear Frances with us to keep up the laugh with her Uncle John and his dear children..."

Sarah Francklin also wrote her relations in Marshfield that their brother and uncle, Nat Thomas, had completed his "new stone house" in Windsor. Sarah had seen him recently. "He was remarkable well in looks and health, and just completed a good stone house, which those who have seen it like much. I have not been in Windsor but three days since I was in Boston." The house was not far from the waterfront. It was a three-story house built of dressed free stone with a garden in the rear of the house.

Sarah requested information about the settlement of Dr. Winslow's estate. In the summer of 1823 she commented: "I shall extremely lament if it must go out of the family." But the situation was not good. Dr. Winslow, though still living in the old "Mansion House," was in a shaky position financially.

Dr. Isaac Winslow continued to live at Careswell until his death in 1819. He was much loved and well respected by the inhabitants of Marshfield and was spared the harsh treatment meted out to other Tories. Unlike Ray Thomas, his estate was not confiscated by the Patriots. Following his death, the Winslow property was sold in 1827 to satisfy his debts.

Dr. Isaac's brother, Pelham Winslow, born in 1737, had graduated from Harvard several classes behind Nathaniel Ray Thomas. He married Joanna White in 1770 and had two daughters who survived. Like his brother Isaac, Pelham the Loyalist did not leave the country and died in 1783 in Brooklyn, New York.

Dr. Isaac's son John who had been born at Careswell in 1774 lived for a time in the old house but then was forced to locate elsewhere because of his health. John died in 1825 in Natchez, Mississippi.

Aftermath

In 1827 Careswell, the mansion house of the Winslows since 1699, was sold to Seth Sprague. Although it is not known as a fact, it is possible that this was the same Seth Sprague who reported on the incident involving Jesse Dunbar and the ox in the month immediately prior to the battles of Lexington and Concord.

Not long after Sarah had informed the Thomases in Marshfield that she had seen Nat and that he was well, her daughter Elizabeth advised her Uncle John: "I am extremely sorry to inform you that my dear Uncle Nathaniel had been very ill. He had a violent bilious attack a few weeks ago but was so much better that he was to have gone out yesterday week, but had a relapse, since which his life has been in immediate danger...Papa took Mama to Windsor last Thursday since when we have not had a line from them." Before sending the letter, though, Elizabeth added a postscript: "I received a letter from Papa last night in which he says: 'Your poor Uncle Thomas is at present very low indeed but free from pain. I fear he cannot hold out much longer.'" Elizabeth was sixteen years old at the time.

Almost exactly a month later, Sarah Francklin wrote to her "dear and only brother." She began: "My daughter Elizabeth wrote you a short time since to tell you that our brother Nathaniel was very ill, and I have now to assure you that he paid nature's last debt on the twelfth of August, just one week after he had numbered 68 years on earth." Sarah then recounted details of the last illness and death of her brother Nat.

"Our brother," Sarah informed John, "about six weeks before his death was brought home from the Court House where he was Custos [Customs Officer] very ill, spasms in his stomach. The Doctor thought him dangerous, but Mrs. Thomas was not alarmed and only thought it an old attack. He remained ill for about a week when a blister was applied to his side but the Doctor thought him greatly better. Mr. Francklin went to Windsor but I did not accompany him as not a word had been said about wishing to see me."

Sarah continued her report. "From my husband I heard constantly but not anything flattering. When Mr. Francklin and others came from Windsor, they said our brother was getting better, and I had promised myself the pleasure of seeing him in his usual health in a few weeks when I was to have visited him in his new house. On the Sunday week before he died, when he had proposed to go out in the chaise, he was

Aftermath

again attacked by those spasms, and on the Thursday following they sent for me. I found our brother very low, but not expecting to die, nor did his wife seem to contemplate that melancholy event. Our brother, however, grew weaker every hour. He remained perfectly sensible when he awoke, but a constant torpor seemed to sink him to sleep the moment he stopped speaking. In this state of ease, he sank into death without one struggle or one groan."

Sarah spoke of family matters. Nat's daughter Sarah she called "a fine girl...she did not seem to realize that her dear father had actually left her forever. The stone house," which had but recently been finished, "which was built to please Mrs. Thomas is certainly a noble one, calculated to spend two thousand [pounds] per annum on. You know that our brother's children have been comfortably provided for by their grandfather, the late B. DeWolf, Esq."

A whimsical touch enlivened Sarah's letter. "William Gray, our nephew, married a good young woman in England. An aunt of Mrs. Gray's came to visit her. She had every article on board a vessel to sail for Jamaica where she has a sister and many friends, when a young divine, with whom she had long been acquainted, went on board the vessel and prevailed on her to come on shore and marry him. All her things were re-landed, and she actually gave her hand to the Rev. Mr. Morris who is fifteen years younger than the lady he has married, and they are gone to live at Parrsborough. What cannot love do?"

With the spring of the year 1825, Sarah Francklin reported to John Thomas in Marshfield that Nat's widow, Sarah *DeWolf* Thomas, and her son Charles and daughter Sarah proposed going to Boston that July. They intended visiting John and his family at Marshfield. Of herself and family, she wrote: "Mr. and Mrs. Francklin, being on the wrong side of 60, look and feel <u>oldish</u>, but we have a thousand blessings to give thanks for and are very well. Elizabeth is a stout girl, such a one as you might fairly doubt being the little puny mortal that visited you, with us eight years ago."

Frances Cunningham also wrote to her Uncle John from Saulsbrook near Windsor that Nat's family were about ready to sail for New England. "I am sure you will be delighted with Sarah [Nat's daughter], who is a very pleasing, amiable girl, and very pretty." Writing to her Uncle brought back memories for Frances. "I often think of the delightful corn which I enjoyed so much at Marshfield and of the apples which you

Aftermath

used to say would kill me from being so unripe, but which I thought excellent. I have never tasted any corn so good since." She remarked that she hoped that he would see her Aunt, who would be visiting her friends in Dorchester near Boston, where she would probably remain until autumn.

Sarah *DeWolf* Thomas and her children arrived in Dorchester in mid-July. On July 1st Sarah Cunningham, who was then in Dorchester visiting her parents, Honorable and Mrs. Perez Morton, had written to Nova Scotia, that she was soon expecting to see Mrs. Thomas and her children. "I have told them [her parents] that they would find a beauty in Sarah; of course I say nothing of Charles for where I could not commend I would rather be silent when among strangers." This was an early intimation that Nat's son was a strange and difficult boy.

Sarah Cunningham's father, Perez Morton, Attorney General of Massachusetts, had assisted John Thomas to recover his mother's dower right in the Thomas lands in Marshfield. Her mother Sarah Wentworth *Apthorp* Morton was a noted beauty and well-known poetess. They lived in Dorchester, but Nat's family were staying with Mrs. Smith in nearby Milton. So Sarah Cunningham and her mother "went in to see Mrs. Thomas immediately, and I am surprised to see how extremely well she looks, younger and more animated than I have seen her since the death of her husband... Charles looks burnt and has lost all his skin from his nose, owing I suppose to the heat from the salt water, for he tells me he has not been sick."

Sarah *DeWolf* Thomas and her daughter were quite social during their visit and managed to see people and be seen. Young Sarah was not averse, apparently, to watching out for suitable beaux or, more appropriately perhaps, members of the opposite sex who might make suitable husbands. At one point Sarah Cunningham reported on progress in this quest, which, however, was not particularly propitious. "Sarah Thomas has made one conquest at least, and will no doubt have an opportunity of refusing, for I do not think that she would marry the gentleman. His name is Henshaw. He is of a good family, has a respectable character and is said to be worth $50,000. But, on the other hand, he must be at least twice her age, and has a voice that I would not be in the constant hearing of for any sum of money. He is a wholesale druggist." No more was heard of Mr. Henshaw.

Aftermath

Not long after the Thomases had arrived from Nova Scotia, they set out for Marshfield and a visit to John Thomas and his family. They spent some weeks there. Early in September they were back in Milton. On September 9, 1825 Sarah Rachel Thomas [Nat's daughter] thanked her Uncle John: "Believe me, I shall ever recollect you and all your dear family with the greatest affection and nothing will give me greater pleasure than to hear of the health and welfare of my kind relations."

As with her grandmother and her father and her aunts and uncles, Sarah endeavored to persuade her Uncle John to visit his relations in Nova Scotia. "I should think myself most happy and favored if I could persuade you to visit us in Nova Scotia. You may always feel assured of a hearty welcome and a comfortable home and we should feel delighted to return in part a portion of those civilities and that hospitality we met with at your house...We were quite sorry that you did not bring Aunt Thomas to Milton last month to the grand party. I am sure you would have found it very pleasant. There were upwards of eight hundred people here and a great deal of gayety."

She remembered her Marshfield cousins. "I wish I had leisure to answer Betsey's kind letter, but I have not till I arrive in Nova Scotia, when you must not be surprised if you sometimes receive one of my scrawls. I have a pair of scissors I took by mistake from Cousin Ruth's and now send them and two little dolls, one for Lucy, the other for little Sarah Thomas, my Cousin Sarah's daughter. Mamma sends a little bag for Sarah Ford with her best love..." "Little Sarah Thomas" was the young daughter of Sarah *Thomas* Thomas, and Waterman Thomas, her husband, who lived at the Neck. She was the great-granddaughter of Sarah Thomas, the wife of Nathaniel Ray Thomas.

Two years later, Elizabeth Francklin, Sarah's daughter, wrote to her Uncle John Thomas in Marshfield, giving details of some of the social activities in Halifax. "Halifax is always very gay during the winter season," she began her description. "There are little dances almost every evening and, as Frances Cunningham is spending the winter with us, we go out together which makes it much pleasanter for me. We have a sleighing club here called the Royal Acadian Club. Most of the sleighs are very handsome and ornamented with beautiful skins. Some drive four and even six horses, and then gentlemen ride as postillions, with scarlet jackets, which make quite a dashing appearance. Others have tandems, etc."

Aftermath

Elizabeth was enthusiastic. "There was a most delightful party at the Bedford Inn two or three days ago. It is three miles from town. We all went (between fifty and sixty persons) in sleighs, and after partaking of a most sumptuous dinner we danced until ten o'clock to the music of the band belonging to the 52nd Regiment, which is stationed here, and then sat down to an elegant supper; after which we returned home by moonlight, without having encountered any other disaster than an upset, which one of the four-in-hand sleighs met with in passing over some very high snowdrifts, but none of the party were at all injured."

More details were forthcoming. "There was a grand ball given here this season by the officers of our garrison at the Artillery mess room, at which all the gentlemen and ladies appeared dressed in the Highland costume which was universally becoming. The ballroom was fitted up in the style of an armory with the swords, bayonets, and guns, etc., arranged in the form of stars, crescents, and circles, which when lighted up were very brilliant and looked beautifully. These were interspersed with the skins of various animals which were suspended round the room according to the custom of the Highlands, and, I assure you, our belles attired in the Scotch bonnet and scarf looked quite irresistible, I often wish that Betsey and Ann were here to partake of some of our events they would possess the charm of novelty."

In the fall of 1827 Sarah Francklin told a correspondent that she had just completed her sixty-fifth year. Along with that she advised that her niece, Sarah Rachel Thomas, was engaged to be married to "a gentleman of the Bar, by the name of Wilkins [Lewis Morris Wilkins], son of Judge Wilkins..." And she had comments about the controversial Charles Thomas, her nephew and son of her late brother Nat. "Charles Thomas has lately got a commission in the 81st Regiment, which is in New Brunswick at present. I trust and hope that Charles may not disgrace himself and his friends. Hitherto he has been an <u>extraordinary</u> boy."

Likewise, that fall of 1827 Elizabeth Francklin, Sarah's daughter, communicated with her cousin Elizabeth Packer Thomas, [John Thomas's daughter] Betsey as she was known to family and friends. Elizabeth was writing because she had heard that Betsey intended to be married, but she knew little of the details. During the previous summer, Elizabeth informed Betsey, she had spent six weeks with their relations in Windsor. She had a delightful visit, she said, and rode horseback a great deal. "...I became so <u>wild</u> and <u>scampered</u> about the country at such a rate that Mamma is almost afraid to let me go again. Our cousin

Aftermath

Sarah is also engaged, but I believe she is not to be married for a long time. The gentlemen's name is Mr. Lewis Wilkins; he is the eldest son of Judge Wilkins and is a remarkably fine young man, possessed of excellent abilities, a good temper, and an amiable disposition so that I think they have every prospect of being happy."

Elizabeth also had something to say about Charles Thomas, Nat Thomas's son. "Charles Thomas has just obtained (through the interest of our Governor, Sir James - - , who has been particularly kind in procuring it for him) an Ensigncy in the 81st Regiment of Foot, which is now stationed in New Brunswick." Concerned about John Thomas's health, she wrote: "We were quite distressed to hear of dear uncle John's indisposition, but I trust that ere this he is perfectly recovered and able to laugh as heartily as he used to when we were at Marshfield." Elizabeth Francklin sent her "most affectionate rememberances to Uncle and Aunt Thomas, and all my dear Cousins..."

Contrary to the expressed belief by Elizabeth that her cousin Sarah Thomas would not be married for a long time, that young lady was married within three months. Elizabeth's father, James Boutineau Francklin, wrote in his journal under date of January 30, 1828: "Miss Sarah R. Thomas married to Lewis M. Wilkins, Esq., in St. Paul's Church by the Bishop of Nova Scotia. Sir James Kempt gave the lady away. The happy couple left town for Windsor at 11 o'clock immediately after the ceremony and arrived there at 1/2 past 6 o'clock in the evening."

Sarah Francklin wrote her brother and sister-in-law in Marshfield in the late summer of 1829: "That you may sometimes think of Elizabeth and myself, in spite of yourselves, I shall ask Mrs. Fales to take charge of two little profiles which we sat for, but which are not the best likenesses in the world. Its like her as far as the nose upward, but mine is like all old persons, looking a little grumpy. That, however, you must not mind."

In a second letter that fall of 1829, Sarah congratulated the Thomases on the marriage of their daughter Ann to Dr. John Porter of Duxbury where they had established themselves some three miles from their home. "This is delightful for all parties," Sarah added. "Indeed, I think all your daughters have been most fortunate in the choice of their husbands and it comforts me to reflect on having once seen them all happily settled around you. It must, however, be a great loss to you and

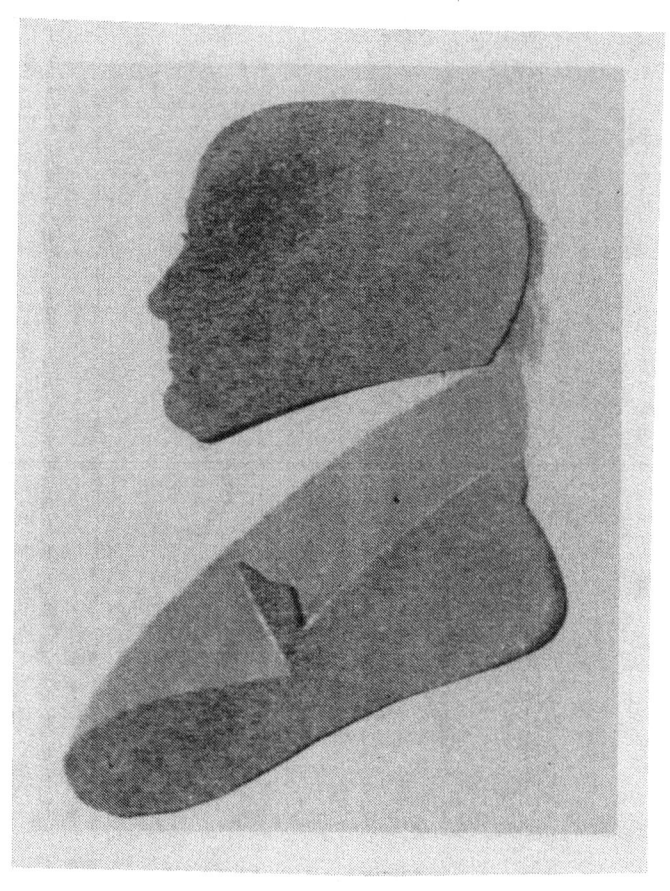

Nathaniel ("Nat") Thomas, son of Nathaniel Ray Thomas.

Elizabeth Packer Thomas, daughter of Captain John Thomas.
Granddaughter of Nathaniel Ray Thomas.
Courtesy of Mrs. Paul Peterson.

Mount Uniacke, Nova Scotia. Home of the Uniacke family. Photograph by William H.B. Thomas, 1989.

"Profile" of Sarah Thomas Francklin, daughter of Nathaniel Ray Thomas.

"Profile" of Elizabeth Gould Francklin, daughter of Sarah Thomas Francklin. Granddaughter of Nathaniel Ray Thomas.

Ann Thomas Porter, daughter of Captain John Thomas. Granddaughter of Nathaniel Ray Thomas.

Aftermath

your dear wife to have parted with all your girls, for after all girls are a prime comfort as boys must necessarily move from home."

She also had news of Charles Thomas, who, she said, was visiting in Windsor when the Francklins were there. "He has become a fine young man in figure. He is a little affected, but that will wear off with age. He was kind to his sister and very fond of her little girl. The 81st Regiment, to which Charles belongs, has been ordered to Bermuda and he came to visit his mother previous to his departure from the other Province."

In the mid-1820s Daniel Webster, one of the country's foremost lawyers and orators and leading statesman, had been in the habit of journeying down to Cape Cod from Boston to enjoy his love of fishing and the outdoor life. Knowing this, a friend suggested he stop at Marshfield and make the acquaintance of Captain John Thomas, as he was by then known, and explore the sporting possibilities there. This Webster did, and he and his wife were cordially welcomed by Captain Thomas and the Thomas family then still at home. For each successive year the Websters made a point of visiting Marshfield and became intimate friends of Captain Thomas, his wife, and their two sons Charles Henry Thomas and Nathaniel Ray Thomas.

By 1830 Webster, having been attracted to young Ray Thomas, his pleasant personality, and his obvious abilities, suggested that the boy go to Boston with the Websters and he, Webster, would place Ray in some business position. Though but eighteen years old, Ray was eager to accept the opportunity. His parents gave their permission. Their other son, Charles Henry, familiarly called Henry, chose to remain with Captain John Thomas and soon became useful to Webster, who, by then, had become interested in acquiring the Thomas property.

In July 1830 Sarah Francklin's daughter Elizabeth was married to the Reverend Fitzgerald Uniacke, son of Richard John Uniacke, the Attorney General of Nova Scotia. Richard Uniacke had been a leading figure in the Province for many years. His family was among the gentry of Ireland. The wedding took place in St. Paul's Church, Halifax, with Elizabeth's cousin the Reverend William Gray officiating. Following the ceremony, the couple breakfasted and then left for Mount Uniacke, the country house of the Attorney General about midway between Halifax and Windsor.

Aftermath

Sarah Francklin described the wedding scene for her brother John and his wife Lucy. "Perhaps ere this reaches you, the news of our daughter Elizabeth's marriage to the Rev. Fitzgerald Uniacke may have reached you. They were united in church on the 29th of last July and, after breakfasting with us at 9 o'clock, they drove to Mount Uniacke, the noble residence of the Attorney General, Mr. U's father, where they spent three weeks. Mr. Francklin and myself were five days at the Mount while Elizabeth was there. The grounds are extremely pleasant to walk over, and had Elizabeth been a queen she could not have been more kindly received by all Mr. Uniacke's family, which is very numerous and a wonderful fine family to look at, very tall and erect. Elizabeth's husband is six feet and four inches."

Almost immediately after the wedding, Richard Cunningham of Saulsbrook died. That was the second of August. Sarah Francklin attended his funeral and described her former brother-in-law as having been "an affectionate friend of our family and E. with myself mourned for him sincerely." Of Richard Cunninghams' widow, Sarah *Apthorp* Cunningham, Sarah Francklin wrote somewhat later: "I do not think Mrs. Cunningham can dispose of her property to live in Boston, as I have no doubt she would gladly do...The family are left in comfort and will no doubt do well as their mother will be their guardian and they think much of her."

Towards the end of 1831 Sarah Francklin wrote to her brother John at Marshfield that their nephew Charles Thomas, who held a commission in the 81st Regiment stationed in Bermuda, had died there the last July. "He was his mother's darling and she is a sincere mourner for him as is his sister [Sarah Wilkins]." He had been a difficult child, had undoubtedly been spoiled by his mother, and the manner of his death is uncertain.

During the years which Daniel Webster and his family had been visiting Marshfield and Captain John Thomas, Webster had become increasingly interested in purchasing the property. Finally, aware that Captain Thomas was in difficult financial straits, he offered to buy the Thomas land, that portion of which the Captain still owned. This he accomplished by the conveyance to him of some one hundred and sixty acres on April 23, 1832. During the negotiations which had taken place for about the previous year, Webster insisted that John and Lucy Thomas continue to occupy the house as their own and sit at the head and foot of the dining table in their accustomed places, while he,

Aftermath

Webster, and his wife would take their places to either side of the table, as would guests.

So the land, or a part of it at least, which the first William Thomas had been granted in 1641 and for six generations had passed down to John Thomas, Eagles Nest as the family called it, went out of Thomas ownership and occupancy. Writing to her brother in 1835, Sarah Francklin commented sadly: "And after all your hard labor upon the poor land at Marshfield, my dear brother, you have been compelled to part with the property. It was better to give it up than to remain under the pressure of debt and so there is a comfort in seeing it in the hands of a gentleman who will improve and embellish it."

In 1835 Seth Sprague sold Careswell, the former Winslow property, to Charles Henry Thomas. Charles Henry, son of Capt. John Thomas, was acting as agent for Daniel Webster and conveyed the land to him a year later. Daniel Webster then became the proprietor of the land of Marshfield's two "remarkable high Tories" - Nathaniel Ray Thomas and Isaac Winslow.

Also in 1835 Sarah Wilkins, Nat's daughter and John's niece, wrote to her uncle. "All my cousins are now married except Ray and I tell him he is too young to think of it yet." [Ray was twenty-three.] "Perhaps some of them will answer this letter, for I know that Ann will not find it any trouble to write. Where is Betsey, and Henry, also, and the Winslow family? How often I talk and think of the happy hours spent with you...I can hardly think of you without tears coming into my eyes and wishing I could go and see you... It seems hard that friends who love each other should be separated so far, but it is the way of the world..."

The next year Sarah Francklin wrote to Lucy: "It gives me pleasure that you have such kind friends in the Websters, and I hope you are able to procure some help when they are with you, as I do not like you to exert yourself too much. I rejoice that your son Ray has a good place and a kind master, and that he has gratified you with a visit, and I can but think it was a great favor that Henry preferred farming to business, as you and his father would be wretched without him."

Then, on July 27, 1837 John Thomas died. Ann Porter wrote immediately to her Aunt Sarah Francklin. Sarah conveyed her sympathies to her sister-in-law, John's widow Lucy. "Since the receipt of dear Mrs. Porter's letter announcing the death of my brother John, I have

Aftermath

scarcely been in a state to do anything as I ought...My brother was an affectionately attached friend of mine and I can but feel his departure from the world deeply..."

From 1838 to the early part of 1840 Captain John Thomas's younger son, Nathaniel Ray Thomas, named for his grandfather, worked for Daniel Webster as confidential secretary and agent for his western land speculation. On January 20, 1840 the twenty-eight-year-old Ray wrote to his former employer from Duxbury:

> In quitting your employment I shall have the satisfaction of knowing that I have discharged the obligation which I was under to you, so far as dollars are concerned. But there are other - and to me higher obligations which I feel I never can discharge; for through all the changes of my changing life I have had the satisfaction of believing that you were my friend, and of never doubting that this friendship was void of selfishness - was pure; and what ever the future may unfold be assured I shall carry with me to the latest hour of my life the purest sentiment of gratitude and esteem.

Then Ray apparently set out for New York and Washington. He had said his farewell to his mother and Henry and his other family and friends.

That Ray had an engaging personality and was an articulate young man is evidenced by a packet of letters written by him to his brother Charles Henry Thomas and carefully preserved wrapped in a sheet of paper marked "Ray's Last Letters after he left home."

Writing from the Astor House, New York, on February 10, 1840, to Henry, Ray remarked: "I have said nothing to John or any body else about my own destitute condition nor do I propose to until I return from Washington. It is a new thing for me to solicit employment and is far more disagreeable than to be sought after, but I suppose I shall be obliged to come to it and will endeavour to do it with as humble a grace as possible." He added: "Oh dear, here I am waiting for dinner which you know we dont get here until 1/2 after 3 o'clock. I have just taken off the sharp edge of appetite with some real corn fed oysters."

Then, with the pleasant touch that marked many of his letters, Ray ended this one: "I wonder how it goes in Duxbury. I should like to call in and see some of the girls, but my course lies in another direction and is

Aftermath

onward, so I will pause only to put my <u>love here</u> and request you to hand it over to Mother and consider it transferable to all that love me. Yrs truly, N. Ray Thomas."

By February 14th Ray had reached Washington. He recalled for Henry one of the incidents of his trip. "I must not forget to mention that we were delayed 24 hours at the Susquehanna River by the running ice which swept all before it rendering it unsafe and indeed impossible for the boats to cross." The travelers were delayed. "Most of the passengers returned to Philadelphia, 60 miles; but myself and two or three others preferred stopping at a fourth rate country tavern, which, in the state of Maryland, is not <u>quite</u> the thing; however, we had plenty of <u>whaffles</u> and a clean bed and I am not the boy to grumble at such fare as that."

Once in Washington Ray contacted Webster and was overjoyed to find himself again in Mr. Webster's employ. Webster intended to send him West in ten days. In the meantime he would be busy. "...one of the things that I am going to do is to send a good lot of documents to Marshfield and Duxbury. Mr. W. says every voter in Marshfield must have something - let him <u>burn</u> it if he likes. I told him that such things would do much good, so he will frank and I address." Ray went on: "We shall send direct to all the names that occur to me, but we shall send them to you by dozens franked by Mr. W. and you can address them where they will do the most good. See that you are up and doing."

Within a few days Ray was able to report to Henry some of the activities of Congress. "There is not much of interest at the Capitol. Hubbard of New Hampshire has been roaring away all day in the Senate upon Grundy's state debt bill. The debate in the House has been of an incidental nature and of not much interest. Mr. Corwin of Ohio made a very good speech on the Cumberland Road bill yesterday."

Then he informed Henry of a bit of excitement. "We had, too, in the Senate yesterday, a little flare-up between Clay and Calhoun on the occasion of some resolutions being presented from the Legislature of the State of Rhode Island remonstrating against Calhoun's bill ceding the public lands to the state. It was personal enough, I tell you. They called each other the d--d--t kind of scoundrels - only they did it in a <u>genteel</u>, though, peculiarly cutting manner. It made my very blood run cold in my veins to witness the <u>grappling</u> of such giant minds."

Aftermath

By the 26th of February, Ray had received one letter from home, although, as he wrote Henry, he had sent eight or ten letters to the family. "I think you and mother are over solicitous about my health," he wrote Henry on that date, "for I certainly never was in better health during my life than I am at present and I have great confidence that it may please Providence to extend it to me throughout my journey, but of this we cannot know."

Henry had apparently written Webster about his obtaining a business opportunity. About this, Ray advised Henry that Webster had received the letter, though he did not know when or how Webster would answer it. "I hope it will be favourable to you and that you may be able to remain in your house and arrange your business as to secure a profitable occupation where you are, and I am not without hope that Mr. Webster may do something for you yet, more than you have <u>asked for</u>, but I would not rely upon it, but go straight ahead and secure for yourself a business somewhere."

Ray set down again his thoughts about politics. "I have not forwarded any documents yet, but have a lot here directed which will be <u>franked</u> in a day or two. I send you enclosed a list of the names of persons in Duxbury and Marshfield to whom I have addressed the Life and public services of Wm. H. Harrison, and some of them also, Judge White's letter to his constituents. We have a lot of Gov. Davis' speech, a very popular one, upon the subject of labour. It is the right kind of thing to circulate and I am going to send a lot of them in packages to you and Knowles, I am glad that you are going to form an association; it is the right thing to dispense the truth. I will arrange before I leave here with one or more members to keep you well supplied with the true doctrine."

Ray ended his letter of February 26th to Henry: "tell Mother I thank her for her letter...Never forget to remember me kindly to the <u>Point</u> [Powder Point, Duxbury, where doubtless Ray had a girl in whom he was interested], to Louisa [Henry's wife], and all that I love. Yours always, N. Ray Thomas." This was the last letter of the packet marked, "Ray's Last Letters after he left home." A few days later, he fell sick.

On the 10th of March Webster wrote to Henry. "Ray has not got along so fast, as I hoped, but still he seems to be growing better. His attack was severe, and he is much reduced. He has a tolerably comfortable room at Brown's...we shall take care that he has every thing comfortable. Dr. [Leavell?] says he is in no danger, now, and recovering as fast as could

Aftermath

be expected. Indeed he has never thought him in danger. I told Ray if he did not recover faster, I should send for you to come to him, but he did not think at all necessary. I shall write you every day, until he writes you himself."

But on March 17, 1840, at the age of twenty-eight, Nathaniel Ray Thomas died. The following morning at eight o'clock Daniel Webster wrote a letter, probably to some member of Ray's family. "The scene closed, a few minutes after 11 o'clock last Evening, when Ray breathed his last breath. No great change preceded this event, but for some time he had been more quiet...I yet hear nothing from Henry; and am obliged to act on my own judgment, under these melancholy circumstances. I have directed everything to be so prepared and arranged, as that he may be taken to Marshfield, and buried by the side of his father...I feel a good deal overcome; and can only send you all my deepest sympathy. The loss of Ray is to me like the loss of a son. But God's will be done. It is a mysterious Providence; but what we know not now, we shall know hereafter. Danl Webster."

Two days after writing that letter, Webster composed a letter of condolence to Ray's mother, Lucy Thomas. "I have been greatly troubled, since Ray's death, to know how I ought to act. For two days, I have looked anxiously for Henry, but he does not come. And it is now necessary either to inter the body, or send it home. I have thought, upon the whole, it would be more agreeable to you and the family, that it should be sent home..."

Then, in conclusion, Webster wrote: "I pray you, my dear Mrs. Thomas, to support yourself, as well as you can, and help to support others under this affliction. For myself, I feel as if I had lost a beloved son. With great sympathy, and much respect and affection to you all, I am, dear Mrs. Thomas, Yours, D. Webster." The death of young Ray shook the whole family, for he had been to his family the particularly beloved son, the proud hope of all, in very much the same way that his Uncle Charles Thomas had been to his in that distant year of 1797 when he had been cut down in his youth.

Fifteen years passed, during which members of the family in Nova Scotia and Marshfield, exchanged letters. In May of 1855 Elizabeth Uniacke, daughter of Sarah Francklin, wrote to her cousin Elizabeth Packer Thomas, who had married Ichabod Sampson of Duxbury. "Do, my dear Elizabeth," Elizabeth Uniacke said, in part, "write me a few lines

Aftermath

soon and tell me how Aunt Thomas is, and how you all are, for every little thing will be interesting to me. I often think of the many happy days we passed together under your hospitable roof at Marshfield and of your great kindness to me when I was such a miserable, delicate little child, and can scarcely believe that so many years have elapsed...give my best love to your mother and all my other dear cousins, none of who are forgotten by me, tho from my having been silent so long, you may have been led to think so."

Several years earlier, on July 31, 1847, Sarah Francklin, aged eighty-four years, widow of James Boutineau Francklin, had died at the Rectory of Saint George's Church, Halifax, Nova Scotia. Sarah Francklin was the last surviving child of Nathaniel Ray Thomas and Sarah *Dering* Thomas to die. She had been born in Marshfield at Eagles Nest, the family estate that had descended to her father in direct inheritance from the first of the family, William Thomas, in 1641. She had witnessed the riotous time that had led up to the American Revolution, the war and the estrangement of family and friends. She took part in the removal of the family to Nova Scotia as refugees in exile. She had assisted in the efforts of her father Nathaniel Ray Thomas, to secure compensation from the British government for his losses. She had suffered through the deaths of her brothers and sisters and her father and her mother. And finally, she had rejoiced in the reunion of herself and other of her relations in Canada with her brother and his children and grandchildren in Massachusetts.

It had truly been, for all, a destiny apart.

A Note About Sources and Methods

For information on the source for the title of this book, see passage from John Andrews' Barrell Correspondence (Massachusetts Historical Society, Proceedings Vol. 8, pp. 396-397, 1865).

CHAPTER ONE

For the source of the title for Chapter One of this book, see Loyalist Papers, Public Record Office, London, England.

My papers of the Thomas family which provided much primary source material relevant to this book, including all the letters of Sarah *Dering* Thomas and Nathaniel Ray Thomas with exceptions as noted, have been subsequently deposited with the Pilgrim Society at Pilgrim Hall, Plymouth, Massachusetts. These papers date from the 1690s to the middle decades of the nineteenth century. They were collected by cousins of mine who became fascinated with the story of Nathaniel Ray Thomas, a notorious Tory of Marshfield, Massachusetts in the Revolutionary War, and his wife, Sarah *Dering* Thomas. These cousins, Dr. Azel Ames, and Mrs. Ames, the former Sarah A. Dering Ames, became so wrapped up in their story that Mrs. Ames changed her maiden name legally to Sarah Dering Thomas Ames. They worked over the collection, made copious notes and wrote innumerable letters to correspondents in Nova Scotia and elsewhere in Canada, England, Bermuda, and, of course, the United States. After the deaths of Dr. Ames and his wife, the papers were inherited by their daughter, Mrs. Louise Ames Norman. It was she who, claiming that she herself was neither able to continue the work of her parents nor had any family member sufficiently interested in doing so, gave the collection to this writer.

Other manuscript collections with important items pertaining to the Thomases are the General John Thomas Papers in the Massachusetts Historical Society, Boston, Massachusetts; the Dering Family Papers in the William L. Clements Library, University of Michigan, Ann Arbor, Michigan; the Harvard College Faculty Records, Harvard University Archives, Pusey Library, Harvard University, Cambridge, Massachusetts; Marshfield Town Records, Town Hall, Marshfield, Massachusetts; the Loyalist Papers, Public Record Office, London, England; and N. B. Shurtleff and David Pulsifer, eds., Records of the Colony of New Plymouth in New England 1620-1691, 12 vols. (Boston, Mass. 1855-1861). The printed collections which contain important primary sources are: Massachusetts Historical Society, Collections, (Boston, 1792-) and Proceedings, (Boston, 1859-); and the Publications of the Colonial Society of Massachusetts (Boston, 1895-). These publications contain a wealth of valuable source material too numerous to cite individually. With this grouping should be included the Journal of the House of Representatives of Massachusetts, 1715-1749, 25 vols. (Boston, 1919-1950).

These primary sources, while noted for Chapter One, are equally applicable to Chapter Two and succeeding chapters.

Among the many printed books and articles, relevant to this book and written by recognized authorities, generally in the order in which they relate to the text, are:

L. Vernon Briggs, History of Shipbuilding on the North River. (Boston, 1889, reprinted 1970).

Lyman H. Butterfield et al., eds., Diary and Autobiography of John Adams, 4 vols. (Cambridge, Mass., 1961).

Robert McC. Calhoun, The Loyalists in Revolutionary America, 1760-1781. (New York, 1965, 1969, 1973).

Colonial Society of Massachusetts, Publications (1895-) vol. 22, Plymouth Church Records 1620-1859. pp. 71-80 (Boston, 1920).

Anne Rowe Cunningham and Edward Lillie Pierce, Eds., Letters and Diary of John Rowe, Boston Merchant 1759, 1767, 1764-1779. (Boston, 1903).

Alice Morse Earle, ed., Diary of Anna Green Winslow: A Boston School Girl of 1771. (Boston and New York, 1894).

Joseph C. Hagar, Marshfield: The Autobiography of a Pilgrim Town. (Marshfield, Mass., 1940).

Cynthia Krusell and Betty Bates, Marshfield: A Town of Villages 1640-1990. (Marshfield Hills, Mass., 1990).

Cynthia Krusell, Of Tea and Tories. (Marshfield, Mass., 1976).

Benjamin W. Labaree, Colonial Massachusetts: A History. (Millwood, N. Y., 1979).

_____, The Boston Tea Party. (London and New York, 1966, 1975).

E. Alfred Jones, Loyalists of Massachusetts. (London, 1930).

George D. Langdon, A History of New Plymouth 1620-1691. (New Haven and London, 1966, 1969).

David E. Mass, Divided Hearts: Massachusetts Loyalists 1765-1790. (Boston, 1980).

John C. Miller, Sam Adams: Pioneer in Propaganda. (Stanford, Calif. 1936, reprinted 1966).

Lysander S. Richards, History of Marshfield, 2 vols. (Plymouth, 1901).

Darrett E. Rutman, Husbandmen of Plymouth: Farms and Villages in the Old Colony, 1620-1692. (Boston, 1967).

Eugene D. Stratton, Plymouth Colony: Its History and People (1621-1691), 2 vols. (Salt Lake City, Utah, 1986).

Marcia A. Thomas, Memorials of Marshfield. (Boston, 1854).

The basic contemporary work on the beginnings of Plymouth Colony is William Bradford, Of Plymouth Plantation, Samuel E. Morison, ed. (New York, 1987).

Newspapers which contain pertinent information are:

Boston Gazette and Country Journal, Feb. 5, 1774; Feb. 7, 1774; Jan. 30, 1775.

Boston Evening Post, Sept. 12, 1774.

Massachusetts Spy, Feb. 23, 1774.

CHAPTER TWO

For details about British troops arriving in Marshfield, see John Andrews-Barrell Correspondence, (Massachusetts Historical Society Proceedings, Vol 8, 1865) and Ezra Stiles Literary Diary, 3 vols. (New York, 1901).

For the proceedings at the Town Meeting of January 31, 1774, see Marshfield Town Records under that date and for secondary sources, see Marcia A. Thomas, Memorials of Marshfield (Boston, 1854), and Lysander S. Richards, History of Marshfield, 2 vols. (Plymouth, 1901).

For Bradford's description of Green's Harbor, see William Bradford, Of Plymouth Plantation, Samuel E. Morison, ed. pp. 253-254 (New York, 1987).

For development of Plymouth Colony, see Nathaniel Shurtleff and David Pulsifer, Records of the Colony of New Plymouth in New England, 12 vols. (Boston, 1861).

For the early history of Plymouth, see George D. Langdon, A History of New Plymouth 1620-1691. (New Haven and London, 1966, 1969).

For the history of the Thomas and Winslow grants, see Cynthia Hagar Krusell and Betty Bates, Marshfield: A Town of Villages 1640-1990. (Marshfield Hills, 1990).

Tracing the progress of the Massachusetts Government Act to enactment in England, see The Annual Register or a View of the History, Politics and Literature for the Year 1774. (London 1810, vol. 17, pp. 69-72)

An extremely illuminating article on the meetings and contemporary events surrounding them in Massachusetts is "Documents Relating to the Last Meetings of the Massachusetts Royal Council 1774-1776" by Albert Mathews, Publications of the Colonial Society of Massachusetts, vol. 32. (Boston, 1937, pp. 460-504).

The story of Nathaniel Ray Thomas at Dr. Winslow's and escaping there from the patriots has been handed down in the family of the writer.

For the course of events generally in Massachusetts in 1774-1776, see Benjamin W. Labaree, Colonial Massachusetts: A History. (Millwood, New York, 1979), and Richard L. Bushman, King and People in Provincial Massachusetts. (Chapel Hill and London, 1985).

For English events, see Esmond Wright, Fabric of Freedom 1763-1800. (New York, 1986).

For details about the Boston Tea Party, see Benjamin W. Labaree, The Boston Tea Party. (London and New York, 1966, reprinted 1975).

For the Tories in Marshfield, see Cynthia Hagar Krusell, Of Tea and Tories (Marshfield, Mass., 1976).

For the deployment of British troops to Marshfield, see John Barker, The British in Boston: The Diary of Lt. John Barker (Cambridge, Mass. 1924) and Frederick Mackensie, The Diary of Frederick Mackensie (Cambridge, Mass., 1930).

For the story of the storing of ammunition and powder in "Capt. Willie" Thomas's house, see Lysander Richards, History of Marshfield, 2 vols. (Plymouth, Mass., 1901).

Plymouth County, Mass. Probate Records, Plymouth, Mass.

For the excerpts from the letters of John Andrews, see John Andrews-Barrell Correspondence, (Massachusetts Historical Society Proceedings Vol. 8) and for excerpts from Ezra Stiles diary, see Ezra Stiles, Literary Diary, 3 vols. (New York, 1901).

CHAPTER THREE

For the early history of Plymouth Colony, see Nathaniel Shurtleff and David Pulsifer, Records of the Colony of New Plymouth in New England, 12 vols. (Boston, 1861).

For the controversy between Reverend Arnold and the Thomas's, see above.

For Edward Winslow, see Cynthia Hagar Krusell and Betty Bates, Marshfield: A Town of Villages 1640-1990 (Marshfield Hills, Mass. 1992).

Mellen A. Chamberlain, A Documentary History of Chelsea, 2 vols. (Cambridge, Mass., 1908).

Cornelius J. Moynihan, A Preliminary Survey of the Law of Real Property: An Historical Background. (St. Paul, Minn., 1908).

Robert M. Sherman and Ruth Wilder Sherman, comp. Vital Records of Marshfield, Massachusetts to the Year 1850. (Warwick. R. I., 1970).

For Nathaniel Thomas's account of the deaths by lightning in Marshfield, see Nathaniel Bradstreet Shurtleff, Thunder and Lightning and Deaths at Marshfield in 1658 & 1666. (Boston: Privately printed, MDCCC). This privately printed account of deaths by lightning is rather rare. It is interesting to note that Shurtleff the compiler of the story was also the editor of the Records of the Colony of New Plymouth in New England and that the person that he presented the little volume to was David Pulsifer his co-editor of the Plymouth records.

For Ray Thomas's statement that his land was considerable and in extent and "his family residence was coeval with that town" (Marshfield), see Loyalist Papers, Public Record Office, London, England.

William A. Whitmore, Massachusetts Civil List. (Albany, N. Y. 1870).

M. Halsey Thomas, ed. The Diary of Samuel Sewall, 2 vols. (New York, 1973).

Samuel E. Morison, Three Centuries of Harvard 1636-1936. (Cambridge, Mass., 1946).

Clifford K. Shipton, ed. Biographical Sketches of those who attended Harvard College in the Class of 1715, Vol. VI, (Boston, 1946).

For details about the Matson case, see printed brief of attorney for plaintiff Nathaniel Matson, Isaac Little, Esq. submitted to Superior Court of Judicature. Boston, S. Kneeland, Queen St., 1720.

CHAPTER FOUR

For Ray Thomas's letter of September 21, 1748 and Dr. John Thomas's of October 4, 1788, see General John Thomas Papers, Massachusetts Historical Society, Boston, Mass.

For the quotations from the Harvard College Faculty Records, see Harvard College Faculty Records, I, Harvard Archives, Pusey Library Harvard University, Cambridge, Mass.

For the original accounts of the income and expense of Ray Thomas's guardianship, see guardianship accounts filed by John Thomas, Nathaniel Ray's guardian, in the Registry of Probate, Plymouth, Mass.

For a description of Harvard and details of student life, including the placing of students, see Morison Three Centuries of Harvard, 1636-1956.

For Pelham Winslow's concern about his class "placing", see Shipton Biographical Sketches ..., Vol 13.

For Ray Thomas's offenses at Harvard, see Harvard College Faculty Records, 1, Harvard Archives, Pusey Library, Harvard University, Cambridge, Mass.

Massachusetts Hall Room Lists, 1741-1767, Harvard College Archives, Pusey Library, Harvard University, Cambridge, Mass.

Nathaniel Ray Thomas's discharge of his guardian is in the possession of the writer.

Excerpts from letters of Nathaniel Ray Thomas and Dr. John Thomas are at the Massachusetts Historical Society in the John Thomas Papers.

Robert M. Sherman and Ruth Wilder Sherman, eds. and comp. Vital Records of Marshfield, Massachusetts, to the year 1850. (Warwick, R. I., 1970).

Clifford K. Shipton, ed. Biographical Sketches of those who attended Harvard College...1751-1755. vol. 13 (Boston, 1965)

Samuel E. Morison, Three Centuries of Harvard 1636-1936. Cambridge, Mass. 1946).

William Coolidge Lane, "The Building of Massachusetts Hall, 1717-1720," Publications of the Colonial Society of Massachusetts, vol. 24, pp. 81-90 (Boston, Mass. 1928).

For the translation of the Latin Quaestio of which Ray Thomas took the affirmative side, I am indebted to Rev. William J. O'Conner and Rev. John S. Morris, Saint Jeremiah's Church, Framingham, Mass., through the courtesy of Miss Joan Scolponeti, Marshfield, Mass.

CHAPTER FIVE

For details about the wedding of Nathaniel Ray Thomas and Sarah Dering, see Marcia A. Thomas, Memorials of Marshfield, Boston, 1854).

For Henry Dering's inventory, see Suffolk County Court Files, Suffolk County Court, Suffolk County Courthouse (Boston, Mass.).

Papers of General John Thomas, Massachusetts Historical Society, (Boston, Mass.).

Briton Hammon's Narrative of the Uncommon Sufferings, and Surprizing Deliverance of Briton Hammon, A Negro Man, - Servant to General Winslow of Marshfield, in New England; Who returned to Boston, after having been absent almost Thirteen Years was printed in Boston by Green & Russell in 1760. Two copies of the original are known to exist, one in the Library of Congress and the other at the New York Historical Society. Courtesy of Ms. Lisa Maria Burgess Noudehou of Pittsburgh, Pa.

The petition of the "French Neutrals" to the Governor and Council is in the Massachusetts State Archives, Boston, Mass.

For a typical foray by provincial troops under command of Lt. John Thomas, see diary entry under date of November 17, 1755 in Journals of Beausejour Diary of John Thomas journal of Louis de Courville, ed. John Clarence Webster (The Public Archives of Nova Scotia, Sackville, N.B., 1937).

Benjamin W. Labaree, Colonial Massachusetts (Millwood, N. Y., 1979).

For a contemporary view of Boston, see Walter Muir Whitehill, Boston: A Topographical History (Cambridge, Mass., 1959).

For the interesting relationship between Franklin and Caty Greene, see William Green Roelker, ed. Benjamin Franklin and Catherine Ray Greene; Their Correspondence 1755-1790 (Philadelphia, 1949).

Merrill C. Rueppel, Paul Revere's Boston, (Boston, 1975).

CHAPTER SIX

For the qualifications of Justices of the Peace, see Michael Dalton, Country Justice, (London, 1692).

For excerpts from Hepsibah Edwards' letters, see Thomas Papers, Pilgrim Society, Pilgrim Hall, Plymouth, Mass.

For the excerpts from John Rowe's diary, see Anne Row Cunningham and Edward Lillie Pierce, eds., Letters and Diary of John Rowe, Boston Merchant ... (boston, 1903).

For the oath of allegiance to King George III required by the Act of Settlement, for the oath of a Justice of the Peace and for the oaths required of judges of the Superior Court of Judicature and the Inferior court of Common Pleas of Plymouth County, see The Charter Granted by their Majesties King William and Queen Mary to the Inhabitants of the Province of the Massachusetts-Bay ... (Boston, 1726).

For considerable information about the life and career of General John Thomas, see Arthur Lord's paper on the General. Massachusetts Historical Society Proceedings, Vol. 18, pp. 420-432 (Boston, 1905) and Edward Pierce Hamilton, "General John Thomas", Massachusetts Historical Society, Proceedings, vol. 84, pp. 44-53 (Boston, 1972).

For conditions in England see Carl Bridebaugh, Vexed and Troubled Englishmen 1590-1642 (London, Oxford, New York, 1967).

CHAPTER SEVEN

For Caty Greene's assessment of Ray Thomas's personal financial situation, see Marcia A. Thomas, Memorials of Marshfield (Boston, 1854).

For Ray and Sarah Thomas's letters regarding his financial problems, see Thomas Papers, Pilgrim Society, Pilgrim Hall, Plymouth, Mass.

CHAPTER EIGHT

For excerpts from Anna (Greene) Winslow's diary, see Thomas Papers, Pilgrim Society, Pilgrim Hall, Plymouth, Mass.

For the assessment of taxes, see list in Thomas Papers, Pilgrim Society, Pilgrim Hall, Plymouth, Mass., and for the division deed executed by the heirs of Mr. John Thomas, see the Thomas Papers.

For the Tory resolutions of thanks to General Gage and Admiral Graves and the Whig reaction to them, see Marshfield town records, Town Hall, Marshfield, Mass.

For the town's expressing its wishes by resolution, see Lysander S. Richards, History of Marshfield, 2 vols. (Plymouth, 1901).

For an outsider's account of the British troops at Marshfield, see Ezra Stiles, Literary Diary, 3 vols. (New York, 1901).

For the opening events of the war and successive events of the first year of the American Revolution, see the readable and reliable Allan French, The First Year of the American Revolution (Boston, 1934).

For the role of the British Army in the coming of the American Revolution, see John Shy's thorough work, Toward Lexington (Princeton, N. J., 1965).

A well-researched history of the Revolutionary War as a whole is Willard M. Wallace, Appeal to Arms: A Military History (New York, 1951).

For an important over-view of conditions in the American Colonies prior to the American Revolution, see Charles M. Andrews The Colonial Background of the American Revolution (New York and London, 1924, 1958, 1969).

For a work investigating the social structure of the American Colonies during Revolutionary epoch, see Jackson Turner Main, The Social Structure of Revolutionary America (Princeton, N. J., 1945, 1969, 1973).

For a careful and thoughtful study of revolutionary politics in Massachusetts, see Richard D. Brown, Revolutionary Politics in Massachusetts: The Boston Committee of Correspondence and the Towns 1772-1774 (New York, 1970, 1976).

CHAPTER NINE

For excerpts from Marshfield town records, see Marshfield Town Records, Town Hall, Marshfield, Mass.

For the story of John Bourne, see Lysander Richards, History of Marshfield, 2 vols, (Plymouth, Mass., 1901).

The Sarah (Winslow) Deming letter is in the collection of the Winslow House and is used by permission of the Historic Winslow House Association, Marshfield, Mass.

For George Washington's letters written to and about General John Thomas, see Fitzpatrick The Writings of George Washington, 39 Vols, Vol. 3, Jan. 1770-Sept. 1775, (Washington, D.C., 1931)

For the affair involving Ray Thomas and the cattle and sheep on Long Island in Boston Harbor, see George Washington, The Writings of George Washington, 39 vols., vol. 3, p. 337 (Washington, D. C., 1931).

For meetings of the Mandamus Council and other pertinent data, see Albert Mathews, "Documents relating to the Last Meetings of the Massachusetts Royal Council 1774-1776", Publications of the Colonial Society of Massachusetts, vol. 32, pp. 460-504 (Boston, 1939).

For Nathaniel Ray Thomas's October 6, 1775 letter to General Gage, see William L. Clements Library, University of Michigan, Ann Arbor, Michigan.

For description of the skirmish between militia and British troops, see John Thomas Papers, Massachusetts Historical Society, Boston, Mass.

For John Andrews letter about conditions in Boston, see John Andrews-Barrell Correspondence, Massachusetts Historical Society, Proceedings, Vol. 8, 1865

For Mary Cheseborough's letter, see Thomas Papers, Pilgrim Society, Pilgrim Hall, Plymouth, Mass.

For the situation in Boston of the Loyalists, see Allen French, The First Year of the American Revolution (Boston, 1934).

For reasons for fortifying Dorchester Heights, and the actual operation, see Edward Pierce Hamilton, "General John Thomas", Massachusetts Historical Society, vol. 84, pp. 44-53 (Boston, Mass., 1972) and Arthur Lord's paper on the General, Massachusetts Historical Society, Proceedings, vol. 18, pp. 420-432 (Boston, Mass., 1905).

CHAPTERS TEN AND ELEVEN

For Mrs. Mercy Otis Warren's comment on the plight of the Loyalists in Halifax, see Massachusetts Historical Society, Proceedings, Boston, Mass.

For the deliberations and edicts of the Provincial Congress of Massachusetts, see The Journals of each Provincial Congress of Massachusetts in 1774 and 1775 and the Committee of Safety ... (Boston, 1838).

For entries in Governor Hutchinson's diary, see The Diary and Letters of His Excellency Thomas Hutchinson, ed. Peter Orlando Hutchinson.

For the Marshfield selection of Nehemiah Thomas, see Lysander Richards, History of Marshfield, 2 vols. (Plymouth, Mass., 1901).

John Trumbull's epic poem, "M'Fingal," was published in many editions, one of which was in Philadelphia, Pa., in 1791.

For Nat Thomas and the Port Roseway Associates [subsequently Shelburne, Nova Scotia], see Marion Robertson, Kings Bounty: A History of Early Shelburne, Nova Scotia (Halifax, 1983).

CHAPTER TWELVE

For Benjamin Marston's comment on Nathaniel Ray Thomas, see Winslow Papers, A. D. 1776-1826, William Odber Raymond, ed. (Boston, Mass. 1972).

For Nathaniel Ray Thomas's claims for losses and loss of compensation, see Loyalist Papers, Public Record Office, London, England.

CHAPTER THIRTEEN

The story of the British ship, Shannon putting into the mouth of the North River and the subsequent raid on Waterman Thomas's house on Marshfield Neck by the British crew has been handed down in the family of the writer. Some corroboration of it is found in L. Vernon Briggs' book History of Shipbuilding on North River... (Boston, 1889) at page 51: "He [Capt. Sherman] was an eye-witness of the engagement between the man-of-war "Chesapeake" and "Shannon." Before the battle the British came into North River for provisions; they took three calves from the farm of Waterman Thomas, on Marshfield Neck..."

For life and times in early Nova Scotia, see William Scarth Moorsom, Letters from Nova Scotia, Marjory Whitelaw, ed., (Canada, 1986).

For Daniel Webster, The Thomas's, and Eagles Nest, see Peter Harvey, Reminiscences and Anecdotes of Daniel Webster, (Boston 1877, pp. 265, 268).

"Little Sarah Thomas" was later Sarah Ames, wife of Elijah Ames. They continued to live in Major Briggs Thomas's house at the Neck.

CHAPTER FOURTEEN

The story of the Sunday visits of John Briggs Thomas and his sister Sarah Thomas to their grandfather's, Captain John Thomas at Eagles Nest, has been handed down in the family of the writer.

For the visit of Sarah DeWolf Thomas and her children and Sarah Cunningham to Boston, see Walter Muir Whitehill's article, "Perez Morton's Daughter Revisits Boston in 1825", Publications of the Massachusetts Historical Society, Proceedings, vol. 52, 1970 (Boston, 1971).

For an important book on the interpretation of the American Revolution, see Gordon S. Wood, The Radicalism of the American Revolution. (New York, 1992)

A Note on Methods

With regard to the letters of Sarah *Dering* Thomas which appear in the text, I have let stand the punctuation, spelling, and capitalization of the originals. This may seem to confuse the reader, but by leaving her writing in the manner in which it came from her pen, one catches the flavor of her style. This is particularly true if the letters are read out loud. Also, retaining the phonetic method of spelling which marked her writing adds much to the sense of the original.

I should point out also that the letters transcribed by Mrs. Ames have been handled in the same way. I discovered from a letter written by General Sylvester Dering to Major Azel Ames that General Dering was a cousin since he descended from Sylvester Dering, the son of Sarah *Dering* Thomas's nephew. General Dering possessed three albums in which family documents had been pasted. Among other things the General said was: "Now about these old letters I have and which you wish so much to go through. Do you know I am inclined to make it easier for you to do so, than it will be for you to come to Utica [New York] and do it. I have three volumes of them, as you know. I am inclined to let you have a volume at a time to look over at your house, and when you have had a reasonable time to go through one, you will return it to me intact and I will send you another and we keep this up till you have finished the three." The Ames' agreed to this arrangement and Mrs. Ames undertook to copy the letters in the volumes. Since she was in fact copying originals, I determined to reproduce her copies exactly as she had copied them: spelling, punctuation, capitalization and all. I believe this has kept the spirit and meaning of the letters in as honest and accurate a way as could be. The letter from General Dering to the Ameses was dated March 7, 1907. I have been unable to locate General Dering's volumes as of this date.

INDEX

Abercromby, James 87
Adams
  Abigail 136, 148, 162
  John 1, 31, 109, 136, 152, 166, 168
  Samuel 152
Agricultural Society 225
Amherst, Jeffery 88, 90, 97
Andrews
  Charles 271
  John 34, 131, 137, 159, 175
apples 120, 250
Appleton
  John 50
  Mary 50, 51
  (see also Thomas)
  Samuel 50
Apthorp
  Charles 81, 104, 184
  Grizzell 171
  Jack 116
  James 81, 104, 113
  Sarah Wentworth 171, 186, 194, 204, 210, 251
Arnold, Samuel 43-45, 47
Asher 79, 85
Auchmuty, Robert 179
Bailey 138-141
Baker
  John 4, 132, 247
  William 115
Balfour, Nesbitt 31, 32, 33, 35, 36, 131, 133, 137, 138, 139, 140, 143, 144, 145, 164, 212
Banishment Act 176
Barbicued Hogg 97
Barker
  John 32, 33, 164
  Sally 105, 184, 185
Bay of Fundy 199, 200
Bermuda 236, 255, 256
Bernard, Sir Francis 16, 179
Betty 116
Bisby 79, 80
Black Mount 140
Blackburn, Joseph 109, 110
Blake 184
Blyth, Benjamin 111
Boston Committee of Correspondence 33, 34, 36, 137
Boston Gazette and Country Journal 6, 7, 32, 136
Boston Massacre 104, 162
Boston Tea Party 1, 2, 5, 13, 17, 104, 132
Bourne
  John 1, 2, 10, 145

Bourne (cont'd)
  Mary 59
Bourne's Ordinary 10
Boutineau, James 29, 150, 179, 230, 235, 244, 254, 262
Bowdoin, James 205
Braddock, Edward 87
Bradford
  Gamaliel 130
  Gershom 225
  James 101
  Major 138
  Wllaim 10, 39
Brick Church 73
Brinley, George 113, 116
Britannia 32, 35
britches 77
British troops 30, 131, 144, 145, 166, 212
Broke, Philip 238, 239
Browne, William 29, 150, 153, 168, 179
Bryant, Seth 4, 132
Bunker Hill, battle of 146, 149, 150, 161
Burch, Wlliam 179
Burgoyne, John 171
Burke, Edmund 15
Butler 107
Byles, Mather 61, 62
Caldwell 107
Calef 103
Calhoun, John 259
Campbell
  Colin 213
  John 87
Canada 78, 88, 90, 97, 160, 179, 207, 262
Cape Blow me down 199
Cape Split 199
Careswell 12, 16, 21, 40, 42, 46, 57, 58, 62, 69, 77, 78, 100, 102, 103, 111, 248, 249, 257
Carleton, Guy 193
Castle William 107, 161
Cato 86
Caves of Flanders 87
Charles River 70
Charter 14, 48, 97
Chase, Joshua 141
Chesapeake 240
Cheseborough, Mary 149
Chignecto, isthmus of 78
Clapp, Thomas 130
Clay, Henry 259
Cleaveland, Samuel 166, 173
Coercive Acts 16, 17, 26, 174
Coffin 176
Collfleet, William 153

Collins 148
Committee of Correspondence 27, 33, 34, 36, 137, 145, 167, 169, 175
Committee of Safety 145, 160, 176
Confiscation Act 179, 180, 187
Connecticut 20, 35, 55, 101, 169, 179, 188, 196
consumption 114, 183, 208, 229, 230, 232
Continental Association 26, 29, 135, 175
Continental Congress 25, 26, 29, 31, 137, 148, 152, 160, 166, 167
Conway, Henry 15
Copley, John Singleton 109-111
Corwin, Jonathan 48, 259
Cranberry Island 199
Croade, Thomas 91
Crocker, Francis 141
Cumberland Road bill 259
Cunningham
  Eliza 213, 316, 226-230, 232, 236
  Elizabeth Packer Thomas 246
  Frances S. W. 246, 248, 250, 252
  Richard 213, 214, 225, 226, 232, 233, 236, 241, 242, 244, 246, 247, 252
  Sarah Aphtorp Morton 241, 242, 243, 251, 252
Cushing
  John 58
  Joseph 180, 182
  William 61, 62, 65
Cushman, Elkanah 108
Danforth, Samuel 51
Dartmouth, Earl of 17-19, 28, 29, 32, 35, 137, 149, 150, 162, 153, 158, 164
Dartmouth College 174
Dawes, William 138
Declaration of Independence 168
Deming, Sarah Winslow 105, 107, 146, 147
Dering 36, 72-77, 79-83, 85, 92, 103-105, 107, 110, 113-119, 122, 124-127, 149, 156-157, 169-170, 172-173, 176, 178, 183-184, 186-189, 191, 195-198, 200, 201-204, 208, 210-214, 221-222, 225, 229-230, 236, 238, 242, 244-245, 262
  Henry (first) 72, 73, 122, 124
  Henry (second) 72-74, 107, 116-117, 125, 157
  Sylvester 127, 169-172, 176-178, 180, 183-188, 203, 210-216, 244-245
Dering's Corner 73, 75, 80, 143
Deschamps, George 197, 201, 206, 209
DeWolf, Benjamin 227, 250
Diana 32, 25
Dingley, Jacob 139
Dowdeswell, William 14
dropsy 114
Dudley
  Joseph 61, 63
  Paul 48, 68

Dunbar, Jesse 27-28, 140, 249
Duxbury Mills 103
Eagles Nest 39, 42, 50, 54, 58, 77, 131, 188, 257, 262
Eames
  Benjamin 141
  Jedidah 141
earthquake 83-84, 102
East India Company 4-5, 8, 13
Edson, Josiah 29, 150, 168, 179
Edward, duke of Kent (Prince of England) 215, 218-220, 225
Edwards, Hepsibah 114, 116, 172, 184, 202, 203, 210
Eells, Robert L. 180, 181
Epes, Samuel 61
Erving
  George 29, 150, 179
  John, Jr. 29, 150, 153, 156, 168, 179
Essex Gazette 32
Ewell, Seth 132
Fales 254
Fitch, Samuel 179
Fletcher 221
Flucker, Thomas 29, 150, 179
Ford
  Elisha 4, 33, 132
  Lemuel 141
  Peleg 248
  Sarah 252
  Thomas, Jr. 100, 187
Fort William Henry 87
Fortune 107
Foster, Thomas 130
Fox, Charles James 15
Foxcroft, Thomas 74
France 38, 58, 83, 90-91, 227
Francklin 226, 227, 232, 234, 255, 256
  Elizabeth Gould 236, 244, 245, 252, 254-255
  James Boutineau 224, 230, 235, 245, 249, 254
  Sarah (daughter) 231
  Sarah Dering Thomas 225, 228-230, 236, 244-250, 253, 255-257, 261, 262
Franklin, John 74
French neutrals 86
French prisoners 83
Gage, General Thomas 16-20, 22, 25-26, 28-35, 132-133, 135, 138-143, 147-150, 152-155, 161, 176
Gardiner, Elizabeth Dering 197, 212
George II (king of England) 90
George III (king of England) 14, 89-90, 215
Germain, Lord George 14, 164
Gershom Bradford House 225
Goldthwaite, Ezekiel 81, 82, 92, 189
Gooch
  John 73

Gooch (cont'd)
　Mary Dering 36, 82-83, 105, 125, 143, 145, 156, 171-173, 178-179
Gould
　Elizabeth Wentworth 114, 116
　John, Jr. 113, 114
　John (second) 200
　Polly 201
Government House 195, 216, 218-219
Graves, Admiral Samuel 132, 135, 140, 155
Gray
　Benjamin Gerrish 212, 214, 223-226, 236
　Harrison 29, 150, 179
　Mary Thomas 212, 216, 224-225, 229-230, 236
　William 250, 255
Great Britain 8, 14, 34-35, 90-91, 109, 133, 137, 151-152, 167, 227
Green 105, 107
　Anna Pierce 82, 100
　Caty Ray 74, 118
　Joseph 81-82, 110, 121
Green Harbor (also Green's & Greene's) 11, 23, 39-40, 42-43, 45, 50, 54-55, 57, 59, 118
Green (also Greene's) Harbor Path 36
Green (also Greene's) Harbor River 10, 39-40, 43, 49, 140
Greenleaf, Benjamin 61
Halifax Gazette 219
Hall, Luke 141
Halliburton, Brenton 217
Hallowell, Benjamin 179
Hammersmith House 174, 186, 190, 192, 194
Hammon, Briton 86-87
Harris 59
Harrison, William H. 260
Harvard College 43, 51, 59-62, 65-68, 70-71, 76-77, 79, 81, 91, 96, 99, 102-103, 105, 107-108, 110, 112-113, 129, 138, 143-144, 164, 248
Hatch, Nathnaiel 29, 150, 153, 156, 176, 179
Haviland, William 88
Head, Michael 209
Henshaw 251
Holyoke
　Edward 60, 62, 67-68
　John 61
Hood, Samuel 107
Hope 140
Howard, Martin, Jr. 96-97, 111
Howe, General 155-156, 158, 163-167, 173, 175, 179
Hubbard 259
　Judith Ray 73-74
　Thomas 70, 73-74
Hulton, Henry 179

Hutchinson 72
　Foster 29, 179
　Sally 116
　Thomas 16-17, 25, 125, 150, 160, 173, 179
Inman
　George 112
　Ralph 107, 112
Intolerable Acts 17
Isaac Winslow House 196
Jamaica 86, 116, 250
James, William 176
Jane 86
Johnson, 105
Keayne, Robert 47
Keene, Simeon 132
Kempt, Sir James 254
Kent 105, 187
　Joseph 60, 101, 188
King Philip's War 45
King's College School 211, 236
Kinsman, Jeremiah 101
Knox, Henry 161
Latin College 115
Lawrence
　Charles 78
　James 240
Lawson, John 213
Lechmere, Richard 29, 109, 150, 153, 156, 179
Lee, Joseph 19
Leonard, Daniel 29, 150, 179
Lewis
　Calvin 141
　James 141
Lightfoot, Judge 81
Lion 199
Little 9
　Ephraim 4, 132
　Isaac 52
　Lemuel 132, 141
　Mary 77
　Massy 103
　Nathaniel 188
　Polly 103
　Thomas 132
Longfellow, Henry Wadsworth 111
Loring, Joshua 29, 103, 150, 168, 179
Lothrop
　Isaac 108, 109
　Thomas 108
Loudoun, earl of 87
Low, Jeremiah 2, 9, 37
Lynde, Benjamin 48
Machias 198
MacKenzie, Frederick 32-33, 131
Macomber, William 132, 141
Maine 48-49
Mainwaring, Judith 55
Malbone, Thomas 65-66

Mandamus Council 17, 21, 32, 149, 168, 173, 175-176, 207
Marston, Benjamin 202, 205
Maryland 259
Massachusetts Bay 3, 10, 13, 16-18, 26-27, 29, 39, 43, 47-50, 61, 63, 67, 75-76, 90, 95, 100, 111, 125, 132, 137, 150-152, 155, 160, 175, 179, 238
Massachusetts Charter 14
Massachusetts (Bay) Governance Act 16-18, 26,135
Massachusetts Government Bill 14
Massachusetts Hall 61, 108, 129
Massachusetts Spy 7, 23, 136
Mather, Increase 47
Matson, Nathaniel 52-54, 75, 120
Mauger, Joshua 197
Mayflower 11-12, 38, 108
meazels 51
Memoramcook 83
Merchant Adventurers 11, 38
Minister's Land 43-45
Monckton, Robert 78
Monk
  Ann Dering 113, 116, 125, 191, 201
  George Henry 195, 197, 199-201, 207, 209
  James 73, 81, 119
Montcalm, marquis de 87
Montreal 88, 90
Morris 250
Morton
  Nathaniel 74
  Perez 194, 204, 251
  Sarah Apthorp 236
  Sarah Wentworh Apthorp 251
Mount Desert 198
Mount Uniacke 255-256
Mrs. Prior 79
Murray
  Daniel 20
  James 88
  John 20, 29, 150, 168, 179
Nab Nowit 86
New Brunswick 177, 202, 215, 253-254
New England 1, 41, 62, 70, 74-76, 78, 83, 87, 100-101, 112, 137, 145, 154, 175, 194, 250
New Hampshire 51, 72-73, 103, 110, 113, 127, 173-174, 195, 206, 259
New Plymouth Colony 38-39, 42-43, 48-50, 76, 95, 108
Nigro Man and wife 79
North Carolina 111
North End 71
North River 10, 23, 35, 197, 237-238
Nova Scotia 58, 60, 72-73, 77-78, 81-83, 85, 87-88, 97, 119, 164, 177, 192-198, 205, 210, 214-215, 221-223, 225, 227, 233, 241, 243, 246-247, 251-252, 254-255,

Nova Scotia (cont'd) 261-262
Oakley 162
Old Colony Club 107-109, 111
Old Comers 10, 108
Oliver
  Andrew 16-17, 63
  Peter 16, 111, 150, 179
  Sally 116
  Thomas 18, 29, 109, 150, 152, 155-156, 158, 164, 168, 179
Packer
  Elizabeth 72, 196, 224
  Henry 73
  Thomas 72
Paige 47
Paine
  Robert Treat 109, 130
  Timothy 19-20
Parker, William 67
Parliament 1, 2, 9, 13-14, 16-17, 22, 24, 27, 35, 132, 137, 151, 167, 174, 210-211
Paxton, Charles 179
Pepperell, Sir William 29, 73, 150, 179
Perkins 157
  Elizabeth Wentworth 200
Petersby 107
Phillips 33
  John 46-47
  Nathaniel 132
Phips
  Spencer 67
  William 72
Pitt, William (earl of Chatham) 15, 90
Port Roseway 193-194
Port Roseway Association 193
Porter
  Ann 257
  John 254
Powell, Major 107
Pownall, Thomas 15
Prince Edward (see Edward, duke of Kent)
Prior, Betty 79
Province Charter 48
Puritanism 75, 116
Quebec 87-88, 90, 210-211, 228
Quincy, Samuel 179, 245
Ray
  Catherine (Caty) 74, 118, 120
  (see also 'Greene')
  Judith 70, 73, 82
  Mary 55
  Simon (first) 55, 56
  Simon (second) 55, 70
remarkable high Tories 3, 34, 131, 175, 257
Revere, Paul 138
Rhode Island 55, 61, 65, 96-97, 149, 177, 259
Robinson, John 107, 217-218

Rockingham, marquis & machioness 174
Rogers
  Amos 132, 141
  Elizabeth 17
  (see also 'Gould')
  Nathaniel 16-17, 114-117
Romney 107
Rose 107
Royal Acadian Club 252
Ruggles, Timothy 29-30, 32, 150, 168, 179
salt hay 118, 120
Saltonstall, Richard 61-62, 65, 67
sampler 196
Sampson
  Ichabod 261
  Paul 187
Sandwich Woods 142
sardonyx 74
Scituate Rangers 138
Scott, George 78
Senate 204-205, 259
Servants 53, 79, 85-86, 92, 94, 145, 181,
  188, 191, 196-198, 200, 203, 232
Sever 184
Sewall
  Jonathan 179
  Judith 49
  Samuel 48, 54, 72, 103, 168
Shaw 23, 105, 202, 227, 235-236
  William 196
sheep 31, 147, 149, 157, 181, 225, 233
Sherman, Elisha 132, 141
Shirley, William 67, 78, 82, 87
Shirtliff, William 47
siege of
  Boston 140
  Louisbourg 58, 77, 97
Simple Sapling 32, 136, 143, 149
slaves 57, 86
smallpox 156
Smith 185, 251
snow 79, 161, 226, 253
South Meeting House 167
South River 36, 237
Sparhawk, Nathaniel 108
spasms 249-250
Sprague, Seth 27-28, 142, 249, 257
St. Asaph 15
St. Paul's Church 195, 219, 254-255
Stevens, William 4, 132
Stewart, Duncan 107
Stockbridge
  Charles 82, 105, 109, 129-130
  Elizabeth 208
  (see also Winslow)
Storer 105, 144, 184, 191, 229, 244
  Charles 169, 183, 186, 193, 212
  Ebenezer 110, 143, 152, 165, 179, 185,
    190, 192-193, 210, 212

Storer (cont'd)
  Polly 210
Surinam 174
Susquehanna River 259
Sylvester
  Brinley 122, 127
  Jonathan 141
  Mary 122
Taxes 99-100
Tea Rock Hill 3
The Group 31, 136, 168
Thomas
  Abijah 132
  Anthony 9, 11, 60, 69, 98, 101-102,
    106, 137-140, 169, 237
  Bethiah 43, 52, 59
  Briggs 9, 139, 237-238, 240
  Charles (first) 107, 200, 210-212, 217-223,
    261
  Charles (second) 253-256
  Charles Henry 233, 255, 257-258
  David 141
  Deborah 45
  Elizabeth 43, 52
  Elizabeth Gardner 58
  Elizabeth Packer (first) 107, 178, 210,
    212-213, 224, 236, 242, 246
  Elizabeth Packer (second) 244, 253, 261
  Hannah 97, 187
  Henry Dering 36, 107, 117, 186, 211, 224
  Isaac 36
  John (unrelated) 11, 58-59, 98-101, 118
  John (Dr.) 12, 60, 63-65, 67-68, 72, 78-79,
    83, 88, 97-99, 101, 111, 138-141, 145,
    149, 160-163, 165-166, 182, 187
  John (first) 50-51, 55-57, 68, 102
  John (second), General 58
  John (third) 58, 108
  John (fourth) 107, 204-205, 207, 210,
    212-213, 219, 222-226, 228-230, 232-234,
    236-237, 240, 245-246, 248-258
  John (fifth) 162
  John Briggs 237
  Joshua 180, 182
  Martin Howard 97, 107, 208, 224
  Mary (first) 38
  Mary (second) 43, 55
  Mary (third), "Polly" 107, 117, 145, 178,
    210, 212-213, 224-226, 236
  Mary Appleton 50-51
  Mary Ray 55-56
  Nathaniel (first), Captain 38, 40, 43-44, 46,
    49
  Nathaniel (second), Colonel 42-46, 48-50,
    52, 55, 79, 91, 95
  Nathaniel (third), Jr., Judge 50-57, 75, 91,
    95, 118
  Nathaniel (fourth) Lt. Colonel 57-59, 62,
    68, 77, 97, 102, 108, 187

Thomas (cont'd)
  Nathaniel (fifth), "Nat" 82, 105, 107, 144,
    156-157, 165-166, 171, 183, 193, 203,
    207-208, 224, 226, 233, 235-236, 243,
    247-250, 252-254, 257
  Nathaniel Ray 3-4, 6, 9, 12-13, 16-21,
    23-29, 32-36, 38-39, 55-65, 67-70, 72,
    74-82, 85-86, 91-105, 107, 109-111, 113,
    118-126, 128-132, 136-137, 139-140,
    143-145, 148-150, 152-157, 165-166, 168,
    170-180, 182-183, 185-188, 190-197, 200,
    202, 205, 207-209, 211, 213, 224-225,
    238, 248, 252, 262
  Nathaniel Ray (second) 245, 255, 258-261
  Nehemiah 1, 9, 25, 100, 132, 167, 237
  Polly 36
  Priscilla 96, 108
  Sally (first), Sarah Dering 106-107, 156,
    170, 178, 208, 210-212, 219, 223-225,
    233, 236, 244 250, 256-257, 261-262
  Sally (second) 213, 222, 229-230,
    235-236, 238-240, 252
  Samuel 98
  Sarah Dering 16, 28, 36, 59, 72, 74-76,
    80-83, 85, 92, 104, 106-107, 110, 113-114,
    116-126, 128, 143-145, 156-157, 165-166,
    169-170, 172-173, 176, 178, 182, 184,
    187, 189-190, 192-195, 198, 201-203,
    205-211, 213, 218, 221-226, 228-230,
    232-237, 240-244, 251-262
  Sarah Dewolf 250-251
  Sarah Rachel 252-254
  Simon 56-57
  Waterman 130, 141, 237-238, 252
  William (first) 11, 38-45, 49, 54, 57-58, 76,
    92, 95, 98, 128, 241, 257
  William (second), II 43-44, 46, 52
  William (third) 55-56
  William, "Captain Willie" 11, 36-37, 138
Ticonderoga 87-88, 161
tidal bore 199
Tilden, John 132
tillage 10-11, 120
Tolman, Joseph 180-181
Tonge 243
Tory 3, 5-9, 13, 16, 21-22, 27, 29-30, 32, 35,
  104, 111, 135, 142, 146, 148, 150, 152,
  165, 168, 173, 175-176, 237-238
Tory Row 111
Treaty of Paris 88, 90
Trount, Samuel 141
Trumbull, John 168
Tufts
  Cotton 65
  Simon 60, 65
Turner
  Lucy 232
  William 138-139, 180-181

Uniacke
  Elizabeth 261
  Fitzgerald 255-256
  John 255
  Richard 255
Vassall, John 29, 103, 111
Wadsworth 105
  Peleg 140
Walker, Abraham 105, 132
Walter 1032
Wanton, Joseph 61, 65-67, 96
War of 1812, 237
Ward 59
  Artemas 145, 160, 162-163
Ward's Hill 138
Warren
  James 31, 108, 136, 189
  Mercy Otis 31, 108, 136, 166, 168
Watch, military 156
Waterman
  Esaph 187
  Thomas 169
Watson 184
  Elkanah 96
  John 108
  William ("Will") 16, 61, 65, 91, 103, 189
Webb, Daniel 87
Webster, Daniel 255-261
Wendell, John 63
Wensley, Sarah 21
Wentworth 157
  Benning 51, 115-116, 126
  Elizabeth Dering 16, 81, 104, 110,
    113-114, 144, 156, 173-174, 186, 191, 203
  Elizabeth (second) 113-114, 116, 186, 200
  Frances 110, 193, 226, 234, 236
  Frances Sarah 214
  John (Lt. Gov.) 103, 113
  John (second) 110, 113, 115-116, 144,
    173-174, 192-195, 206-207, 215-216,
    218-220, 234, 236
  Molley 116
  Paul 174, 194, 205-207
  Samuel 73, 81, 92, 103-104, 107, 110,
    113-117
  Samuel (second) 113, 115
  Sarah 76, 81, 104, 186, 251
West 107
White 33, 260
  Abijah 5-8, 16, 100-101, 132, 168-169
  Benjamin 2, 9, 37, 145
  Cornelius 132
  Daniel 132
  Joanna 248
  John 141
  Paul 132
  Suzannah 101
White's Ferry 35, 139, 197-198

Wilkins
  Lewis Morris 253-254
  Sarah Thomas 256-257
  (see also Thomas)
Willard, Abijah 18, 20, 66, 150, 179
Williams 105
Willis 187
Winslow 34, 60, 77, 86, 175, 191, 202, 249, 257
  Anna Green (first) 104, 106, 110, 143, 146, 183-184, 210-212, 228, 241
  Anna Green (second) 104, 106-107, 110, 179, 183
  Edward (the Pilgrim) 11-12, 39-43, 48, 58, 76, 98, 101
  Edward (second) 12, 103, 109, 111-112, 177
  Edward, Jr. 103, 108-109, 177
  Elizabeth Stockbridge 21-22, 196, 208, 228, 231-232, 246
  Isaac (Dr.) 3-4, 11-13, 21, 28-29, 36, 39, 100-101, 105, 109-110, 130-132, 134, 144-145, 177, 179, 188-189, 196, 198, 208, 227-228, 232-236, 246, 248, 257
  Isaac (Judge, Colonel) 11-12, 21, 48, 57-58, 91, 96, 128
  Joanna White 248
  Job 132
  John 11-13, 16, 21, 58, 62, 69, 77-78, 82-84, 86-88, 91, 96-103, 108-111, 128, 130, 147, 177, 202
  John (second) 21, 248
  Joshua 36, 82, 106-107, 110, 117, 143, 145, 173, 177-179, 183-184, 211
  Josiah 45-46, 48
  Kenelm 100-101
  Mary Little 77
  (see also Little)
  Pelham 11, 13, 62, 77, 102-103, 108, 129, 248
  Penny 103
  Sally 103, 177
  Sarah 146
  Sarah Wensley 21
  (see also Wensley)
Winslow House Association, Historic 80
Winthrop, Wait 48
Wiswall 59
  John 61, 65
Wolfe, James 88, 90
Wright, Abner 132
Yale College 35